little festival of the unexpected
of the
unexpected
2000 & 2001

Portland Stage Company

little festival of the unexpected 2000 & 2001

Edited and with an Introduction
by Lisa DiFranza

Plays by

Liz Duffy Adams

William Donnelly

Laura Harrington

Prudence Wright Holmes

Daniel Pinkerton

August Schulenburg

Caridad Svich

Stage
& Screen

Special thanks to Anita Stewart, and to the actors and directors who took part in Little Festival of the Unexpected 2000 and 2001.

The actors:
David Babin, Ron Botting, Lauren Burns, Marc Carver, Todd Cerveris, Aled Davies, Moira Driscoll, Gist Finley, Alice M. Gatling, James Hoban, Prudence Wright Holmes, Robert Jason Jackson, Mike Kendrick, N. Rose Liberace, Abigail Lopez, Sarah "Squid" Lord, Daniel Noel, Keith Powell, Kelli Putnam, Doug Shapiro, Elizabeth Ureneck, Sally Wood

The directors:
R. J. McComish, Lisa DiFranza, Padraic Lillis, Kent Paul, Davis Robinson

ISBN: 0-7394-2927-2

Printed in the United States of America

CONTENTS

INTRODUCTION

Every year, as spring arrives in Maine, Portland Stage Company cele-
brates the season with its Little Festival of the Unexpected. For one
intense, spirited week, this small regional theater devotes its full attention to nurturing playwrights working on fresh, seedling scripts and
supporting the organic, creative, even miraculous process of playwriting. When the theater's doors open, inviting the public to free staged
readings of brand new scripts, audiences eagerly flock to engage plays
and playwrights with sensitivity and attentiveness, eyes and ears wide
open. But how, you might reasonably ask, does a theater invoke and
present "the unexpected" (and whose expectations are we talking about,
anyway)?

To produce the Festival, we at the theater have to shake ourselves
loose at the outset, upturn our own programmed expectations—those
we apply, day in and day out, to the work we do all season long. Whether
we are conscious of it or not, as theater artists we are in the habit of making productions work. We use all available means to spit and polish a
show, hide what is unseemly, sand down the rough edges. In a regional
theater setting, our own expectations often revolve around meeting
expectations of our subscription audience. A production should look a
certain way, make the grade, please, be (to some degree) slick. This is not
rampant commercialism, but a means of survival in an economic climate that is not friendly to the arts in general, and to low budget, non-
profit operations in particular. The chance to risk failure is rare.

By contrast, if Little Festival of the Unexpected is to live up to its
name, we must let go of the habitualized impulse to use the tricks of the
theatrical trade to cover up what might be perceived by an audience as
raggedy. Instead, from the initial selecting of scripts, the Festival
demands that we expose and tap the raw vein of a play in formation,
with no specific finished results in mind, no expectations. Now, our task
is to be active listeners and advocates, boldly supporting the heart of
what writers are writing even if the play's edges are unsanded, or its form
strikes viewers as uncomfortably idiosyncratic or unwieldy.

Attempting to keep our own familiar expectations aside and out of
the way, the ingredients of the Festival are drawn together. Writers and
scripts are matched with directors, actors, and stage managers, and the

Festival company takes shape. This collective explores each play in rehearsal, their mission clearly defined: to take the risk of letting the playwrights' words fly off the page in their own terms. This task is deceptively simple. Our expectations are well programmed, deeply rooted. If the artistic team truly allows the writers' spirits to emerge, undiluted and unrestrained, the Festival will be on the road toward the unexpected.

Discussions with the audience, director, and playwright follow each public reading. As the facilitator of these conversations, I am distinctly aware of our audience's role in the invocation of the unexpected. Their expectations (necessarily significant during the rest of the season) must also be left at the door. Over the thirteen years that Portland Stage Company has produced Little Festival of the Unexpected, this challenge to the audience has been met many times over. The Festival audience has coalesced into an impassioned makeshift community, a significant part of the process.

This volume is a compilation of the work of seven writers. All of them have spent the week in Portland with us, summoning the unexpected. Obviously, the words that have sprung from their minds, hearts, and hands are the root, essential element of the Festival. But the importance of their presence goes even deeper than that. Looking back at the 2000 and 2001 Festivals, it is honest to say that all of the playwrights represented in this book arrived in Maine with a willingness to dive headlong into the process, an openness to what they might discover in their own work, and an inherent instinct to lay aside their expectations. And with this final, most potent ingredient, the unexpected was brought into our midst.

As we worked on these plays, I was stunningly reminded of the amazing, fiery potential that exists when imaginative, passionate people are thrown together without the pressure of internal or external expectations—even for one week! The work was not without struggle, conflict, and anguish, but ultimately, it was extraordinarily productive, creative in the most real sense, and truly joyous. Messy, rugged, developmental work is essential. It fuels theaters with the plays that emerge onto main stages before audiences with expectations.

In putting this book together, and reconnecting with writers, I was struck by the ways that Little Festival of the Unexpected lives on well after the actual event is over. Many writers have made lasting friendships and continued collaborations for months and years following their time in Portland. I have personally continued numerous friendships and partnerships seeded at the Festival. We have produced Laura Harrington's play *Hallowed Ground* on Portland Stage Company's main stage, and assembled follow-up readings of her play *The Bathtub Diaries*, and Liz Duffy Adams' *Dog Act*. The continued relationships between Festival artists are an extraordinarily rich result of this one annual hot box of a week.

The first question most often put to me by playwrights as I contacted them about this volume was "Which draft do you want, the Little Festival draft, or the latest one?" Though I asked each writer to submit the draft they are happiest with, the plays you are about to read remain under scrutiny by their writers. Of course, the identification of a work of art as "finished" is inevitably arbitrary. Even so, it is worth noting how rare and exciting it is to have the opportunity to read plays before they have had the seal of a full production, and that is the case with most of these plays. They are still in construction: vital, breathing, emblems of our time.

This is important, particularly because the two years that this volume represents was not an ordinary span of time. I cannot read this collection of plays in the same way, now that we have crossed the boundary line of September 11th, now that we are forced to question and re-interpret our place in the world. Directly or obliquely, every play in this book actively reflects and re-creates the interior and exterior landscape of contemporary America. Each of the writers imaginatively evokes images formed and shaped by our own particular place in the continuum of time. These are seven extraordinary playwrights writing in America, and they have a lot to say about who we are.

Caridad Svich's play *Archaeology of Dreams* conjures the U.S., 1963— then and now. Her America is seen through the eyes and memory of an innocent witness, one who is just being born. Through the just-opening eyes of the witness, we are surrounded by the music, people, politics, and poetry of the year 1963. Svich swirls them together in a wild, kaleidoscopic vision of a singular year in our history and the ways we are living with its legacy.

Pushing the boundaries of the theatrical form, Liz Duffy Adams' *Dog Act* catapults us to the aftermath of the apocalypse, and into the world of two vaudevillians, Rozetta Stone and Dog, as they wander the barren wilderness somewhere in the northeast of the former U.S., en route to their next gig in China. Under attack from rabid scavengers and other wayfarers, the two must rely on their vaudevillian skills of performance and dexterity to continue on their path in a future America where little of the familiar remains, and nothing is certain. *Dog Act* is a wildly imaginative, deeply soulful, funny play. Combining a rich, idiosyncratic style, deftly manipulated language, and vivid, musical theatricality, Adams takes us on an exhilarating journey.

Do You Want to Know a Secret? by Daniel Pinkerton takes us off of American soil. Set in Berlin, between 1988 and 1993, interweaving film clips with live action, Pinkerton tells the story of Karin and Walter, who fought on opposite sides of the East/West Germany dispute. Despite their political differences, they fell in love, married, and had a child together. Karin is imprisoned for her anti-Stasi involvement, missing the formative years of her daughter's life. Once out of jail, she activates a political campaign for the people's right to read the files the government keeps on them, which include clues to the identity of the people who informed on them. When Karin reads her own file, she uncovers a horrible secret. Pinkerton shrewdly explores how the personal and the political are deeply and inextricably entwined.

Laura Harrington examines our own country's civil conflict in her drama *Hallowed Ground*. Told with the undercurrent of a vivid soundscape, this Civil War story involves a Union soldier, a Confederate soldier, a thirteen-year-old southern girl and her ex-slave. Harrington sensitively distills the enormity of the American Civil War into the personal stories of this unlikely quartet, thrown together by chance, life, and death. In one night, their fates become enmeshed and the lines between North and South, black and white, become blurred.

In *Dr. Sam Is Under Your Bed*, Prudence Wright Holmes tells an autobiographical story of a young girl growing up with a father obsessed with the Dr. Sam Sheppard murder case. Although Burt Holmes may want to blame Sheppard for destroying the American family, the problem isn't that simple. From the war to "women's lib," Ike to Kennedy, America is turning upside down and inside out while father and daughter struggle to make sense of it all. Prudence Wright Holmes (who performs this script herself) draws a deeply touching, if shocking and frightening, picture of the America she knew as a child.

Laura Harrington's second play read at Little Festival, *The Bathtub Diaries*, pulls us into a land of fantasy. Set on the island of St Helena during the last days of Napoleon's life in exile, the play moves fluidly between the actual island and Napoleon's dreams and nightmares. Joan of Arc and Ulysses S. Grant are but two of the characters Napoleon encounters as past and future converge. In *The Bathtub Diaries*, Harrington explores the hollowness of war in a radical stylistic departure from her earlier work, *Hallowed Ground*. Here, she ventures into the matrix where madness and genius, history and legend meet.

Set in an unnamed northeastern American town, William Donnelly's stylish, dynamic, fast-paced, and funny play, *Apocalypso!*, brings us to the very cusp of the millennium. As rumors of the end of the world spin out of control, eight disparate characters begin thinking a little harder about who they've wronged and what steps to take to make things right. From a barstool philosopher to a messenger who is either angel or lunatic (or both), these souls on the brink must evaluate their place in line for judgment.

August Schulenburg courageously addresses race in America in his tender, harsh, honest play, *Kidding Jane*. Here Schulenburg genuinely explores the nature of possibility and the power of hope. After the violent death of their daughter, Jane and Martin search for resolution and are led to Kidd Trick, an angry, troubled, inner-city youth. Kidd's presence in the household generates tension amongst all parties, exposing the couple's subconscious racial prejudices. *Kidding Jane* is about rap and race, secrets and ghosts and, ultimately, it is about forgiveness.

As a director, as well as the producer of Little Festival of the Unexpected, I am deeply grateful for the Festival's reminder each year, that if we are doing our jobs well, fulfilling our responsibilities as makers of theater, we are always working in service to a playwright's vision. In these complex times, it is surely more important than ever to find the means and ways to listen to and support the creative writers among us. It is no wonder to see audiences arriving with almost desperate curiosity to hear what playwrights are writing. We need their voices now. Idiosyncratic, unbound, poetic, dissenting, frenetic, dark, wildly funny, radical, unpredictable, these are the prophets who light the way, so we will have the courage to move forward. In an uncertain time, these are the voices of hope.

Please enjoy the plays in this collection. And leave your expectations behind as you turn this page.

—*Lisa DiFranza*
Literary Manager
Portland Stage Company
April 2002

THE ARCHAEOLOGY
OF DREAMS

A VAUDEVILLE

BY CARIDAD SVICH

No performance or reading of this work, *The Archaeology of Dreams*, in any medium, may be given without express permission of the author. Inquiries regarding performance rights, publication, duplication of any kind should be addressed to: New Dramatists, 424 West 44th Street, New York, NY 10036 U.S. Attn: Caridad Svich.

BIOGRAPHY

Caridad Svich's plays include *Alchemy of Desire/Dead-Man's Blues, Any Place But Here, Fugitive Pieces, Prodigal Kiss, But there are fires, Gleaning/Rebusca,* and *Brazo Gitano,* among others. She is currently working on commissions from Ensemble Studio Theater, and Intar; and in pre-production with The Booth Variations, a solo multimedia collaboration with director Nick Philippou and actor/writer Todd Cerveris. Her plays have been produced by The Women's Project, Intar, HERE, T.W.E.E.D., Primary Stages, and Theater for the New City in New York; Salvage Vanguard Theater, and Kitchen Dog Theater in Texas; Cincinnati Playhouse in the Park and Cleveland Public Theater in Ohio; Perishable Theater; Latino Chicago; Frank Theater; Key West Theater; Hackney Empire Studio Theater, London. Her plays have been workshopped by Actors Touring Company in London, ASK Theater Projects, Mark Taper Forum Theater, Portland Stage, South Coast Repertory Hispanic Playwrights Project, Evidence Room, Printer's Devil Theater, Hourglass Group, Voice & Vision Theater, Blue Heron Theater, New Georges, Repertorio Espanol, Midwest PlayLabs, Royal Court Theater, and Traverse Theater in Edinburgh. *Fugitive Pieces* (a play with songs) is published in TheaterForum; *Prodigal Kiss* and *But there are fires* are published by Smith & Kraus; *Gleaning/Rebusca* is published by Arte Publico Press; *Brazo Gitano* is published in Ollantay Theater Journal; *Any Place But Here* is published by TCG's Plays in Process; *Alchemy of Desire/Dead-Man's Blues* is included in *Out of the Fringe* published by TCG. Caridad is a member of New Dramatists and the recipient of a 2002-2003 Bunting Fellowship from Harvard University/Radcliffe Institute for Advanced Study, an NEA/TCG Playwriting Residency, Thurber House Playwriting residency, Jonathan R. Reynolds Playwriting residency, Rosenthal New Play Prize, PEW/National Theater Translation Fund Commission, California Arts Council Fellowship, TCG Hispanic Translation Commission. She is co-editor of *Conducting a Life: Reflections on the Theater of Maria Irene Fornes* (Smith & Kraus), *Theater in Crisis?,* and editor of *Transglobal Readings: Crossing Theatrical Boundaries* (both for Manchester University Press). Her translations are collected in *Federico Garcia Lorca: Impossible Theater* (Smith & Kraus). She is founder of the performance/media collective NoPassport, and holds an MFA from UCSD.

CHARACTERS

WITNESS/PRESS—premature child, female/media

PONCE—senator, fifty years old, vigorous, volatile

JOHN/ADAM/JIM/BOB DYLAN/
LEE HARVEY OSWALD/GOOD HUMOR MAN—
senator/surfer/aide/singer/assassin/ice cream vendor

JFK/JACKIE GLEASON—president/comic

MOTHER/MARGARET/FIDEL CASTRO—
Louella's mother/Ponce's wife/politician

MANDY/PATSY CLINE/PERRY COMO/PETULA CLARK—
Ponce's mistress/country singer/crooner/pop singer

HENRY/GIDEON/SIMON/ANDY WARHOL/
JOHN LENNON—aide/senator/surfer/Pop artist/singer

LOUELLA/EDITH PIAF/JACKIE KENNEDY—
eleven-year-old girl/chanteuse/First Lady

TIME & PLACE

U.S., 1963: then, now, and parts in-between.
A fluid space where scenes are lit in isolation, and are at times
opened up to include the full company.

In Part 1, everything is in pastels.

In Part 2, the stage takes on more vivid Warholian hues.

In Part 3, silver, black, and white dominate with the rare, occasional splash of intense color.

.

NOTES

This text should be preferably performed with an interval after Part 1. The text may be performed with eight actors: four women, four men, with roles doubled as listed above. Character changes may be indicated simply by switches in physicality or vocal quality.

This play is composed of selective photographic cuts from memory's lens. As such, there is a constant interplay in performance between the visual and the verbal, between the virtual and the real. A strong, specific, shared gestural and physical vocabulary among the actors is to be encouraged.

Thanks to Shelley Berc for support and encouragement of this play, Mitchell Gossett at Bottom's Dream in Los Angeles for development time, to John Diehl and Kimberly Scott for always teaching me so much about my work with their talent and generosity, to Anita Stewart for the opportunity to play a bit with real and imagined versions of my past at the Little Festival and for a company of actors at Portland Stage who allowed me to rediscover much joy.

—C.S.

"*Remembering my birth in infancy, the coughs,*

The swallows, the tear-trees growing

From your eyeballs of shame; the gray

Immense morning I was conceived in the womb,

And the red gory afternoon delivered

Therefrom."

—Jack Kerouac, "89th Chorus"
Mexico City Blues (1959)

THE ARCHAEOLOGY OF DREAMS

PART 1

PROLOGUE

(Out of the darkness THE GHOSTS *appear:* JFK, EDITH PIAF, LEE HARVEY OSWALD, *and* PATSY CLINE. *Each is framed by an archival news photo of themselves in the background. Each is caught in a defining gesture in a column of light. The following is spoken in rough unison, in a staggered manner, sometimes led by one of the Ghosts, sometimes by another: a spoken fugue. Each ghost is trying to make sense of the numbers, to remember a combination forgotten.)*

JFK & PIAF & OSWALD & CLINE: Nineteen sixty-three, Nineteen thirty-six, Thirteen ninety-six, Sixteen ninety-one, Ninety-six thirteen, Ninety-three sixteen, Sixteen thirty-nine, Sixty-three nineteen, Sixty-nine thirteen, Sixty one thirty-nine, Thirty-one sixty-nine, Thirty-nine sixteen, Thirty-six ninety-one Thirty-nine sixty-one . . .

(A wash of light. Music is heard: Patsy Cline singing "Crazy" on a distant radio merging with the Ghost of PATSY CLINE, *singing live. The* WITNESS *steps forward, as* JFK, EDITH PIAF, *and* LEE HARVEY OSWALD *fade.* PATSY CLINE *continues singing softly underneath the following . . .)*

WITNESS: I am standing on a corner and I hear Patsy Cline has died. March, 1963. I hear "Crazy" coming through the radio, and the ache in her voice has never seemed louder and I feel my stomach hurt. Kennedy is on the TV and he's giving a speech, and I can barely see him. I never see him. He always seems faint to me. But Patsy's real. She's realer than anybody. And my mind goes: nineteen thirty-six, sixteen ninety-one, nineteen sixty-three . . . And I think where am I? How could I be listening to "Crazy" now? Before Beverly D'Angelo and Jessica Lange get a hold of it? Before I even know who Willie Nelson is? This is a corner in New Jersey. 54 North 11th Street. It's gray. But this

isn't where I was born. I was born in Philadelphia: The Liberty
Bell, Betsy Ross, and all that. Can you see it? I am standing on
the steps of the museum and I raise my arms like "Rocky," only
that movie won't come out until years later. I am in an incubator. I am premature. In danger. Fragile. There might be something wrong with my brain. They have tests you can take.
Shapes and colors. "Is this a box? Is this a square? Can you name
this?" Cat. "Yes. Good. You're fine." There's nothing wrong with
my brain. "Next child." The Beatles play "I Wanna Hold Your
Hand" right in my ear. I put the transistor radio right up against
my ear. I hear the whirring of the mechanism inside. Grinding.
Buzzing. But the Beatles blast through:

(sings) "I wanna hold your hand . . . I wanna hold your hand . . ."
I am standing on another block. Another corner. This time I
hear

(She sings line from chorus of the 1980s Wang Chung song "Dance
Hall Days.")

"Take your lover by the hand." But it's not the Beatles. It's someone else. A group. Faceless. But with a sneer. In rock n' roll,
there's always a sneer. Elvis taught us that. A woman named
Christine Keeler sleeps with a man named "Honeybear" and
then with a bald guy named Profumo who hides his head
behind a folded-up newspaper. I think to myself "Does he sell
perfume? Why is he called 'Profumo?'" What a fusty name. Fust.
Is that a word? Okay. The doctors have determined there's nothing wrong with my brain, but I should wait a couple of days
before I go home. A couple more days in the incubator.
Thirteen ninety-six, nineteen thirty-six . . . Remember the
Depression? Okay. Cocoon. Bubble. Respirator. Hold me. My
fingers small, and soon on my hips standing on the corner of 54
North 11th Street, and crazy.

(Music fades, as PATSY CLINE disappears. THE LIVING appear:
JACKIE GLEASON, JACKIE KENNEDY, BOB DYLAN, and
ANDY WARHOL. Each is framed by an archival news photo of
themselves in the background. Each is caught in a defining gesture
in light. Each is trying to remember a combination of numbers
long forgotten. Staggered unison here. A fugue . . .)

GLEASON & JACKIE KENNEDY & DYLAN & WARHOL: Nineteen sixty-three, Nineteen thirty-six, Thirteen ninety-six, Sixteen ninety-one, Ninety-six thirteen, Ninety-three sixteen, Sixteen thirty-nine, Sixty-three nineteen, Sixty-nine thirteen... (THE LIVING *fade. The* WITNESS *remains.*)

SCENE 1

HOME

(Flowered curtains and a console. MOTHER *fusses with her dress.)*

MOTHER: Louella, get the cake.

LOUELLA: But, Mom!

MOTHER: The Warrens are going to be here any minute and they've got to have their cake.

LOUELLA: But it'll get stale.

MOTHER: Lemon cake never gets stale. And don't forget the plastic cups with the flowers on them. "Dixie," they're called.

LOUELLA: Mom.

MOTHER: What, dear?

LOUELLA: You can't serve Dixie cups.

MOTHER: Why ever not, dear?

LOUELLA: They're for the bathroom.

MOTHER: You're wrong, dear.

LOUELLA: It says so on the box. *(holding up box)* See? Bathroom.

MOTHER: Oh dear. But they're so pretty. With flowers and everything. What am I going to use? Our glasses are all stained and chipped.

LOUELLA: You want me to go to the corner?

MOTHER: No. That's all right, dear.

LOUELLA: I could go. It'd be no trouble.

MOTHER: Turn the radio on, dear.

LOUELLA: What?

MOTHER: I have to think. The only way I can think is with the radio on.

(PATSY CLINE *appears in a spot singing "Crazy." This is sung live.*)

Turn that woman off.

LOUELLA: But, Mom, you just told me to—

MOTHER: I don't like that woman, Louella. She's forward. Singing like that, she's very forward.

LOUELLA: Everybody else likes her.

MOTHER: Turn it off now.

(PATSY CLINE *stops singing.*)

Put a record on. Perry Como. Yes.

LOUELLA: I hate Perry Como.

MOTHER: He helps me think, dear.

(PATSY CLINE *turns into* PERRY COMO, *and sings "Catch a Falling Star" underneath the following . . .)*

MOTHER: That's better. Oh. What a little Perry Como can do.

(*sings*) "Catch a falling star and put it in your pocket, never let it fade away . . . "

LOUELLA: What are you doing, Mom?

MOTHER: I'm singing, dear. Singing and thinking.

LOUELLA: You're weird.

MOTHER: What did you say?

LOUELLA: Nothing.

MOTHER: Okay. I've figured it out.

This is what we'll do.

LOUELLA: What?

MOTHER: If we fill the Christmas glasses up with Koolaid, the Warrens won't be able to see the poinsettias on the glasses. The Koolaid will cover everything.

LOUELLA: Mom, lemon cake and Koolaid don't go together.

MOTHER: They go fine, dear.

LOUELLA: It's tacky, Mom.

MOTHER: Don't use that word with me. "Tacky." Now get the Christmas glasses and mix some Koolaid.

(MOTHER *dances to* "Catch a Falling Star." LOUELLA *throws a silent temper tantrum.* WITNESS *appears from behind the console, as Perry Como fades.*)

WITNESS: Red Ranger pajamas and red slippers for boys, pink fuzzies for girls. On the TV, it's black and white, and I can't make out anything: Brillo. Brillo pads, and Borax, and a man named Mr. Clean sweeps a linoleum floor with a T-shirt on and an earring in his left ear. On the record player: Perry Como, and The Singing Nun. And outside: the ice cream truck. Bells. The Good Humor man always drives by at two o'clock.

(*The* GOOD HUMOR MAN *appears in light.*)

I clutch a dollar and race down the steps: One-two-three, skip a step down to the yard, and the ice cream truck is waiting. And there are all these kids. Kids I never see. They only come out when the ice cream truck comes by, and then they disappear into their homes down 54 North 11th Street. I hope he has strawberry shortcake. With pink, red, and white chips on the outside. Vanilla and strawberry. Please, please. The other kids are shouting and I can't be heard. There is no sound coming out of my throat. I try to catch the ice cream man's eyes, but he's got his head down in the barrels inside the truck. He starts to pull away. I hit the side of the truck with my hands, beating on the face of Good Humor.

(*The* GOOD HUMOR MAN *looks at her.*)

The truck stops and I point to the strawberry shortcake bar which is pasted on the outside of the truck along with the chocolate éclair and the almond one that tastes like butter. Ick. And the Good Humor man shakes his head and says

GOOD HUMOR MAN: Sorry. All out.

(GOOD HUMOR MAN *laughs, and fades in light.*)

WITNESS: He pulls away, the bells of the truck ringing a tune I can't name.

(PERRY COMO *fades back up in spot singing* "Catch a Falling Star" *softly.*)

The dollar bill is tight in my hand, sweaty. Now I have to wait until tomorrow for the ice cream man to come back again.

(Bells. LOUELLA *runs out.* MOTHER *pushes console away.* PERRY COMO *fades.* WITNESS *pulls down the curtains to reveal . . .)*

SCENE 2

OFFICE

*(*JFK *is smoking a cigar.)*

JFK: Take that down, Henry.

HENRY: But, Mr. President—

JFK: I don't want some goddamn picture of a bull terrier in my office. Christ. It's bad enough I have to look at all those dead Presidents on the wall. Damn George Washington. What'd he ever do for me?

HENRY: It's down, Mr. President.

*(*HENRY *with picture frame in hand . . .)*

JFK: Well, put it away. Don't stand there like a school-boy. You're worse than my brother Bob.

HENRY: Yes, Mr. President.

JFK: And tell Andy Warhol that painting of Jackie stinks.

HENRY: I thought you liked it, Mr. President.

JFK: I don't know who that Warhol thinks he is. Jackie's my wife, goddammit. He's got her painted like a damn Koolaid baby. What's that, Henry?

HENRY: Sir?

JFK: On your lapel. Is that dust?

HENRY: It must've fallen when I was trying to put up the picture, sir.

JFK: Jack. The name's Jack. Can't you call me that?

HENRY: Yes, sir. Jack.

JFK: Well, clean yourself up, Henry. I don't like dust. Nothing but particles. Dead particles, Henry. Spare atoms messing up the ozone.

HENRY: I'll brush myself off, sir.

JFK: And get Castro on the line.

HENRY: Yes, sir.

JFK: He's a goddamn nightmare. Charming. Damn charming. But he's made Cuba a goddamn hell. You know, I used to go down there. Before Jackie. Hell. We all used to go down there. Isn't that right, Henry?

HENRY: Oh. Yes.

JFK: You could get any piece of ass you liked. Now Castro's ruined it. For everybody. Goddamn can't go anywhere anymore. Cuba, Indochina . . .

HENRY: No, sir.

JFK: The world's fucked, Henry.

HENRY: Yes, sir.

JFK: No one can set it right. . . . Put the hi-fi on, would you, Henry? I need some of that Patsy Cline. I need to listen to her just now.

HENRY: Yes, sir.

JFK: She's some woman.

HENRY: . . . Shall I get the First Lady, sir?

JFK: No. It's just me and Patsy right now.

HENRY: Yes, sir.

(HENRY *exits with frame.* PATSY CLINE *appears in a spot, singing "Walkin' After Midnight."* JFK *turns away, and masturbates.* LOUELLA *appears in a spotlight.*)

The Letter

LOUELLA: You don't know me, but I'm your biggest fan. Even though you're dead. My mother says I'm being morbid thinking about you all the time, but I don't think about you all the time. Just sometimes. I like your voice. Your "ache," I guess folks call it. I don't know how you got to be called "Patsy." But it sure is a perfect name. For you. For your voice. And smile. I've seen pictures of your smile. Sometimes I stand in front of the mirror and practice your smile, even though my teeth aren't great or big or wide. I try to put my mouth just like yours. I even warble a bit. Not like you. No one in the whole world will ever sing like you. With that ache. I wish I had an ache. Like that. So big it could fill my voice. Can you see me, Patsy? Up there in the sky? Can you see me from your plane the same way Buddy and the rest of them that died? I'm listening to your voice on the AM. It's singing

(sings) "I go out walkin' after midnight . . ." And I can see myself walking just like you.

(Spotlight fades on LOUELLA, *and* PATSY CLINE. *Silence.* LEE HARVEY OSWALD *appears in the distance. He sings a variation of "Walkin After Midnight." He sings simply.)*

OSWALD: I go out walkin' after midnight, in the spotlight, in the belly of your hum. I go out walkin' after midnight searchin' for you . . .

*(*JFK *turns back. A smile crosses his lips. He doesn't see* OSWALD. *Light change.)*

SCENE 3

OUTSIDE THE OFFICE

(Three Senators shift through garbage.)

JOHN: Hey. Bazooka.

PONCE: Throw that out, John.

JOHN: A whole pack of gum, Ponce.

PONCE: Out.

JOHN: Could use gum.

GIDEON: I think I . . .

PONCE: What did you find, Gideon?

GIDEON: . . . Brillo pad.

PONCE: Anything in it?

GIDEON: Just dirt.

PONCE: We have to keep looking, gentlemen.

JOHN: Maybe it's not here, Ponce.

PONCE: I saw it. I know I did.

   A thin cord, a microphone . . .

GIDEON: Nobody's tapping you, Ponce.

PONCE: Don't be so sure.

GIDEON: If they were tapping you, they'd be tapping me.

JOHN: And me.

PONCE: Why would they wire-tap you, John?

   You practically just got into the Senate.

JOHN: I know.

PONCE: They got nothing on you, John.

JOHN: You think?

GIDEON: Dixie cups.

   (GIDEON *tosses Dixie cups to the side.*)

PONCE: I've got secrets, John.

JOHN: Everyone's got secrets. Our country's built on secrets. You
   think Jefferson didn't have a whore or two?

PONCE: I'm not talking about women, John.

   I'm talking about secrets.

GIDEON: You mean the Russians?

PONCE: Not from my lips.

GIDEON: But that's what you mean, isn't it?

PONCE: Gideon, you have my word . . .

JOHN: I'm standing here in aluminum cans and cabbage leaves
   for some Russian shit?

PONCE: It's not like that, John.

JOHN: What is it, then?

GIDEON: What Ponce here is trying to say is that it's more than
   that, isn't that right, Ponce?

PONCE: A cord, a microphone . . . Ah!

JOHN: What?

PONCE: Son-of-a-bitch.

(PONCE *pulls a shoelace out of the garbage.*)

JOHN: That's a shoelace, Ponce.

PONCE: It is. It certainly is, gentlemen.

JOHN: I don't—What's a shoelace—?

PONCE: Who did this shoelace belong to, gentlemen? Think.

GIDEON: I'm not following you, Ponce.

PONCE: Who followed me out of the Senate the other day?

JOHN: The new intern?

PONCE: Shush about her. Think, gentlemen.

GIDEON: You have a new intern, Ponce?

PONCE: A perk. Nothing more. Come on, gentlemen. Think.

JOHN: What's her —? Mandy?

PONCE: This is not about women, John.

GIDEON: Then who, Ponce?

PONCE: Khruschev's men.

JOHN: Khruschev?

PONCE: His men.

GIDEON: They were following you, Ponce?

PONCE: They wore heavy shoes, remember? Thick soles.

JOHN: Are you saying —?

PONCE: This is a Russian shoelace, gentlemen.

GIDEON: Yeah?

PONCE: See the end twist in the cord? Only in Russia.

JOHN: I don't believe . . .

PONCE: Things are escalating, my dear gentlemen.
They are escalating indeed.

(PONCE *places shoelace in his pocket. LIGHT SHIFT.*)

SCENE 4

OFFICE (1)

(JFK *is kneeling before* JACKIE KENNEDY.)

JACKIE KENNEDY: You'll bruise my knees.

JFK: How will I do that?

JACKIE KENNEDY: With your teeth. Now, get up. The Press will be here any second.

JFK: Screw the Press.

JACKIE KENNEDY: Jack.

JFK: You're a hard woman, Jackie. Harder than when we got married.

JACKIE KENNEDY: I don't want them to come in here and see us like this.

JFK: We're married, aren't we? Nothing's illegal if we're married.

JACKIE KENNEDY: Depends which state you're living in.

JFK: I'll make a law. "Cunnilingus in the fifty states."

JACKIE KENNEDY: If the bastards let you.

JFK: They'll let me. Between me and LBJ . . .

(*He disappears under her skirt. Lights shift.*)

SCENE 5

PRIVATE

(*Three senators in the bath-house. Steam rising.* JOHN, GIDEON, *and* PONCE.)

PONCE: Get me a phone!

GIDEON: For Christ's sake, Ponce, can't you rest for a minute?

PONCE: I can't sit, Gideon. A man has to move. You want to sit there and let the steam come up into your brain and dull you to nothingness, go ahead. I'm getting a phone. The Russians aren't going to wait for us to finish opening our pores.

GIDEON: The Russians don't even know we're here. Besides, they're Soviets now, Ponce.

PONCE: Well, what else am I going to call them? It's Russia. That's the name of the country. The word "Soviet" has no history to it. None at all. It's a made-up word. Thought up by some lunatic.

JOHN: Bolshevik.

PONCE: Damn useless word.

(Phone appears.)

Ah!

JOHN: You should rest, Ponce.

PONCE: No rest for anyone, John. Not if you want to win.

JOHN: You sound like my father.

PONCE: I could be your father. You ever think of that? *(on phone)* Margaret? Ponce here. How are you, dear? . . . Nothing. Cleaning the pores . . . What? . . . Yes, Gideon's here . . . You want to talk to him? . . . This is business, dear. Not some bloody social . . . All right. All right. *(off phone)* . . . Gideon?

GIDEON: What?

PONCE: Margaret. She wants to speak to you.

(GIDEON takes the phone.)

GIDEON: *(on phone)* Margaret? Yes . . . Yes . . . Oh, yes. Some time . . .

PONCE: Off the phone, Gideon.

GIDEON: *(on phone)* Lovely day. Yes . . .

JOHN: Margaret likes talking to him.

PONCE: What has this got to do with you, John?

JOHN: Nothing.

PONCE: Then shut up.

GIDEON: *(on phone)* I never said that, Margaret . . . When did I? . . . Okay. Okay . . . Your hair . . . Right.

PONCE: Give me the phone, Gideon. The whole country is going to pot, and you're talking about Margaret's damn . . .

GIDEON: *(on phone)* Yes, Margaret . . . All right.

(PONCE grabs the phone.)

PONCE: *(on phone)* Margaret? Margaret? . . . *(off phone)* She hung

up. The bloody bitch . . . *(redials, and . . .)* The phone's dead.
(PONCE throws phone to floor.)
Goddamn nothing works here. Whole country . . . straight down in a piss stream.

JOHN: We'll get another phone, Ponce.

PONCE: I don't want another phone. Not now. I don't want to talk to anyone now. Fucking Khruschev could be calling, I wouldn't answer it.

JOHN: Why would he call you, Ponce?

PONCE: Don't push me, John. Don't push me.

GIDEON: Your stomach's all swollen, Ponce.

PONCE: What?

GIDEON: You have a tumor or something?

PONCE: What the hell are you talking about?

GIDEON: Look at it.

(PONCE looks at his stomach.)

PONCE: It's always like that.

GIDEON: You should get it checked. If I were you –

PONCE: You're not me, Gideon.

So do your best to keep your hands off my wife.

GIDEON: What are you—?

PONCE: I heard you. "Margaret. Yes . . . "

GIDEON: She wanted to say hello, Ponce.

PONCE: You shouldn't speak to her.

GIDEON: What?

PONCE: She likes men, Gideon. She's got a sickness. Sex. All the time. But it's nothing. Understand? She doesn't mean any of it.

JOHN: She doesn't seem sick, Ponce.

PONCE: Do you live with her?

JOHN: No.

PONCE: Then you don't know.

GIDEON: She seems fine at parties, and—

PONCE: At parties. Yes. She's on medication. She's sedated. All the men are the same at parties when it comes to Margaret. But get her in a room at home, you'll see what I mean.

JOHN: You're never home. How would you know anything about Margaret?

PONCE: I work, John. I have a job.

JOHN: Exactly. Which means you can't be home all the time. You can't know everything about Margaret.

PONCE: What do you know, John?

JOHN: Huh?

PONCE: You know something? Seen something? Done something with my wife?

JOHN: She's not my type, Ponce.

PONCE: Son-of-a-bitch.

GIDEON: Take it easy, Ponce. Your stomach . . .

PONCE: What the hell is wrong with my stomach, eh? You want to kill me? Stab old Ponce in the bath-house, then go to the Russians with everything I've got on the satellite project?

JOHN: We'd never do that, Ponce.

PONCE: I'm not Profumo, gentlemen. Profumo got caught because he wanted to get laid. I don't need to get laid, you understand? I got Margaret. Sex. All the time. So whatever you two think you're up to . . .

JOHN: Margaret's too smooth.

PONCE: What?

JOHN: Her face. It's like marble. I can't stand that.

PONCE: Traitors. Both of you. Adulterous sons of bitches.

GIDEON: Your stomach, Ponce.

(PONCE *doubles over in pain.*)

PONCE: Christ. Bloody Christ . . .

JOHN: It's your ulcer, Ponce.

PONCE: I don't have an ulcer . . .

(PONCE *collapses. After a beat, the phone rings.* GIDEON *and* JOHN *look at each other. The phone keeps ringing. Steam rises.*)

SCENE 6

THE HEBRIDES

(Out of steam, the sky's tip is seen. Slowly it opens wide, vast, cold. ADAM and SIMON with surfboards. They are suspended.)

ADAM: Nothing but sky.

SIMON: We're at the fucking end of the earth.

ADAM: More like the top.

SIMON: Eh?

ADAM: The Hebrides.

SIMON: You're fucking insane. How are we going to surf here?

ADAM: We'll surf the sky. Look at that cloud.

SIMON: What?

ADAM: Just look at it.

SIMON: I'm not riding any clouds, Adam.

ADAM: We'll stay here on this pin-point spot, this fucking end coordinate, and take our boards and pitch them on the clouds. And then we'll see if we can land back on this spot whole, with nothing broken, except our heads, full with riding the biggest fucking wave you can imagine. Something like that song.

SIMON: Eh?

ADAM: *(sings)* "Fly me to the moon . . . and let us surf among the stars . . ."

SIMON: Yeah.

ADAM: *(spoken)* Only with less swing and more bop, kind of like Elvis on a good day before he's doped up.

SIMON: Yeah.

ADAM: And then we'll touch down with our shoulders high and our boards up. Or better yet, with our boards cracked.

SIMON: What?

ADAM: Split open. Split to infinity. And we'll be like fucking kings, Simon, kings of the earth. Cause who else would think of coming here? to this cold place full of stars and nothing else. Who else would think of riding these fucking clouds? And we can just keep riding, keep surfing, *(sings)* "Let me see what stars are like on Jupiter and Mars . . ."

SIMON: *(sings simultaneous with* ADAM *on . . .)* "on Jupiter and Mars . . ."

ADAM: *(spoken)* until there aren't any more clouds left, until everyone has gone through the portals of hell, and it'll be just us, bouncing against each other in pockets of diaphanous waves we can't even see, caught in the random bliss of the Hebrides.

SIMON: . . . You drink something, Adam?

(Light Shift.)

SCENE 7

SPACE

(WITNESS is drinking a can of Tab soda.)

WITNESS: Blame it on the blue lava in my brain but I can't think straight. Not like this. I mean, you got ZaSu and Plath and Patsy Cline dying,

(Crash pad. ADAM *and* SIMON *with surfboards.* WITNESS *walks in, continuing.)*

And where do I fit in, huh? I feel cursed. I mean, here I am, drinking Tab, right? And I don't even know what's in it. I mean, what is Tab? It doesn't taste like Coke. Tastes liquid, strange, and yet I'm supposed to like it. Because it's good, right? Everyone else says it is. And then I got these quasars. Somebody comes up with quasars and I don't even know WHAT . . . But they are already making TV's with them. Quasar Vision. Martian kind of stuff. And I'm just trying to miss being bombed out. By everyone. The Soviets, the Cubans, the Viet Cong. I'm thinking, can't I just go out, meet somebody, and go dancing?

(WITNESS exits.)

ADAM: Quasar in the head.

SIMON: What?

ADAM: Just now. Hit me in the head. It's gone now.

SIMON: Invisible-like?

ADAM: Speeding comet.

SIMON: I thought you said it was a quasar.

ADAM: Like a speeding comet. Fast.

SIMON: Where did it hit you?

ADAM: On the crown.

SIMON: Got a bump?

ADAM: Don't know yet. Feels funny.

SIMON: Sit down.

ADAM: I got to hit the waves.

SIMON: You can't hit the waves with a bump on your head. You'll kill yourself.

ADAM: Feels like lava coming out of my brain. Like when I was a baby and got that fever . . .

SIMON: You should have it checked.

ADAM: What?

SIMON: The lava.

ADAM: It's imaginary lava, Simon.

SIMON: Oh. Can I touch it?

ADAM: What?

SIMON: Your head.

ADAM: It's hot. Watch out.

(SIMON *touches* ADAM*'s head.*)

SIMON: It is.

ADAM: I told you.

SIMON: Maybe it wasn't a quasar.

ADAM: Eh?

SIMON: Maybe it was a drop of mercury.

ADAM: You don't believe me?

SIMON: I didn't see anything, Adam.

ADAM: I told you. It was fast. You couldn't have seen a quasar.

SIMON: Would've felt it, though.

ADAM: How?

SIMON: Would've felt a rumble or something like that.

ADAM: A rumble?

SIMON: Yeah. Like a train.

ADAM: Quasars are silent.

(Caught in light: the crash of WITNESS crushing the can of Tab with her foot. PERRY COMO appears in a spot singing "Catch a Falling Star," fading into . . .)

SCENE 8

REMAINS (1)

(Cocktail party chatter. In the background are seen JACKIE GLEASON, JACKIE KENNEDY, FIDEL CASTRO, ANDY WARHOL, PERRY COMO, and the WITNESS. During the scene PERRY COMO and ANDY WARHOL will fade out of party, as will the WITNESS. In the foreground: PONCE is drinking. JOHN is at his side.)

PONCE: I miss the Russians, John.

JOHN: How's that, sir?

PONCE: I understood them: their music, their drinking. Now I don't know who the hell I'm talking to. Soviets? They're a different breed.

JOHN: They've been around a long time.

PONCE: Christ. They're our enemies, John. Am I supposed to like my enemies now?

JOHN: No.

PONCE: Damn right.

JOHN: But we have to work with them, sir.

PONCE: We have to beat those motherfuckers out of the water. Off the goddamn planet. They've ruined everything. I used to go to Cuba three, four times a year, get me the best pussy. Now I can't go there. I have to look at Margaret all day. With her bone china and frosted pink lipstick. She's fucking ice, John.

JOHN: Marble.

PONCE: Yes. So, I dream of Cuba. You know I went to school with Castro? In New York. We went to bars, strip clubs. He was a regular fellow, one of the boys. But he hooked up with Che and the Soviets, and that was the end of him.

JOHN: Keep your enemies close.

PONCE: Who said that? Jack? I don't want to talk about him, John. You want to upset me talking about a Catholic? Do you?

JOHN: No.

PONCE: Then don't talk about him. Christ. He's destroyed everything, everything our country stands for.

JOHN: You should stop drinking, sir.

PONCE: What?

JOHN: Somebody might hear you.

PONCE: What? I can't talk anymore? This is a free country, John.

JOHN: I know.

PONCE: We're not in the USSR.

JOHN: I know that.

PONCE: And if fucking Marilyn can go in and out of the White House any time she wants, then I sure as hell . . .

JOHN: Certain things, Ponce.

PONCE: What?

JOHN: You wouldn't want someone to hear.

PONCE: You're like a son to me, John.

JOHN: I know, sir.

PONCE: . . . Remember when we went fishing that time?

JOHN: I packed my bait.

PONCE: Right off the coast. The cool rush of the Atlantic.

JOHN: Everything was gray.

PONCE: You held your own.

JOHN: I held my breath.

PONCE: You stood firm against the sudden waves.

JOHN: I couldn't let go of the line. I was afraid.

PONCE: Damn miss those days.... Godammit. My head feels hot.

JOHN: Could be the quasars, Ponce.

PONCE: Quasars?

JOHN: They've put quasars in the security cameras. Upgraded the mechanism.

PONCE: Burning...

JOHN: It's technology, sir. You want to lie down?

PONCE: You put something in my drink, John? You're trying to poison me like poor-ass Julius Caesar?

JOHN: I've done nothing, Ponce.

PONCE: You slipped me a mickey.

JOHN: What?

PONCE: It's an expression. You never—?

JOHN: No. Maybe when I was a kid...

PONCE: That's right. I'm old.

JOHN: I didn't mean it like... just the term... I've never...

PONCE: You're a goddamn spy, aren't you, John? You've been cavorting with Philby and all the rest of them. With that goddamn Honeybear...

JOHN: I don't know what you're talking about, sir.

PONCE: Why do you want to keep our enemies close, John?

JOHN: Strategy, sir. If you keep your enemies close, you keep their secrets in your pocket.

PONCE: What the hell does that mean?

JOHN: The Russians, Ponce.

PONCE: The Soviets?

JOHN: Yes.

PONCE: You're an agent. Is that what you're telling me? You sleep with the Soviets, and then wash their laundry out here?

JOHN: I don't wash laundry, Ponce.

PONCE: You iron it?

JOHN: I place it in paper bags and send it to the cleaners.

PONCE: Someone else irons it.

JOHN: I think they fold it. You have to pay extra for ironing.

PONCE: I knew it. Son-of-a-bitch. You're on our side.

JOHN: What other side would—?

(PONCE *lifts* JOHN *up, kisses him.*)

PONCE: You're going to get Cuba back for me, aren't you, son?

JOHN: Well, I . . .

PONCE: Carry on, son. Carry on. The day I sit on the white Cuban sand, I'll tell all the brown-eyed whores that you are their rightful savior. And you know why I will do that? Because I respect you, son. Down on my knees I will respect you.

JOHN: Let me go, sir.

PONCE: What?

JOHN: Let go of me.

PONCE: Sorry, John.

(*He does so.*)

It's affection. You understand?

You're like a son . . .

JOHN: Yes, sir. I know.

PONCE: I've taught you everything.

JOHN: We should stop drinking now.

PONCE: Huh?

JOHN: We have that meeting. With Jack. You know how he doesn't like you to drink.

PONCE: Coward. Fucking coward.

JOHN: Let's get you ready, Ponce.

PONCE: Only he can get drunk. We have to stand around and watch.

JOHN: Let's go, Ponce.

PONCE: You're going to get Cuba for me, John. Remember that. You're going to get her for me.

JOHN: I'll do my best, sir.

PONCE: And we'll play on the sand.

(PONCE *and* JOHN *exit.*)

SCENE 9

INTERLUDE

(Cocktail party chatter from previous builds to a feverish pitch, a wall of sound, then a crash of glasses. On a loudspeaker is heard: "And now: JACKIE GLEASON, JACKIE KENNEDY, *and* FIDEL CASTRO." JACKIE GLEASON, JACKIE KENNEDY, *and* FIDEL CASTRO *step forward. They are slightly drunk. They sing the following to a mutation of the song "Those Lazy, Hazy, Crazy Days of Summer.")*

GLEASON & JACKIE KENNEDY & CASTRO: Roll out those lazy, hazy, crazy days of living On the sand On the beach On the shore . . . Of life. Oh, oh, oh, what can one, one do but go on spinning? To the beat To the bop To the bass . . . Of strife?

(spoken) Exhibit A.

*(*GLEASON & JACKIE KENNEDY & FIDEL CASTRO *point to:* ADAM *and* SIMON *with beat-up surfboards.)*

ADAM: He crashed into me. He did it on purpose. He wanted to ruin my board.

SIMON: You'll get another.

ADAM: And you didn't do anything, did you? You let the bastard crash into me.

SIMON: I didn't know he was going to do it.

ADAM: You could've sensed it.

SIMON: How?

ADAM: You got a gift, don't you? You sense things.

SIMON: I get thoughts sometimes. Yeah.

ADAM: You could have pushed him out of the way. Let him crash.

SIMON: I can't sense people, Adam. Only things.

ADAM: Fucking useless, that's what you are.

SIMON: Hey.

ADAM: Fucking quasars out to get me. Crashing into my life.

SIMON: Come on now, Adam.

ADAM: Hopeless.

(ADAM *walks away from* SIMON, *exits.* SIMON *is left. Shift to* THE LIVING. *This is half-sung.*)

GLEASON & JACKIE KENNEDY & CASTRO: Roll out those lazy, hazy, crazy days of living On the sand On the beach

CASTRO: On the crap . . .

GLEASON & JACKIE KENNEDY: Of life.

GLEASON & JACKIE KENNEDY & CASTRO: Oh, oh, oh, what can one, one do but go on spinning? To the beat To the bop

CASTRO: To the stink

GLEASON: *(spoken)* Exhibit B.

(GLEASON, JACKIE KENNEDY, *and* CASTRO *point to:* PONCE *and* JOHN . . .)

PONCE: Mongrel.

JOHN: Hold on, Ponce.

PONCE: You put me down and forget about me, make me miss my meeting?

JOHN: I thought you were sleeping.

PONCE: Now I've got Jack on my ass. Goddamn Catholic.

JOHN: I'm sorry.

PONCE: Goddamn mongrel. I should've never taught you anything, the way you've paid me back.

JOHN: I thought if you slept . . .

PONCE: You didn't think anything. Stupid bitch. What happened to Cuba, huh?

JOHN: I'm working on it, Ponce.

PONCE: Castro's got you by the balls. Hopeless, that's what you are. I put all my faith and trust in you, and it turns out you're hopeless. A goddamn fag.

JOHN: I'm not a . . .

PONCE: You were looking at me, weren't you? While I was sleeping?

JOHN: Well, I . . .

PONCE: Only thing it could mean, John. You think about that.

(*Beat. Shift to* SIMON.)

SIMON: Adam loves the waves. More than me. I look at him sometimes, when he's staring out at the ocean or watching TV, and think "Would he let me touch him?" I want to touch him sometimes. On the shoulder. Chest. But something stops me. I think it's the waves. So, I light up a joint. I let the smoke curl around me, and let the smoke become Adam's fingers touching me, squeezing my hard nipples. Waves mean nothing to me. But smoke? Smoke is Adam. And how he touches me.

(Shift to PONCE *and* JOHN.)

JOHN: You ever try surfing, sir?

PONCE: What?

JOHN: It's a sport. Like fishing. Only a helluva lot more relaxing.

PONCE: I can't swim, son.

(Shift to THE LIVING.)

GLEASON & JACKIE KENNEDY & CASTRO: *(spoken)* Ladyboy, ladyboy, come into my room. Come into my room tonight. *(half-sung)* You'll get a lazy, hazy, crazy fuck of glory . . . *(spoken)* that you'll remember straight through your whole life.

(Orgy. GLEASON & JACKIE KENNEDY & CASTRO & SIMON & PONCE & JOHN: *each assumes a semi-pornographic pose, and freeze as* PATSY CLINE *is seen on a platform singing "Sweet Dreams" to an unseen audience.* WITNESS *appears.)*

WITNESS: Five times seven, four times twelve, twelve times nine . . . The multiplication tables are written on the left side of my tablet, as I copy them on the right. The girl on the other side of the room is left-handed, and is being told by the teacher that she must learn how to write with her right hand, because being on the left is no good. She has short hair like Audrey Hepburn in "Roman Holiday," and she smells of pine. I look at her knees. Four times six, six times eight, ten times . . . The numbers fall from my lips. Particles in space. She turns the tablet over to adjust her hand, and keeps writing with her left. I copy her. In ten years, I will forget my multiplication tables completely.

(Lights fade on WITNESS, *and* PATSY CLINE *singing "Sweet Dreams." The orgy's end: bodies of* GLEASON & JACKIE

KENNEDY & CASTRO & SIMON & JOHN *break out of their poses.*
PONCE *remains prone on the ground. Cocktail party chatter
resumes. A wall of sound.*

GLEASON & JACKIE KENNEDY & CASTRO *disappear midst the
swinging lights.* SIMON *walks away.* JOHN *nudges* PONCE. *No
response.* JOHN *shrugs, walks away in the direction of the swinging lights. Sound stops abruptly.* PONCE *wakes.*)

SCENE 10

REMAINS (2)

(Time shift. Open space.)

PONCE: I want my pride back. I know it's a foolish word these
days. Old-fashioned. That's what they say. "You're from another
time, Ponce. You remember the Russians? Who remembers
them anymore? Who drinks vodka?" Pride. I hold it inside me.
Sometimes when I'm playing golf, out in the open, or down in
the rough, I think "Yes. Pride's come back." And then I swing,
and the iron flies out of my hand, and the ball lands in a sand-
trap, and I think "Not yet. Not now." Margaret won't look at me.
She's got her Mary Quant dresses and manicured hands. She
doesn't have time for me. I haven't made time . . . Damn politics. All my life.

(Shift to GIDEON *framed in light.)*

GIDEON: Margaret was standing in a corner with her hands
caught in the middle of a sentence. I walked across the room,
past the silver trays of Norwegian cheese, and touched
Margaret's shoulder, her exposed shoulder in her slim dress.
Without a bra. I could see. I kept my hand. She dropped her
eyes. Cold zipper down her back, down to the bone.

(Shift to PONCE.)

PONCE: And for what? I've worn more black this year than I care
to think. The whole damn country is in mourning.

(Shift to WITNESS.)

WITNESS: Blame it on the blue lava in my brain but I can't think straight. Not like this. I mean, you got Zasu and Piaf and Oswald . . .

PONCE: Perpetual Sorrow. Our Lady of the Perpetual Sorrows. I pray to her now, and I'm not even Catholic. Can you understand that?

(*Back to* GIDEON.)

GIDEON: I had Margaret on the terrace and there wasn't a scruple that would stop me.

(*Fade on* GIDEON. *Back to* PONCE.)

PONCE: I got this chow. This dog. He rests his head on my foot. I think "This dog, this chow, has pride." I hope some of it rubs off on me.

(*Shift to* ADAM.)

ADAM: Quasars on the TV. Infecting my brain.

(SIMON *appears, smoking.*)

SIMON: You want a hit, Adam?

ADAM: Everything looks the same. Nothing but waves.

SIMON: You let smoke go up into the air, it'll catch you on the way down.

ADAM: I can't think anymore, Simon.

(*Lights begin to slowly narrow their focus on* PONCE.)

PONCE: Five o'clock. Time for a drink. You like vodka? It's Russian, if that's all right. I take it with these pills. They help my nerves.

(*Shift to* ADAM *and* SIMON.)

SIMON: Take a hit, Adam.

ADAM: Huh?

SIMON: Kill the waves.

(ADAM *takes cigarette from* SIMON. *Shift to* MOTHER *and* LOUELLA *in a corner of home.*)

MOTHER: I wonder if Perry Como is married, dear.
He's got such a lovely voice.

LOUELLA: He'll never sound like Patsy.

MOTHER: Shush. What'd I say about her?

LOUELLA: It's true.

MOTHER: Don't use that tone with me, Louella.

LOUELLA: What tone?

MOTHER: You know perfectly well what I mean.

WITNESS: Red Ranger pajamas and red slippers for the boys, pink fuzzies for the girls. On the TV, it's black and white . . .

WITNESS & ADAM & LOUELLA: I can't make out anything.

(Shift to PONCE *more isolated now in light.)*

PONCE: I'll fix you a vodka. Straight up. Straight up. What do you say? It's going to be a long night. I can see it. I can see it from here. And this time, I don't want to wake up. Not this time.

*(*PONCE *downs pills and vodka.)*

WITNESS: When you're premature, when you're kicking to get out and into the world, you're more likely to get a fever than not.

(The GHOSTS *are glimpsed in shadow. This is a soft fugue.)*

JFK & PATSY CLINE: . . . ninety-three sixteen, sixteen thirty-nine

JFK & PATSY CLINE & ADAM & SIMON & LOUELLA & MOTHER: Sixty-three nineteen, Sixty-nine thirteen

JFK & PATSY CLINE & ADAM & SIMON & LOUELLA & MOTHER & WITNESS: Sixty-one thirty-nine, Thirty-one sixty-nine, Thirty-nine sixteen, Thirty-six . . .

*(*PONCE *collapses. Lights fade on all except* PATSY CLINE *who remains caught in a mere fragment of light. She starts to sing "I Fall to Pieces.")*

END OF PART I

PART 2

SCENE 11

PARADE: HOME AND AWAY

(Lights on WITNESS *in a frame.)*

WITNESS: Flat, black, with thin straps: Mary Jane's. From Buster Brown. They were better than Stride-Rite. They were more expensive. I placed my feet inside the cool leather and thought of the cardboard cut-out of Buster Brown and his dog at the front of the store. And how I wanted my hair to be just like that. How I wanted to be a boy in my Mary Jane's.

(Shift to MOTHER *with camera.)*

MOTHER: Louella, dear. Please sit up straight. And stop fussing with your Mary Jane's. Child, I bought those for you yesterday. You're going to ruin them if you keep fussing with them like that. Now, look over here. That's right. Don't look up, dear. Your eyes are tilting. And smile.

(Freeze on MOTHER *and* LOUELLA. WITNESS *steps out of the frame.)*

WITNESS: I don't want my face to be inside a Sears frame. Not ever. Not again. Ever since I was born, I've had my face stuck inside frames that come from the portrait studio at Sears. And they always look the same: Painted-on smile, locked eyes, and stiff hair. There is a shelf in my parents' house of pictures of me. And every time I think of it, I look in the mirror to see if I still look like that, the way Sears wanted me. Even though I know I don't look like that anymore. In fact, I never looked like that. It was the pictures that made me.

(Shift back to MOTHER *and* LOUELLA, *who break out of their freeze.)*

MOTHER: Oh dear, how do you work with this thing?

LOUELLA: It's an Instamatic.

MOTHER: Don't confuse me, dear. Don't confuse me.

LOUELLA: Just press the button, Mom.

MOTHER: Louella, honey, smile, all right? I'll figure it out. Don't I always figure it out?

LOUELLA: Yes, mother.

MOTHER: Smile.

LOUELLA: *(through clenched teeth)* I'm smiling.

(Flash. Fade on LOUELLA and MOTHER. Time shift. A million flash-pots go off. Red carpet and the stars. WITNESS is now the PRESS with camera in hand.)

PRESS: Miss Cline, Miss Cline, over here.

(PATSY CLINE appears. Pose.)

PATSY: CLINE: Take that picture, honey. Take that picture, son-of-a-bitch.

(Flash. PATSY CLINE walks away, and poses to one side ... ANDY WARHOL appears.)

WARHOL: All I want is to get my picture taken. There's no other point to life.

PRESS: Mister Warhol?

WARHOL: Yes?

(Flash.)

PRESS: Mister Warhol?

WARHOL: Yes.

(Pose. An extended close-up.)

I painted her Koolaid colors: Jackie. A woman like her doesn't deserve black-and-white. Jack? I don't think he minds. He understands Jackie and I were twins in some other life. Magenta. Ultra-violet. Pink. We all could use a little color under the glare of the lights.

(Flash. ANDY WARHOL walks away, and poses to one side ... EDITH PIAF appears. She is in desperate need of pissing.)

PIAF: Scum. Nothing but scum. These Americans don't even let you piss when you want.

PRESS: Miss Piaf, Miss Piaf. Over here.

PIAF: La vie en shit.

PRESS: Miss Piaf?

(Pose.)

PIAF: Merde. Tout merde.

PRESS: Why don't you sing us a bit of something, will you?

(BOB DYLAN appears.)

DYLAN: If you sing for your supper, you fall on your face.

PRESS: What was that, Dylan?

DYLAN: I am a certified bastard of the ruling class who wears shades on the inside and jangles on my feet. Nothing in my pockets but a stick of gum and an itchy forefinger. What do I got to owe you, eh? Bastard children of loose-lipped America, loose-hipped wanderers with acid leaves? My family's from a town I don't want to remember. I'm the accidental child, entrusted to rumors. I've made up my tongue, this rasp, snake wail and clenched-teeth drawing out of indigent words from another time I am the bastard prince born of a bastard king out of the belly of nothing but a stack of old records and mutable beliefs. Call me as named. Expect nothing of me. But take my picture. Please.

PRESS: What was that, Mister Dylan?

PATSY CLINE & WARHOL & PIAF: Merde.

PRESS: Right.

(Flash. Flash. Flash. Flash. PATSY CLINE, ANDY WARHOL, EDITH PIAF, and BOB DYLAN exit. FIDEL CASTRO appears, cigar in hand.)

CASTRO: One should never underestimate the power of a photograph. After all, it is the record of a time. A smile can say so much to someone looking at a photograph fifty years from now, and so little.

PRESS: Castro, give us a smile.

(Flash. JFK appears.)

JFK: Here for the party, Fidel?

CASTRO: You know I never miss a party, Jack.

JFK: How about a cigar, Fidel?

CASTRO: For you, my friend? Always.

(FIDEL CASTRO hands JFK a cigar. Flash.)

PRESS: Mr. President, Mr. President, one more word.

JFK: That's enough, gentlemen.

PRESS: But, Mr. President, for the country, sir. One word for the country.

JFK: Merde.

PRESS: What was that, sir?

(JACKIE KENNEDY *appears.*)

JACKIE KENNEDY: Shit. Or can't you speak English? Come on, Jack.

(*Flash. Flash. Flash.* CASTRO, JFK, *and* JACKIE KENNEDY *exit.* LEE HARVEY OSWALD *appears.*)

OSWALD: I just want to say this: everyone here is full of shit. No one person deserves to be standing.

(JOHN LENNON *appears.*)

LENNON: You're awfully cynical. Aren't you, chap?

OSWALD: The name's Lee Harvey Oswald. A record speaks for itself.

LENNON: What kind of record is that? 45 or 78?

(*Flash.*)

PRESS: John Lennon, John Lennon, over here. Over here, John.

LENNON: "Over here." That's a bloody song, isn't it?

(LENNON *poses.* PONCE *appears.*)

PONCE: It was "Over There," son. "Over There."

LENNON: You're a regular quiz show muff, aren't you?

PRESS: Hold that pose, gentlemen.

OSWALD: No picture. No picture. You do not see me.

(*Flash.*)

Faceless, I am.

PRESS: One more, gentlemen. One more.

PONCE: (*To* LENNON) What did you say, son?

LENNON: Lick me.

PONCE: What was that?

LENNON: Lick me. Lick me. Lick me.

PONCE: Now, son?

LENNON: What other time is there?

(PONCE *is about to lick* LENNON *when Flash, Flash.*)

PRESS: Thank you, gentlemen.

LENNON: My pleasure.

PONCE: That wasn't for the public record, was it?

PRESS: Everything's for the record, sir.

PONCE: Son-of-a-bitch.

LENNON: I'm like any other son.

(LENNON *walks away, singing "Love Me Do" softly.*)

PONCE: Christ.

(LENNON *exits.*)

OSWALD: I just want to say this: There is no record of me. I was never here. I will blur and be made counterfeit before my blood dries.

PONCE: What?

(*A million flash-pots go off as* OSWALD *exits.* PONCE *is left standing to one side. Time shift. Back to home's corner.* MOTHER *has taken* LOUELLA*'s picture.*)

MOTHER: See, baby, that wasn't so hard.

LOUELLA: I think I blinked.

MOTHER: What was that, dear?

LOUELLA: I think you took a picture of me with my eyes closed.

MOTHER: Always fussing, dear. Always a fuss.

LOUELLA: I'm going to look stupid.

MOTHER: . . . You want an Italian ice or don't you?

LOUELLA: Italian ice?

MOTHER: I said I'd treat.

LOUELLA: Mom, you're the best.

(MOTHER *and* LOUELLA *exit. Back to red carpet and the stars.* JACKIE GLEASON *enters on cue, flask in hand.*)

GLEASON: "Baby, you're the greatest!"

PONCE: They're all inside, Jackie.

GLEASON: How do you like that? They've crapped out on me already. *(offering flask)* Care for a drink?

PONCE: No, I'll be fine.

GLEASON: I got Russian vodka.

PONCE: Real Russian?

GLEASON: Given to me by Khruschev himself.

PONCE: Khruschev?

GLEASON: He played a killer of a game of golf at Boca. *(offers flask again)* What do you say, Ponce?

PONCE: . . . No, I'll be fine, Jackie.

GLEASON: Yeah?

PONCE: I can live through anything.

GLEASON: How about your wife, Ponce?

PONCE: My wife?

GLEASON: Margaret. She's quite a woman.

PONCE: Yes. Well, she couldn't make it tonight, Jackie.

GLEASON: She's in another orbit, am I right?

PONCE: What?

GLEASON: "To the moon, Alice. Straight to the moon."

(Flash. GLEASON *exits.* PRESS *holds up camera.)*

PRESS: Senator Ponce Quarry Simmons Modesto King?

PONCE: Yes.

(Flash. PRESS *exits.* PONCE *is left standing as . . .)*

SCENE 12

FLOATING (1)

(Hum and chime of the cool glass serene. MARGARET *is in a mall.)*

MARGARET: Things slip. I don't know how. They just do. Ponce and I have stopped speaking to each other. No more than ten words in five days. Ponce likes to tell people I'm on medication. "Margaret? She's sedated," he says. But the truth is, I make small talk with anyone just for the comfort of words, lies, drinking too much . . . I couldn't tell you what I dream. But I often think of paradise: an atrium, a high ceiling, the smell of flowers and rows of neon: a mall. *(as if pointing out objects in the store)* Cosmic green eyeshadow, flats, mules, and Mary Janes. I miss words, the simple ones like "tell me" and "give me a hand." But I don't say anything. I shop. At peace.

(Up the escalator, and MARGARET *disappears.)*

SCENE 13

LANDING

*(*PONCE *and* MANDY *before the TV.)*
MANDY: I'd like to fuck one.
PONCE: What?
MANDY: Astronaut, cosmonaut. I could get inside one right now.
PONCE: What about me, Mandy?
MANDY: I've had you. But an astronaut . . . Look at him.
PONCE: Gordon Cooper? He's a damn headache.
MANDY: Twenty-two orbits. No one's ever done that before.

(Shift to crash pad: ADAM *and* SIMON *watching TV.)*
SIMON: He must be dizzy, don't you think?
ADAM: He's specially trained, Simon. He's a fucking astronaut.
SIMON: Still must be . . . Twenty-two times around . . .
ADAM: You want to try it?
SIMON: What?
ADAM: Twenty-two waves. Non-stop. Twenty-two orbits.
SIMON: It's damn thundering.
ADAM: You don't think Gordon Cooper had the elements to contend with?
SIMON: He was in a capsule, Adam.
ADAM: It's all a matter of gravity. What's larger than air. If you can ride that, you can get through anything.

(Fade on ADAM *and* SIMON. *Back to:* PONCE *hits the TV.)*

MANDY: Hey. What'd you do that for?

PONCE: I don't make time for you, Mandy, so you can sit around and watch some Oklahoma kid fly around in space.

MANDY: Say my name again.

PONCE: What?

MANDY: Say it.

PONCE: Mandy.

MANDY: I like how you say it.

PONCE: You're a sweet girl, Mandy.

MANDY: Is that all I am?

(WITNESS *appears in light.*)

WITNESS: Something lifts, something moves, and I'm in the air. A cowboy has gone into space, and I feel myself spinning. Twenty-two orbits . . . I start to move my arms, legs . . . The incubator falls away. I am kissing everything.

(*Back to . . .*)

PONCE: You're a doll. I don't know what I'd . . .

MANDY: Shh . . .

(*Back to* WITNESS.)

WITNESS: When I look down, I hear a man named Nikita at the other end of the earth cursing.

(WITNESS *fades. Back to . . .*)

MANDY: Hey.

PONCE: Hmm?

MANDY: Call I call you Nikita?

PONCE: Damn Soviet—?

MANDY: I'll fuck you again if you let me call you Nikita.

PONCE: Why that . . . ?

MANDY: I have to call you something when I come.

PONCE: . . . What about me? What do I call you?

MANDY: Mandy.

PONCE: You don't get to change?

MANDY: No.

PONCE: Why not?

MANDY: Cause this is my game. Pucker up, Nikita.

(MANDY *kisses* PONCE. *Time shift into . . .*)

SCENE 14

ORIGINS

(PONCE *watches* MANDY *as she walks away.* JOHN *is revealed in light. He watches* PONCE *watching* MANDY.)

JOHN: It's all arbitrary, Ponce.

PONCE: What's that?

JOHN: What happens to us, what comes down to us in time.

PONCE: I like Mandy, John. There's nothing arbitrary about her. She's a permanent part of my life.

JOHN: Now.

PONCE: You can't have her, John.

JOHN: Time moves in a continuum. Think about it. One day you're spinning a hula hoop, the next day you're standing at a hospital door and you don't even know why.

PONCE: A hula what?

JOHN: Hoop, Ponce.

PONCE: What's got into you, John?

JOHN: Numbers, dates . . . they don't mean anything. They're just particles in space.

PONCE: Who have you been talking to?

JOHN: No one.

PONCE: Well, I have to believe in something, John. If I don't, I wouldn't get up in the morning, understand? I have to get up, check the ballot box, see if I got another term down the line . . . or if I have to move out of the Tudor house I bought and move me and Martha into a red brick shingle roof number in Maryland somewhere. Dammit. That's not arbitrary, John. That's life. Cruel and definite.

JOHN: You should really try surfing, Ponce.

PONCE: What?

JOHN: Riding the waves.

PONCE: You are turning into some kind of . . .

JOHN: What?

PONCE: . . . I don't even recognize you.

JOHN: Ease up, Ponce.

PONCE: The months I showed you around this town, the time I've spent on you . . .

JOHN: When were you born, Ponce?

PONCE: Huh?

JOHN: Year, date?

PONCE: Must've been nineteen-twelve, nineteen . . .

JOHN: You don't know?

PONCE: My folks hid all my papers in a box. I think I'm registered somewhere . . .

JOHN: Arbitrary.

PONCE: I know my age, John.

JOHN: Your body maybe, But there's a whole cacophony of atoms, and subatomic particles dancing in space mindless of whether you were born or not, of whether what you're doing is useful or not, of whether what you do means anything to the overall construct of a world that's falling apart anyway.

PONCE: Did Jack give you a talking?

JOHN: Nobody needs to tell me anything.

PONCE: Humility, son. That's something you still have to learn.

JOHN: Like you and Mandy?

PONCE: . . . Look, I'll talk to Jack. Whatever you've done, I'll help you through it.

JOHN: Goddamn loyalty . . .

PONCE: I don't like the son-of-a-bitch, but I'll talk to him. For you. You got a hell of a future, son.

JOHN: You know what I like about you, Ponce? You don't stop. You still believe "talking things out" will make a difference.

You're under a fucking cloud.

PONCE: Look at me. Look at me, John.

JOHN: What?

PONCE: I've been loyal to you. I've . . . put my faith . . .

JOHN: Right.

(JOHN *walks away.* PONCE *grabs him.*)

PONCE: Look at me!

(PONCE *hits* JOHN.)

. . . I'm sorry. I don't know what . . .

JOHN: Doesn't make a difference whether you're fifty or five, does it? It's all the same.

(*Shift to* WITNESS *found in light.*)

WITNESS: I think it was the radio. Petula Clark singing "Downtown" and Bobby Darin crooning shortly after. I remember the radio, and my mother's voice: Spanish. Clear. Crystalline. "Duerme, nina. Duerme . . . " Lullaby words in a clear voice with the radio in the background blaring: (*sings*) "When you're alone and life is making you . . . You can always go downtown." (*spoken*) I loved to dance to that song. I didn't know what it meant then, But I knew dancing.

(WITNESS *dances. Fade on* WITNESS. *Back to* PONCE *and* JOHN.)

PONCE: I don't know what I'm doing anymore, John.

JOHN: Give me your hand, Ponce.

PONCE: What?

JOHN: Your hand.

PONCE: What are you—?

JOHN: It's time you went dancing.

PONCE: You've lost your mind. Everybody's damn lost their mind.

JOHN: Forget the ballot box, Ponce. Forget everything. Let's go (*sings*) "Downtown . . . downtown . . . "

PONCE: What are you singing?

JOHN: A song.

PONCE: I've never heard of it.

JOHN: It won't be out for another year. *(sings)* " . . . Forget all your troubles, forget all your cares and go downtown . . . "

PONCE: You're crazy, John. How'd I ever get stuck with you?

JOHN: Let's dance, Ponce.

PONCE: What?

JOHN: Spin me.

PONCE: Now?

JOHN: I want to feel the air between my lungs.

(PONCE *spins* JOHN. PETULA CLARK *appears through a Warhol screen in the distance singing "Downtown."* JOHN *spins and spins and spins and spins, as the music blares . . .)*

SCENE 15

HOME AND SPACE (2)

(From home's corner: LOUELLA *is in her room, watching TV, and smoking a joint.* MOTHER *is heard in Voiceover.)*

MOTHER (VO): What are you watching, dear? Is that another astronaut?

LOUELLA: Gordon Cooper, Mom.

MOTHER (VO): I don't know why everyone is going into space, dear. There's plenty of space here. What's that funny smell, dear? Are you smoking in there?

(Fade on LOUELLA. *Shift to* GIDEON *and* JOHN *in a corridor.)*

GIDEON: We send him up. Into orbit. And what does he see? UFO's.

JOHN: Maybe he did see them.

GIDEON: What are you saying, John?

JOHN: He has the vantage point, Gideon. Gordon Cooper's been in space. All we can do is speculate.

GIDEON: Coop is cracked. Like our friend Ponce.

JOHN: Ponce's not cracked.

GIDEON: He will be.

JOHN: Did Coop see saucers, Gideon? I like saucers. The idea of them. Floating around.

GIDEON: Did you smoke something, John? The Democrats smoke all the time. They got weeds up their trouser legs. Pull one up. You'll see. You can catch them in the toilet. Reeking of it.

JOHN: I got nothing to do with the Democrats, Gideon.

GIDEON: Then who?

JOHN: Cosmonauts.

GIDEON: You're still talking to them, John?

JOHN: They've been looking at the sky for a long time, Gideon.

GIDEON: They sent a damn pooch into orbit, John. Made fools of us with that Sputnik crap.

JOHN: Well, I don't talk to dogs, Gideon.

GIDEON: Who do you talk to, John?

JOHN: It'd be a breach of ethics if I told you that.

GIDEON: Fuck the breach. Are you turning into a Soviet, John?

JOHN: Keep your voice down.

GIDEON: There will be no one left. If this keeps up, we'll all end up in Dylan's basement.

(GIDEON *walks away. Light shift as* JOHN *turns around and . . .*)

SCENE 16

INTERLUDE

THE BASEMENT

DYLAN: Look around, walk in I got all the dead here in my basement: snatches of bluegrass, be-bop, piano rags, jug bands, playing claw-hammer, jackrabbit, getting high and talking down. This is the ballroom of the dancing dead. You see, the floor caved in and landed in my basement.

(*He sings a mutated version of the 1931 blues song "Pick Poor*

Robin Clean.")

How was I to know? How was I to know I'd have to come here to pick a poor robin clean?

(DYLAN *spins a 78 rpm record out of a stack on the floor and sends it orbiting through the air. The basement is now a ballroom. In the background, a scrawl on a screen reads "January." The scrawl merges with archival photos of the dancing ghosts, the living (as they appear), and the assorted dead recalled.* PATSY CLINE *and* EDITH PIAF *are dancing to a fractured, ambient waltz.* DYLAN *stands to one side.* JFK *appears, followed by* ANDY WARHOL *and* FIDEL CASTRO. *The* WITNESS *floats in, and dances among the living and the dead.)*

JFK: Robert Frost?

PATSY CLINE & PIAF: Dead.

JFK: Jack Carson, Dick Powell, Sylvia Plath?

(The scrawl turns into "February" and "March," as more photos merge.)

PATSY CLINE & PIAF: Dead.

JFK: Patsy Cline?

PATSY CLINE: Dead.

JFK: William Carlos Williams?

PIAF: William Carlos who?

JFK: William Carlos Williams.

PATSY CLINE & PIAF: Dead.

(The scrawl turns into "May" and "August, " as more and more photos merge and faces of the assorted dead become indistinguishable from each other.)

WARHOL: Monty Woolley?

PATSY CLINE & PIAF: Dead.

WARHOL: Whoa. Whoa. Whoa. Dead?

PATSY CLINE: Dead. Monty Woolley is dead.

(Beat.)

CASTRO: Clifford Odets?

PATSY CLINE: Dead. Just croaked.

PIAF: Last breath.

JFK & CASTRO & WARHOL: Whoa.

DYLAN: Whoa indeed.

   (Beat. The scrawl becomes indecipherable.)

CASTRO: What are we going to do, Jack?

JFK: Go on living.

WARHOL: Like this?

PATSY CLINE: With Piaf,

PIAF: And Cocteau,

PATSY CLINE & PIAF:And Oswald to go.

   (Beat)

DYLAN: What are we going to do, Jack?

CASTRO: What are we going to do, Jack?

PATSY CLINE: What are we

PIAF: What are we

WARHOL: What are we going to do, Jack?

JFK: *(half-sung)* "How was I to know I'd have to come here to pick a poor robin's breast clean?"

   (Basement door slams. Ballroom disappears. PIAF, PATSY CLINE, WARHOL, CASTRO, JFK and WITNESS fade. DYLAN remains. Some confetti loose on the ground. PONCE walks in, drink in hand.)

PONCE: Hey. I heard there was some kind of party down here. Where the hell . . . ? *(To DYLAN)* What are you doing here, son?

   (DYLAN sings to the tune of "Walkin' After Midnight.")

DYLAN: I go out walkin' in the headlight, in the Klieg-light, in the rattle of your mind. I go out walkin' after midnight cryin' over you . . .

   (DYLAN blows PONCE a kiss, and walks away.)

PONCE: What the hell are you singing, son? What the hell . . . ?

   (Basement door slams, and shift to . . .)

SCENE 17

HOME (3)

(PONCE *is drinking.* MARGARET *watches him.*)

PONCE: I cried all night. Put myself to sleep like a baby. Best thing I could have done.

MARGARET: You want to tell me what this is, Ponce?

PONCE: I don't think I want to tell you anything, Margaret. It's not the first time I cry. You've heard me.

MARGARET: How am I supposed to know you're crying. If you have your back turned against me?

PONCE: Well, what do you think I'm doing?

MARGARET: I don't know, Ponce. I know not to ask.

PONCE: You don't care. You never have.

MARGARET: Ponce . . .

PONCE: I'm not complaining. Like I said "Crying's the best thing . . . "

MARGARET: And why's that, Ponce?

PONCE: Because suffering is good. Don't you know that?

MARGARET: Fatalist bullshit.

PONCE: I'm not a fatalist.

MARGARET: You're a grown man, Ponce. Not some child, some beatnik.

PONCE: That word's gone out of style, Margaret. I thought a woman like you would know that.

MARGARET: What word are you talking about, Ponce?

PONCE: "Beatnik."

MARGARET: You know what I mean.

PONCE: Yes. I do know what you mean, Margaret. And you know what? I don't care. I'm a free man. You're getting your big old divorce, like you always wanted.

MARGARET: Not always, Ponce . . .

PONCE: And I'm going to cry and drink and be free. I'll burst my

gut, while I'm at it. Would you like that? Would you like to see
my gut burst?

(PONCE pulls a pistol from his pocket.)

MARGARET: What the hell is that?

PONCE: This is a pistol, Margaret. Ruby-inlaid. It was given to me
by Nabokov.

MARGARET: You're drunk.

PONCE: You didn't know I knew Nabokov, did you? I know all
sorts of people, Margaret. I'm an important man.

MARGARET: *(indicating gun)* Put that thing away.

PONCE: Why? Don't you want to suffer, Margaret? Even just a little bit?

MARGARET: You're being foolish. Stop.

PONCE: Suffering is integral to life.

(He fires a shot. It hits a vase.)

MARGARET: Christ.

PONCE: Feel something now?

(Another shot. It hits the lamp.)

MARGARET: Christ.

PONCE: I haven't heard you speak the Lord's name so much since
the day we got married, Margaret.

(Another shot. It hits the TV.)

MARGARET: Look, let's settle this right now. You keep the
house, I'll move out.

PONCE: I don't want the goddamn house. Keep it. Sleep with
your lawyer. Sleep with Gideon. Screw the whole goddamn
country. I'm going out on the street, see the world . . .

(Another shot. He's hit.)

MARGARET: I'll call an ambulance.

PONCE: It's just a scratch, Margaret . . .

MARGARET: *(at phone)* Damn cord is tangled. I can't get anything to work in this house.

PONCE: What are you doing, Margaret?

(She is trying to untangle the phone cord.)

MARGARET: Everything's in knots ...

PONCE: I got blood coming out of me, Margaret.

MARGARET: Ah. There. *(dials. On phone:)* Emergency? Yes. Yes
  ... What?

  (Lights fade.)

END OF PART 2

PART 3

SCENE 18

TRIO WITH SOLOS ON THE SLIDE

(A green hospital room. PONCE *is lying on a thin bed.* MAR-
GARET *is near him.)*

PONCE: Green. Everything's green. There are dandelions on the
trees. Everything's falling on me.

MARGARET: Can you breathe?

PONCE: The dandelions are mean. They have evil faces. They
want to eat me.

MARGARET: Ponce?

  (Sound: riff on a slide guitar. WITNESS *appears hovering over*
  PONCE.*)*

WITNESS: It's small right now. A thin layer of flesh over my skull.
My brain is the size of a tennis ball bouncing off the strings of
a wood racket, not the power ones made of steel like we have
now, but wood, like in the days of Rod Laver, Margaret Smith,
and Billie Jean King. It rests on the small cushion that serves as
the makeshift bed in the incubator, and records all it hears:
hums and beeps and fingers wriggling.

  (Surfer riff on the slide guitar. ADAM *and* SIMON *appear from
  under the hospital bed.* SIMON *is reading a newspaper.)*

SIMON: Hey, Adam, you hear about this guy?

ADAM: What guy?

SIMON: Senator Ponce. Tried to kill himself.

ADAM: Like the explorer?

SIMON: Eh?

ADAM: Ponce de Leon?

SIMON: I don't know. It says here he's got to "battle his nerves."

ADAM: Where does it say that?

SIMON: Right here. See?

(*Projection on the hospital wall, a headline: "Senator Ponce Quarry Simmons Modesto King Battles Nerves."*)

ADAM: Fucking twisted way to put it.

SIMON: I didn't write it.

ADAM: Why can't they call things by their proper name?

SIMON: What's that?

ADAM: A "crack-up." That's what he had.

SIMON: Oh. Is that the term?

ADAM: Quasars in the brain.

WITNESS: "Let me out," my brain says. "I have fifteen languages bursting and two already on my tongue."

(ADAM *and* SIMON *disappear under the bed. Projection fades. Slide guitar riff.*)

MARGARET: I held his hand. Was that wrong? Maybe I should have cleaned up. The house was a mess. But I don't clean. Silvie does. I held his hand until the ambulance came. Then I put on my hat. The one with the blue trim. I wore it to a party once. Gideon liked it. Ponce couldn't stand the sight of me in that hat. Made him feel weak, he said. I wore it just for him. To see his face. And now he can't recognize me.

PONCE: (*semi-conscious*) Mandy . . .

(*Slide guitar riff. From behind the hospital bed appear* GIDEON *and* JOHN, *smoking cigars.*)

JOHN: She's taking it well, Gideon.

GIDEON: Margaret?

JOHN: Yes.

GIDEON: She's a strong woman, John.

JOHN: Were you going to tell him?

GIDEON: What?

JOHN: That you screwed her.

GIDEON: There's no point in hurting a man, John.

JOHN: Isn't lying worse?

GIDEON: You are turning into a fucking boy-scout.

JOHN: I don't know a thing about making a fire.

GIDEON: You could learn.

PONCE: *(semi-conscious)* Traitors . . . Sons-of . . .

(GIDEON *and* JOHN *disappear under the bed. A pillow of cigar smoke in the air. Sound: erratic beeps of a racing heart.* MAR-GARET *rises.*)

MARGARET: I need a drink. Tall with black ice. Liquor the color of blood.

(MARGARET *exits through the green hospital doors.*

Lights dim in the hospital room.)

WITNESS: The lights go out. Incubator bubble lets air in through a coiled tube. My brain tries to sleep. I think of Kim Philby seeking exile in the USSR on a warm evening in July. I think of four little black girls walking to church on a September morning before all is blown out, and there's nothing but fragments on grass. I think of the Hebrides: Islands suspended in the near frozen Scottish sky, and how somehow everything belongs there, because there's nothing but sky.

(*Riff on the slide as* WITNESS *flies up, and disappears into the green sky.* PONCE *reaches up toward the sky with his arm.*)

PONCE: Margaret . . .

(*Lights fade.*)

SCENE 19

PRIVATE (2)

(PONCE and MANDY on the sofa.)

PONCE: Venus. That's what you are, Margaret.

MANDY: Mandy.

PONCE: What?

MANDY: You called me Margaret.

PONCE: I've a lot on my mind, Mandy.

MANDY: And I don't?

PONCE: Be kind with me.

MANDY: I don't want to be.

PONCE: Then spank me.

MANDY: Done that.

PONCE: Bored already?

MANDY: You never tell me anything.

PONCE: What do you want to hear?

MANDY: About what you do, Nikita.

PONCE: Stop.

MANDY: You're a big-time senator, aren't you? You must know all sorts of things. Eh, Nikita?

PONCE: *(pushing her away violently)* No. I don't like it!

MANDY: I'll get dressed.

PONCE: Wait . . .

MANDY: I can't stay in this house all the time, Ponce.

PONCE: But I bought you this house. We had an arrangement, Mandy. *(She's dressed. Quick, simple, stunning.)* Look at you.

MANDY: You bought the house, Ponce. You didn't buy me. You bought sex. Remember? The sex I give you when I want.

PONCE: It was my money. I paid for this house with my money.

MANDY: Don't crack up again, Ponce.

(MANDY starts to walk away.)

PONCE: Did John say something to you? Mandy?

(MANDY *exits. Beat.* PONCE *begins to tear up the sofa.*
Shift to a corridor where GIDEON *and* JOHN *stand.*)

GIDEON: He's lost his mind.

JOHN: Sad.

GIDEON: He's a relatively young man, if you think about it.

JOHN: For someone born in nineteen thirteen.

GIDEON: I thought he was older.

JOHN: He's always in the past.

GIDEON: Yes. Remembering too much. Bad sign.

JOHN: He's even lost Mandy.

GIDEON: Is that right?

JOHN: I don't know how many times I told him to ease up, slow down.

GIDEON: He won't listen.

JOHN: He wouldn't listen to anybody. Stubborn man.

(*Sofa stuffing everywhere.*)

SCENE 20

STATIC

(*Home. Another part of the house:* LOUELLA *and* MOTHER.)

MOTHER: Where are you going, Louella? You're never home. You don't play in the yard. You don't even listen to that goddamn Patsy Cline anymore.

LOUELLA: Don't you curse at me, mother.

MOTHER: I'm not cursing.

LOUELLA: Just leave me alone.

(*Door slam.*)

MOTHER: Well, I . . . Louella

(WITNESS *comes up from behind the console.*)

WITNESS: Pain in the dead center of my forehead. Nobody knows what it is. I try to tell the doctors it feels like when the bullet breaks through Mick Jagger's face in that movie "Performance." But they don't understand. My tongue doesn't work, and the movie isn't out yet.

(Back to . . .)

LOUELLA: I broke the piggy bank, Mom.

MOTHER: You mean Topo Gigio, dear?

LOUELLA: His face is cracked.

(Shift to a party on the terrace: ANDY WARHOL *and* JFK.)

JFK: Warhol, take my picture.

WARHOL: I don't take pictures, Jack.

JFK: Do me a close-up. Like you did with Jackie.

WARHOL: I could throw paint on you, Jack.

JFK: Blue eyeshadow?

WARHOL: Glitter. And a red back.

(Shift to . . .)

WITNESS: That's how I feel. Red glitter-chips through my skull. My brain is swelling. My chest expands over my painted Koolaid heart. I see Andy Warhol and JFK getting ready for a close-up. I see a senator and a woman named Mandy caught in the stale blue of a D.C. bedroom, thrashing. I see Topo Gigio's head cracked open, on the floor of a girl's room, like a bullet through the skull. I see. I see . . .

(Sound: heartbeat, heartbeat. Acceleration.)

LOUELLA: Over. It's all over, Mom.

MOTHER: We'll get a new piggy bank, Louella.

LOUELLA: They don't make them anymore, Mom.

 This was the original Topo Gigio.

MOTHER: It's just a ceramic mouse, dear.

LOUELLA: You don't understand. Everything's dead now. Everything's destroyed.

(Back to . . .)

WARHOL: I could cut out your eyes.

JFK: What's that?

WARHOL: Freeze them in a silver gelatin print painted to look black-and-white. You've got great eyes, Jack. Great, sad eyes. Like Elvis.

JFK: Well, I always said he stole my act.

WARHOL: Look over here, Jack. Look at me. Haunt me. That's right.

(Camera flash. A rain of glitter. Everything is black and white. A Warholian portrait of JFK *is blown up to cover the entire back of the stage. Shift to* LOUELLA *and* MOTHER *and a mountain of pennies.)*

LOUELLA: What am I going to do with all these pennies, Mom? What am I going to do?

MOTHER: Don't cry, Louella. Oh dear. You're just a girl. My little girl.

WITNESS: It's mid-day. The hand of a nurse rests on . . . *(Sound: heartbeat deceleration.)* I have pissed all over the thin cot. Wet, stinking piss like a cat's. The nurse rests her hand on my sex, and wipes me with a cold cloth that feels like sand. I'll be all right. Everything's going to be . . .

(The face on the JFK *portrait disappears. Only the eyes are left. Disembodied. Static on the TV console. White blur drowns out everything.* PONCE *steps through the disembodied eyes into . . .)*

SCENE 21

OFFICE (3)

PONCE: You wanted to see me, sir?

JFK: Call me Jack.

PONCE: Yes, Jack.

JFK: Would you like a cigar, Ponce?

PONCE: Cuban?

JFK: The only kind.

PONCE: Thank you, Jack.

JFK: Light up. That's right. Let the smoke fill the room.

PONCE: Is this peach, Jack?

JFK: Whiff of peach.

PONCE: Peach cigar. Never tasted the kind.

JFK: You don't like it, Ponce?

PONCE: It's fine, sir. Jack.

   (Beat)

JFK: You've been to Cuba, Ponce?

PONCE: Before Castro. Well, we all went before . . .

JFK: Damn right.

PONCE: Is that what you wanted . . . why you wanted to see me?

JFK: Settle down, Ponce. I just want to talk. Don't you just want to talk sometimes, when you're with Margaret, and the like?

PONCE: Is this about Mandy, sir? Cause if it is . . .

JFK: Mandy's fine. She's a fine girl. My brother Bob . . . well . . . we all like Mandy. She knows what she wants. Question is, do you know what you want?

PONCE: I don't believe I . . .

JFK: Do you believe in forgiveness, Ponce? It's a Catholic thing.

PONCE: Forgiveness?

JFK: People say all sorts of things when they're tired, drinking. Vodka, is it? You're a vodka man?

PONCE: Habit, sir.

JFK: Yes, I know all about that. But Margaret, you see . . .

PONCE: Did Margaret talk to you?

JFK: Calm down, Ponce. Margaret and Jackie have gotten to be friends. Jackie needs friends. You know about loneliness, Ponce? Mandy and her stockings around your throat.

PONCE: How'd you know—?

JFK: Now, I think Margaret and Jackie should stay friends, and you should try your hand at forgiveness.

PONCE: I'm afraid I . . .

JFK: Forgive me, Ponce.

PONCE: You, sir?

JFK: I could use it just now.

PONCE: I don't understand . . .

JFK: Come to Dallas with me.

PONCE: What did Margaret say to you?

JFK: She said nothing, Ponce. Nothing at all.

PONCE: I would never do anything, Jack. Not against you. I talk sometimes to Gideon and John . . .

JFK: Mandy's a fine girl.

PONCE: And Mandy. Yes. But . . . I would never . . .

JFK: You come down to Dallas, Ponce. All is forgiven.

(Lights fade.)

SCENE 22

THREE VIEWS

1) ANATOMY

(PONCE is packing his suitcase.)

PONCE: Ponce Quarry Simmons Modesto King: a. Assiduous b. Boisterous

(One by one, MANDY, GIDEON, MARGARET, *and* JACKIE KENNEDY *appear. They watch* PONCE *pack.)*

MANDY: c . . . Captive.

GIDEON: d . . . Difficult.

MARGARET: e . . . Egotistical.

PONCE: f . . .

MANDY & GIDEON & MARGARET & JACKIE KENNEDY: Flatulent.

PONCE: g . . . Giving.

JACKIE KENNEDY : h . . . Hat.

GIDEON: i . . . Inquisitive.

MANDY: j . . . Jealous.

PONCE: k . . . .

MANDY & GIDEON & MARGARET & JACKIE KENNEDY: Kleptomaniac.

MARGARET: l . . . Loving.

PONCE: m . . . Manic. n . . . Nauseous.

2) DIAGRAM

(WITNESS *appears from inside the open suitcase.*)

WITNESS: I remember the letter "m." Eme. That's how I would say it. Eme. Eme. Eme. It was a bad word in Spanish. Like when folks say "f" in English, but you know they mean something else.

(MOTHER *in Voiceover:*)

MOTHER (VO): Watch that mouth, young lady. You're starting to say some rude things. Look at the yard. The ants are crawling all over . . . shit.

WITNESS: "Eme. It means "shit." "Mierda." Eme. Eme. Eme. That was the first word I learned in this world. Shit. Things were bad from the start, and I didn't even know it.

(WITNESS *disappears back into the suitcase.* PONCE *continues to pack.*)

PONCE: o . . . Obstinate

MANDY & GIDEON & MARGARET & JACKIE KENNEDY: p . . . Parenthetical.

MANDY: q . . . Quarrelsome.

JACKIE KENNEDY: r . . . Restive.

GIDEON: s . . . Secretive.

MARGARET: t . . . Tolerant.

PONCE: u . . . Undecided.

(PONCE *finishes packing. Shuts suitcase. Fade on* PONCE.)

3) AUTOPSY

(Spot on JFK *at a podium. Translucent body, transparent veins, and a tie.)*

JFK: Ask not what your country Mothers all want their sons to grow up. Those who make peaceful revolution. Let the word go forth from time to time. From time to place Ask not what your country. But they don't want them to become politicians. My brother Bob. My brother Bob. My brother Bob. My brother brother brother. Promised Dad he'd go straight. Rushing into the future. But History will not permit it. Mankind must put an end. A torch has been passed on to a new generation. Try to hold fast hold fast hold fast or you will be swept aside. We once lived. My brother Bob. My brother Bob. My brother brother brother promised my Dad he'd go straight. In a country of men tempered by war. But history will not permit it. History is a relentless master. Only the past only the past only the Friend and foe alike pass the torch to the new end to mankind Let the word go forth from this time and place that we helped make the world safe for violence Let the word go forth brother brother brother that we once lived.

(Lights fade.)

SCENE 23

LEAVING THE DEAD

(Outside the house. On the veranda. JIM *is standing with the suitcase.* PONCE *enters.)*

PONCE: You look just like my wife standing there with that look. What are you doing?

JIM: Waiting for you, sir.

PONCE: Just like my wife.

JIM: I don't mean to . . .

PONCE: No. It's all right. I can talk about her. She's not here. I can talk about her as much as I want. "Negotiable difference," as they say.

JIM: What's that?

PONCE: It's an expression. You haven't heard of it?

JIM: No.

PONCE: It's an expression people use to resolve things. "Negotiable difference." That's what Margaret and I had.

JIM: I see.

PONCE: What is it you see?

JIM: Sorry?

PONCE: The ring, the house, the fucking . . . Everything was negotiable. Including our differences. Understand?

JIM: Oh.

PONCE: Where'd they train you, son?

JIM: Sorry?

PONCE: Slowest fucking aide I've ever met. You won't even sit down. What is that smell?

JIM: Hmm?

PONCE: Like death. Coming from the house.

JIM: Maybe it's the rain, sir.

PONCE: What rain?

JIM: The coming rain.

PONCE: It's like someone died.

JIM: Want me to check, sir?

PONCE: I can't stand it.

JIM: I'll check, sir.

(JIM *sets suitcase down, and goes toward house.*)

PONCE: John? John!

JIM: The name's Jim, sir.

PONCE: Jim. Right.

JIM: . . . I'll go check, sir.

(JIM *goes inside the house. Lights change.*)

SCENE 24

LOWER DEPTHS

(ADAM *in the basement of the Texas School Depository in Dallas. A small window.*)

ADAM: Can't see anything here. Except feet. High heels. I think I recognize them. No. That's not her. Looking at feet through a grate. Fucking parade. Someone died. I can smell it. I can't see anything except feet. And ankles. Big heavy ones with ridges and nylons coming down. Police cars now. Sirens. I think someone died. But I can't see anything. Everything's white now. Like the Hebrides. Except there's only feet, and sirens. Kennedy. Kennedy's been shot.

(*Lights shift to . . . .*)

SCENE 25

FALLOUT

(LOUELLA *stands against a schoolyard fence.*)

LOUELLA: Black hair. Black lipstick. And blood down my pants. I got my period today and everyone knows it. The blood has seeped down the back of my pants: A wet patch right in the center of my ass. My hair is pulled back in a ponytail. And my bangs have the frizzies. Sun beats down on a November day. And I cannot take off my pants. Not at school. I have nothing else to wear. Everyone is looking at me. I'll never wear pants again.

(*Fade on* LOUELLA. *Shift to beating sun, and* DYLAN *through a bus window.*)

DYLAN: Hey hey hey, Jack. What do you want? Ain't nothing here but the bus backing up and making a turn, a scarf lost and torn on the pavement. Time to get a move on, slip yourself under a fringe of hair made of ash. I've got slits for eyes, and songs inside my skin. "Hey hey hey, Jack." That's what I'll sing. But I won't believe it. Not a word. I don't believe anything anymore.

(*Fade on* DYLAN. *Shift to* PONCE *standing in a doorframe.*)

PONCE: I held my head down. I didn't think of anything except the back of his head blown out, as she sat in the car. Then I thought of Margaret. I thought "Margaret is going to scream. She'll scream like bloody Jesus in front of all those Democrats and ruin my chance . . ." I wish I shot him. That'd be something to scream about now, wouldn't it? At least I'd have done something to be remembered by. But I can't even shoot myself right. and Margaret's my goddamn grievance.

(Camera flash on PONCE. *Fade. Time shift.* ADAM *and* SIMON *on the grounds.)*

ADAM: Looks like peanut shells, Simon.

SIMON: They're bullet shells.

ADAM: Huh?

SIMON: Dead particles all around. Did you see anything, Adam?

ADAM: I saw feet.

SIMON: Feet?

ADAM: Spare parts of a body. Through a window. Hey. What's the temperature now?

SIMON: Late. It's late, Adam.

ADAM: I'm cold.

SIMON: We could go to the Hebrides.

ADAM: I can't look up at the sky, Simon. Not anymore. It's fucking freezing.

SIMON: Quasars again?

ADAM: Everything's turned to static.

(Fade on ADAM *and* SIMON. *Shift to* WITNESS *in a distant lens.)*

WITNESS: The letter "a" is gone. It fell out of the alphabet. Just now. No more Amor, agua, acorn. Everything's going down: Anxiety, anticipation, antediluvian, antiquity . . . Apples. No feeling in my mouth.

(strikes a match.)

Light. *(blows out. Strikes a match.)*

Light. *(blows out. Lights fade.)*

SCENE 26

Exile

(Winter. On the veranda. Deck chairs.)

PONCE: One drink. What's it going to hurt? Vodka for me. Scotch for you. That all right?

JIM: Yes. That's fine.

PONCE: You're Scotch, aren't you, Jim?

JIM: What?

PONCE: Your family.

JIM: Way back.

(PONCE hands JIM the drink.)

Straight up, sir?

PONCE: Only way to drink it. You want rocks?

JIM: I thought . . .

PONCE: Wears it down, Jim. Wears the whole content of the malt down. . . . Where were we?

JIM: Kennedy, sir.

PONCE: Fucking Catholic. Died a Catholic death. Margaret said I orchestrated the whole thing. Forget Oswald. The puny punk. It was me. You should've seen her. "I denounce him." Like a goddamn fury.

JIM: I'm not sure I follow . . .

PONCE: My wife, goddammit.

JIM: Your ex-wife, sir.

PONCE: Ex. Yes. You want another drink? You could use another to strengthen you up. You're nothing but bloody bones, son.

JIM: Yes, sir.

PONCE: Call me Ponce, will you? Would you do that, son? That's all I will ever ask of you, Jim.

JIM: Yes, Ponce. What were you saying about your ex-wife, sir?

PONCE: Huh?

JIM: Margaret.

PONCE: Spy. All the women in this town are spies. Mandy and all the rest of them.

JIM: Who's Mandy, sir?

PONCE: *(serving another drink.)* Mandy, son?

(Lights dim on PONCE *and* JIM. *Shift to . . .)*

SCENE 27

LOOSING

WITNESS: I cannot remember anymore. Thoughts move in and out of the fallen "a" that has dropped out, and come to rest on a discarded blanket. I am an only child, right smack in the middle of my parents. My mother speaks Spanish and my father speaks a broken tongue of mumbles and smiles that I will later understand to be English. I had a sister once. An elder sister without a grave I can point to. Without a name.

*(*WARHOL *appears.)*

WARHOL: Jackie and I were twins in some other life. Magenta. Ultra-violet. Pink.

WITNESS: She had brown hair and hazel eyes, black hair and blue eyes, brown, white, yellow, red, olive skin. She is my phantom sister, my unspoken twin.

(Fade on WITNESS. JACKIE KENNEDY *appears, as if startled from sleep.)*

JACKIE KENNEDY: September. Four little girls were found on the sidewalk outside the church in Alabama. Their arms were split from their chests, their eyes staring. Four little black girls in dresses visit me.

WARHOL: September fifteen. Four little girls among the leaves. Denise, Carol, Cynthia, and Addie Mae.

*(*WARHOL *begins to paint, his hands moving through the air.)*

JACKIE KENNEDY: Denise, Carol, Cynthia, and Addie Mae. On the other side of the street.

WARHOL: On the other side of Pop, four girls in white dresses died senselessly.

(JACKIE KENNEDY *and* WARHOL *are framed inside a painting that fades and fades. Shift back to . . .)*

SCENE 28

EXILE (2)

(From before. Winter. On the veranda. Deck chairs.)

PONCE: Nothing left now.

JIM: And Mandy?

PONCE: She used me, son.

JIM: You used her.

PONCE: I don't see her in goddamn exile, John. I mean, Jim. I don't see her looking out onto a cold deck that smells of vomit. She's walking around getting some other fool to take state funds to buy her a goddamn house, and then leaking on him. I can't even walk into Senate now. Ponce Quarry Simmons Modest King kicked out. Fuckin LBJ. Like he doesn't have a whore in his pocket . . .

JIM: Yes, Ponce.

PONCE: Five o'clock. Time for another drink. You like vodka? It's Russian, if that's all right.

JIM: That's fine.

PONCE: I take it with these little pills. They help my nerves. You're not an agent, are you, Jim?

JIM: No, sir.

PONCE: If you are, I'd like you to go down to Cuba for me, talk to that snake Castro. He's damn ruining the beaches down there, making one hell of a mess.

JIM: Yes, sir.

PONCE: Call me Ponce, would you? Say my name.

JIM: Ponce.

PONCE: That's right. *(indicating drink)* Straight up. What do you say?

JIM: That's fine.

PONCE: You know whatever Margaret tells you . . . I didn't kill him.

JIM: We got our man, Ponce.

PONCE: Puny punk. He had myopia. Did you know that? Oswald couldn't see straight.

JIM: I wouldn't know, Ponce.

PONCE: It's going to be a long night. I can see it. I can see it from here. And this time, I don't want to wake up. Not this time.

(PONCE *downs pills and vodka. He collapses. Darkness.*)

SCENE 29

A CLEARING

WITNESS: Some objects never travel. I know. I've seen it happen.

(PONCE *in a coffin. Funeral service in distance presided over by* GIDEON, MARGARET *and the others on the periphery.*)

GIDEON: Ponce Quarry Simmons Modesto King.

WITNESS: Objects will remain sometimes for years. Unmoved. From the place they were first put.

GIDEON: Born Tampa, Florida in nineteen-thirteen.

WITNESS: Prisoners of circumstance, and folly. The folly of the owner who placed them there—On a table-top, bureau, chest of patterned leaves . . .

MARGARET: Favorite singer: Patsy Cline.

WITNESS: And the folly of the objects themselves Who through the comfort of habit, refuse to move.

MARGARET: He was a good man, I think. I married him when I was nineteen. Ponce Quarry . . . hardly the man of anyone's dreams.

WITNESS: Traveling involves distance. Motion. And time.

(ADAM *appears from the periphery.*)

ADAM: If you go up to the Hebrides, you can see the whole world
... And ride the biggest fucking waves this side of Hawaii.

(ADAM *fades into the sky.*)

WITNESS: A voice on the radio

(*Music is heard: Patsy Cline singing "Crazy."*)

A sound on the breeze.

(*From home's shadow, in voiceover:*)

MOTHER (VO): Louella! Louella, dear, where are the Dixie
cups?

WITNESS: Some objects simply do not have the will to move.
They do not have endurance. So, they sleep.

(JFK *in a rocking chair in the distance.*)

JFK: Henry, leave me be for a while. Let me listen to Patsy.

WITNESS: They sleep in one place. Surrounded by the same
objects. The same air. The same stale year after year

(MANDY *poses from the periphery.*)

MANDY: I got me a fur coat. Mink. Can you smell it? I think it's
still got blood on it. Gideon, John ... they'd do anything for me.

WITNESS: And out of this sameness, sometimes, another thing
grows.

(*From home's shadow,* LOUELLA *fishes something out of a waste-
basket. In voiceover:*)

LOUELLA (VO): Mother, what's this? Did you throw out Daddy's
shoelaces again?

WITNESS: A kind of film that covers the object. An imperceptible
layer that reflects time. The eyes sink. Reason disappears.

(*From the coffin:*)

PONCE: Green. Everything here is green.

WITNESS: And you begin to see the object for what it is.

(JACKIE KENNEDY *appears.*)

JACKIE KENNEDY: Eme. Eme, eme, eme. Or can't you speak
English?

WITNESS: As years pass, the object is more and more itself And less what your eyes bring to it.

MARGARET: I couldn't tell you the color of his eyes. Not now.

(JIM *appears out of the sky's edge.*)

JIM: Green. Everything about him was green.

WITNESS: The recognition of the object, of seeing it for what it is, after time, deepens your understanding of it. "This was a vase," you say.

JIM: Everything was on the dot: at five, ten . . . I was like a son, he said. I watched him.

WITNESS: This is a vase. A true vase. It sat on the dresser for fifty years. And the recognition makes you proud, Even as it cheapens your appreciation of the object's worth. For, you know, to have withstood time, To have endured . . .

LOUELLA (VO): Mother? Whose shoelace is this?

WITNESS: Without the possibility of motion . . . (WITNESS *pulls a shoelace out of her pocket, looks at it.*) is to have withstood the terror of never seeing beyond your reach. I am in an incubator. I am premature. The year is nineteen sixty-three. The year of Patsy, Piaf, and Lee Harvey, and four little girls in white dresses.

MARTHA & GIDEON & JIM & MANDY: (softly underneath) nineteen thirty-six, thirteen ninety-six, sixteen ninety-one, ninety-six . . .

WITNESS: My fingers reach out barely the length of a shoelace. I peer out of my bubble.

MARTHA & GIDEON & JIM & MANDY & JFK & JACKIE: *(softly underneath)* . . . sixty-nine thirteen, sixty-one thirty-nine, thirty-one . . .

WITNESS: There are two surfers hung on the sky's tip. Waving at a young woman in a fur coat. Who smiles at a man who goes by the name of Ponce.

MARTHA & GIDEON & JIM & MANDY & JFK & JACKIE: (softly underneath) . . . thirty-nine sixty-one, thirty-one ninety-six, ninety-one, nineteen sixty . . .

WITNESS: I reach again. The respirator hums a beat. Hold me.

(The funeral service breaks into a carnival-esque frame where ALL *except* WITNESS *freeze.).*

This is my story, the story of what I remember the year I was born.

(Music comes up blaring: Beatles sing "I Want to Hold Your Hand." WITNESS *takes a photo of the frozen frame with her camera. The song mutates into a sonically altered, contemporary version, as the frame dissolves.)*

END OF PLAY

DOG ACT

A PLAY WITH MUSIC

BY LIZ DUFFY ADAMS

For Nancy, Abigail, and Charles

BIOGRAPHY

Liz Duffy Adams' plays include *Dog Act* (staged readings at Portland Stage Company's Little Festival of the Unexpected 2000 and New York Theater Workshop, Finalist for the Clauder Competition 2001); *The Train Play or The Reckless Ruthless Brutal Charge of It* (a Clubbed Thumb production at Ohio Theater, Finalist for the Clauder Competition 1999); *A Wrinkle in Time* (adaptation commissioned and produced by Syracuse Stage); *A Fabulous Beast* (One Dream Theater); *Teacup for a Shallow Apocalypse* (Santa Monica Playhouse); and the short plays *Greeks & Centaurs, The Last Woman on Earth*, and *Aphra Does Antwerp* (The Women's Project and Productions). Her *Poodle with Guitar and Dark Glasses* was recently published in Applause's "Best American Short Plays 2000-2001" anthology. She is a graduate of NYU's Experimental Theater Wing and the Yale School of Drama, and a member of New Dramatists.

CHARACTERS

ROZETTA STONE (ZETTA)—woman
DOG—young male; human by birth, dog by choice
VERA SIMILITUDE—gray-haired woman
JO-JO THE BALD-FACED LIAR—girl, semi-feral teenager
COKE & BUD—two scavengers; men

TIME & PLACE

Later on. A wilderness in the Northeast of the former U.S.

SONGS

Walking to China (Zetta, Dog)
The Wang-Tailed Wallow (Zetta, Dog)
Weed World (Vera)
Sing Yo, Street Harriet (Zetta, Vera, Jo-Jo)
Human Blues (Zetta)

NOTES

A single set, mostly bare. The major element is Zetta's cart. It is large enough for the characters to enter, with wheels, a fold-out stage, awnings, painted drops and posters, and hanging lanterns. In front there are poles to pull by, and a pulling harness. It may be cobbled together from partly recognizable objects originally of other uses (a stainless steel coffee wagon?). It is bursting with costumes, props, musical instruments, cooking utensils, and flotsam and jetsam of past ages, such as but not necessarily: books, broken clocks, a Russian Orthodox icon, a laughing Buddha, a Menorah, an Agent Mulder Action Figure, a tattered Keith Haring barking dog umbrella, a *Star Trek* lunch box, a banged-up computer monitor with the glass removed to serve as a puppet stage, puppets made from plastic flamingos, a Gumby, voodoo dolls, and botanica saints; things with unknown purposes made of spare parts from obsolete objects like toaster ovens, doorknobs, telephones, CDs, a Statue of Liberty pencil sharpener, and so on.

The musical instruments are handmade from various found objects, and may function similarly to guitars, horns, xylophones, percussive instruments, etc. while being clearly unique and makeshift.

The weapons, similarly, are salvaged, low-tech variations on bow and arrows, spears, knives and so on. Perhaps a rifle has been turned into a crossbow, or a pistol serves as the handle for a long dagger.

The vaudevillians dress in layers of mismatched theatrical costumes, threadbare and much-repaired. They may have some scars and tattoos. Jo-Jo may wear a battered old Etch A Sketch around her neck on a bit of rope. The Scavengers wear light armor cobbled together from found objects, including barely recognizable flattened-out and scratched-up Coke and Budweiser cans.

The "e" in vaudevillian should be pronounced as a separate syllable.

DOG ACT

ACT I

(Autumn. Night. Wilderness. ZETTA *enters cautiously.)*

ZETTA: *(stage whisper)* Dog. Dog. Where you, Dog?

(She whistles low. Noises off, screams and yells. ZETTA *falls flat and lies still in the shadows. Two Scavengers,* COKE *and* BUD, *run in with a large, heavily filled sack.)*

COKE: Fuck this fucker, fuck-all heavy.

BUD: Fuck yeah. And will not cease to struggle, thou fuck. *(Strikes sack)*

COKE: Yoi! Do not thou fuck with my prize, I want it lively for the sacrifice.

BUD: Thy prize?

COKE: Fuck yeah, mine. I saw it, I fucking caught it, I will fucking eat its fucking brains at fucking midnight, and the gillies will all fucking compete to fuck me, yeah.

BUD: The fuck you say.

COKE: The fuck I do say.

BUD: Thou fuck-lobe, I saw it first.

COKE: Fuck thy freeze-dried scrotum, it's mine.

BUD: In a mutant's anus, thou quark-witted son of a three-eyed stump-licker.

COKE: So's yer mother.

BUD: FUCK.

(They drop the sack and begin attempting to throttle each other. A girl we will later know as JO-JO *crawls out of the sack, snatches up another bag and scrambles off. After a moment,* COKE *breaks away and sees what's happened.)*

COKE: Yoi! It scramoosed!

BUD: With our caboodle to boot, the god-fucking whore of a god-fucked fucker!

COKE: Let slip the hound-droogs, ah-oooh!

BUD: Ah-oooh!

(*Howling, they turn to pursue—and discover* ZETTA, *possibly by falling over her. A very tense pause. Then* ZETTA *performs a little dance, ending with a flourishing bow.* THE SCAVENGERS *exchange disgusted looks.*)

COKE: It's a fucking vaudevillian.

BUD: Fuck that.

(*They resume their howling pursuit and exit. As the sound of them dies down* ZETTA *whistles again for* DOG.)

ZETTA: Here, boy. Here, boy. Damn you, Dog, come the hell on!

(DOG *has entered behind her.*)

DOG: Hey.

ZETTA: (*jumps*) DAMN. Dog. Where you been?

DOG: Sniffing around.

ZETTA: Anything?

DOG: Bad place.

ZETTA: No joke, puppy. Scavengers on the roam, and where you? "Sniffing around." Come when called, next time, damn the bitch what bore you, hey?

DOG: Okay, Zetta. Where's the cart?

ZETTA: Back there. Wait. What you smell?

DOG: All clear. Hunt moved on southward.

ZETTA: Okay. Good Dog. Go on.

(DOG *goes off.* ZETTA *looks around, listening, and begins to sing quietly:*)

Sing yo, street Harriet
Comin' four o'clock to my door
Sing yo, street Harriet
Come in for the four o'clock show

(DOG *enters pulling the cart.* ZETTA *lights a lantern hanging from it, and they take what they need to get comfortable, all the while:*)

I tell you what, Dog, this do suck. This do suck like a succubus suck.

DOG: At least we still have the cart.

ZETTA: So the god-fugged what? We got cart, we got costume, we got strum-strings and jing-jang-whackers and we got fug-all with we got no bodies to go with! Ever since Smack and Jelly got eaten up in Kinarsey and the freaks defected to the N'orlin Freak Kingdom we been down to the bare wish-bone.

DOG: Got me.

ZETTA: A dog act. One one-dog dog act. One one-trick one-dog dog act. Listen oh listen, I have seen and been better days and ways. I have seen and been. How we going to perform for the King of China when we get there? No Mortality Play, no orchestramie, no dancing gillies, no freaks not even!

DOG: Nada mucho.

ZETTA: You have said it.

DOG: Rub my head.

ZETTA: *(doing so)* What will the King of China say when he sees solemente us, bare-ragged, foot-fagged, lacking all but the least of entertainment necessities?

DOG: What indeed?

ZETTA: He be sans speech. He be disappointed down to his DNA and have no not a word to exsanguinate his soul-sadness forth, by with.

DOG: DNA?

ZETTA: Damn Near All. Don't Nock Ale. Dust Not Answers. De Nasty Ain't. So on. He be heart-busted.

DOG: Anyway, any luck we won't get there.

ZETTA: Won't need any luck for that. Just the self-same brand of anti-luck we be running with.

(DOG begins to play one of their makeshift instruments.)

Hey, now, Dog, we got to keep it on the quiet.

DOG: It's safe, Zetta. Trust me.

(DOG sings the first line of the song:)

Don't ask me why *(Pause. He starts again:)* Don't ask me why

ZETTA: *(singing)* Don't ask me what

ZETTA & DOG: *(singing together)*

Don't ask me nothing nothing nothing nothing but
Hoo hoo, hoo hah
We're walking
Just walking
Walking to Chi-i-na

The King of China
He sent to me
A messenger of such immense civility
Hoo hoo, hoo hey
Just walking
Yeah walking
Walking to Chi-i-na
No one know where

That China be
We only know it where the sun come out the sea
Hoo hoo, hoo hoh
We're walking
Just walking
Walking to Chi-i-na
Said Dog and Zetta!
Nobody better!
Walking to Chi-i-na!

(After the big finish, DOG *keeps playing and* ZETTA *dances, but almost at once, the earth wobbles violently, signaled by a sound-effect like booming thunder. They start to lose gravity, then:)*

ZETTA & DOG: WOOOOOOH!

(They stagger and fall down. It is abruptly much colder. Maybe even some flakes of snow.)

ZETTA: Damn-all, winter again? Winter last week.

DOG: *(shivering)* Frrrrrrrrr.

*(*ZETTA *pulls out warm costume pieces, and the remnant of a velvet stage curtain for them to huddle under.)*

ZETTA: Here, Dog, bundle. *(stamps on the ground)* Settle out and fly straight why dontcha?

DOG: I hate when it does that. *(sneezing)* Ach-ooo!

ZETTA: Okay, there, Dog, get under there. Damn thing got the wobbly shakes and we got to shake along with. Time we get to the sea it be all spilt out, this rate.

DOG: Tell me something, Zetta.

ZETTA: Tell you what?

DOG: Tell me about the sea.

ZETTA: I told you.

DOG: Tell me again.

ZETTA: The sea. *(pause)* It the Big Wet. It the prime-odial stuff of all stuff. It got the roar of a monster and the harsh of a whisper. It thicker than blood and fiercer than weather. It draw you to it, and then it drag you in and make you drink, and when you drink you want to stay, and never breathe no rank old air again, and then it got you and you stay got. It deep and cold and fat and wild and I will know it when I see it.

DOG: When will we see it?

ZETTA: Maybe in the spring.

DOG: Maybe tomorrow.

ZETTA: We smell it first. The sea may be smelt from afar.

DOG: What's it smell like?

ZETTA: It smell like a come-on meeting a want-to, like a knife's edge meeting a peach, metallic hoo-hah and salt.

DOG: It's been a long time since I've had salt. Or a peach.

ZETTA: I never had neither. Where you have salt, Dog? Dog?

DOG: We have any of that food left?

ZETTA: What, that squirrel?

DOG: Wasn't a squirrel.

ZETTA: Don't start. What was if not squirrel?

DOG: No squirrel ever had scales and gills.

ZETTA: Well, ain't no fish ever got a fluffy tail and run up a tree. Call it a squish if you want to, we ate the last of it yesterday.

DOG: Squish. Flurrel. Flurrel is better.

ZETTA: Flurrel. Write it down, why not.

DOG: We haven't seen any others, no point in noting anomalies.

Anyhow. Dogs don't write.

ZETTA: A-nom-u-lee. I bet you can write, Dog.

DOG: Not anymore.

ZETTA: But I bet you can—

DOG: Grrrrr . . .

ZETTA: *(warning)* Dog . . .

(He stops growling. But she drops the subject.)

We go hunting first-light, catch something to eat. Fug-hat, soon's the sky's clear and we get some star light we start out walking, hey? Faster we get outa this the better. Scavengers got no proper appreciation of culture. Get someplace a little bit organized, hey? Got to be a tribal boundary around here somewhere, find us a town some kind, put up your act and a song. Maybe somebody be ready to bust out of tribe, come on the road, train 'em up for the play, hey? Damn-all, wish it ain't winter again.

DOG: Never know, might be spring any minute.

ZETTA: Any minute or never what-all. Spring mighta got lost in the trans-nation, caught in the gears o' time, never to be seen, felt nor smelt again. Might could stick on winter for good and all, till our froz-ed toes snap like twigs and when we get to the sea he froze too.

DOG: Like to see that.

ZETTA: Hell you would.

DOG: Spring'll come, Zetta.

ZETTA: You cheering me up, snoopy?

DOG: Don't know. Am I?

ZETTA: Shut it, Dog.

(slight pause)

DOG: Tell me about China.

ZETTA: I don't know. I don't know what-all about China.

DOG: You do. You know all, Zetta.

ZETTA: That so?

DOG: You know you know all, Zetta. You could add it to the bill.

Ask The Amazing All-Knowing Zetta, No Question Unanswered.

ZETTA: I do. I do know all. Know why?

DOG: Because you are unfettered by any fanatical reverence for facts. I mean. I mean. Why, Zetta?

ZETTA: I know all. Because. I got the cart. And with the cart come ancient wisdom and knowledge and know-how and the sacred-freaking-flame of the olden days and ways and the lore of the golden age, the silver age, the brassy age and the age of plastic, you follow me, puppy?

DOG: Sure, Zetta. Say, Zetta, what's this China I've heard you speak of?

(slight pause)

ZETTA: Say, Dog, glad you asked. Who-all has not heard of that wonder-ous city, and yet who-all has seen it with they own eyes and can so say? Far and so-so-far-'n-fablisimo: Chi-na: even the name a very chime of phantas-no-goria. Across a vasty-wide plain-old plain, a many-days slog of dry empty nada-mucho, no food, no drink, no rest from weary nor longing nor gathering gut-gloominess of burdened spirit and foot-drag. Only just when hope be not just lost but found again then tramped down spat on beat all to fug-hat and back, only then: a glimmer is seen on the edge of far-off. Is it? Oh my sacred and profane golly yes. A glimmer comes a gleam, a gleam a glitter as nearer we come. Then you in China, and it like nothing you ever thought you might of maybe one time dreamed. Every step bring a eye-goggling wonder. There a pointy tower so high when you climb up there you can see tomorrow. There a stone woman higher even nor that, and from the top you look out her eyes and see day after tomorrow. All around, buildings tall, old and old, gold stone higher than you can see, shimmer-shammyin' in the tender old sun. But the most important thing about China of all and all? The people. And the most important thing about the people: they wise. They so wise. They know the past, they imagine the future. And this because in the very center of China, there a very particular building. Stone. Old stone. Big around as would take half a day to walk. Door guarded by two vasty-big beasts, monster-osities of the old times, last of their kind. You want to enter, got to get past them, and if you want to get past them, you got to answer their question. No one know what that question be; it can't be remembered what-all. Get it right, you in with a fin. And then you really someplace. That building be filled with everything ever forgotten, everything ever known, everything can be known. Filled with fine, fine, moo-ie fine info-mation, yeah. It be the reservoir. It be bliss. But. You can't answer the question? Beasts devour you on the spot. Critter on the left take off your head in one clean bite. Critter on the right swallow your body. Snap, crunch, gulp, gone.

And that be what-all I know about China.

How 'bout you, Dog?

DOG: What?

ZETTA: What do you know?

DOG: About China?

ZETTA: About anything what-all.

DOG: I don't know anything. Dogs don't know anything, Zetta.

ZETTA: Dog, I tell you history, I tell you songs, I tell you stories, I tell all the info-mation I got and you take it. But you don't tell nothing back.

DOG: I pull my weight.

ZETTA: Nobody say you don't. You a good dog.

DOG: That's right.

ZETTA: I just want to know, * Dog—

DOG: (*overlapping) Leave it alone, * Zetta—

ZETTA: (*overlapping) WHY you a dog, Dog, and what * you know—

DOG: (*overlapping) Leave it alone, Zetta, or I'll be one of those dogs that don't even talk.

(slight pause)

ZETTA: Stars'r out. Let's walk.

(They start putting stuff away. ZETTA starts humming. She sings a line, DOG repeats it on an instrument—then they're singing.)

ZETTA & DOG: (singing)

The wang-tailed Wallow caught the 32-snup
Say hey and a hey till you bust a stangle
And it made it all the way to the ante-up
Ho, ho, the wrangle.

The Wallow and the Ju-jee caught the 84-snap
Say hey and a hey till you bust a stangle
Then the gazabo copped it up the hinky-hap
Ho, ho, the wrangle.

The Jujee pulled a woolly on the 22-snout
Say hey and a hey till you bust a stangle
So the Wallow hollered sammy till they cheesed it out
Ho, ho, the wrangle.

The limp-a-lone snooker snagged the Jujee's last bap
Say hey and a hey till you bust a stangle
But the bulls biffed Cokey so they tipped the tap
Ho, ho, the wrangle.

(Instrumental bridge. They play and do a comic dance. Unseen by them at first, VERA *and* JO-JO *enter, stand watching.)*

DOG: *(seeing them. Not barking, actually shouting the word "bark")* BARK! BARK, BARK! BARK!

*(*ZETTA *has a weapon in her hand we didn't see her reach for.* VERA *holds her hands out, palms up, and nudges* JO-JO *to do the same.)*

ZETTA: Okay, Dog. Good boy.

DOG: Grrrr . . .

JO-JO: Told you, Vere, a man.

ZETTA: Keep your hands out. And he a dog.

JO-JO: Oh. Sure?

ZETTA: *(to* VERA*)* What you be? What tribe?

VERA: None.

ZETTA: *(still to* VERA*)* I asked you.

JO-JO: No tribe. Believe it. She don't lie. She a Vera.

VERA: Vera Similitude. At your service. Only truth told.

ZETTA: Yeah? Tell the future?

JO-JO: Future? Har. She do better an that. She tell the present.

VERA: My young associate and I intend no harm. We are vaude-villians, like yourselves, or so I surmise from your apparatus.

ZETTA: Gear on the ground. Go on.

(They place everything they carry on the ground between them-selves and ZETTA.)

Check 'em out, Dog.

(DOG *goes over and starts to frisk and sniff them carefully.)*

So. You roadsters? Where your company?

JO-JO: Long story. Don' ask don' smell.

ZETTA: Asking you, Vera.

VERA: We were down to only five of us. The others men. We found ourselves in a perilous predicament, having wandered unwittingly deep within the tribal borders of a militaristic matriarchal free-market slave-economy. They were profoundly interested in the breeding potential of our compatriots and ulti-mately we found it irresistibly advantageous to part with them.

ZETTA: You sold 'em?

VERA: One might perhaps more precisely express it as a irrefus-able reward for accepting gracefully an unavoidable event and eschewing the shedding of blood which would undoubtedly in the circumstances have been our own.

ZETTA: That what truth sound like?

VERA: You may have absolute confidence in the meaning of my content, but you must forgive me my elaborations of form, my dear. When only truth may be told, obfuscation of style is very strongly advised.

ZETTA: Huh. What happen to your cart? And what you doing * round here—

JO-JO: *(*interrupting) HEY FUCK this askin askin I ain't talk no more KEEP YER DOG OFF I CUT HE SNIFFIN * NOSE OFF

VERA: *(*overlapping) Now, now, now . . .

ZETTA: *(at the same time)* Come 'ere, boy. *(to* VERA) What's her deal?

(JO-JO *sits on the ground with her back to them and calms her-self with her battered old Etch A Sketch.)*

VERA: Allow me to present Jo-Jo, The Bald-Faced Liar. Stories told, ancient and marvelous, no veracity guaranteed.

ZETTA: Story-teller?

VERA: She holds them verbatim in her teeming brain, however unlikely her demeanor may strike you, and she can recite same, for proper remuneration.

ZETTA: Huh. Soothsayer and story-teller. What else you got?

VERA: Perhaps, before we satisfy more of your no doubt justifiable curiosity, it would be well to establish new parameters for our group dynamic. We saw your cart and supposed you might be moved to view us in the light of tribal kinship, and offer us succor, if not a merging of the ways. May we not establish at least a temporary peace?

(ZETTA *considers this, then puts her weapon down.* DOG *and* JO-JO *tense. She takes a step toward* VERA, *who takes a step toward her. They both ritualistically display "nothing up my sleeves," then bow, maintaining eye-contact until the last moment, lowering their heads for a bare instant then snapping them both up warily. This trust rite completed, they step back.*)

VERA: (*cont'd.*) May I receive it then, that my assumption was correct? You are of the trade?

ZETTA: I am Zetta Stone, and THIS (*she pulls a rope on the front of the cart and a painted banner appears*) is ROZETTA STONE'S POST-'POC SNAKE-CIRCLING TRAVELING VAUDEVILLE & FREAK SHOW, SONG AN DANCE EXTRAV-NO-GANZA WITH DOG-ACT AN MORTALITY PLAY CURRENTLY UNDER CONTRACTUAL OBLIGATION TO THE KING OF CHINA, SECOND TO NO-ONE AND NO MONEY BACK.

VERA: I am extraordinarily gratified to make your acquaintance.

ZETTA: This Dog. He don't bite.

VERA: Dog.

DOG: Madame Similitude.

VERA: Jo-Jo. These are now friends. A greeting.

JO-JO: Yeah. Just: dog or no dog, he lay a paw on me he pay, one way or other.

DOG: Trust me.

ZETTA: Okay then.

(They all take up and put away their weapons. They sit down, still in wary, separate pairs, as if to a parlay.)

Let's see what you got. How's this truth-telling? You answer any question?

VERA: Assuredly.

ZETTA: Why the earth wobble?

VERA: I don't know.

DOG: What's the meaning of life?

VERA: I have no idea.

ZETTA: How the stars stay up?

VERA: Not a clue, my dear.

(slight pause)

ZETTA: Not much of an act.

VERA: Sadly, that is also true.

ZETTA: How 'bout a story from your little short-fuse there?

(JO-JO lurches instantly to her feet and launches rapidly into her story.)

JO-JO: "ONCE IN THE LONG AGO TIME Fox went looking for a wife. He was poor, he had only one horse, because he was lazy. So he went looking for a rich wife. He heard of a woman, the daughter of a chief that no one wanted, because she was a witch. He went to that village on the plains, where they live in clay houses. He sat with the chief and they smoked together. He said, I will marry your daughter. But you must give me one hundred horses. The chief agreed. The daughter was sent for. Fox was pleased. She was beautiful. And he had one hundred horses. The next day they set out to return to Fox's home. When a little time had passed he thought to count his horses. There were only ninety. But ten ducks were flying back the way they had come. After more time had passed he stopped to count again. There were only seventy horses. But twenty snakes were wriggling back the way they had come. Some time later he counted again. What do you think? Only forty horses, and thirty hornets buzzing back the way they had come. By the time they reached Fox's home he had only the horse he had started with, and his new wife. He was angry, and raised his knife to kill her. She became an eagle and flew up, but he threw his knife, and hit her in the wing. She fell back. She became a woman again. He put her in a dark pit. He told her, you are a witch. But you will be my witch, and help me avenge myself on your father for tricking me. Every day she grew weaker. One day he let her back into the light, and he pointed at the sun: See how bright the moon is tonight? She said, That is the sun. He put her back in the pit. Another night he let her out again, and he pointed at the moon: Isn't the sun hot today? She said, That is the moon. Back into the pit. The next time he let her out he said, Do you see the moon? She said, Yes, there is the moon. He said, Are you blind? That is the sun. She said, Forgive me. It is the sun. It is whatever you say it is. Then Fox knew she was his witch. He gave her some food, and they set off toward her father's village. As soon as she had eaten she grew stronger. As soon as she grew stronger she turned into a wolf and she killed Fox. She was not his witch. He had been wrong about that."

(JO-JO sits again. Slight pause.)

ZETTA: Not bad, what-all. Socko finish.

DOG: What's it mean?

JO-JO: Huh?

DOG: What's the story mean, what's it about, what do the man and woman represent, what is witch a metaphor for, is the sun/moon dichotomy significant in gender terms, what's it mean?

(Slight pause. JO-JO stands up again.)

JO-JO: "ONCE IN THE LONG AGO TIME, Fox went looking for a wife. * He was poor—"

VERA: *(*overlapping)* That will do, my dear, never mind.

ZETTA: *(to DOG)* What-all's with you?

DOG: Sorry, sorry, never mind, I'm sorry.

ZETTA: What else you got?

VERA: For select and sophisticated audiences of mature age we offer a special curiosity for an additional fee: "The Tableau of Human Tenderness."

(VERA *and* JO-JO *form a tableau, a tender embrace. There is nothing remotely salacious about it. They hold for a moment, then bow.*)

ZETTA: Huh. We could use that. Set up a peep show behind the cart, hey, Dog?

DOG: I guess.

VERA: Also: singing, dancing and pretending to feel things, of course.

ZETTA: What do ya sing?

VERA: We have an extensive repertoire of standards. Do you know "Weed World?"

(*She hums a bar, and* DOG *begins to play.*)

VERA: (*singing*)
I'm just a weedy girl
In this weedy seedy world
With not much left to do
But survey the gloomy view
Of the end of what we knew
So I'd like to say to you . . .

In this age of slow decline
don't you decline to be mine
In this era of decay
Won't you say with me you'll stay
And as a weedy girl and boy
What's left of weed world we'll enjoy
For I would gladly be extinct
If my epitaph when inked
read: she went the way of Dino
But she loved a boy divine-oh!

(*As* DOG *continues to play,* VERA *and* JO-JO *do a brief soft-shoe, then* VERA *continues the song.*)
Yes I am just a weedy girl
In this seedy weedy world
But if you say you love me true

I'll gladly cling to life with you
Till cockroaches and zebra mussels
Are all that's left for us to stew
I won't boo-hoo . . .
If I have you . . .
In weed . . . weed . . . world

ZETTA: Class act. Moo-ie jiggie.

VERA: And when the market is propitious Jo-Jo rents out her body for sexual purposes.

ZETTA: She keep that or pool it?

VERA: Oh, pool, assuredly, after a top-share. Jo-Jo is a team-player. That is, in a sense, and taking into account, and so on.

JO-JO: Choose my own tricks.

ZETTA: Yeah, sure. And you-all know the Mortality Play, got your parts down stone?

VERA: Naturally.

ZETTA: Well, there, now, Vera, don't mind saying it: you a true vaudster, and welcome to walk along with. Shake-down tour, anyhow, see how we fit. Sound okay?

VERA: Indubitably, a most welcome invitation.

ZETTA: Okay, then, no blinding contract, but we a patch-company for now and for sure. Come on, critters, company-greet.

(*They perform a brief, ritual version of theatrical greeting, with kisses: first* ZETTA *approaches* VERA, *a highly-stylized mock-embrace, they each speak the word* Darling *quite deadpan. Meanwhile* DOG *and* JO-JO *do the same, reluctantly.*)

ZETTA: (*to cap the ritual*) Show must go on!

DOG, VERA & JO-JO: We go on!

ZETTA: Have a drink!

DOG, VERA & JO-JO: Don't mind if I do!

ZETTA: Too bad we got no drink, but that'll hold her for now.

JO-JO: TALK TALK TALK FUCK this I'm HUNGRY you got FOOD or WHAT

VERA: Yes, yes, my dear, a very good point. (*to* ZETTA) I must confess a sympathy with Jo-Jo's observation.

ZETTA: We hungry too. Were just about to go hunt when you-all snowed up.

VERA: To cement our new fellowship, allow me to observe that before joining you, we passed a small body of water possibly containing edible wildlife. We will provide, in demonstration of our gratitude.

(Producing a small fish spear as if by magic from her clothes.)

Come, Jo-Jo.

(VERA and JO-JO exit.)

ZETTA: Well, well, well! Now we talkin'. What say, José! Back in business and no Miss Snake! Heh, heh, heh-heh-heh! *(notices DOG)* What?

DOG: What?

ZETTA: Don't what me what, what's with? Why all long in the snout?

DOG: Nothing. Reinforcements. Hurray.

ZETTA: Dog, you smell something, you speak. Hear me?

DOG: I hear you, Zetta, but it's nothing.

ZETTA: Yeah?

DOG: Trust me.

(slight pause)

ZETTA: Come on. Make a fire case they catch what-all.

(They start to build a fire. To herself:)

Nothing. Nothing, Zetta. Damn-all shut-mouth for a talking dog.

(Lights up on VERA and JO-JO elsewhere on the stage. JO-JO is fish-stalking with concentration.)

JO-JO: *(low, to the fish)* Fish, fish, fish, fish, fish, fish, fish.

VERA: Well, well, well. So far, not entirely without advantageous possibilities. Our new colleagues are certainly very nicely set up. Very nicely indeed. You did well, my dear, in stumbling across them. Such a talented little savage.

JO-JO : Fish, fish, fish, fish, fish, fish, fish.

VERA: Still. Finding is one thing. Using is another. Remember what I spoke to you about? Hm? Keep your head, my dear.

JO-JO: Fish, fish, fish, fish, fish, fish, fish.

VERA: *(quietly)* Are you listening to me, Jo-Jo?

JO-JO: Listening. You want fish?

VERA: I want fish. And I want you to keep that violence of yours in check until it's required. If it's required. There are many ways to exfoliate a feline. Or a canine for that matter.

JO-JO: You know that mutt somewhere before?

VERA: What an extraordinary question. Where would I have known him?

JO-JO: The fuck I know? Got a feeling.

(slight pause)

VERA: Fish.

(slight pause)

JO-JO: Fish, fish, fish, fish, fish, fish, fish.

(Back to the others. They've built a fire.)

DOG: Zetta?

ZETTA: Uh huh.

DOG: You haven't forgotten about China?

ZETTA: Forget China? Why you ask that? Course not, what kinda dumb-fug question?

DOG: Okay.

ZETTA: Why you think I let these sorry refugees join in? Now we got almost the whole she-bang an ma-gilla, enough bodies for the Mortality Play and everything. "Forget China."

DOG: Okay.

ZETTA: What-all's biting you, puppy?

DOG: Maybe

ZETTA: Come on, boy. Speak!

DOG: Maybe you're trusting them too fast. Maybe they could be dangerous.

ZETTA: Oh, well. That Jo-Jo got a loose spoke, but she just a little thing. Savvy moolah's on you, push come to gloves, hey?

DOG: Sure.

ZETTA: No change, Dog. You still a headliner. Top-share and all. They good, but they no talkin' dog. You and me, pupster. Walkin' to China. Hey?

DOG: Yeah, sure, Zetta.

(Slight pause. ZETTA *begins a slower, a capella version of their song.)*

ZETTA: *(singing)* Don't ask me why

(Slight pause. She starts again:)

Don't ask me why

DOG: *(singing)* Don't ask me what

ZETTA & DOG: *(singing together)* Don't ask me nothing nothing nothing nothing but

ZETTA: Tell you one thing: this so-called Vera may be the truth, but she no whole truth so far. "Vaudevillians shall freely exchange all manner of useful info-mation as geographical data, tribal boundaries, recent and on-going armed conflicts and any and all knowledge that may aid a fellow vaudevillian, what-so-never." That the code.

DOG: There's a code?

ZETTA: Why not? So fret not. If she know what-all about the forward route, she be worth fetching along, even with her little loose-canon. What?

(DOG has tensed, looking off.)

DOG: Just them. Smells like they caught something.

(VERA and JO-JO *reenter.)*

VERA: Veni vidi vici, my dears. Here is food, or so I hope. I had been led to believe that there are only half a dozen aquatic creatures to be found on our vasty continent, but this asphyxiating fellow is unknown to me.

ZETTA: Now, that a squish.

DOG: *(sniffing it)* Edible.

VERA: Jo-Jo will eviscerate. She is deftness itself with a knife. Go on, my dear.

*(JO-JO *pulls out an ugly-looking blade and goes off with the squish.)*

ZETTA: Well, now, then, Vera. Soon's we eat I want to be back on the road. No trade round here 'cept rough trade, and they don't pay. So, what-so-never you know in the way of routes and obstacles, spill now or forever expect no peace.

VERA: But of course, my dear. I am delighted to share what poor scraps of knowledge I've acquired, to further our now combined fortunes. What was your intended destination?

ZETTA: China.

VERA: China?

ZETTA: Chi-na.

VERA: Ah. Yes. On foot?

ZETTA: Not walkin' on our hands.

DOG: We have an engagement.

VERA: Ah.

ZETTA: We been workin' our way north some while now, veering eastward. Out on our usual routes, and we don't know what-alls to come. What's your circuit?

VERA: We were working primarily the South-west to West.

ZETTA: That so? Long time since I been out that way. What's the latest?

VERA: Trouble, upheaval, dark, dark times. The Lone Star Libertarian Army is attempting another invasion of the Pan-AmerIndian Casino Nation.

ZETTA: Again? Stubborn sons, got to give 'em that.

VERA: Naturally, they're quite doomed. Casino Nation possesses Technology, you know.

ZETTA: Sure. Played there once with my Mam's troupe when I was coming up. Never forget it. Elec-trixity, Dog.

VERA: Can you imagine that, Dog?

DOG: No.

(slight pause)

VERA: Well. Ever since the Nuevo Aztecs ejected them from what used to be called Texas, the Lone Stars have been, how shall I say? martially resistant to historical trends. Despite the inequality of the struggle, it has dragged on long enough to wreck bloody havoc, and our fragile little troupe was caught in the crossfire. Casino Nation's Technology being both deadly and none so accurate, it was perhaps not surprising, however distressing, that we came under friendly fire—that ancient ironic phrase—and lost half our players in one fiery blast. And our cart with all its precious cargo.

ZETTA: *(softly swearing)* Jesse fug-it Crisco.

VERA: Indeed. Clearly, there was no safety to be had in the entire region, and no great demand for our noble art. So we buried what we could find of our fallen comrades, shouldered the remnants of our belongings, and steered our course due north, hopeful of mended fortunes. We perambulated fearlessly as far as the very shadow of the Great Canadian Barrier Wall, but, alas, we soon found ourselves performing only the cliched fire/frying pan scenario. The tribes of the Mid-North and North-West are unspeakably diverse and dangerously agnostic regarding the sacred person of the Vaudevillian. Radical-Agrarian-Utopians. Paranoic-UFO-Communing-Separatists. The Skinhead-Skateboarders Union. Millennial-Revisionists.

ZETTA: Never heard on 'em.

VERA: Oh, yes, they're quite fascinating. They refuse to believe the Apocalypse has come and gone, it having failed their expectations, and every year their priests solemnly postpone the deadline. Well, as I previously related, our career reached its nadir when we lost the surviving male members of our troupe to the procreational demands of the sisters sans merci. All told, by the time we'd emerged into the blessed wilderness of the blasted East, we were as you find us: sans troupe, sans props, sans very nearly everything—and most disastrously of all, sans cart.

(JO-JO comes back with skinned and gutted squish on a stick. DOG goes to take it from her. She recoils, holds up the knife.)

JO-JO: *(hissing at him)* Sssssss

VERA: Jo-Jo.

DOG: *(to JO-JO)* It's all right. I was just helping. We have a fire, see?

VERA: Give it to him, Jo-Jo.

DOG: It's all right. You cook it.

(He retreats. JO-JO *goes to the fire, holds the squish over it.)*

JO-JO: *(muttering)* I fucking caught it.

VERA: If I may, Zetta, be so bold as to venture a query . . .

ZETTA: What-all, speak free.

VERA: You referred earlier to a dog act. I have heard, as who has not? of this fabled wonder of the dim and glorious past, but I have never been privileged to witness one, dogs in general being so sadly declined and brutish in our jaded age. I confess it, I burn with vulgar curiosity.

ZETTA: Hey now, fair enough. Dog don't mind, hey, Dog? Hey? Dog?

DOG: My throat's a little hoarse. From the smoke.

ZETTA: Oh, now, that don't matter. Do the short version. *(to* VERA *)* It one hell of an act, never fail. *(to* DOG *)* Come on there, Dog, snazzle us all ready.

*(*DOG *mounts the stage of the cart.)*

ZETTA: *(cont'd.)* Oh, you in for something now. Some places, we can't barely pull the cart for what-all they throw at us, after they catch an ear-load a Dog there.

DOG: Doubt that the earth quakes. Doubt that the sun shivers and flares. Doubt that the moon broke free of our doubtful gravity to fall endlessly into the endless night, but never doubt that I am yours and more constant than earth, sun or treacherous moon. Can words encompass my love? Shall I debase the immaculate ardor of a perfect flame to say "I love you?" Don't listen to my words. Words can lie, words are made for betrayal, the same word may issue from the mouth of a saint and a villain. Listen to your own heart, beating in rhythm with mine. It will tell you what is in my heart, for two hearts as one can keep no secrets. You are the air I breathe, the life's blood in my veins, you are every thought and dream and longing that shake this poor frame, weak with groaning for you, with not sleeping for calling your name. You are love itself and I am your slave. You are life itself and I worship you. Don't speak, never speak, and I may wait for ever in the exquisite hope of your love and never know the torment of being cast out of your light. I love you. I love you. I love you.

(DOG *bows.* VERA *and* ZETTA *applaud.* ZETTA *tears a strip off the cooking squish and tosses it to* DOG, *who pops it into his mouth and comes off the stage.)*

ZETTA: Good boy. Good dog.

VERA: Amazing. One would almost believe he actually understands what he's saying.

ZETTA: *(patting him)* Who's a good dog?

DOG: I am.

ZETTA: *(to* VERA*)* How about that, hey? Ever seen what-all to beat that, hey?

VERA: Never.

ZETTA: Never what-all. Well, now, then. Where we at. You got nothing on the North-East road, then?

VERA: Well, nothing recent. But I was once very familiar with these parts. Intimately familiar. You've never come this far?

ZETTA: Said not.

VERA: Not even your Dog there? Perhaps before he joined your enterprise?

ZETTA: He'd a said if so. Hey, Dog?

DOG: I would have said.

ZETTA: Why you ask?

VERA: Merely seeking clarification on the point. Well. Many years ago, not far from here, there was a small tribe living in the fortified remnants of what used to be a sort of . . . cathedral.

ZETTA: Cath-e-dral?

VERA: An ancient place of worship. But this was a secular cathedral. For the worship of knowledge. When I knew them, they were a benign people. Making their home among the books. They could all read. Imagine that. And they were safe. Marauding savages would come to the gates, but the gates were strong, and the walls were high and the place easily defended. They were happy enough, as the world goes.

ZETTA: Sounds like people might appreciate a show. How far? Could you find it?

VERA: Not far. It's on the way to the sea. And I'm entirely certain I could never forget the way, however long ago I last saw it.

ZETTA: Damn-all this stop-still, then, let's move! Eat walking, come on there, girl, put out the fire. Dog, shake it, pack up, let's go!

(Another violent earth-wobble)

ALL: WOOOOOH!

(They all fall down. It's suddenly very hot, and everyone begins stripping off outer layers.)

ZETTA: Summer! Fug-hat! Where-all spring?

JO-JO: Hot hot HOT

VERA: Ah, grateful warmth.

ZETTA: Come 'ere, Jo, I'll show you where to stow your stuff and all.

(DOG in the front of the cart pulls the harness over his shoulders. VERA moves closer to him, unobserved by ZETTA, who is helping JO-JO in the back.)

VERA: I know you.

DOG: No.

VERA: Oh, yes, perfectly. Just as perfectly as you remember me.

DOG: I don't. Leave me alone.

ZETTA: *(coming back around)* All ready, hey? Then lead on, Mizz Duff! An audience awaits! Play us off, Dog.

(They pull the cart around in a circle and off, DOG playing a walking beat. As soon as they're gone, COKE and BUD enter, looking after them.)

BUD: Fuck this, for-fuckin-sooth, let us fuck off home. My feet are fucked.

COKE: Hast no fucking guts? That's our fucking prize.

BUD: Art thy eyes and ears be-fucked? They're fucking vaudevillians.

COKE: So fucking what? And watch thy tongue.

BUD: Watch it for me, thou fuck-sucking roach-cunt, dost think I shut up at thy fucking decree?

COKE: Not now, not now, not fucking now, I'm trying to fucking think.

BUD: Oh, fuck this then, we'll be here till we're fucking bones.

COKE: That's it, thou'rt fucked.

(Promptly pushing Bud down, sitting on his chest and holding a thumb to his eye.)

BUD: Ah, fuck.

COKE: Dost hear me now, thou limp-dickied would-be sister-fucker?

BUD: Ay.

COKE: Then attend. One: why should these fucking vaudevillians be not fair game and sport for a bold scavenger? Who should say me fucking nay if I choose?

BUD: Our divine leader protector and mother of us all THE WENDY, thou fucking freak, that's fucking who—

COKE: Ah, ah, wouldst speak with that tongue?

BUD: Thorry, thorry. *(Coke lets go of his tongue.)* And yet, if thou will hear me . . . they're off-fucking-limits. The Wendy forbids it. Fuck knows why, but it's always been so.

COKE: *(getting up)* Wendy's fucked, isn't she? Dead and gone and broken up to spare fucking parts, praise her usefulness.

BUD: Praise it. But there'll be a new one, soon as someone scrounges her up. Wendy's * Here To Stay.

COKE: *(simultaneously joining in on the ritual phrase)* Here To Stay.

BUD: *(continuous)* That's what we ought to be looking for, not footling afar after one scrawny runt of a ratty prize that's taboo to boot.

COKE: Not so scrawny. And I fucking caught it, dost hear? My fucking prizes stay fucking caught or what the fuck am I? As for so-called taboo, that brings me to two. Two: The rest of them may be fucking vaudevillians. But that prize is none.

BUD: What means thou? We saw its fucking act. It sucked squirrel anus, but—

COKE: It's been trained, what the fuck does that prove? It's been with them long enough, but it didn't start out with them. Dids't mark its cleverness? Fuck, it got away from me. From me!

BUD: And me.

COKE: And boosted our boodle on the fly! I fucking say it—it's one of ours. It's a born scavenger, and fuck me bloody if I don't get it back or break its neck trying.

BUD: Well but if it's one of ours, we can't fucking eat it, can we? So what's the fucking point?

COKE: If thy fucking head weren't full of fucking shit thy fucking skull would collapse. It's female, right?

BUD: Ahh . . .

COKE: Fucking right, ah. It's too small for a Wendy, but I know where it would fit. Ah? Ah?

COKE & BUD: *(roaring lewdly)* AARRHH!

BUD: What are we fucking around for, then, let's fucking after it!

COKE: Easy, easy, for fuck's sake. The prize took our fucking weapons, dost remember?

BUD: Fuck, right, yeah. Fuck. And there's but we two against . . . *(concentrating, counting on his fingers, then giving up)* more of them.

COKE: And one a fucking dog. Fuck it, by thy mother's tits, the taboo fits not a fucking dog. I'll take my chances with the next Wendy—I'll have that hound's heart in my belly before the seasons change, the fuck I won't.

BUD: It looked a fierce mean dog, withal. Oh, yeah, but fuck it, I'm with thee! Fuck, yeah!

COKE: Come on, then, but keep thy fucking tongue still, or I'll have it for a fucking garnish. We'll follow apace, and watch our moment.

(They exit.)

END OF ACT I

ACT II

(From off we hear a drum beat, a steady walking rhythm, and then the vaudevillians singing "The Wang-tailed Wallow" as a walking song. They enter, pulling the cart. VERA is walking in front. She stops and the others stop singing. There's a brief silence, as they all take in the ruins before them.)

ZETTA: Sad old place, this.

VERA: Indeed.

ZETTA: Grievous old ju-ju went on here. Anything, Dog? Dog!

DOG: What?

ZETTA: What you smell?

DOG: I don't know.

VERA: Old smoke. Long-spilt blood. Treachery, catastrophe, death. Even my poor nose can smell that much in these ruins.

ZETTA: Well, what-ever-all this is, it be nothing to us. Let's get on, hey? Think we can make your cath-ee-drell by dark? Hey? Vera? Damn-all, everybody turn to stone here?

VERA: I beg your pardon, my dear. I was adrift in bitter nostalgia. For I must inform you, to my infinite regret, that we have reached our destination.

ZETTA: No. This-all? This rubble? Fug-hat, this it? Hang on, now, this dev-no-station old and old. Weeds are well-grown to bury all. Whatever disaster came down on here was long ago.

VERA: So it seems. I did say, it was long ago that I last was here.

ZETTA: You did say. Must have followed fast upon your exit. Guess you did well to leave.

VERA: I did well to live. Many here did not, by the look of it. See, where the window frames are splintered, and blackened by soot? A savage fury tore this place apart stone by stone, and burnt what could burn. What would we find, do you think, if we were to wander amongst the ruins and dig, just a little, among the choking vines? A single shoe? Rain-rotten pages of what were books, rewritten now by weather and ignorance? Bones, do you think? Surely we would find bones, lying, sinking into the yielding dirt, where people fell. Where they died. Their terrible, surprising deaths. When the walls were finally breached. Or however it happened.

DOG: *(quietly)* Zetta. Let's walk on.

ZETTA: All right, there, Vera. No more on that. We walking on bones every day we walk the earth. This a bad place, sure, and I disappointed too, but what be, be, and old news is nothing to us here and now, 'cept we got to think of what next. It be dark soon. And the unknown road's the darkest, they say. Better sleep here and start fresh.

DOG: Let's walk on, Zetta, please.

ZETTA: Well, que pasa, Dog? What is it? You know something I ought to? *(He doesn't answer.)* You just spooked, pupster. Wore out from a long haul. Make no sense what-all to keep on now, hey? Lookit, you rest up, I'll take Jo-thing to gather firewood.

DOG: No, I'm not tired. I'll come with you.

ZETTA: *(Looks at him. Then, to* VERA:*)* We going for wood. You-all make camp.

VERA: Avec plaisir, mon capitane.

*(*ZETTA *and* DOG *exit.* JO-JO *pulls her bag off the cart and pulls out a weapon, sits on the ground and begins to sharpen, oil or otherwise refurbish it.* VERA *opens the cart and begins to explore the contents.)*

VERA: Instruments, of an unusual nature. Costumes. Bedding. Hmm, books. I would have wagered our intrepid leader was fully as literate as a squish. Perhaps she enjoys perusing the illustrations. . . . Very nice. Very old. And what have we here? Fascinating. Quite a collection of ancient artifacts. By the looks of it, the contents of this cart have been passed down through many a generation. A true aristocrat of the trade, our Zetta. What are you doing, Jo-Jo?

JO-JO: Nothin'.

VERA: I don't remember that weapon.

JO-JO: It's mine.

VERA: Jo-Jo. Where did it come from?

JO-JO: It's mine. I found it.

(VERA *comes down off the cart.*)

VERA: Jo-Jo. I asked you before, and now I think, true to your name, you were less than truthful with me: when you went missing those few hours, the other day. And came back scratched and bruised.

JO-JO: Fell asleep ina tree. Fell out.

VERA: Look at me, Jo-Jo.

JO-JO: Fell. Fell outa tree.

VERA: Look at me.

JO-JO: FELL OUTA FUCKIN TREE

(VERA *looks at* JO-JO, *never raising her voice.*)

VERA: A little liar. But not a good one. I can see right through you. Right through you, Jo-Jo. I can see right through you.

Where did the weapon come from, Jo-Jo?

JO-JO: Took it.

VERA: From whom, Jo-Jo?

JO-JO: Scavengers.

(*slight pause*)

VERA: Scavengers.

JO-JO: They caught me. Went to take a pee, fuckin' caught me. But I got away. They were stupid. Hah. I got away, and I took their stuff. See?

(*She holds her bag open to show* VERA.)

See? Gotta whole buncha their stuff. Hah.

VERA: And you're very pleased and proud, aren't you? To have scavenged a Scavenger?

JO-JO: Two of 'em.

VERA: You unspeakable little half-wit. One, two, an army of Scavengers. What they find, they do not relinquish. Recycle, reclaim and reuse, but never, never relinquish. You belong to them now, you troglodytic wretch.

JO-JO: No.

VERA: Yes, my dear, you are lawful Scavenger prize. No doubt they have been tracking you ever since. This is an unwelcome development. You might have told me sooner.

JO-JO: I'm not theirs. I have their weapons. I'll fuckin' kill them.

VERA: Yes, yes, you're the fiercest creature in the forest, I know. Well, after all, there may be a way to turn this to our advantage.

JO-JO: I'm with you now. I'm a vauder now. You said.

VERA: All right, all right, there, there. I know what it is to take refuge in an assumed identity. We neither of us were born to the life, but for a long time now it has been a haven to me, and served my turn, and it will yet for both of us. I don't suppose you're prepared at last to explain your origins to me? From whence you sprang, before I found you that long-ago day?

JO-JO: Told you. Don't remember.

VERA: And that may even be true. Enough for now. I must think. Keep your eyes open, hm? And that evil-looking object at the ready.

(VERA *goes back into the cart, while* JO-JO *strikes ferocious poses with the weapon, standing guard. Lights shift to another part of the stage, where* ZETTA *is binding together a large bundle of branches with strips of cloth or leather.* DOG *is nearby. Maybe he's lying on the ground, like a sick* DOG.)

ZETTA: Hey. Hey, Dog. Smell that? Maybe . . . yeah, there he is. That the sea, Dog. I knew we getting close. Man, oh man, if that ain't the smell of all change nor possibility. I ever tell you, Dog, the one time I smell the sea? Ever tell you that one? Long and long ago. Back in the day when it my mam's cart, and we a dozen strong almost. Oh, we could make an entrance then, razz and dazz, tribe knew it when we came in. I had three daddies then, Dog, Mam's three men. Sword-swaller, acro-gnat and the little old odd-jobber, who sewed costumes, pulled teeth need be, cooked, mixed medicines, what-ever-all. Clever son. They all nice to me, but I remember him most, some reason. Mam's busy, running things, but Jemmy had time for me. Well so Mam always kept us inland, said there's plenty land to keep us working, no need to get too close the edge, where who knows? Might wind up on a piece ready to fall off. Said sea's a treacherous critter, never trust him. Said sea's always nagging at the land, biting and tugging, and jumpin' up and over. Said there's tribe and tribe used to be, now lying under, deep and deep. And that's true enough, Dog. In the books. You know that, Dog? Well. One time, we were out on our usual circuit by a few days, detouring for a tribal offshoot wanted us specially, celebrate making it through the first year on their own. Way and away down south and west. High summer, plenty to eat, nice tribe. Day after day they kept us on. Everybody happy. Good gig. But day we going to leave, all a sudden, wind changed. Blew up wet and strange from the south. Jem smelled it. Next thing, he packed up separate and ready to walk. Mam so pissed, but nothing she can do. She worked on him, talking herself blue. All he said, he come from down there, down by the sea, and now he smelled it again, he had to see it too. Just had to. Said it was pulling and tugging and he had to go. You ever felt like that, anything, Dog? Well so maybe we sat and talked and maybe it all took days, but way I remember, that was it for Jem. He walked away and kept on walking, and we watched him walk, and that the end on it. Mam told me it was because he wasn't a true roadster. She said, one of those things you can't help. Where you belong got a gravity and it going to pull you hard. But fug-hat, Dog. Why this sea-smell making me think? I followed Jem a ways. But Mam was right. I went back, and we went away back inland. Maybe, though, nothing was the same. And one by one company died or got ate or went off and started new companies. Mam died with half the others, that drought summer when we had to drink what we could find, and it bad water, turned out. Well. All that long ago, and we doing fine and fine. Hey, Dog? So this stop-over a slosh-out, we got the gig of gigs ahead. King of China'll lavish us with rewards be-fitting and laissez le bon ton roulez once more. You know it, Dog. We better shake out the Play with the new hires, scrape off the rust, hey? Polish her up. Been a while. Wish I knew what eating you, damn-all if I don't.

Look up there, Dog. Getting dark down here, but sky still fat with light, glowing all kind colors. Something, hey? Wicked old world, but she ours.

(Pause. Back at the cart, VERA *is lighting lanterns,* JO-JO *completing a fire-circle of rocks. The stage of the cart has been folded*

out, and some cushions and blankets arranged on it.)

VERA: I want you to take whatever opportunity may present itself, Jo-Jo, to sequester our benefactress some little while. I need a quiet word with the two-legged mongrel. Given the possibly imminent invasion by your savage acquaintances, I can no longer afford to take my time as I might prefer, pursuant to our aims. Acceleration seems advisable. Do you understand?

JO-JO: Get mizz Zetta away so you can work the dog.

VERA: A fair approximation.

(ZETTA & DOG return with bundles of sticks, which they dump beside the fire circle.)

ZETTA: Make the fire there, okay, Jo-girl?

DOG: I'll do it.

ZETTA: No, Dog. You sickening for something. Go lie down. I said, go lie down, Dog.

(He goes and lies down on the cushions.)

You can make a fire all right, hey, Jo-critter?

JO-JO: Course I can.

ZETTA: Okay, then.

(Leaves her to it, goes up to VERA. They look at the sky.)

Look clear enough what-all, hey?

VERA: Assuredly. And yet, I don't quite like that yellow in the northwest. In my experience, it is an ill portent.

ZETTA: Can be. But no wind. Maybe we get wet sometime tomorrow, but nothing to fret over.

VERA: Agreed. Barring unexpected shifts, our night, at least, will be calm.

JO-JO: *(low, starting the fire)* Fire, fire, fire, fire, fire, fire, fire. *(it lights)* Fire.

(VERA goes and sits by the fire with JO-JO. ZETTA gets out a small sack of smoked squish, gives some to DOG.)

ZETTA: Here, Dog.

(He takes it, but doesn't eat. She joins the others around the fire. The little sack of food gets passed around as they speak.)

Vera, should have asked before. These people used to be here, they friends of yours?

VERA: One could say so.

ZETTA: Long time ago. But tray desolay. My sympathy, and what-all, you know.

VERA: Thank you.

(slight pause)

ZETTA: Damn-all hot, still. Just when you ready for a season-change, she turn stubborn, hey? Get stuck on summer who know how long.

VERA: Quite.

(slight pause)

ZETTA: Good fire, Jo-thing. Say now, Jo-ster, what say you give us another out on your repertoire, hey? Night for a story, if ever.

(Again, JO-JO goes instantly into her story-telling mode.)

JO-JO: "ONCE IN THE LONG AGO TIME there were two broth-ers. One was Coyote and one was Gopher. One day when Coyote was off hunting, an old woman came to the brothers' tent, where Gopher was sitting in the sun. The old woman said, I am thirsty. Gopher said, there is no water. Old woman said, I am hungry. Gopher said, there is no food. Old woman said, I am tired, let me rest in your tent. Gopher said, go away old woman. There is nothing here for you. Old woman then became what she was, that was a wolf. Gopher ran away, but Wolf caught him, and ate him in two bites. When Coyote came home from hunting, a young woman was sitting in front of his tent. Where is Gopher? he asked. The woman did not answer. He looked at her, and he desired her. She said, I am thirsty. He gave her water. She stayed. After many years, he woke one night and she was not in the tent. He went out, but he could not see her. All he heard were wolves howling. The next day he said to her, I woke in the night and you were not here. She said, you dreamed. He said, no. Where were you? She said, you dreamed, husband. Do not ask me anymore. Coyote became angry then, but he said nothing. That night, he pretended to sleep. In the night she went out. He followed. She became what she was, that was a wolf. He saw her. He saw her."

(She's finished.)

ZETTA: Well? What happens next?

JO-JO: Don't know. How it ends.

(They sit in silence for a moment. Then ZETTA *begins a soft scratchy percussive sound, by scraping something against something else.* JO-JO *joins in, making some quiet sound that complements the first sound.* ZETTA *begins to sing, to the tune of "Swing Low, Sweet Chariot.")*

ZETTA: *(singing)*

Sing yo, street Harriet
Comin' four o'clock to my door
Sing yo, street Harriet
Come in for the four o'clock show

(VERA joins in)

ZETTA & VERA: *(singing)*

I looked over Wanda
And what did I see
Comin' four o'clock to my door?
A band of wastrels
Shootin' up at three
Comin' for the four o'clock show

(JO-JO joins in)

ZETTA, VERA & JO-JO: *(singing)*

Sling joe, fleet Cherry-Anne
Comin' four or five on the floor
Sling joe, fleet Cherry-Anne
Commissar don't want you no more

ZETTA: Now, that an old one, for sure and all.

VERA: One of the oldest.

(slight pause)

JO-JO: Still hungry.

ZETTA: I did see some berry bushes, getting the wood. Could pick some in the dark, maybe.

JO-JO: *(getting a look from* VERA*)* Oh. Um. Yeah. I'll help you.

Let's go. C'mon.

ZETTA: Well, there, Jo-girl, coming out on your shell, aren't ya? Sure, what-ever-all, let's go get some berries. Bring that lantern.

DOG: Zetta.

ZETTA: We be back in a jump-jack-flash, Dog. Stay.

(ZETTA *and* JO-JO *exit. Slight pause.*)

VERA: Strange, isn't it? It must be perfectly surreal, not to say nightmarish, for you, finding yourself here again, after so long. It's strange enough for me. Quite numbingly painful, even for me, at first.

DOG: I don't, I don't know what, what you

VERA: It's possible, I grant, that you don't remember me. You were young. Still of an age to find most adults interchangeable. I slept on the far side of the, what did we call it? The campus. I think it was over there, my tower. Though it's curiously difficult to get my bearings. It's so much altered. The place where we both were born. Where I grew up, worked, made plans. Till the sky fell and everything ended.

DOG: I've never, never been here, never seen, you, or this, place

VERA: Do you not remember who I am? Now, I mean to say, who I am now. I cannot lie. I tell only the truth. Not the whole truth, but nothing but the truth. You may not remember me. But I know you. I know what you did, boy.

(slight pause)

DOG: Are you going to kill me?

VERA: Is that what you want?

DOG: It doesn't matter.

VERA: Are you inviting me to pity you?

DOG: No.

VERA: How did it happen, precisely? I've so often wondered.

(slight pause)

Am I not entitled to know?

(slight pause)

DOG: If you had asked me yesterday, I could have honestly said I didn't remember. I've been a dog a long time. But seeing the place . . . I wanted to know. What was outside the walls. Everyone said terrible things. But I knew that grown-ups didn't always tell the truth. I didn't believe them. I wanted to know. So I slipped away. I went to the South Gate. I knew the watchman that time and day was my uncle Fig. I knew he got sleepy after lunch. I waited till he dozed off and I opened the gate. I only meant to look. But there was that little ridge, that I couldn't see over. I found I had to just see what was on the other side. And there were woods, and there was something through the trees, and I found I just had to go see what that was. It was a stream, running off down a slope, and I followed it. After I'd walked for a while I got tired, and I lay among some ferns to rest. And I fell asleep. When I woke up it was nearly dark. I was worried. I'd have been missed by then. How would I explain? I followed the stream back, and went through the little woods, and climbed up the ridge. I began to hear a noise. I came to the top of the ridge.

VERA: You'd left the gate open.

DOG: I'd left the gate open. How did you know it was me?

VERA: Some of the women they didn't kill. They took us out the South Gate. I saw it hadn't been forced. You'd been looked for that afternoon. Your mother assumed you'd gone off among the stacks in one of the towers, reading, as you'd do. Then I saw you, cowering among the trees, and all of that came together in my mind. I often, later, wondered what became of you.

DOG: I became a dog. My mother. Was she.

VERA: She fought too valiantly to be captured. An arrow pierced her brain, through an eye.

DOG: Why weren't you killed? Didn't you fight too?

VERA: Oh, no. I surrendered instantly. By the end of the first day's captivity I was the slave of the head-man. At the end of a week, he was mine. I wasn't beautiful, mind you.

DOG: I know what you were.

VERA: Are you judging me?

DOG: No.

VERA: Surely it isn't necessary to remind you.

DOG: No.

VERA: I held a precarious sort of power among our conquerors for a brief time. But there was limited scope for my abilities. It may be better to rule in hell, but demons were surely never so dull. I found my chance when I persuaded my pet marauders from massacring a passing vaudeville troupe. In gratitude, they took me with them, and apprenticed me. In due course I became their leader. And so I've passed the years. Not surprising that you fetched up, after what ordeals I shudder to imagine, in the business yourself. Not many places for an over-educated boy, or dog, now the university tribes have fallen.

It is strange, being here again. If I didn't know better, I would say there's a feeling here of unquiet ghosts. Do you feel that? Restless spirits of the betrayed and unavenged.

DOG: They. They wouldn't have wanted.

VERA: Wouldn't have wanted revenge? They were a gentle people. But they were most ungently served. No doubt you imagine that your own suffering, your voluntary demotion from humanity, your willful unconsciousness of the past are sufficient to shield you from your own past deeds. It doesn't work that way, dear boy, as you ought to know. It is a matter of consequences. Not a moral question at all. There are things that forgiveness cannot touch. There are things that once done cannot be undone. Do you understand me? Feeling any amount of guilt or anguish, performing any little rites of expiation, all that is quite beside the point, because it isn't a sin, a personal moral drama—it is a historical fact. A miniature civilization lies here in ruins and decay. Because of you. I stand here as the sole survivor of your act of thoughtlessness and selfishness. The sole surviving member of your own tribe. Your only kin in this world, and your victim. Can you look at me and deny me anything? Can you look at me and not know that you belong to me, body and, for what it's worth, soul?

(slight pause)

DOG: No.

VERA: That's right. I'm glad we've had this chance to talk. I'm sure it's a relief to you, in a way. You've come home. All you need do now is remember where your allegiance lies. I won't ask anything else from you. Do you understand me, Dog?

DOG: Yes.

(We hear ZETTA *and* JO-JO *returning.*)*

VERA: Do you, Dog?

DOG: Yes, Vera.

JO-JO: *(*beginning off, continuing as they enter)*
And y' never eat the white ones, or the red ones, or the black ones, or the yellow ones, or the orange ones, just the blue ones, right, or the purple ones, or the big red ones, but not the little red ones, right, cause the little red ones'll kill you but good and the black ones'll—

(They've entered the camp by now, and seeing VERA *and* DOG, JO-JO *falls silent.)*

ZETTA: That's right, Jo-girl, you got berries down stone. Hey, now, Dog, feeling a tad better? Hey, Vera. Berries for all. People here must of cult-no-vated them, more than we can pick if we picked all night.

VERA: A very welcome addition to our repast. Good work, Jo-Jo.

ZETTA: Here, pupster, eat something. We ate plenty while picking. Never foraged in the dark before, but Jo-girl's got sharp eyes on her, could be a nowl of old.

(DOG takes the berries offered, but doesn't eat.)

JO-JO: Nowl?

ZETTA: Nowls were big fierce bad old birds, could see in the dark an fly silent, pick off anything came out at night. If you too big to eat, they ask: Who? Who? And then watch out, cause nowls harbingers of death.

JO-JO: Harb-a-gers?

VERA: Forerunner sign messenger outrider warning herald.

ZETTA: First you see nowl, soon next you going to see death come up say: "hey." Who? Whoooo.

JO-JO: HEY. HEY.

ZETTA: *(laughing)* Hey there, Jo-ster, easy up. No nowls round here.

VERA: Not for a long, long time. Have you ever seen one, Dog? Have you ever seen an owl, Dog?

DOG: No, Vera.

ZETTA: Well, now, there, Vera. Thinking. About time we took the Play out for a spin, see how she fits with the new group. Hey? Early yet, may as well rehearse before weather changes on us again.

VERA: That, my dear, is a perfectly marvelous conception. We stand ready.

ZETTA: All right then. Set-up!

(A flurry of activity ensues, as costumes are put on, props and costume changes laid out, musical instruments checked, tuned and readied, non-essential items like the berries tidied away. JO-JO's *bag containing the Scavengers' weapons ends up to the side of the cart, upstage. As this begins,* VERA *takes the opportunity to speak to* JO-JO *in an aside:)*

VERA: I have muzzled the mutt. Now is the time to act. You will find your moment and give our brave vaudevillian the hook, at the point of your knife.

JO-JO: Vera. How come. I mean. Why not. I mean.

VERA: Have you an objection, Jo-Jo?

JO-JO: Why we can't just go like we are? With Zetta? She and Dog. They not so bad.

VERA: *(rapidly)* I would have thought even your small wit could have puzzled that out without a pause for exposition. But, attend, I will illumine: we have lost our cart and everything we need to live; Zetta will share, up to a point, but it is her cart and her properties and her sufferance; they could chase us off whenever they pleased, and we would revert instantly to desperate need; not to mention that I am no one's supporting player. It is true that I could take it all, but slowly, so she would not know at what moment it ceases to be hers and becomes mine; I could enslave her, as I have her mongrel, without spilling a salty droplet. I have done it before. But I am no longer as patient as I once was, I am not patient at all and I will have it, I will take it, I will not wait. Marauders are at the gate again and we must be

ready. So. Yes? Do you understand? May we go on now? When
we come to The Tower scene, when you come on as the plagues,
switch the prop knife: let your blade be real, and let it be swift.
The dog won't hinder you. Then when your Scavengers show up
they can have her body to recycle. Instead of yours. Go on, now.
Prepare.

(The preparations continue and now ZETTA *and* DOG *speak
apart.)*

ZETTA: Give me a hand with this, hey, Dog? This just what-all
you need; you be a new critter with the show-juices flowing
again. Long time since we done the thing all the way through.

DOG: Zetta, listen, there are things. There are things you don't.
Listen there are things you don't know about me.

ZETTA: No kidding. You picking this moment out of a blizzard-
ness of moments to spill a revelation? Hey? Well, okay, snoops,
spill away.

*(*DOG *doesn't speak.)*

Now, you listen a me, pup. Speak, don't speak, it your own story
to tell or keep shut-mouth on. You know me, I want to know
any-all info-mation going, add it to the stockpile. But fug-hat,
if it be the past wigging you out, my advice? make your peace
and move along. History's a bitch to have at your heels. Smell
that sweet old night, Dog? Feel that old earth of ours underfoot?
Enough, can't it be? Okay, all I'm saying, you got to figure it out
your own self. For me, you my dog and I take you as you are,
don't need the back-story, nevermind the pedigree and filigree
and narrative hoo-hah. Hey? Okay then.

(She moves off about her tasks. DOG *looks after her.* JO-JO *sidles
up.)*

JO-JO: Sorry.

DOG: What?

JO-JO: I'm sorry.

DOG: Why?

(slight pause)

JO-JO: FUCK OFF aright JUST FUCK OFF

ZETTA: Hey, hey, got the jittabugs there, Jo-thing? C'mere, let's get you set up. I got your prop knife for the Tower, c'mon, now.

(JO-JO *goes upstage to* ZETTA. VERA *speaks aside to* DOG.)

VERA: Our little liar is volatile, but you needn't fear her. She is a weapon that I have the aiming of, and the trigger.

DOG: Are you aiming her at Zetta?

VERA: What is that to you? You don't belong to her anymore. Your silence proves it. You would have told her everything by now if you were still hers. But you don't speak, because you know very well that if she knew what you are, she would, very rightly, no longer trust you. She would hold you in contempt. Anyway, she isn't of your tribe. I am. Remember that, and no harm will come to you.

ZETTA: Well now so, think we all good to go here. Stop if need be, but let's try to get right through her in one gallop, hey? Get the feel of her. Places! Hit it, Dog.

(DOG *begins to play, and the others take their places. There is a brief—no more than a minute or two—colorful explosion of opening number/overture/prologue here. If the actors have any skills such as juggling, tumbling, stilt walking, etc., these should be displayed simultaneously. Otherwise they may parade about in costume and perform a lively dance. Then* ZETTA—*in costume, possibly low stilts—comes forward to declaim:)*

ZETTA: Listen all and you shall hear
A tale to make you quake with fear
A story full of woe and pity
The rise and fall of human-ity
The breathless rise and tragic fall
Of those before who made us all
Listen well, and learn once more
The misery that lies in store
For those who will forget the past
May perish in a fiery blast
Listen well but blame us not
It was not we who wrote the plot
Have mercy on we players poor
If we offend, forbear to roar

And if you roar, forbear to rage
Remember all the world's a stage
We do our best, look you do too
Or we will in our turn judge you

(Exeunt to music. While everyone is occupied, we see the Scavengers sneak on upstage, steal back the bag of weapons and exit. A painted sign is revealed, reading; "Act 1: Adam and Eve's Evolutionary Comedy." VERA *and* JO-JO *step forward with a musical introduction played by* DOG *or* ZETTA.*)*

VERA/ADAM: Say, Eve, what's all this I hear about the origin of the species?

JO-JO/EVE: Say, Adam, glad you asked. It's all very simple. First came Who, an amoeba, and then came What, a fish, and third, I Don't Know crawled onto land and grew feet. See?

VERA/ADAM: What a minute, wait a minute. Who came first?

JO-JO/EVE: That's right. Who came first.

VERA/ADAM: That's what I'm asking.

JO-JO/EVE: Who.

VERA/ADAM: You tell me.

JO-JO/EVE: I'm telling you.

VERA/ADAM: Who?!

JO-JO/EVE: That's right, who!

VERA/ADAM: You tell me!

JO-JO/EVE: Okay, hold on now—

VERA/ADAM: Jeez!

JO-JO/EVE: It's simple, Adam, now listen. What came next.

VERA/ADAM: What?

VERA/ADAM: That's right.

VERA/ADAM: WHAT?

JO-JO/EVE: A fish! And who crawled onto the land and grew feet?

VERA/ADAM: I don't know!

JO-JO/EVE: That's right! I don't know!

VERA/ADAM: One of these days, Eve! Bang, zoom! To the moon!

(DOG enters as the snake, juggling apples)

DOG/SNAKE: Say, Adam and Eve, ya hear the one about the origin of the species?

VERA & JO-JO: *(turning on him)* Aw, shaddup!

DOG/SNAKE: Awright, awright! *(offering an apple)* Anybody hungry?

(Vera and Jo-Jo haul off to smack Dog, who ducks so they clock each other instead; a frenetic slapstick fight ensues, with Zetta doing comic sound-effects. It ends with Dog victorious, and Vera and Jo-Jo on the ground with their heads wobbling. Dog takes a big bite of an apple; Zetta makes a loud, ominous sound-effect like thunder; the other three look up to the sky anxiously. Then Zetta plays a flourish of exit music, they jump up, bow and run off. A new sign appears, reading: "Act 2: Rozetta Stone sings The Human Blues." During the song—if not before—unnoticed by the players and even by most of the audience, the Scavengers creep in downstage right and sit watching.)

ZETTA: *(singing)*

Critter in the bushes, critter in the sky
Don't know nothing, they just live and they die
Critter in the river, critter in the sea
Don't know nothing and they happier than me
I know one thing, know it chapter and verse
However bad it been, it gonna keep getting worse
I got the human blues
O-o-o-oh the human blues

The apple of Eden is a sour old fruit
Filled with bitter wisdom from the twig to the root
That apple it leave an evil taste in the mouth
Once it get in it ain't never get out
I know one thing, know it upside and down
When the water rise, everybody get drown
I got the human blues
O-o-o-oh the human blues

Know enough to mutter, know enough to moan
Know enough to know I can't never go home
Know enough to holler, know enough to howl

Know enough to know I know nothing at all
I know one thing, got it nailed to the floor
Although it do me no good, I always got to know more
I got the human blues
O-o-o-oh the human blues

(The song finished, ZETTA *takes a bow and exits. New sign: "Act 3: The Tower or The Tragedy of the Fall."* VERA *comes forward in a somber costume as the narrator and chorus. She beats a drum. A painted backdrop is lowered, showing a high, unfinished tower in a desert.)*

VERA: So long ago the stars were not yet cold
There was a land all desert, parched and dry
The people there were clever, we are told
And longed to look their dread god in the eye
And ask him why they were condemned to dwell
In such a desperate land, so hard and hot
That nothing was to choose 'tween it and hell
They loved their god, but feared he loved them not
And so in grief and anger did they bake
A thousand thousand bricks of straw and mud
Forgetting what befell the lord's own snake
When he presumed to know more than he should
But as they built their tower high and wide
It pleased them so, their rage turned into pride

*(*ZETTA *in costume as* THE BUILDER, *and* DOG *as* THE WORKER, *come on.)*

ZETTA/BUILDER: Stupendous! Magnificent! The tallest thing in existence! You know, Worker, when I look at what we've done, I marvel. It must be the greatest wonder of the universe.

DOG/WORKER: If you say so.

ZETTA/BUILDER: It started slow, but every day we're building faster and faster. A brilliant achievement: a tower to trump the heavens!

DOG/WORKER: I'd rather stay on the ground.

ZETTA/BUILDER: What are you complaining about? You'll be paid for your labor.

DOG/WORKER: That's what I'm afraid of.

ZETTA/BUILDER: Shut up and get back to work. We want to finish this level by nightfall. There are some who say that soon we'll be high enough to look God in the eye and demand some answers. About time!

DOG/WORKER: I'll work, but if any God-teasing goes on, I'm out of here.

(VERA bangs the drum again, and DOG and ZETTA do a working-mime-dance. VERA makes a scary thunder-effect with her drum, and they stop and look up.)

ZETTA & DOG: Uh oh.

VERA: *(continuing the sound-effect)*
The tower rose, and waked their sleeping god
Who raged to see how high they'd dared to go
He'd made them to be meek and tread the sod
And so he sent down plagues to bring them low

(DOG and ZETTA cower as JO-JO enters in costume as THE PLAGUES. She runs around them, shrieking horribly—and then stops short, having run downstage right and come face-to-face with THE SCAVENGERS. THE SCAVENGERS rise. There's a moment of dead silence. Then JO-JO turns to dive for the weapons bag, only to find it gone. THE SCAVENGERS raise their weapons.)

DOG: *(belatedly)* Bark! BARK BARK BARK.

COKE: Be-still thy fucking dog or I'll be-fucking-still him for good.

ZETTA: Dog. C'mere, Dog.

COKE: Know thou all, it is thy glory to be the prize of the great, the grasping, the rapacious Coke, scavenger of scavengers.

BUD: And me. Bud the scavenger. Fuck yeah.

COKE: My eyes are keen, my feet tireless, and my hands loose not their grip for fuck-all. What-ere I see, that do I possess, and re-possess. I can wring usefulness from the very stones, from the very air if I choose! Be thou all assured, you will be well used, and never wasted. Pack all that was thine, now mine, that we may return in triumph.

VERA: A moment, if I may speak. Can it have escaped your notice that we are vaudevillians? Surely you must respect the sacred protected status of the traveling player.

BUD: Fuck. Yeah. What I fucking said, Coke.

ZETTA: That's right, there, lord scavenger. Only ignorant old savages don't know better nor that.

COKE: *(to BUD)* Thou useless fuck, be fucking still. *(to VERA)* We know about vaudevillians. But our Wendy is dead and recycled, praise her usefulness.

BUD: Praise it.

COKE: And the next one yet to be found. See? Betwixt and between and all bets off. Thou'rt raw material to me, nothing more. *(to ZETTA)* Insult me again and I'll lay thee open like a gutted fish. Pack it up.

(He has spoken. THE VAUDEVILLIANS *slowly turn to obey. But:)*

BUD: Well, but, fuck. What about the play?

COKE: What?

BUD: What about the rest of the play? I would see it. I would see how it ends. Dost not thou want to see it? *(to* THE VAUDEVIL-LIANS*)* Play fucking on, or know the wrath of Bud!

ZETTA: You want to see the rest of the play, it your call and all, just slay the word.

COKE: Ah, fuck yeah. I would see it finished. Let the play proceed. But fuck with us and thou'rt dead fucked, dost hear?

*(*ZETTA *bows slightly and draws the other* VAUDEVILLIANS *with her a bit upstage)*

ZETTA: *(aside)* Command performance, if ever. But an audience an audience, what-ever-all. Give me time to think, one thing. You all okay to go on?

VERA: Most assuredly. As you say, time to think. After all, anything can happen in the theater.

COKE: Shut fucking up and act!

ZETTA: *(aloud)* From the entrance of the plagues. When-ever-all you ready.

(They resume their places. VERA *plays the thunder-effect,* ZETTA *and* DOG *cower.)*

VERA: And so he sent down plagues to bring them low.

(JO-JO *runs in again as* THE PLAGUES, *and circles* ZETTA *and* DOG. *She wears a half-mask of exaggerated hideousness and performs a grotesque dance, brandishing a knife, as* VERA *speaks, beating her drum before each plague.*)

VERA: The Plague of What-You-Lookin-At's

The Plague of Big Ideas

The Plague of Flag-Waving Border-Raving Killer Toads

The Plague of Rockem-Sockem Godheads

The Plague of Sick Machines

The Plague of Tiny Blood Bugs

The Plague of Crashing Techno-Rocks From Space

The Plague of Dinosauritis

The Plague of Neighbor-Slaughter

The Plague of Long-Distance Rains O' Terror

The Plague of Accidental Armageddon

The Plague of The New Darkness!

(ZETTA *confronts* JO-JO.)

ZETTA/BUILDER: Why do you torment us?

JO-JO/PLAGUES: You know why.

ZETTA/BUILDER: Why did he make us, if he was going to destroy us?

JO-JO/PLAGUES: It's your own pride that destroys you.

ZETTA/BUILDER: Why does he hate us?

JO-JO/PLAGUES: He loves you but you betray him.

ZETTA/BUILDER: He betrays us!

JO-JO/PLAGUES: You never know when to stop, do you? It's too late. Your day is done. Your tower will be shattered, your workers decimated and scattered into the desert, never to build again.

(*She turns her back to* ZETTA *and raises the knife.* DOG *looks at* VERA, *back to* JO-JO.)

And you, builder, architect of defiance, you must now pay for your sins. You wanted to speak to God. Come and see him now!

(JO-JO *turns to stab* ZETTA. *But* DOG *suddenly puts himself in the way and is stabbed. There is a moment of confusion.* DOG *holds the knife in his chest. He stares at* JO-JO. *Then crumples to the ground and is still.)*

ZETTA/BUILDER: *(ad-libbing)* Laborer, it is not your part to die.

(ZETTA *kneels down and touches* DOG. *Breaking character:)*

Dog? Hey, Dog?

Knife real. He dead.

VERA: *(to* JO-JO*)* Fool!

ZETTA: *(to* JO-JO*)* That my death he took, meant for me. Why?

(JO-JO *doesn't answer.* ZETTA *looks at* VERA.)

Well? You the true hand on the hilt. How about some of your famous truth?

VERA: But of course. You have only to ask.

ZETTA: Why you want me dead?

VERA: The usual reason. For what you have that I want. All rather moot now of course, but trust Jo-Jo to stick to a plan regardless.

BUD: *(to* COKE*)* This play fucking sucks.

COKE: *(to* VAUDEVILLIANS*)* Yoi! This play fucking sucks!

VERA: Our heartfelt and profound apologies, gentle viewers. The play has come to an untimely end. Not to put too fine a point, one of the actors is dead.

COKE: What, truly dead? Dead in fact? Not playacting dead?

BUD: What the fuck?

VERA: Truly dead, dead in fact and not in fiction. Lamentably, yes.

BUD: Thou overacting fuck-up, why-fucking-for didst thou so?

COKE: The dog was our prize, not thine to sacrifice. Hadst cause? Speak.

(*All eyes are on* JO-JO. *After a beat, she goes into her story-telling mode—but for the first time, inventing.*)

JO-JO: Hadst cause? Hadst fucking cause? Listen, thou fucks, and thou shalt know that this dog, this dead dog, this dead fuck of a dead-fucked dog was the evilest, vilest, badest dog of all. He could not be trusted, no, not so far as fuck-all. No one was safe from this heinous marauding brute. He woulda ripped out thy throats as thou slept, brave scavengers, first chance, or tried, and win or lose we'd a been fucked. If fail, thou'd a figured we were in on it and kill us all. If he succeed no odds for us, he'd get us sooner or later too. It was a wicked blood-thirsty man-eating monstrous wicked cruel beast of a bad, bad dog and I did us all a fucking favor.

(Slight pause. JO-JO *and* COKE *have locked gazes)*

BUD: What a load of stinking fuck-all.

COKE: *(to* BUD*)* Shut thy fucking hole.

BUD: It's a lying little fuck! Let's gut it and teach it a lesson.

COKE: Touch her and die slow and horrible. *(to* ZETTA *and* VERA, *referring to* DOG*)* Pack up the meat, and make haste. We must return to make the feast before it spoils.

(Since last speaking, ZETTA *has been on the ground by* DOG's *body. Now she stirs.)*

ZETTA: No.

BUD: Fuck, another fucking tribe heard from.

COKE: What false understanding of me gives you this foolish courage, prize?

ZETTA: No false info, Coke, but something I know you don't. Kill me, you live and die an ignorant fuck.

(Coke seems prepared to risk this, but BUD *holds his arm.)*

BUD: Stay, stay, for fuck's sake. I would know what it thinks it knows.

COKE: Speak, before you die.

(ZETTA rises, taking her moment.)

ZETTA: Your Wendy dead, and you chasing through the wide world for what, such poor prizes as seedy old vaudsters and dead dogs? You see, but you blind. You hear, but you deaf. This-all's your lucky day, deserve it or not. What you most of all need be under your noses, inside your reach, here to bring you glory to the end of your days for being the ones to scrounge it. Still don't know what-all? I should let you go on plain old dumb-fug as you are, but for pity's sake I will speak and end all suspense. Your Wendy dead but she rise again, recycled and good as new, ready to guide you. Where she? you long to learn. I tell you: She here!

(She turns and unexpectedly indicates VERA. *General amazement, including from* VERA.*)*

Conceal yourself no longer, O Useful One. The moment for reveal-ation be at hand. Tell what only the Wendyness of all Scavengers know. Expound the reason for the vaudevillian taboo, and so they will know you.

*(*VERA *and* ZETTA *regard each other.)*

Your moment be come, O Most Resourceful. Recycled soul of the Wendy joined with your own. Cast off your temporary guise of the Vera, and speak free. The truth will save us all, the truth as only the Wendy know it.

(slight pause)

VERA: *(decisively, to* THE SCAVENGERS*)* I had intended to observe you yet a while longer in my disguise, to see for myself the state of my scavenger kingdom. This wretched player has revealed me precipitously, and yet perhaps the moment has indeed come. The soul of your late Wendy, Praise her Usefulness—

COKE & BUD: *(automatically)* Praise it.

VERA: —has been recycled and restored good as new in me. Great and wise are the two who have found me. You will have glory when we return. Your usefulness will be much admired and rewarded.

*(*THE SCAVENGERS *hesitate.)*

BUD: *(to* COKE*)* Is't true, think you?

COKE: If be so, as may be, that you are our salvaged leader, tell us this. Why are vaudevillians taboo? It is something only the Recycled One can explain.

VERA: Did not your previous late Wendy ever elucidate this question for you?

COKE: She forbade, under pain of terrible retribution.

BUD: She never explained fuck-all.

VERA: And now you expect me to reveal what she in her wisdom left shrouded? You are treading on the hem of a great mystery. I will say this, my children, listen thou well. The vaudevillian is the repository of all that was and all that may be. She is the key. She is the translator of our souls. More than this, more than all, listen thou, dear scavengers: she is that rare and precious pearl lying in this dark, drear, perilous sea: she is *entertainment*. Further than this I cannot nor I will not speak. Kill us all and be damned for ignorant outlaw barbarians. Or accept me as your Wendy, and let us return to scavenger territory where you will be feasted in triumph for your brilliant resourcefulness in having found me, where you will have the choice parts of every sacrifice and the intense and pliant admiration of anyone you fancy.

(THE SCAVENGERS *exchange a pragmatic glance.*)

COKE: Fuck yeah.

BUD: Fucking right.

COKE & BUD: *(a roar)* FUUUUCK.

COKE: Right. Thou'rt her all right. Anyone doubt it, is fucked.

VERA: Splendid. Well, let us delay no longer. Come, Jo-Jo.

BUD: *(referring to* JO-JO*)* Tarry a fucking moment. What is it? Prize, scavenger or vaudevillian?

ZETTA: She's mine. She killed my dog. Leave her to me.

VERA: A sort of justice in that, I concede . . .

COKE: She's mine. I fucking caught her.

JO-JO: Fuck you. I'm not your fucking prize.

BUD: What the fuck art thou then?

COKE: My prize or my mate. Choose.

(*Everyone else is dumbfounded.* JO-JO *looks from* COKE *to* ZETTA, *and back again.*)

JO-JO: If mate, keep my own weapons?

COKE: Fuck yeah.

VERA: Jo-Jo, if I may interject—

JO-JO: Fuck when *I* say, or thou'll feel my knife.

COKE: *(to* BUD*)* Witness it.

BUD: Witnessed.

JO-JO: *(to* COKE*)* Deal.

*(*COKE *tosses her one of the weapons. She brandishes it.)*

Fuck yeah!

JO-JO, COKE & BUD: *(a celebratory roar)* FUUUCK.

VERA: Well. If the wedding's over, let us depart.

*(*ZETTA *and* JO-JO *exchange a look. Then* JO-JO *turns and strides off,* THE SCAVENGERS *following.* VERA *lingers a moment, looking at* ZETTA *on the ground by* DOG*'s body.)*

VERA: You do have a gift for improvisation.

A happy ending, all things considered.

I never would have expected it of him.

Best of luck in China, my dear.

(She exits. Slight pause. ZETTA *touches* DOG*.)*

ZETTA: Okay, Dog. They gone.

*(*DOG *comes back to life.)*

DOG: Close one.

ZETTA: Quick of you, playing dead and all like that.

*(*DOG *shrugs)*

You thought that a real knife, didn't you? Hey?

DOG: No. I don't know. Yeah.

ZETTA: Damn-all, Dog, what kinda dumb-fug trick?

DOG: Vera told me—I thought—

ZETTA: I know. Jo-Jo spilled the cat out the bag, while we setting up for rehearsal. I was going to take a dive, get Vera off guard.

DOG: You could have let me in on it.

ZETTA: Well, you not being all so comunicado your own self! What you get for being a stubborn old close mouthed mutt.

DOG: It was complicated!

ZETTA: Yeah, yeah.

DOG: Dammit, Zetta!

ZETTA: Don't you dammit me! Man! Gonna have to keep you on a tighter leash, pulling dum-fug sacrificial tricks like that.

DOG: Never again, trust me!

ZETTA: Damn right!

(Another violent earth-wobble)

ZETTA & DOG: WOOOOOOH!

(They fall down.)

DOG: Ow.

ZETTA: *(re: the change of season:)* Hey. What you think?

DOG: Feels like spring.

ZETTA: It do, it surely do. About time.

DOG: You said we might get to the sea in the spring.

ZETTA: I did so say. And we close. Sans doubt, we could do it.

DOG: And then China?

ZETTA: Sure, Dog. China be next.

DOG: I might not be a dog anymore.

ZETTA: Oh. Yeah?

DOG: Yeah. I might. I might become, you know. Human.

ZETTA: Well, it your call.

DOG: I know.

ZETTA: It'd change things. You and me. Be different.

DOG: I know.

ZETTA: Might not be bad. Might not be bad what-all.

DOG: I'm going to think about it.

ZETTA: Okay. You let me know.

You want to stick around here day or two?

DOG: No. No, let's hit the road.

ZETTA: Pack it up, pup-man.

(They throw everything into the cart as ZETTA *plans:)*

We get to the sea, there be people to ask. Always people close to the sea, poor dumb-fugs. Ever now and again they get all swallowed up, but more come to take their place. That people for you. But so there'll be a town, we can give 'em a show, get ourselves directions how to head toward China.

(Ready to go, they take a look around.)

You okay, there?

DOG: Yeah. Yeah.

ZETTA: Come on, then.

(DOG *slips the harness over his shoulders, begins to play percussion, as* ZETTA *pushes or pulls too. They exit, singing in a walking rhythm:*)

ZETTA & DOG: *(singing)*

Don't ask me why
Don't ask me what
Don't ask me nothing nothing nothing nothing but
Hoo hoo, hoo hah
We're walking
Just walking
Walking to Chi-i-na

END OF PLAY

DO YOU WANT TO KNOW A SECRET?

BY DANIEL PINKERTON

For Ariel—a great role model

BIOGRAPHY

Daniel Pinkerton, a California-born and Minneapolis-based playwright, holds advanced degrees in playwriting and European history. A core member of the Playwrights' Center in Minneapolis, he was awarded a National Endowment of the Arts Fellowship for his opera libretto *Dance of Death* and a Jerome Fellowship in Playwriting. *Do You Want to Know a Secret?* was an O'Neill Conference 2000 finalist, and has been workshopped at Red Eye Theater's Works-in-Progress Series (Minneapolis), the Jungle Theater Reading Series (Minneapolis), the Portland Stage Company's Little Festival of the Unexpected (Maine), and will be read by Undermain Theater in New York in 2002. His latest play, provisionally titled *Alles Klara*, was workshopped at the Playwrights' Center in June 2001, and he is at work on a ballad opera, *The Ballad of Mary Mallon*, based on the life of Typhoid Mary (with composer Chris Gennaula).

CHARACTERS

WALTER BERGER

ERIKA BERGER—his daughter

KARIN BERGER—his spouse

ANJA HORNUNG—KARIN's best friend

WOLF NIEDERMANN—KARIN's father

TIME & PLACE

The action takes place in Berlin between 1988 and 1993. The filmed monologues in Act I take place earlier.

The setting is divided into three playing areas: The Bergers' apartment, center stage; a space containing a desk and two office chairs, downstage left; an empty space into which small pieces of furniture can be moved as needed, downstage right. (At the end of Act I, the desk could be moved offstage, so that scenes not occurring in the Bergers' apartment could be played either downstage right or left.)

The back wall of the Bergers' apartment (upstage center) is a screen where video footage is projected from behind. The projected images should be much larger than life-sized, taking up almost the entire wall. The furniture should be arranged to ensure minimal blocking of the images.

NOTES

Do You Want to Know a Secret? was written with support from the Playwrights' Center Jerome Fellowship Program, Minneapolis, Minnesota. I would like to extend a special thanks to the Playwrights' Center and to Megan Monaghan, former Director of Playwright Services, for developmental assistance and financial support for my participation in The Little Festival of the Unexpected.

I am also indebted to numerous sources for information about the Stasi and life in East Germany. Three particularly helpful published sources were Timothy Garton Ash's "The Romeo File" (*The New Yorker*, April 28/May 5, 1997) and his memoir, *The File* (New York: Random House, 1997); "East Germans Face Their Accusers," by Stephen Kinzer (*New York Times Magazine*, April 12, 1992); and *The Haunted Land* by Tina Rosenberg (New York: Random House, 1995). Although the larger historical events mentioned did take place, this play is a work of fiction and any resemblance between its characters and any person, living or dead, is coincidental.

—*D. P.*

Think, in your head, now, think of the most . . . private . . . secret . . . intimate thing you have ever done secure in the knowledge of its privacy. . . . Are you thinking of it? Well, I saw you do it!

—Tom Stoppard
Rosencrantz & *Guildenstern Are Dead*

The key to betrayal is trust.

—Timothy Garton Ash
The File

DO YOU WANT TO KNOW A SECRET?

ACT I

(On a large screen, we see a video of WALTER BERGER *filmed in extreme closeup, against a bland white background. Occasional jerky cuts give the video an informal, "homemade" look.* WALTER *is about thirty, has longish hair and a scruffy beard or goatee. He smokes as he talks confidentially to the camera.)*

WALTER: I first met Karin six months ago, at the parade that opened the Twenty-First Annual Week of German-Soviet Friendship. Who could forget such an event? The tall, bearlike Comrade Brezhnev himself, leader of our "friends," bent down to kiss Secretary Ulbricht, a hundred pigeons were released, and billions of Ostmarks' worth of Russian-built tanks, fresh from the invasion of Prague—excuse me, the "August Assistance"—began rolling down Unter den Linden, followed by row after row of soldiers in perfect formation, their bayonets gleaming in the morning sun. The sight of so much "security" was a stirring visual metaphor for our German Democratic Republic.

Well, undoubtedly you were there, too. It was *dienstlich*—our duty. And in the middle of all this goodwill and celebration of everything that keeps us safe from capitalism, I saw . . . Karin. Blonde hair, little wooly cap, marching at the head of a ragged band of perhaps twenty foolish citizens. I've no idea who they were. I didn't want to know who they were. But there was something very . . . arresting—(*smiles*) sorry!—about Karin. For one thing, she carried an enormous sign proclaiming END STASI TORTURE.

How should I know? I proof the party paper, but I don't really follow politics. Still, a sign like that makes you wonder: Do the police really torture people? And then—as I'm sure you know—the Stasi fired rubber bullets and tear gas into the crowd. Now I make no judgements. But people panicked and began to flee, and what did the Stasi do? They moved in with gas and truncheons, spoiling the mood of "peace through strength" that the parade had engendered. I daresay Comrade Brezhnev was not pleased.

I myself did not flee. I found myself moving toward Karin, which is quite unlike me. But I wanted to become involved. . . . In the clash? No. With Karin. I was attracted to her. So I pushed my way through the crowd. My eyes were smarting from the gas, but I managed to keep sight of Karin's sign. And just as I reached her, a policeman swung a club at her, and she fell to the street and dropped it.

This was my chance. I could have lifted up Karin. I could have picked up the sign. But I was frozen—suspended between desire and fear. She looked, at that moment, quite helpless. And yet I knew she was strong, possibly intoxicating, and certainly dangerous. As the police dragged us both away, I knew that I had failed some sort of test, that I was too . . . careful to ever be a part of Karin Niedermann's world.

(The screen goes dark.)

MAY 1988

(Lights up on the Bergers' flat in East Berlin. A beat-up couch and a dining room table with a few chairs around it. Stage left is where people enter from the hall; stage right, where they exit to the rest of the apartment. A telephone sits on the table. WALTER *is at the table playing chess with his 15-year-old daughter* ERIKA. WAL-TER *is definitely older than he was in the video—his dark hair and goatee are shot through with gray.* ERIKA, *like* WALTER, *is tall and dark-haired, though she has pink streaks in her hair. She is dressed in black.)*

ERIKA: Check.

(The telephone rings. WALTER *answers.)*

WALTER: I'm sorry. We have no fresh fish. (WALTER *hangs up, examines the chessboard.)* Hm. I suppose you think you're clever. He looks up and smiles at her. Well, you are . . . but . . .

(The telephone rings. WALTER *answers.* ERIKA *sighs.)*

I'm sorry. We have no fresh fish.

(WALTER *hangs up. He examines the chessboard again.*)

WALTER: Now. What was I saying?

ERIKA: You were lecturing about the art of typesetting.

WALTER: I was not. We were playing chess.

ERIKA: *(rolls her eyes)* Sort of.

WALTER: Whose move is it?

ERIKA: Yours, dad.

(The telephone rings. WALTER *reaches for it.)*

Hey. Are you gonna like, play chess or be a dope?

(WALTER *looks at* ERIKA *as if to say "okay, we'll do it your way." So the telephone keeps on ringing and ringing.* WALTER *starts to move his rook.*)

I'd think twice about that, dad.

(WALTER *keeps his hand on his chess piece, looking around the board more thoroughly. The phone doesn't stop ringing. Finally,* ERIKA *can't stand it any more. She answers the phone.*)

Berger residence. *(Beat.)* Shit.

WALTER: Language!

ERIKA: *(to Walter)* Sorry! *(into phone)* Sorry. But we don't have any fresh fish. *(Beat.)* Yeah? Well, eat my shorts!

(ERIKA *hangs up.* WALTER *frowns.*)

That's not swearing. Have you figured out your move yet?

WALTER: Just give me some time.

ERIKA: I'm goin' nuts, dad!

WALTER: Sorry. I don't mean to be slow. But—

ERIKA: You're slow because you can't think. Nobody can with this damned—

(The telephone rings.)

WALTER: Language!

ERIKA: AAUGGH!

(WALTER *answers the telephone.*)

WALTER: I'm sorry. We have no fresh fish.

(WALTER *hangs up the telephone.*)

ERIKA: I don't get it. Why are people still calling us all the time? Mom's in prison! They've got her! The Stasi can drop the whole campaign—there's no one here to harass.

WALTER: There's me.

ERIKA: Dad. You don't actually march or anything.

WALTER: Not now. But before you were born, I was quite a familiar figure in meetings and on the streets.

ERIKA: Yeah, right.

WALTER: Young lady. Maybe I wasn't as infamous as your mother, but I spent a few nights in jail. And I got a stern talking to from my editor. I almost lost my job.

(The telephone rings. ERIKA *lifts it up and puts it down.)*

WALTER: Erika!

ERIKA: Like it was really mom.

WALTER: Erika. Your mother isn't allowed visitors anymore. This telephone is her only link to us.

ERIKA: Yeah, and our only link to her. So we get punished for her crimes.

WALTER: Heroism.

ERIKA: Whatever.

(Telephone rings. ERIKA *reaches for it.)*

WALTER: No. Let me take it.

*(*WALTER *answers the telephone.)*

I'm sorry. We have no fresh fish. . . . Schnauzer puppies? No, that was last week. And we didn't have any of those, either.

*(*WALTER *hangs up.)*

ERIKA: See? I say we just rip out the goddamned phone.

WALTER: Language!

ERIKA: Sorry. But it drives me nuts!

WALTER: Apology accepted. Me too. *(sighs)* You know, the worst thing is that it's just not personal.

ERIKA: Not personal? But isn't grandpa in charge of all the spies?

WALTER: Well, not on a day-to-day basis. This is too trivial for the great Wolf Niedermann. Some lieutenant with dreams of pro-

motion thought this one up, and now some little man somewhere has to place a want ad every week. He probably doesn't
know why. And if he does, he may not know that your mother
is in prison.

ERIKA: But grandpa knows she's in prison, doesn't he?

(Beat. The telephone rings.)

Doesn't he?

WALTER: Yes, I'm sure he does.

(WALTER answers the telephone.)

I'm sorry. We have no fresh fish.

ERIKA: Can't he just let her go?

WALTER: I'm afraid not, sweetheart. There are people above him
who would be very unhappy. Honecker would have his head on
a platter.

ERIKA: Honecker! I hate Honecker.

WALTER: *(fingers to his lips)* Shhh.

(The telephone rings.)

Now we're in for it. They heard you say that.

(WALTER winks at ERIKA, answers phone.)

WALTER: I'm sorry. We have no fresh fish. *(Beat.)* A case of condoms? What do you think we are, millionaires?

(WALTER hangs up.)

Well, the Stasi have outdone themselves this week. We're going
to get more calls than ever.

*(ERIKA makes a strangled, impatient noise and puts her head in
her hands.)*

WALTER: There goes the chess game, I suppose. But, after all,
you're growing up. Playing a game of chess with dad isn't as
exciting—or, face it, as challenging—as it was when you were
little.

ERIKA: It isn't fun because we're trying to play chess while the
Stasi are trying to drive us insane.

WALTER: They'll never succeed.

ERIKA: They'll never succeed because we're taking the chess set to the park. Where there are NO TELEPHONES!

(WALTER *opens his mouth to speak.*)

Hey. I don't want to miss mom's call, either. But just an hour or two. We can do it. We need to do it.

WALTER: But . . . well, why not? It's a lovely day.

(They gather up the chess set and throw on their coats. Telephone starts ringing.)

ERIKA: Come on, dad. Please.

(ERIKA *takes* WALTER'*s arm and pulls him offstage. Sound of door shutting firmly. Telephone keeps ringing. Quick fade to black.*)

(On the screen, we see WALTER *again, smoking and talking. This time, he is smiling and almost giddy.)*

WALTER: Yes, yes, you were right. It was easier than I ever dreamed possible. I actually ran into her one afternoon at a tram stop. Just like that. The same wooly cap and blonde hair. I was nervous; she looked anything but vulnerable at that moment.

Still, I—well, I suppose I did it just the way you suggested. I just . . . smiled. And she smiled back! (*giggles*) Really! She said, "Do I know you from somewhere?" and I said, "Yes, we were hauled into a van together a few months ago." She nodded and laughed, remembering—but then she became puzzled and rather suspicious. "What were you doing there?" she asked. "You're not part of the movement." Well, what could I do except tell the truth? "No, you're absolutely right. I'm not. I could never be brave." But then I—I lied a little. I didn't want to tell her I came to help but lost my nerve. "I was just in the wrong place at the wrong time." She nodded again, this time more sympathetically. "A lot of people were. I'm sorry." Then she turned to go. I could see this chance slipping away and I could hear you saying, "Walter. It's really not that difficult. Just ask her."

Well, I quickly said, "I don't suppose you'd like to go out for a cup of coffee or a meal sometime." I don't think she was expecting this. She turned and stared at me. "Do you know who the hell I am? I'm fucking Karin Niedermann. Mister, if you're not brave, you'd better stay six blocks away from me." But I told her that I didn't actually want to take an active part in her politics, I just . . . wanted to have a meal with her. Because she seemed dangerous and courageous and untamed . . . just the opposite of me. It wasn't much of a sales pitch. A bit self-deprecating, really. But she said yes! I couldn't believe my ears. I blushed and grinned . . . just like I'm doing now.

Next Tuesday. And she insisted on meeting at a wurst stand and walking down Unter den Linden. No standing still. No sitting anywhere where there might be microphones. And before she walked away, she said, "And if I should ever find out my father sent you, I will cut you open and feed your entrails to the crows."

(He frowns for a moment, then grins again.)

And I have a date with this woman! Thank you. I am so glad to have a friend who knows something about women.

(The screen goes dark.)

OCTOBER 1988

(Visitor's Day at KARIN'*s prison. Downstage right, a table with a mesh screen running down the middle of it and one chair on either side of the screen. Lights up on* WALTER *sitting in one chair.* KARIN *shuffles wearily in. She is about forty, with blonde hair. She wears prison overalls and no makeup; but she's attractive and gives the impression that she could be glamorous if allowed to be.)*

KARIN: Walter . . . ? (KARIN *sits down at the table on the other side of the screen from* WALTER.*)* It *is* you.

WALTER: Yes. At last.

KARIN: How did you . . .

WALTER: I complained. Politely, of course.

KARIN: It's been a long time. Couldn't you have been a little less polite?

WALTER: One must always be polite. That's one of the things I've learned during the past ten months.

KARIN: Ten months, two weeks, and three days.

WALTER: I've also learned a good deal about the virtues of patience. And how to stay alert and awake during long hours spent sitting in offices of various prison officials and party functionaries.

KARIN: There's a useful talent. It will come in handy if you ever end up where I am. But you won't, will you? Tell me you've profited from my mistakes. Tell me you're being careful.

WALTER: I don't have to be careful. I'm good. I don't betray the state in word or deed. Indeed, I have a newfound respect for our civil servants. I got a very close view of some of them when I was fighting to be allowed to visit again. They're eating well, though most spend too much time on their—

KARIN: Walter. You needn't have put the state through so much trouble. When you stopped showing up, I knew exactly what was going on. I followed the fox's stratagem. I said to myself, "Big fucking deal. That Walter—he wasn't so great. I don't really need him."

WALTER: Ah. Yes, I know how strong you are. Really, I did it for my sake. I wanted to try a simple experiment.

KARIN: And you needed me to perform it?

WALTER: Yes. I wanted to know whether or not two people who touched a screen, like so . . .

(They both move their hands so that their fingertips touch the screen)

. . . could generate sufficient warmth to bring the metal up to body temperature. The scientist in me is curious.

KARIN: This place drains the heat from me. I doubt if I'm warm enough to be of any help.

WALTER: You underestimate yourself. Your fingers are radiating more heat than the pipes in our flat. And extremities are frequently colder than the rest of the body, so we can infer that the rest of you is warm.

KARIN: Unfortunately, that can't be verified empirically.

WALTER: No. I must rely on logic and memory to produce a body of theory.

KARIN: I do worry that I won't have enough heat for you and Erika when I get out. I try to hoard it, husband it, in order to survive.

WALTER: Just concentrate on the present. Think only of our fingers.

(They both concentrate on the "experiment.")

You know, if the state could only harness this, they wouldn't have to build nuclear plants.

KARIN: Are we doing that well?

WALTER: Yes. I'm noting a number of . . . *(he fidgets in his seat a bit)* interesting phenomena.

KARIN: I'm afraid I can't quite keep my thoughts on the present. Walter, do you remember that warehouse in Prenzlauer Berg where we used to go before we were married? Nobody would ever believe me, but I didn't go there for the predictable reform-movement political discussions. I went there because they played music from scratchy, forbidden records. I was happiest of all when they would play something jazzy and slow. You and I would dance and I could feel your warm breath on the side of my neck. I was nervous. I was embarrassed. But you . . . you were calm and happy enough for both of us.

(Beat.)

(seductively) However, I want you to know that prison has reformed me, and made me a more productive citizen. I no longer dream of such decadence. The idea of seducing you to music played by foreigners fills me with shame.

(sighs) Let's change the subject. How is Erika?

WALTER: Tall.

KARIN: Yes, I imagine so.

WALTER: Impatient.

KARIN: She's a teenager.

WALTER: With a striking temperamental resemblance to her mother.

KARIN: Pure coincidence. She hasn't seen me in almost six years.

WALTER: Still. I think it's genetic. Plus, she has ten years of your influence to draw on.

KARIN: Yes. If I am lucky, she'll recognize me when I see her again.

WALTER: Of course she will.

KARIN: And if I am very lucky, she may still love me.

WALTER: Please. Don't be maudlin.

KARIN: Sorry. I try not to be.

(Beat.)

Well. Tell her to be strong.

WALTER: I will.

KARIN: Tell her ... tell her that she had better be good. Brush her teeth. Go to bed on time. Or she could end up like her mother.

WALTER: I'll be sure to give her proper moral guidance.

KARIN: And about your experiment?

(KARIN kisses her hand and presses it to the screen again.)

I think I just corrupted the data.

WALTER: Then I will have to return to collect more.

(Fade to black.)

(On the screen, we see WALTER again, smoking and talking.)

WALTER: Karin and I have been on vacation. We took the Trabi and drove to a small cottage a few kilometers from the Czech border. It's beautiful there ... deep in the wooded hills, yet close to the Elbe. I've never visited such a peaceful place in all my life.

The first couple of days we walked through the forest, swam naked in the river at midnight, and fell asleep in front of a crackling fire. We could feel all the cares of Berlin slipping away: the dirt, the soot, the Premier's awful spelling, the low-level Party functionaries who put slugs in the coin dish ... but more than anything, it was unbelievably exhilarating to know that no one was watching.

True. One never does know, really, but during our vacation Karin went away for ... a long bicycle ride. If someone had been watching, she never would have gotten away. Or never returned. But five days after she left, she came riding down the road on Anja's bicycle and my heart grew so light it nearly floated up out of my throat. That night, I proposed to her. I told her that I loved her . . . that the scent of her hair, the curve of her lower back meant more to me than all the volumes of philosophy I'd ever read—and you know how I feel about philosophy. I told her I wanted to love her and support her in whatever way I could for the rest of her life. She laughed and pointed out that, given the life expectancy for enemies of the state, that would be an easy commitment to honor.

It had taken me a month to work up the nerve to ask her out and two years to reach the point of proposing; I was disappointed by her answer. I must have shown it, because she took my face in her hands and kissed me, and told me she was moved by my commitment to social justice . . . and to her. After that, neither of us said anything for a while and we began to make love. When we were naked and I reached for the condom, Karin took it from my hands and threw it across the room. And for the rest of our stay, we never used one again.

(The screen goes dark.)

JANUARY 1990

(Lights up on the Bergers' apartment. KARIN *and* WALTER *enter from the hall.* KARIN *is wearing street clothes.* WALTER*'s arm is around her. He carries her small valise. He puts it down near the table.)*

WALTER: Here we are again.

KARIN: I'll be damned.

(She looks around.)

I outlasted the bastards. *(She laughs.)* They locked me up to save themselves and their empire collapsed before my sentence was up.

(WALTER *takes* KARIN *in his arms. They hold each other for a moment.)*

KARIN: But where is Erika? I thought she'd be here.

WALTER: I wanted a moment alone with you. I told her to come home immediately after school. But school is over now. She should be here any minute.

KARIN: Oh, God, I can hardly wait. Will I know her? Will she know me?

WALTER: Relax. Relax.

(Beat.)

I must unfortunately go to that job interview now, but I should be back in an hour. I'm sorry to—

KARIN: I'll be fine.

WALTER: Really?

(KARIN nods.)

WALTER: I'll see you tonight, then. Maybe we'll take the U-Bahn to West Berlin. See an Arnold Schwarzenegger film.

KARIN: Arnold Schwarzenegger?

WALTER: *(laughs)* Or Wim Wenders. Whatever you want.

(KARIN nods. WALTER kisses KARIN tenderly on the cheek, then exits. KARIN watches him go. Sound of door shutting. Music fades up as KARIN goes to the table. She runs her hands along the side of it, kneels under the table, carefully running her hands under the whole surface. In the same manner, she examines the chairs and the chess set, including the underside of the board and each individual piece. She examines the telephone and unscrews the caps of the receiver. She puts nothing back together. She then goes to the couch, lifts up cushions and begins to search the couch. She looks around all sides of it and then tips it on its back to look under it. When she is finished, she collapses on the floor. Music fades out. ERIKA appears in the apartment doorway with a small bouquet of flowers.)

ERIKA: Mom?

KARIN: Erika?

(ERIKA looks around at the mess.)

ERIKA: What the hell happened here, mom? Did somebody break in?

(KARIN raises her head.)

KARIN: No.

(ERIKA kneels next to KARIN.)

ERIKA: Are you all right?

KARIN: Yes. (KARIN *looks up at* ERIKA.) I always do this. Or at least I used to.

ERIKA: You mean before . . .

KARIN: Yes.

ERIKA: When I was little.

KARIN: Yes.

ERIKA: Wow. Are you sure? I don't remember it ever looking like this.

KARIN: I made sure you didn't. But I was younger then. And faster.

ERIKA: Did you ever find anything?

KARIN: Once or twice. When I did, I would do this. (KARIN *rolls over, puts her face to the couch, and bellows.*) RRRAAAAGGGHH!

(KARIN *rises.*)

Right into the microphone. It was always very cathartic. Then, of course, I would rip them out.

ERIKA: Cool.

KARIN: Well, in some ways it was a satisfying little ritual. But I never really knew if anybody was listening. Still, I had to assume the worst—which, let me tell you, made me very paranoid about what we said in here virtually twenty-four hours a day.

ERIKA: In our own home? That's cold.

KARIN: I'll say. So I can only hope that once in a while I made somebody's ears ring for a few minutes.

ERIKA: I wish I could find the guys that did all that shit. You know I'd kick some serious butt.

KARIN: Ha! Your father was right. You do have my temperament. But they were in the business of being invisible.

(KARIN *notices flowers.*)

Are those flowers for me?

ERIKA: Duh. Welcome home, mom.

(ERIKA *hands* KARIN *the flowers.*)

KARIN: Thank you. They're beautiful.

(KARIN *looks carefully and wonderingly at* ERIKA, *like a naturalist finding a new and beautiful species.*)

And you are, too.

(KARIN *takes a pink lock of* ERIKA*'s hair in her hand.*)

Your father never told me about this.

ERIKA: Oh, man. Don't tell me you're gonna make me get rid of it.

KARIN: No, no. It's—fun. Harmless. You know, you're not so different from what I imagined you might look like. You're older than I want you to be but younger than I feared you'd be.

(KARIN *gives* ERIKA *a long hug.*)

ERIKA: Well, you don't look or sound much different. I was afraid they might have beat you to a pulp in there. But you don't look crippled.

KARIN: No, no. I was very careful and kept my mouth shut.

ERIKA: Wow. You can do that?

KARIN: Smartass.

(KARIN *winks and squeezes* ERIKA*'s hand.*)

KARIN: *(contd)* Did you miss me?

ERIKA: Yeah. I mean, we got by. But . . . yeah. A whole lot, mom.

KARIN: Good. I missed you, too.

(KARIN *pats* ERIKA*'s hand.*)

I'll never forgive those bastards.

(KARIN *takes a deep breath, then looks around at the mess she's created.*)

This place really looks like hell, honey.

ERIKA: It kind of freaked me out at first. But don't sweat it. You find a vase for the flowers and I'll straighten up.

KARIN: I can't let you do that.

ERIKA: Hey. I do lots of stuff around here. I'm a big kid. Some people even call me an adult.

KARIN: Then we'll do it together. That's what your father and I would have done.

ERIKA: Oh, man. All right, but I'll do the heavy work. You're too old and slow.

KARIN: And the flowers?

ERIKA: They'll be okay for five minutes. Come on. Let's get moving.

(KARIN *laughs and nods.* ERIKA *starts to right the couch and* KARIN *starts to put the phone together.)*

KARIN: Erika . . . who is Arnold Schwarzenegger?

(Lights fade slowly to black.)

(On the screen, we see WALTER *again, smoking and talking.)*

WALTER: Karin and I were married last Saturday. It was a small wedding. Just a few close friends . . . Professor Hornung, Professor Rothmann; Dr. Langer; that woman from the Transportation Ministry, Petra something-or-other; and, of course, Father Poppe—he had nothing to lose by performing the ceremony.

(WALTER *gives a short laugh.)*

No, her father did not come. She didn't invite him and he couldn't have attended anyway. I'm sure he knows every detail of the ceremony. No doubt one or two of the guests present were on his payroll, or he had the hall bugged. There are probably some grainy wedding photos taken with a surveillance camera in her file now, and he may even have his own personal copies. Perhaps he has one framed on his parlor wall. I like to think that General and Frau Niedermann are sitting at home, thinking, well, he's a nice young man who proofreads the Party newspaper—maybe he'll be a settling influence.

It was a lousy day for a wedding—cold, gray, and blustery. Father Poppe was late and he had the key to the hall, so the small group of us huddled with our backs to the wind, trying to muster up some lightheartedness and gaiety. I don't recommend a March wedding to anyone, but what could we do? We were in love. We would have married eventually. And Peter—or Erika if it's a girl, but it's sure to be a boy—is on the way. One has to do the honorable thing.

(The screen goes dark.)

MAY 1990

(Lights up. KARIN *and her friend* ANJA HORNUNG *are sitting downstage right at a café table together.* ANJA *ought to be a bit older than* KARIN; *though an intellectual, she dresses somewhat flamboyantly: dark glasses, perhaps a wide-brimmed hat, heels, bright red lipstick, and a very colorful dress.)*

KARIN: Franz Handlbauer.

ANJA: Karin.

KARIN: You don't think so?

ANJA: I don't care.

KARIN: I'm deeply disappointed, Anja. I thought you loved gossip.

ANJA: Since this is neither current nor salacious, it hardly qualifies.

KARIN: I find it invigorating.

(Beat.)

Anita Eichinger.

ANJA: Karin. I love you, but you're beginning to bore me.

KARIN: Anita Eichinger.

ANJA: Anita was arrested a year after you.

KARIN: Really? I never heard about that.

ANJA: Didn't that husband of yours bring you any news?

KARIN: We didn't usually talk about politics.

(Beat.)

Prison or exile?

ANJA: Anita? Exile.

KARIN: The lucky bitch.

ANJA: I'll say. They took my datscha and then my job.

KARIN: And my freedom. And while we were sitting around on our asses—

ANJA: —yes, the Wessis were giving Anita a flat and a juicy pension. Which is probably why dear Walter never mentioned it to you.

(Beat.)

KARIN: Rudi Weissenbacher.

ANJA: Can we talk about something else?

KARIN: Of course.

ANJA: Good.

KARIN: I'm not obsessed.

ANJA: If you say so.

KARIN: Why should I be? I've only lost seven years of my life.

ANJA: *(shrugs)* Yes, but it must have been a hell of a homecoming.

KARIN: Actually, it was a little odd at first.

ANJA: *Naturlich.* So much light, so much space, so much flesh . . .

KARIN: And so much of the mental scum of prison clinging to me. But after a few days, when Erika was at the movies with some of her friends . . .

ANJA: Aha! You and Walter had a proper celebration.

KARIN: Well. Not "proper." More like . . . uninhibited.

ANJA: You? Uninhibited?

KARIN: *(laughs)* Yes. It was like the old days at your datscha. No cameras, no microphones . . . I tell you, privacy is a real aphrodisiac. Although certain muscles are a little out of shape after all this time—

ANJA: Then you'll simply have to get more exercise.

(They both laugh.)

KARIN: Of course, there are the nights when even sex can't take my mind off things.

ANJA: Prison?

KARIN: Worse. Nights when I relive the days before prison, looking for clues. When Walter slides his hand across my behind and I think of, say, Martin Binder. Do you remember Martin?

ANJA: Who could forget the son of a bitch? He put his hand on the ass of every woman in the movement.

KARIN: You're not kidding.

ANJA: *(nods)* Anja, was Martin an informer?

ANJA: He was a sexist asshole. Please: Tell me you never trusted him with anything important.

KARIN: I didn't. But still . . .

ANJA: You're becoming tiresome again, Karin. I really don't know.

KARIN: Nobody knows—except the Stasi. But what do you think?

ANJA: Who cares? Why not ask your father, the all-knowing Wolf Niedermann?

KARIN: He'll never tell. And you can bet there's no paper trail leading to him. That's long since been burnt. On the other hand, the files we do have might make it possible to find all the little people—my so-called friends—who, in exchange for money or favors, gave my father the evidence he needed to lock me up.

ANJA: No doubt. So the Wessis will get their hands on them, declare them off limits, and use their contents to fuck every Ossi in the ass.

KARIN: Not necessarily.

ANJA: It will be Prague all over again. Anyone whose name is reportedly in the files will become persona non grata.

KARIN: Some of us have a plan. We want to give everyone the right to read their own file, and nobody else's.

ANJA: And how will you do that?

KARIN: For starters, I'm going to run for the Bundestag.

ANJA: Ah well, it was only a matter of time. You've always been involved in politics. Might as well get paid for it.

KARIN: And we'll fight to have the files turned over to an independent commission. Run by an Ossi.

ANJA: That will be one hell of a fight.

KARIN: I'm not a coward.

ANJA: For better or worse. Well, keep your back to the wall.

KARIN: I've been doing it for years. I'm not about to stop.

(Blackout.)

(On the screen, we see WALTER *again, smoking and talking.)*

WALTER: Last week was Erika's first day of school . . . and, interestingly enough, Karin's last day of work. I'm a little surprised.

I thought the state liked the idea of Karin Berger as a washroom attendant. Yes, they've caught her inserting messages in the towels, and—as they see it—they've no choice but to fire her. But have they really thought this through? Now that Karin has the whole day free, she'll have even more time to devote to her reform movement. Erika? Of course she'll devote time to Erika. But she won't neglect the country. Karin will demonstrate her love for Erika—and me by working for a better future, and by taking the risk involved in that work herself. You never believe me when I tell you this, but she even spares me most of the details about people and places, and Erika is told only the rudiments of what causes Mama to be away from home so often. In fact, I had to convince Karin to let me warn Erika that the Stasi may try to influence her through her teachers. I'd like to avoid a Bandhauer tragedy, thank you. A seven-year-old child can be very vulnerable, and if the teacher fills his head with tales about his parents, things like that will happen.

No, no one never said so, but who else would do such a thing? Frankly, I'm disgusted. Children?

(The screen goes dark.)

MARCH 1991

(Lights up on KARIN*'s office downstage left: a desk and a chair opposite it.* KARIN *sits at the desk. A knock on the door and* WOLF NIEDERMANN *enters, a stocky 70-year-old gentleman with silver hair and a relaxed, good-humored manner.)*

WOLF: Good morning, Mrs. Berger.

KARIN: Good morning . . . Mr. Niedermann.

(Beat.)

It's been a very long time.

WOLF: Too long.

KARIN: If you say.

WOLF: Mrs. Berger, I want you to think of me as just another constituent. An unremarkable retired gentleman.

KARIN: You're a little different from most, I'd say.

WOLF: But I have the same concerns, the same problems as other elderly Berliners. *(making a show of sharing a confidence)* The government has drastically reduced my pension.

KARIN: The organization that originally funded your pension has gone belly up.

WOLF: Ah! Too true, too true. I suppose I shall have to rely on my savings.

(Beat.)

I don't suppose, as my representative to the Bundestag, you could—

KARIN: Out of the question. Now if that's all you've come for—

WOLF: No, no. Of course that isn't why I've come. Even you cannot deny that I am a pragmatist.

KARIN: Then why—

WOLF: *(shrugs)* Call it a joke. Call it a testing of boundaries. Call it what you like.

(WOLF *indicates one of the chairs.)*

May I sit?

KARIN: *(glancing at her watch)* I told the receptionist to let you in. But I do have a meeting.

WOLF: I won't take much of your time. I promise.

(WOLF sits.)

Nice quarters. Much more elegant than the old GDR.

KARIN: You got to work in your home town.

WOLF: Ah, well, one day Berlin will be the capital of Germany again, and you can see your family all the time. Family is important.

KARIN: But not as important as one's job.

WOLF: No. Apparently we both think so.

(Beat.)

I suppose that I've come to congratulate you.

KARIN: Really? I didn't see your name on the list of campaign contributors.

WOLF: I didn't want to hurt your chances. I gave anonymously.

KARIN: Bullshit.

WOLF: *(shrugs)* How do you know? It wouldn't be the strangest thing I've ever done.

KARIN: Why would you want me to sit in the Bundestag?

WOLF: Well . . . it would make me very proud. You may not believe this, but I have always admired you.

KARIN: Oh, please.

WOLF: It's true. And if I have to be swept into the dustbin of history, I'd like you to be the person holding the broom.

KARIN: Because I might go easy on you?

WOLF: Karin. Don't condescend. I know you. I know what to expect from you.

KARIN: So on the basis of this small comfort, you come to my office to give me your hearty congratulations.

(Beat.)

It stinks. Get out.

WOLF: I'm sorry. You know, I had hoped that all this . . . my fall, the unification, your election . . . might have given you a sense of triumph. I hoped we might begin a working through and eventually reach a reconciliation.

KARIN: And that's why you came here.

WOLF: It is the only thing I want from you.

KARIN: I'm not ready yet.

WOLF: But you hold all the cards. If not now, when?

KARIN: After I read my file.

WOLF: Ah yes. The files. Now that the rabble have got ahold of them, I expect you'll be making them public property. Like books in a library.

KARIN: More or less. That way the whole country can begin to grapple with the past. And ultimately—I hope—to heal.

WOLF: Ah, well, you were always an optimist. I'm glad to see that you haven't changed.

(Beat.)

KARIN: I do have a meeting.

WOLF: Yes, yes. Well, I'm glad you're a public servant. As long as I'm polite, you can't refuse to see me.

KARIN: I can always have you thrown out for loitering.

WOLF: That will be difficult. I know how to be courteous.

KARIN: Yes, and I've always hated you for that.

WOLF: I know. Thank you for your time.

(WOLF *stands and bows. He turns to go, then turns back.*)

Ah! How could I forget? Your mother sends her love.

KARIN: Does she? Well, send her mine. Tell her to come visit me sometime.

WOLF: I will, I will.

KARIN: And remember: You're not going to get any special favors from me.

WOLF: Did you ever get any from me?

KARIN: No.

WOLF: Did you ever want any?

(*Beat.*)

KARIN: No.

WOLF: (*tips his hat*) Wiedersehen.

(WOLF *exits. Blackout.*)

(*On the screen, we see* WALTER *again. He doesn't look so good; scragglier, scratchier, maybe a touch of gray.*)

WALTER: Please . . . please excuse me. I just haven't been out of the house much. Erika's upset. I'm upset. I thought . . . well, I thought exile for sure. But prison? For ten years?

(WALTER *can't go on. He chokes up, then covers his face. We hear a tear or two. Jump cut. He is shakily lighting a cigarette, somewhat more composed.*)

If it were exile, the Wessis would have picked up the tab, given her a decent living allotment, maybe even given the GDR a pile of deutschmarks so Erika and I could go west, too. . . . I don't want to go live in the west. But I want my wife . . . Erika wants her mother . . . don't they have any pity at all? The girl will be twenty-two before her mother is freed.

Me? I'm a good citizen, a decent man. I don't understand how a state can be so cruel to me, of all people . . . and yet, at the same time, so kind. Schnittke—my supervisor—actually gave me time off to go to the trial. After the sentencing, of course, he wrote a stinging editorial condemning Karin and praising the state's swift justice. Or so I thought. He called me into his office the next day and explained to me that he himself had not actually written it. The Stasi had supplied the story and suggested it be published under his byline.

A lovely woman, he said, not looking directly at me. She must be charming, in her own way. Of course you love her, even if she is—and here he paused—because the word was distasteful? because he felt sorry for me?—a traitor. It's unfortunate, he continued. Her father is well-positioned. She might have been a party favorite. He walked over to me and put his hand on my shoulder. This all must be very upsetting to you and your daughter. You need some time alone together. And so he gave me the rest of the week off.

And this is the man who runs the Party's newspaper . . . no fanatic, but a human being. I wish we had more like him. Then I don't think Karin . . . would be . . .

(WALTER *covers his face again.*) I'm sorry.

(*The screen goes dark.*)

JANUARY 31, 1992

(*Night.* WALTER *and* KARIN *are lying in bed, downstage right, moonlight playing over them.*)

WALTER: What are you thinking about?

(KARIN *strokes* WALTER*'s chest.*)

KARIN: Your skin.

WALTER: Really?

KARIN: I can't tell you how much I miss it when I'm in Bonn. How reassuring and electrifying I find it when I'm here. And most exhilarating of all is the fact that when I go to Bonn . . . when I am forced to forgo the pleasure of your company and your skin . . . it's my choice. I can dream about you all I want because I control what happens when I wake.

WALTER: No one ever completely controls their own life. For instance . . . I might like it if you spent more time here, but it's not entirely my choice.

(KARIN *is a bit taken aback by this statement.*)

KARIN: Walter, you have more power than you think. Talk to me about it.

WALTER: Erika is nineteen. She'll want to get a place of her own soon. She might even want to go to a university outside of Berlin. Outside of Germany. And your biggest battles have been won. Communism is dead. Germany is united. The files will open tomorrow.

KARIN: There's work to be done yet.

WALTER: There's always work to be done. You don't have to do all of it.

KARIN: I . . . suppose I don't.

(*Beat.*)

Why haven't you mentioned this before?

WALTER: I would never ask you to forgo your crusades and quests for me. But the files. They were your last personal campaign. But now what? Did you ever think about that?

KARIN: Mm-mm. I'm still focused on my file.

WALTER: I thought you were focused on my skin.

KARIN: I was! When you asked me.

(KARIN *kisses* WALTER *and rolls onto her stomach.*)

Rub my back.

(WALTER *begins to gently massage* KARIN*'s bare back.*)

Now: How can we spend more time together? I suppose I could retire undefeated. Find a new job in Berlin that requires my particular skills. After all, you did.

(*Beat.*)

Of course, you could also move to Bonn.

WALTER: Become a Wessi?

KARIN: No, just live in the west when the Bundestag is in session.

WALTER: But the west . . . it's nice to visit, but to live in? It's so garish. Commercialized. Frantic.

KARIN: Bonn is a charming little town. Ask Erika. She liked it.

(WALTER *says nothing.*)

Well, it's only a suggestion. I do want us to be together more often. And I think we can successfully negotiate which one of us will make the sacrifice.

WALTER: I don't want any "sacrifices." I'm sick of that word.

KARIN: I don't mind it. I've made sacrifices for my country. You've made them for me.

WALTER: No, I haven't. I've made deliberate choices because I love you.

KARIN: Mmmm . . .

WALTER: I love our child.

KARIN: Mmmm . . .

WALTER: And I admire your politics.

KARIN: Please. Don't say that.

WALTER: Why?

KARIN: My father claims to "admire my politics." I hate that phrase.

WALTER: All right then. I have always believed in the justice of your reform movement. In your quest for personal freedom.

(KARIN *rolls over, rises to her knees, and puts her arms around* WALTER.)

KARIN: And I have always appreciated that. You've done more than I asked. You've volunteered before I asked. I couldn't have survived without your support.

WALTER: You flatter me.

KARIN: No. What I said is true. Even now, I still might not be able to survive without it.

(KARIN *and* WALTER *kiss. They kiss again. They fall back onto the bed locked in an embrace and continue kissing. Blackout.*)

(On screen we see WALTER, *smoking and talking. He looks haggard but is more composed.)*

WALTER: Yes. I'm much better, thank you. I'm sorry, but—no, I'm not sorry. A man has only one love.

Thank you. You're a true friend.

I thought about your advice. I would like to take control of my own destiny. I only wish there were a way I could help free her. But I have no secrets big enough to get Karin freed. And it may be dangerous to say this, but I don't trust the people who have thrown my wife in jail. No, I will simply have to be strong.

No, my spirits have not been raised simply by the passage of time. Professor Hornung came to see me today—just to comfort me. And as she was leaving, she squeezed my hand, saying, you must be steadfast and courageous now, for both Karin and Erika. But, she said, you need support as well. Small domestic tasks sometimes bring great comfort. She kissed my right cheek and whispered, start by cleaning the sugar canister. She kissed my left cheek and whispered, one should always be certain there are no foreign objects in the sugar.

I dumped the sugar into a bowl. At the bottom of the canister was a letter from Karin.

*(*WALTER *pulls a note out of his pocket, unfolds it, puts on glasses. As he does so, downstage left of the screen,* KARIN *walks onstage with a banker's box. She sets it down at the desk, pulls out a fat manila folder. During the next section, she examines individual sheets, scanning each one carefully before going on to the next.)*

"Dear Walter,

If you are reading this, the tragedy we never dared to imagine has struck. If I am alive, the twin suns have been blotted from my sky, for it may be many years before I see you and Erika again. If I am dead, we will never be reunited. Let us hope that the end came quickly and mercifully.

"You and Erika will talk about me—and when you do talk about me, please remember: I did everything for love. I wish I could have done as you did, you who speak of love with your words, your eyes, your tongue, the tips of your fingers. I wish I could have let you see my desire, loneliness, and vulnerability. But I lack your emotional eloquence; I have declared my love in the only way I know how and now we will all pay the price.

"Separation or even death cannot destroy the gifts you have given me. Your unconditional love has brought me peace, emotional security, an outlet for my passion, and the great relief of knowing there is one person I can absolutely trust. Please know that my heart is filled with the same kind of unconditional love for you.

(KARIN *stops at a page, concentrates.*)

"I may never be able to voice this in person, so please: Keep this letter close to you for spiritual nourishment, as a reminder of the gifts I would like to bestow on you. It is my secret declaration of love that no one else has ever read and no one else will ever read. In this time and place, such an intimate commodity is as precious as diamonds.

(*From the file folder,* KARIN *lifts up the same note that* WALTER *has been reading.*)

WALTER AND KARIN: "All my love, Karin."

(*Onscreen,* WALTER *looks at the letter, then reluctantly looks up and holds the letter straight out, as if he is about to hand it to someone. On stage,* KARIN *stares at the letter. Quick fade to black onstage, blackout onscreen.*)

END OF ACT I

ACT II

(*On the screen, we see* WOLF *in a medium closeup. He is impeccably dressed, and sits in a comfortable modern chair with a background that suggests the set of a television talk show. He does not speak straight into the camera, but to an unseen person just out of camera range.*)

WOLF: That's an interesting question, Peter . . . yes, I was proud of the work I did. It was my job to protect the people of the

German Democratic Republic from those who would destroy the country. This I did well. I don't doubt that there were some excesses; just as I felt pressured by the minister for state security, so my subordinates must have felt pressured by me. Most of them responded by conforming to both the letter and the spirit of the law . . . no, that does not mean that I condone torture . . . such a course was legal, but we managed to avoid it almost all the time, and I personally encouraged agents to use other, more benign methods to gather information. It is, I think, within this context, that we have to examine the issue of paid informants. Were they not helping their country? Were they not saving their fellow citizens from physical danger? They were patriots.

Peter, let me illustrate this point. One morning in the late 1970s, I went to Frau Winderl for my daily massage. The poor woman looked exhausted and her eyes were swollen from crying. "I'm sorry, General Niedermann," she told me, "but I don't think I can take care of you this morning." I asked, "What is the matter?" and she replied, "It is my boy Thomas. Oh, General, I am so ashamed and so frightened." Well, it seems that her son had been staying out later and later . . . not telling her what he was doing or who he was seeing. She was certain it was not a love affair. She was afraid—in her words, mind you—that he was "running with a dangerous element" and that he was headed for trouble. I said that I was certain her fears were unfounded, but I would have a man make a few discreet inquiries. Frau Winderl broke into tears, thanked me, and kissed my hand . . . it was a bit embarrassing, actually. But such scenes occurred many times, and the average citizen was grateful for the safety and stability that we provided.

(*The screen goes dark.*)

FEBRUARY 2, 1992

(*The Bergers' apartment.* WALTER *and* ERIKA *are playing chess at the table. Door slams.* WALTER *turns.* KARIN *enters, carrying a fat manila envelope. Her expression is impassive, though her eyes are red and puffy.*)

ERIKA: Hi, mom.

(Beat.)

Jeez. You don't look so good.

KARIN: It's been a hell of a day.

(WALTER rises, goes to kiss her. She slides away from him, throws the envelope on the table.)

Don't.

WALTER: Why not?

KARIN: Walter. I am going to give you an opportunity here. Is there nothing . . . nothing you'd like to tell me?

(Beat.)

WALTER: Only that I love you.

KARIN: Oh, God, Walter. Nothing . . . more?

WALTER: Well, let's see. Chopped beef was on special, so we're making a spicy goulash.

KARIN: Don't do me any favors.

WALTER: But I love to cook. And I love you.

KARIN: Walter, if you don't stop saying that, I'm going to vomit.

ERIKA: Mom?

KARIN: You think you can spout this meaningless drivel over and over again. You think I don't know that it's just fucking words.

ERIKA: What's got into you?

WALTER: Your mother's tired.

KARIN: You might say that. *(to Erika)* I've been looking at my file all day.

(ERIKA lets out a low whistle.)

ERIKA: Wow. That sounds depressing.

KARIN: It was. Especially the part about . . . Jason. Walter: Tell us about Jason.

(KARIN looks steadily at WALTER. He gives her a small half-smile, then looks away.)

WALTER: I've no idea what you're talking about.

KARIN: Don't give me that bullshit!

WALTER: Erika. I think you'd better go to your room.

ERIKA: Hey. I'm not a child.

WALTER: Your mother and I are about to have a serious argument.

KARIN: *(to Walter)* Over what? You don't know what I'm talking about.

WALTER: *(to Karin)* No, I don't. But you're upset—and I would like some privacy.

KARIN: *Fuck you and your privacy! (to Erika)* Don't you move. I want you to hear every goddamn word.

(KARIN *circles around* WALTER.)

You're a lucky, lucky man, Walter. Despite my infamous reputation, my scandalous activities, you managed to remain an employee of the Communist Party newspaper. How did you manage that?

WALTER: I don't really know. My supervisor, Schnittke . . . he was a decent man.

KARIN: And perhaps he was. But he . . . and his superiors . . . might have had a good reason to keep you on the payroll.

WALTER: I doubt it. But I'll ask Schnittke.

ERIKA: Mom. The Party guys were all assholes, but dad had to feed us.

KARIN: Erika. Only people who cooperated were allowed to work for "those assholes."

ERIKA: What about Anja?

KARIN: Anja lost her job and her cottage. Walter kept the flat, the Trabi, and everything else.

ERIKA: So what are you trying to say?

KARIN: I think you know.

ERIKA: No, I don't.

KARIN: Then I'll spell it out. I read over 200 pages of my file today. I read about my political activities—most of which were more or less public—and about my private, even intimate affairs. And I kept running across reports by an unofficial collaborator who betrayed me time and time again. His code name was Jason.

ERIKA: And you think—

KARIN: I *know* that your father was Jason.

ERIKA: That's a lie.

KARIN: I wish it were.

ERIKA: That's a fucking lie!

KARIN: I know it's not. Your father is a vicious, two-faced, schizophrenic peeping Tom—

ERIKA: He is not!

KARIN: —who sucked the dicks of his Stasi bosses—

ERIKA: *(covering her ears)* Stop it!

KARIN: —through our entire marriage, and he took away seven years of my life, the heartless, gutless bastard!

WALTER: I did no such thing!

(KARIN *slaps* WALTER.)

KARIN: *Liar!*

ERIKA: Mom!

KARIN: Anyone who disagrees with me can look in the envelope on the table. Twenty years of information from grocery lists to pillow talk.

(ERIKA *rushes over to the table, opens the envelope, rifles through the documents. She pulls out a sheet and reads.*)

ERIKA: "Unofficial agent 'Jason' reports that he and Fräulein Niedermann vacationed in Bad Schandau at a cottage belonging to Professor Anja Hornung, well-known antigovernment agitator. He further reports that he proposed marriage to Fräulein Niedermann. This is a very promising development for the Ministry."

(Beat. ERIKA *is stunned.)*

You did it.

WALTER: Not really.

KARIN: What the hell do you mean by that?

WALTER: The Stasi came to me. I met with them. But I merely chatted.

ERIKA: Why?

WALTER: What was the alternative? They might have thrown us in jail.

KARIN: They did throw me in jail.

ERIKA: I—I don't get it. When mom went to prison, you cried your eyes out for months.

KARIN: And yet he kept on spilling his guts to them every week, even after I was in prison.

ERIKA: You did? Why? Why didn't you stop?

WALTER: You can't imagine the pressure.

KARIN: I think I can.

ERIKA: So you kept talking because . . . you had no choice?

KARIN: Everyone has a choice, honey. They could hold a fucking gun to my head and I would not give them one word.

WALTER: *(to Karin)* Yes, but I am not Karin Berger. I never claimed to be. *(to Erika)* And I couldn't stop whether I wanted to or not. They would have exposed me. I would have lost you and Karin. So I decided to help the movement from the inside . . . I thought that if I talked persuasively enough to my operative about Karin . . . about the philosophy of the movement . . . that I could bring him around to our side.

KARIN: So. You were really a double agent.

WALTER: In a manner of speaking, yes.

ERIKA: Really?

(WALTER nods.)

Well, I guess that makes sense, but—

KARIN: Oh, yes. It's a very logical story.

(KARIN swings again for another hard slap. ERIKA grabs her wrist. KARIN lunges for WALTER's face with her other hand. ERIKA wasn't expecting this and can't hang on. KARIN knocks WALTER to the floor. ERIKA screams. The rest of the dialogue comes quickly and characters overlap each other.)

KARIN: You bastard! You son of a bitch!

ERIKA: Mom—dad—stop it!

(KARIN is clawing WALTER's face, and he is trying to pull her hands away.)

WALTER: Karin—for God's sake, think of Erika—

(But KARIN *is raving uncontrollably.)*

KARIN: I didn't see sunlight for nine months—I didn't see another human being for six months—

WALTER: Calm down—

KARIN: They rewarded any prisoner who would beat the shit out of me—

ERIKA: Don't hurt him, mom!

KARIN: They broke my hand and two ribs—

ERIKA: Please!

KARIN: And you tell me to calm down!

*(*ERIKA *tries to pull* KARIN *away.)*

Well, it's your fucking turn now! *(to Walter)* I swear I'll kill you—

ERIKA: You will not!

KARIN: —with my bare hands, you—

ERIKA: You will not.

*(*KARIN *twists around to look at* ERIKA. *She is crying, but firm.)*

He's my father. And you will *not* kill him.

KARIN: For God's sake, Erika. Don't you want to kill him, too?

ERIKA: I don't want to kill anybody.

(Beat. She turns to WALTER.*)*

Honecker. Mielke. Grampa. But you? . . . I really looked up to you. I used to tease you about not marching, but I thought you were just as brave as mom. How could you?

WALTER: They . . . they made promises.

KARIN: Oh, Jesus, Walter. If you believed them, they were playing you for a sucker.

*(*WALTER *rises to his feet.)*

WALTER: That's not true! I was in control. I was helping.

*(*KARIN *leaps up.)*

KARIN: How? By telling those thugs exactly where and when you and I stopped using condoms?

WALTER: Karin, Erika—

KARIN: *(louder)* That I liked to have sex on parquet floors?

WALTER: —Erika is listening—

KARIN: *(louder)* That my favorite position was—

ERIKA: Stop talking about sex!

KARIN: Are you embarrassed? Humiliated? Well, so am I.

(KARIN *turns to* WALTER.)

All right. I'll talk about something else. Walter! What about my gift to you? The letter more precious than diamonds, that no one else would ever read? Where is it?

WALTER: I . . . the Stasi . . . they break in, they steal things . . .

KARIN: But not our letter.

(Beat.)

You gave it to them.

WALTER: They made—promises . . . it was harmless . . .

KARIN: Harmless? Walter, you haven't just betrayed me, you've stripped me naked and fucked me in front of the entire Ministry of State Security—including my father. And for what?

WALTER: For you. For Erika.

KARIN: Look at Erika.

(ERIKA *is sitting on the floor with her chin resting on her knees, staring at them. Tears and mascara are running down both cheeks.)*

ERIKA: Don't. Don't anybody look at me. Don't anybody talk to me.

WALTER: Erika. I love you.

ERIKA: I don't know what you mean by that.

WALTER: It means that we are a family and we can work through this.

KARIN: No, we can't. Because, Walter, you are a spineless coward. I despise you, Walter. I loathe you.

(KARIN *spits in* WALTER's *face.* ERIKA *shuts her eyes, buries her head.)*

If I were you, I'd leave right now, because I'm going to start throwing everything of yours that I find in this apartment out of the living room window. You want it, you pick it up off the sidewalk and stuff it in that goddamned Trabi.

(Beat. Reluctantly, WALTER *starts to walk offstage. In one last effort, he turns back to* KARIN.*)*

WALTER: Karin—

KARIN: Get out, Walter.

*(*WALTER *exits. Sound of a door shutting.* KARIN *walks to* ERIKA, *bends down to put her arm around* ERIKA.*)*

ERIKA: Don't.

KARIN: I'm sorry.

ERIKA: I coulda lived my whole life without this.

KARIN: Yeah. Me too.

(Beat.)

ERIKA: I've never seen you freak out like that.

KARIN: I fought long and hard for the freedom to do it.

ERIKA: Yeah. Well, I learned a lot tonight.

*(*ERIKA *wipes her cheeks and pushes* KARIN *away.)*

I gotta lie down.

*(*ERIKA *stands up, picks up her jacket. She heads for bedroom, changes her mind.)*

I gotta throw up.

*(*ERIKA *exits toward front door. Sound of a door slamming.* KARIN *watches her go, then turns to the chess game. She strikes it with all her might, knocking the board to the floor and scattering pieces everywhere. Blackout.)*

(On the screen we see KARIN *in front of a group of microphones. Flashbulbs are repeatedly going off and we hear the sound of clicking camera shutters under her speech. She has a prepared statement but does not always read from it.)*

KARIN: I spent the entire day at the Gauck Commission yesterday. It was an extraordinary experience. Biermann was at the table next to me, beginning an examination of the tens of thousands of pages comprising his file. His original file may have been even larger—after all, he was a highly visible singer and poet—but alas, some material has been lost forever.

I am, however, not here to discuss Biermann's file, but my own. It is a more modest file, perhaps two or three thousand pages. I have only looked at the first two hundred pages, but already I have an important announcement to make.

(ERIKA *walks onstage. Back to the audience, she watches* KARIN.)

On the basis of what I have read, I have come to the inescapable conclusion that Walter Berger—my husband, my lover, the father of my child—was also my personal—very personal—Stasi spy, code-named "Jason." I have copies of some pertinent material here for anyone who wishes to consult them.

I realize that this public exposure may damage his life and cause him financial hardship, but I feel it is important that a man of such moral cowardice and so little regard for those closest to him be cast out of German society.

(*A hubbub of voices in the background.* ERIKA *strides angrily off-stage.*)

One at a time—please!

(*The screen goes dark.*)

FEBRUARY 4, 1992

(*Three a.m. in the Bergers' apartment.* KARIN *is sitting on the couch in the dark, illuminated only by light from outside the window. Door opens and shuts.* ERIKA *enters slowly, wearily. She stops behind* KARIN.)

KARIN: It's late.

ERIKA: Yeah. It is. What're you doing up?

KARIN: I was worried. You're supposed to call if you're going to work late. . . . What's that smell?

ERIKA: Nothin'. I threw up all over myself in the women's room at the Chicago Bar.

KARIN: Erika! Are you all right? You didn't ride your motorbike home, did you?

ERIKA: Maybe. And no.

(ERIKA *sits at table. She picks up a chess piece.*)

How 'bout a game? I'll give you a handicap.

KARIN: Chess is your game, not mine.

ERIKA: Yeah, but c'mon. It's dark. I'm still kinda woozy.

(ERIKA *peers at the chess pieces.*)

And we're missing a black bishop.

(KARIN *shakes her head.*)

Hey. I'll play black.

KARIN: I'm too tired.

ERIKA: Funny. It used to be nothing could wear you down. Sticks, stones, tear gas. Man, they'd let you have it with both barrels and there you'd be: Karin Berger, stronger and prouder than ever. Of course, this time you're the one dishing it out. Maybe that's more tiring.

KARIN: What are you talking about?

ERIKA: I saw you on TV today. Awesome performance. I especially liked the way you reinvented yourself as Karin Berger, the Christ of the Ossis. Made it clear to the voters that all their pain was personified in your suffering.

KARIN: I did not hold that press conference for political gain!

ERIKA: Course not. You held it for revenge.

(KARIN *starts up out of her chair toward* ERIKA.)

(*calmly*) Go ahead. Hit me too.

(KARIN *stops, turns away.*)

KARIN: Why are you being such a little shit? What is it that you expect of me? My whole life has just imploded!

ERIKA: Yeah. Mine too.

KARIN: Well, aren't you angry?

ERIKA: Yes, I am. At you.

(KARIN *turns back to* ERIKA.)

KARIN: Me? What about your father?

ERIKA: My father's been a total dick. But he didn't hold a press conference about it. You did.

KARIN: And why shouldn't I?

ERIKA: Because you hurt me. What do you think happened the minute your press conference was over? The fucking reporters were on me like cockroaches. They came swarming around the taxi, begging me to give them the inside dope on you two. That's why I got the day off. That's why I didn't make a cent.

KARIN: I . . . I'm sorry. I didn't think about you.

ERIKA: Yeah. No shit. Well, thanks for the apology, but it's a little late. I'm a fucking celebrity now.

Jesus, mom, what's gonna happen? At this table I can think eight, ten moves ahead, see what's coming every step of the way, and be prepared. But this whole thing with you and dad . . . I don't have a goddamned clue. I don't like being famous. Not as Erika Berger, daughter of the notorious Karin and Walter Berger. But thanks to you, I am. When I got to the Chicago, everybody had seen your goddamned press conference. Poor kid, they said. Drink up, they said. On me! No, on me! They were so fucking sorry but they all wanted to know more about us. Our family secrets. Our goddamn business. And I couldn't tell them to shut the fuck up. So I took their money and drank till I puked.

When I came out of the toilet, I think they all felt a little bit guilty. The place was quiet as a fucking library. I said, "If you got any more questions, you might find the answers on the floor of the women's room."

(KARIN *walks to* ERIKA, *puts her hands on* ERIKA's *shoulders tenderly.*)

KARIN: I'm sorry, darling. Is there anything I can do for you?

ERIKA: Turn back the clock.

KARIN: I wish I could. I didn't mean to hurt you. It was just an unintended side effect.

ERIKA: Yeah. Like death from extra pure heroin.

KARIN: It won't be quite that bad. These scandals pass quickly. The public will want a fresh one.

ERIKA: I dunno, mom. This is pretty juicy. And you're pretty high profile. Shit. I'll probably lose my job. Of course, if I act soon,

Stern will give me 20,000 marks for an exclusive interview. More if I have a picture of the family in happier times.

(Beat.)

Jesus. This whole thing stinks. It wasn't heroic, wasn't brave . . . not at all like when I was a child, when you were marching, being attacked, imprisoned, whatever. I was proud of you for all that, and I let the whole world know. But, today . . . y'know, for the first time ever, I didn't want to hold up my head and say "Karin Berger—that's my mom."

KARIN: I am sorry if it seems distasteful to you. I'm sorry if it hurt you. But I had a duty.

ERIKA: Bullshit. The minute you found out about dad, your first instinct was to go on TV and tell the whole world what an asshole your husband was, knowing that because you were the famous Karin Berger, they'd listen. I mean, that's the beauty of the setup: You are sincere, you have suffered, your anger is justified. You have every right to publicly ream him and no one can see what a cheap trick it is.

KARIN: Erika, listen to me. Your father is the worst kind of—

ERIKA: I don't care. I love him. *(Beat.)*

KARIN: You what? How can you?

ERIKA: Well, I don't know! It's just . . . he's my dad. He did all that kind of dad shit, y'know? Took me to the park, tucked me in at night, read to me. Taught me how to play chess and football. And sometimes he did mom stuff, too. Taught me how to cook. Held me when I cried.

KARIN: Things I might have done if he hadn't sent me to prison.

ERIKA: I know he betrayed you, mom, and me too, but—

KARIN: Then whose side are you on?

ERIKA: Your side. Dad's side. My side. Don't you know what I mean? Didn't you love dad?

KARIN: Of course I did! But I . . . *(shakes her head)* Let me put it this way. I once loved a man. Let's call him "Walter." He was extraordinary—selfless, supportive, and . . . yes, even sexy. I married this wonderful, nearly perfect man and was happy for twenty years. Two days ago, I met a loathsome, spineless coward. Let's call him "Jason." I was apparently married to him, too. Jason would share cups of coffee with his wife's mortal enemies, tell them tales no self-respecting person should tell strangers, and arrange to have her locked up for ten years.

ERIKA: Can't you just love Walter?

KARIN: I wish. I really wish . . . but Jason has poisoned my relationship with Walter because they aren't separate people, and I can't look at Walter without seeing Jason. *(Beat.)*

ERIKA: So how long is it gonna be before you can forgive him?

KARIN: Haven't you been listening? Your father violated me, and I will never, ever forgive him.

ERIKA: Never?

KARIN: Not ten or even twenty moves from now. *(Beat.)* I'm sorry. I know you're going to miss him.

ERIKA: Whaddya mean?

KARIN: When we relocate to Bonn, you'll never see him again.

ERIKA: Bullshit.

KARIN: Oh, Erika. Erika. Tell me you're not going to . . . I mean it's one thing to love him, but another thing to see him. Jesus. Are you doing this just to get back at me?

ERIKA: Mom. Get real.

KARIN: That bastard is not setting foot in my home.

ERIKA: Well, duh.

KARIN: And I am not giving you money to go visit him.

ERIKA: You won't need to. I'm not going to Bonn.

KARIN: What?

ERIKA: I'm nearly nineteen years old. I got a full-time job. For now, anyway. It's time to get my own place. Y'know?

(Beat.)

KARIN: He's done it. The son of a bitch has done it. He put me in prison and took you away from me.

(ERIKA walks over to KARIN.)

ERIKA: He didn't take me away from you. I just grew up. Like kids do.

KARIN: While I wasn't looking. Couldn't look.

(ERIKA *whispers in* KARIN'*s ear.*)

Don't be afraid. I love you, too, mom.

(ERIKA *exits to bedroom.*)

KARIN: *(after Erika has gone)* Then why aren't you on my side?
(Lights fade to black.)

(*Onscreen,* ANJA *is sitting at a table. She has an ashtray and cigarettes in front of her.*)

ANJA: Oh, Christ. I have never been opposed to the Gauck commission or to opening the goddamn files. Will you write that down? Now? And perhaps even tell your friends? Thank you ... now, does anyone have a question about my book?

(ANJA *points at someone in front of her, unseen by the camera.*)

Oh, Christ. If I were Stasi, don't you think Karin Berger or Anita Eichinger or Franz Handlbauer would have Gaucked me by now? I simply don't want to look at my files. Yes? ... Oh, God. All right, all right. I will answer that question on one condition: That when I am done, we discuss this book that I've written ... agreed?

(ANJA *looks around for a moment, then nods. She lights up a cigarette, then speaks.*)

Going to the Gauck Commission . . . looking at one's files . . . confronting one's betrayers . . . this is supposed to be intensely private, isn't it? Well, bullshit. It's not private at all. Anita Eichinger looks at her files, sees that our mutual friend Gretchen Zinzindorf informed on her, and of course she tells me. As a matter of fact, she tells everybody in the fucking world. Why should I spend hours looking through the tedious minutiae in my file? It must be boring as hell. Forget that shit. I'll go to the coffeehouse, park my ass at a sunny table, and wait for all my friends to tell me everything I need to know. And if I'm too lazy to go to the coffeehouse, well I can just stay home and watch television while I wait for Karin Berger's kiss-and-tell book to come out. So that's reason number one. I'm a lazy bitch.

But I'm not a stupid lazy bitch. You think I don't know that Gretchen was selling out? She had a great job, she got to travel anywhere in the East Bloc that she wanted. Christ, the rest of us were losing our jobs, going to prison. Everybody suspected her. So ninety percent of the names that show up don't surprise those reading the files, and don't surprise me. That's reason number two: It's not news.

And now that we know who they are for sure, what do we do? Damned if I know. Most of these people were small potatoes. Not evil, just cowards. And of course, the higher up the ladder they were placed, the less likely it is that they'll be punished. So since we'll never have justice, fuck it. If any of my friends or lovers has, in a moment—or a lifetime—of weakness, betrayed me, to hell with them. I hope they're terrified at the prospect of being Gaucked. I hope that they're genuinely repentant. I hope they'll spend the rest of their days treating me like the goddamned queen of the universe to soothe their consciences and to show their gratitude. As for me, I'll be looking toward the future, not the past.

So. There's reason number three. And all the fucking explanation you're going to get out of me. Now, goddamn it, we are going to talk about feminism and the postwar German novel!

(*The screen goes dark.*)

MAY 1992

(*Lights up. Downstage right,* KARIN *and* ANJA *sit at a café table. A manuscript wrapped in brown paper sits between them.*)

KARIN: So. You didn't like chapter one.

ANJA: (*arches an eyebrow*) "The Monster in the Bed"?

KARIN: It's a working title.

ANJA: Well, darling, it promises lots of good dish, but I'm afraid I've heard it all.

KARIN: Jesus. What made me think you'd be willing to give a friend an unbiased opinion?

ANJA: Oh. You want my opinion? Give back the advance.

KARIN: You condescending bitch.

ANJA: You're welcome.

KARIN: Just tell me what's wrong. All right? I'll fix it.

ANJA: You can't fix it, darling. It's the concept. Revenge is sweet, but obsession is oh, so sour. Look, do you really need—

KARIN: It's not about what I need.

ANJA: Oh, please.

KARIN: Well, not completely. It's also about what Germany needs.

ANJA: A kiss-and-tell book about the Cold War? Yes, that's guaranteed to win admirers.

KARIN: So? I don't have any now.

ANJA: Don't play the martyr with me, darling.

KARIN: Well, some days it feels that way. Even in my own party, the old boys hate me because one, I'm a woman, two, I'm an Ossi, and three, I helped form a bipartisan coalition to open the files. Bipartisan! One might just as well say "child rapist."

And, of course, so many secrets have been revealed, so many families and reputations destroyed, that even my natural allies—women, young turks—think that we opened a Pandora's box, and are trying to distance themselves from the whole issue of the Gauck Commission. Oh, they smile. They're frequently cordial. But they don't ask me to join them for a beer. They hesitate before putting me on the guest list for their parties.

Some days I feel as if I was Gaucked. I've lost my comrades, my husband, and my daughter.

ANJA: Now you've gone too far. You have not lost Erika.

KARIN: Yes, I have. Seven crucial years of her life are simply a blank to me. I really don't know who she is, and she doesn't understand me, either. No wonder she loves him more than she loves me.

ANJA: What makes you think that?

KARIN: She visits her goddamned father!

ANJA: She does not.

KARIN: What?

ANJA: Walter seems to have vanished without a trace. No one knows where he's living.

KARIN: Maybe he isn't. Maybe the asshole's dead.

ANJA: *(shakes her head)* We'd have heard. But I know Erika isn't visiting him.

KARIN: Well. That's a day brightener. *(Beat.)* Oh, what the hell does it matter? She'd visit him if she could. She loves the son of a bitch.

ANJA: She loves you both.

KARIN: She can't. He's the one who tore this family apart and sent me to prison.

ANJA: Did he?

KARIN: What the fuck do you mean by that?

ANJA: Well, if I'm not mistaken, Walter was reporting to the Stasi for twenty years. But for the first twelve or thirteen years, nothing much happened beyond the occasional clubbing, gassing, or night in jail. So clearly somebody else—perhaps your father, General Niedermann?—got sick and tired of you mouthing off in public and decided your number was up.

KARIN: Oh, so it was just "fate"?

ANJA: That's not what I'm saying. I'm saying that opposing the state is always risky business, never more so than in the dear old GDR. Anybody could have sent you to prison.

KARIN: Yes, but "anybody" turned out to be Walter.

ANJA: You don't know that.

KARIN: I do, too! There may be very few things I know for sure, but I know that Walter betrayed me. Jesus. You're on his fucking side, too.

ANJA: Really, Karin—

(KARIN shoves the manuscript into her briefcase and stands.)

KARIN: You think he's so fucking charming, such a prince—

ANJA: I am not on Walter's side—

KARIN: —that you want to take my money away and stop me from showing the whole world what a—-

ANJA: Karin, what do you want me to do—hate him?

KARIN: Yes! *(Beat.)* I can't bear this burden alone. I want one, just one, other person to hate him as much as I do.

ANJA: I can't do it, Karin. I never loved him as much as you do.

KARIN: I don't.

(KARIN drops the briefcase and collapses back into her chair.)

I don't. I hate him. I did everything I could to get rid of him. I hit him, kicked him out of the flat, went into therapy . . . but his ghost haunts all my soft organs. The memories that sustained me while I was in prison: feeling his soft breath on my neck, pressing my lips to his, having him up inside me, makes my skin crawl. And I want him to know what he's done to me. I want everyone to know what he's done to me.

ANJA: So you're going to lift your skirt and let all of Germany see your internal and external wounds. The nation and your family will be grateful, and you will be healed.

KARIN: It doesn't sound like such a great plan, does it? But I don't know what else to do. It's either this or kill him.

ANJA: I'll give you this much credit. Writing a book is a better idea than killing him.

KARIN: I appreciate your support.

ANJA: I'm always happy to dish up faint praise.

KARIN: Hard-ass bitch.

ANJA: Hard-assed but not cold-hearted. I am your friend.

KARIN: I know that. I do. Oh shit, oh shit, oh shit. *(KARIN sits up, runs her hands through her hair.)* What was I thinking? I don't have the mental or physical energy to sit at a goddamned computer every day. And even if I could—if I hired a ghostwriter and actually finished it—what if it's decent? What if it's actually moving? Profound?

ANJA: All right. For argument's sake, what if?

KARIN: A book tour. Chat shows. And a daughter who really does hate me for the rest of her life. You win. You all win. I won't write the damn book.

(Fade to black)

(On the screen, we see WALTER *against a brick or concrete wall.)*

WALTER: Please. I'd rather not. Speak to my wife instead. She'll tell you all you need to know. My side of the story? My, how kind of you. But I'm afraid there isn't much to tell. He was a nondescript, pleasant man. Like you. We met in a basement room in the building where I worked. He always offered me a cup of coffee. Very good coffee, too. Strong, flavorful. I'd never tasted anything half so good.

He apologized for the uniformed police. Said if I would voluntarily come to see him once a week, he would dispense with them. When they had gone, he told me a secret. He said, "Honestly, Walter, I work for an insufferable bureaucracy that wouldn't know vital information if it kicked them in the rear." Those were his exact words. He said the quality of the information in Karin's file didn't matter, only the quantity. "So," he said, "Tell me about your Fräulein Niedermann. Tell me anything you want. And don't tell me anything you feel uncomfortable sharing with me."

And that was what I did. All I did. For twenty years. It was nothing at all, really. I grew more comfortable, began to share more, but nothing that was really political. Nothing Karin could possibly object to. So I never told her about it. Why should I?

But then came Gorbachev. The GDR fell like a house of cards. And in the harsh light of the new, unified Germany, such decisions look . . . different. More deceitful. Perhaps unforgivably so.

Did I know that all along? Is that why I never told her? Is that why I can't argue with her now?

Please. I want to stop talking about these things.

(He walks off camera. Blackout.)

JULY 1992

(Downstage right: two rows of two chairs represent a taxi. ERIKA *sits in the front seat on the driver's side, reading a book. After a beat,* WALTER *slides quickly into the back.* ERIKA *does not look up from her book.)*

ERIKA: Sorry, bud. You gotta take the cab at the head of the line.

WALTER: I'm not really going anywhere.

ERIKA: Dad!

(ERIKA *tosses her book down and twists around in her seat to face* WALTER.)

WALTER: Erika, I'm sorry—

ERIKA: *(finger to her lips)* Sshh.

WALTER: All those journalists—

ERIKA: *(as before)* Sshh.

WALTER: I was afraid—

ERIKA: *(as before)* Sshh. You talk too much, Dad.

(*Beat. They look at each other.*)

So where the hell have you been? I didn't even hear from you on my birthday.

WALTER: Life has been . . . difficult.

ERIKA: Oh, life is tough for everybody. Don't give me that shit. What makes you think your pain is so special that you can like, disappear for five months and then just pop up again? I've kicked guys in the balls for less.

WALTER: I was afraid you might want to do that anyway. *(half-smile)* Happy birthday.

ERIKA: Don't push your luck, dad. I got boots on.

WALTER: Well, why don't you just give me a few swift kicks and get it over with?

ERIKA: I should. I really fuckin' should. *(She grins.)* But mom did it for me on TV.

WALTER: She certainly did. I suppose I deserved it, in a way.

ERIKA: I'm not sure you did. And I know I didn't. Man, between the two of you, my life has been nuts.

WALTER: I'm sure. Mine, too, if it's any consolation.

ERIKA: But hey: Here's good news for both of us, dad. She handed back her advance. She's not gonna write a book about you.

WALTER: Well. That's some relief. Why . . . ?

ERIKA: Not because she's gone soft on you. I think she's just tired.

(*Beat.*)

WALTER: Erika, it's not easy for me to apologize—

ERIKA: It doesn't seem to be easy for anyone. But thanks.

WALTER: I haven't been a very good father, I'm afraid.

ERIKA: The past five months? Yeah, you've been a shitty father. But before that, you were the best.

WALTER: How can you say that after . . . after what happened?

ERIKA: Good question. What you did to mom . . . really devastated her. Me, too. I just wanted to vomit. Hell, I did vomit. I just couldn't believe that my dad—who I loved, who loved me—was so fucked up.

WALTER: It must have been quite difficult for you.

ERIKA: It was at first. And I don't just mean the scene at home. But after the press conferences, the fucking reporters got in my face all the time and asked for dirt about you. I woulda spit in their faces before I gave 'em any, but I gradually came to realize that I didn't have any. Y'know? You were, like, a really good dad. So I just told them about how you took care of me and educated me. But it never came out quite right in the press. It always seemed to make you look more duplicitous.

WALTER: So you're on the record as saying "father was duplicitous."

ERIKA: Well, you were. I tell ya, dad, I still don't know how to reconcile it all. I mean, I used to think that there were good people and bad people and a bunch of in-betweens. And you were good to me. So how could you do something so horrible for so long? Am I, like, being stupid? Should I just admit that you're actually an awful man?

I want to believe that you're not, that you just . . . picked a really stupid strategy. Like a real-life version of the Budapest Gambit: You sacrificed a piece hoping that it would gain you something. And just like in chess, it didn't get you jack shit. You gambled with us all and lost big time.

WALTER: And so you hate me.

ERIKA: No. I love you. Your actions were unforgivable, but I forgive you.

WALTER: But I was—

ERIKA: (*finger to her lips*) Sshh.

(Beat.)

ERIKA: *(contd)* You talk too much, Dad.

WALTER: But I want you to understand. This is not like the Budapest Gambit. It's worse than that. It's a game that you've lost the minute you agree to sit down to play. But you don't know that until you've tentatively made that first harmless move—pushed that pawn out one simple square.

ERIKA: Then why—?

WALTER: Because two men knock on your door. Because it is suggested that you should regularly meet with Stasi. Because the threats and implications are tangible yet horrifyingly vague.

ERIKA: So you really don't know why.

WALTER: Not any more. If I ever did.

ERIKA: Well, now you know you don't know. That's a good thing. You're, like, a step further down the road.

WALTER: Yes, but the road to where?

ERIKA: Out of the past. Can't say more than that.

(ERIKA reaches out and touches WALTER's chin.)

Come on, dad. Look me in the eye.

(WALTER raises his head. ERIKA slides her hand onto his cheek. The two of them slowly break into a smile. ERIKA leans across and kisses WALTER on the cheek. He puts his hand on hers.)

WALTER: Erika, I . . . I'm going away.

ERIKA: That's what you think.

WALTER: I'm serious, Erika. Life in Berlin has become too . . . unpleasant. I can't get a job as a proofreader since your mother Gaucked me, and I have very few friends. People I'm ashamed to associate with seek me out for comradeship and I'm utterly humiliated. I've been offered a job in a little town in Saxony. They don't know about my past, except that I was a Communist. But they don't mind. They're only looking for a gardener.

ERIKA: What the hell do you know about gardening?

WALTER: My father was a gardener. I know as much about soil, water, pruning, and the like as you know about chess. Although

I may be a bit more out of practice than you.

ERIKA: So what's your new address?

WALTER: I don't have one yet.

ERIKA: Damn. Damn. I knew it! You're gonna run away again. You really are a coward.

WALTER: Erika.

(WALTER *pulls a scrap of paper out of his pocket and hands it to* ERIKA.)

This is the telephone number of my new employer. If you call in a few weeks, they will have my number and address. But I'll call you first. I swear I will. Just promise me one thing: that you will never share this number with anyone.

(*She looks at the paper, then at* WALTER.)

ERIKA: Well, dad. We're just gonna have to trust each other.

(ERIKA *stuffs the number in her pocket. Quick fade to black.*)

(*On the screen, we see* ERIKA *in a coffee shop. A murmur of partons in the background.*)

ERIKA: Oh, what the hell. For that kind of money I'll give you five minutes. But that's it. So. What do you want from me, Mr. Big-Shot-from-*Stern*?

Why I'm going to Cambridge? Shit. That's way easy. It's a good school. With an awesome philosophy and mathematics faculty. My test scores are phenomenal, my English is fuckin' excellent, they're salivatin' for me. That's all. Piss off.

Fuck. You. I love my father. I love my mother. I'm just . . . twenty years old, y'know? It's time to take off. Go someplace where nobody knows who the fuck Walter and Karin Berger are. Hell, it's *you* guys I gotta get away from. *You're* tearing the goddamn country apart.

Oh yeah, yeah, right . . . Mom has this whole rap about "healing," too. I don't buy it. This is all about selling papers, getting TV ratings, and in the case of some of these assholes, collecting big fees from people like you for their public confessions. You tell me how much my grandfather has made since the first of the year. Jesus. We're not promoting healing by creating this cottage industry of accusers and accused. We're just picking at our scabs . . . causing them to get infected and fester.

You're probably right. That is way simple. Germany is suffering a complicated disease. Not the kind you can cure. The kind you just get sick and die from. So fuck it. Keep your goddamn thousand marks and buy a wreath. Every word has been off the record. Publish it and I sue your ass.

(ERIKA *puts her hand up to the lens, blocking the camera's view. The screen goes dark.*)

JANUARY 1993

(*Lights up on* KARIN *standing in the moonlight downstage right. Her arms are folded protectively around her. After a beat, we hear* WOLF's *voice from offstage.*)

WOLF: *(off)* Hello? Who's there?

(WOLF *steps onstage, dressed in shirtsleeves. He sees* KARIN *and breaks into a smile.*)

WOLF: Karin! What an unexpected pleasure.

KARIN: I'm here to see mother. If that's allowed.

WOLF: Oh, I no longer tell anyone what they can and cannot do. Including your mother.

KARIN: Really? Then why hasn't she been to see me?

WOLF: You live in Bonn.

KARIN: She could phone.

WOLF: Your mother doesn't trust the telephone.

(*Beat.*)

May I join you?

(KARIN *shakes her head.*)

Another visit, perhaps?

KARIN: I think not.

WOLF: As you wish.

KARIN: I didn't actually want to come back here until . . .

WOLF: Until I was dead?

KARIN: Maybe. I don't know. But I thought, why should mother have to wait?

WOLF: That's kind of you. Well . . . I'll just stroll to the corner. Have a glass of beer. Smoke a pipe. Chat with Ernst. You two have a good visit.

KARIN: Thank you.

(Beat. KARIN doesn't move.)

What did you know?

WOLF: About?

KARIN: Me. Walter.

(WOLF gestures expansively.)

WOLF: When I was at the peak of my power I rarely had to tell my subordinates what to do. They anticipated my needs and took appropriate action.

KARIN: Did you ever look at my file?

WOLF: I had no time for such things. I saw only summaries. A few photos.

KARIN: I see. Well. Enjoy your pipe and your beer.

WOLF: I intend to. Perhaps one day you and I could . . . go down to the corner. I would even leave my Meerschaum at home. A pity, but I know how you feel about pipes and cigars.

KARIN: Yes. Of course you know. Well, I won't deprive you of your Meerschaum.

(KARIN exits. WOLF remains onstage. Blackout.)

(Onscreen, we see KARIN sitting in a comfortable chair. At the beginning, a medium shot, slowly zooming in during her monologue.)

KARIN: First of all, as I look back after a year, I can see that the life I lived before I opened my file—and maybe the entire history of the GDR—was one long dream. Parts of it had a nightmarish quality, and parts of it were beautiful enough to make me cry, but none of it was real.

Take this example: On January 15, 1990, a pro-democracy mob descended on the Stasi headquarters. They were 100,000 strong, they were angry, they were delirious with newfound freedom in the temporary anarchy that existed after the collapse of the GDR and before unification. The crowd broke open the doors and poured into the deserted compound, found the hated files, tore them apart, dumped them out windows, and even set some on fire. Finally, cooler and more rational leaders managed to convince the mob to leave the files alone, that this evidence would be needed to punish Stasi members. Ultimately order prevailed, although between the material the Stasi managed to destroy beforehand and the material that the crowd destroyed in its fury, a lot of gaps exist in the Stasi record.

(WALTER *steps onstage into a soft pool of light. He turns to the screen.*)

WALTER: *(live) (a whisper)* Karin. What I did—it was definitely not good. But I came to think it was good.

KARIN: *(onscreen)* So what? you say. Freedom means loss of control. It's unfortunate, but that's democracy. But what if I tell you what we now know . . . that one half of those 100,000 were on the Stasi payroll.

WALTER: *(live)* Or if not good, better than if some malevolent stranger were twisting your words, presenting you in an unflattering light. I saw myself as protecting you, helping myself, sheltering Erika.

KARIN: *(onscreen)* What did this mean? It's hard to say. Perhaps those files weren't destroyed by accident on January 15. Perhaps the mob was perfectly controlled—by its Stasi contingent. Maybe people like my ex-husband weren't cowards but unsung heroes. Maybe they did convince their Stasi handlers that the GDR was corrupt and reform was necessary.

Or perhaps the reform movement didn't exist. After all, the Americans manufactured a Red Scare to provide full employment for their secret police; did the Stasi manufacture a dissident organization for the same purpose?

WALTER: *(live)* But in the end, I don't know what I accomplished or wanted to accomplish at any given moment. I did not plan ahead. I wasn't playing chess—or not well.

KARIN: *(onscreen)* There are only two things I know for sure.

First, I believed in my dream—the work I was doing, the future of my country, my personal code of ethics, my family's love.

WALTER: *(live)* It is no longer possible to explain my motivations or circumstances. Absolution is unattainable. And yet I want absolution. I need absolution.

(KARIN's face now fills the screen. WALTER reaches out to the screen.)

KARIN: *(onscreen)* And second, Walter was kind and loving and utterly without courage.

(A tear rolls down KARIN's face.)

Dammit, I knew that. Right from the beginning. . .

WALTER: *(live) (whisper)* A man has only one love . . .

KARIN: He was so careful. So very ordinary.

(WALTER is kissing KARIN's image. She is crying. The screen and stage go dark.)

END OF PLAY

HALLOWED GROUND

BY LAURA HARRINGTON

BIOGRAPHY

Laura Harrington's award-winning plays, musicals, operas, and radio plays have been produced regionally, Off-Broadway, and in Canada. Some recent credits include: *Hallowed Ground*, Portland Stage Company, 2002 World Premiere; *Martin Guerre* (Music: Roger Ames), Hartford Stage Company (directed by Mark Lamos), Nomti Festival 2001; *The Heart of an Emperor, Dress Right, Universal Soldier*, and *Flag Girls*, Boston Playwrights Theater; *The Bathtub Diaries*, Portland Stage's Little Festival of the Unexpected, 2001; *Resurrection* (Music: Tod Machover), Houston Grand Opera 1999 World Premiere, Boston Lyric Opera, 2001, Pacific Opera, 2003, CD available from Albany Records; Joan of Arc (Music: Mel Marvin), Boston Music Theater Project, Wellesley College Theater, ACTF Finalist 2001; *The Perfect 36* (Music: Mel Marvin), Tennessee Repertory Theater, Hartt School of Music; *Marathon Dancing*, (directed by Anne Bogart) En Garde Arts, NYC, and Munich, Germany; *Lucy's Lapses* (Music: Christopher Drobny), Portland Opera Company, Playwrights' Horizons; *The Song of the Silkie* (Music: Elena Ruehr), Rockport Chamber Music Festival, 2000; *Babes in Toyland*, Houston Grand Opera; and *Sleeping Beauty* (Music: Roger Ames), North Shore Music Theater.

Ms. Harrington is on the faculty at M.I.T. and is the winner of the 1998 Massachusetts Cultural Council Playwriting Fellowship, and a two-time winner of the Clauder Playwriting Competition (1996 for Mercy and 2001 for *Hallowed Ground*). Other awards include a Boston "IRNE" Award for Best New Play, 2001, a Bunting Institute Fellowship at Harvard/ Radcliffe, a Whiting Foundation Grant-in-Aid, the Joseph Kesselring Award for Drama, Opera America development and commissioning grants, a New England Emmy, and a Quebec Cinemateque Award.

CHARACTERS

JACK WALKER—25, a Union soldier/doubles as the
Confederate soldier Tom

MICAH—19, a black woman

LIZZIE PEAKE—15, a white woman

JUBAL HALEY—19, a southern conscript, a ragged, hungry
boy/man, unschooled, odd, doubles as Sam English, a
Union soldier

Two to three extras play Confederate soldiers, including Jimmy,
15, in Scene 1, and dead soldiers, as needed

TIME & PLACE

Fall, 1864. Georgia, between Atlanta and the sea.

THE SET

The set is bare, elemental, simple, fluid, suggestive rather than
literal. Sound and light evoke a feeling, an era, a mood,
a world of loss, a landscape of unbearable human
and natural destruction.

I don't see an actual house, for instance, but I do see a wooden
floor, a treasured box, flames, the suggestion of a riverbank, the
play of light on water, moving shadows beneath a willow tree.
A brilliant sound design will create the landscape of this play far
more effectively than any literal representation we might see.
I hear the caw of crows, the sound of their wings beating,
marching feet, riderless horses, the groans of the dying; the
subtle, haunting sounds of a world blanketed in death.

The action of the play takes place during one long night
and the following morning.

"We moved forward stumbling over the dead and dying who lay thicker than I ever saw them . . . It was hard to keep off of them in the darkness. I'll never forget the terrible groans of the wounded, the mournful sound of the owl and the awful shrill shrieks of the whippoorwill . . . These birds seemed to mock at our grief and laugh at the groans of the dying."

— from *Bloody Roads South:*
Wilderness to Cold Harbor, May-June 1864,
by Noah Andre Trudeau

"The scenes on this field would have cured anybody of war."

— William Tecumseh Sherman, after Shiloh

"I am the enemy you killed, my friend."

— Wilfred Owen

HALLOWED GROUND

ACT I

Sunset

(*WE HEAR men forming up into battle lines, the clang of muskets, the distinctive sound of a ramrod shoved home, coughs, the creak of leather, the sound of horses.*

Drums begin . . .

WE HEAR a collage of confederate soldiers' voices as they wait for the battle to begin. JIMMY, *kneeling, sobs. Offstage a soldier sings an old Baptist hymn which underscores the following.*)

TOM: Got any tobacco? Goddamnit, Jimmy Hicks, get up!

JIMMY: Folly. It's all folly.

TOM: You got anymore of that good tobacco?

JUBAL: All right. All right. I can stand it.

TOM: I am gettin' too old for this business.

JIMMY: I wish it was this time tomorrow.

TOM: It's a damned long ways over there.

JIMMY: Shut up! Shut up! You are a damned lie!

TOM: A long ways to walk and nowhere to run.

JUBAL: I wish I was a bluebird. I'd fly me to the gulf.

TOM: Shut up, you peckerwood.

JIMMY: I have loved you boys.

TOM: You shut your mouth!

JIMMY: Say, any of you all seen my coat?

JUBAL: This ain't gonna be my burying ground.

JIMMY: If you are killed, can I have your watch?

TOM: No!

OFFICER: (*o.s.*) Load and prime! Load and prime, boys. Move smart. Keep your muzzles up there . . .

(*WE HEAR men loading muskets, priming, setting caps.*)

JUBAL: *(under his breath)* Jesus Christ, my hands are shaking. I need another powder packet. *(drops it)* I need another powder packet! Goddamnit! *(searches frantically for another packet)*

OFFICER: *(o.s.)* Fix . . . . bayonets!

(WE HEAR hundreds of bayonets rattle home on hundreds of muskets.)

JUBAL: Steady. Steady. We have done this before.

TOM: Well, old boys, we have come to that moment once again.

OFFICER: *(o.s.)* Silence in the ranks there!

TOM: My, my, the young general is snappish today.

(laughter)

OFFICER: *(o.s.)* Remember to keep your dress.

(echoing down the line)

Keep your dress . . .

Keep your dress . . .

Keep your dress . . .

JIMMY: What's the matter, Jubal?

JUBAL: Nothin'. Nothin' is the matter.

TOM: Take it easy. It ain't that far. Just a little walk and we'll be done.

JUBAL: Just a little walk . . .

TOM: We done it lots of times before.

OFFICER: *(o.s.)* Silence in the goddamned ranks! Shoulder . . . arms! Right—shoulder—shift . . . arms!

TOM: Get your ass in the wagon, boys, we are goin' into town.

(WE HEAR the soldiers move into line. The color bearers shake out their flags. The flags snap in the wind. More drums.)

OFFICER: *(o.s.)* Forward, quick time . . .

TOM: Oh, shit.

JUBAL: Let it commence. Let us all cross that river and see what it is to die.

JIMMY: Oh, sweet Jesus. Oh, sweet Jesus.

TOM: Easy there . . .

OFFICER: *(o.s.)* . . . march!

(The drums increase in tempo and intensity as . . .

WE FOCUS on a confederate soldier, JUBAL, *barefoot, moving in line. A cornet strapped to his haversack slaps against his thigh as he walks.)*

JUBAL: We wait all day. Forming up in the dying light. Glares off our bayonets. Lights us up like Christmas. Great target. One great bloody lit up target.

JIMMY: *(panicked)* Did I load my musket? Damn! I can't remember . . .

TOM: Do you have to puke every time? There's nothing in your stomach anyway . . .

JIMMY: I can't remember! I can't remember! Jubal! Did I load my musket?

JUBAL: They look like ghosts comin' through the trees.

JIMMY: Don't tell me not to cry! I'm keepin' up! I'm keepin' up!

JUBAL: I don't want to see their faces. I don't want to see at all.

TOM: Get out of my country! Bastards!

OFFICER: *(o.s.)* Guide center, boys! Dress it up!!

TOM: How'd they get the good goddamned land?

JUBAL: The breastwork's too high.

TOM: It's always too high. Son of a bitchin' bastard! You fixin' to die in that meadow?

JUBAL: I'm flying through that meadow. I'm flying over their works. We're all flying. You watch me fly.

(the band strikes up "Annie Laurie")

JIMMY: I can't remember! Jubal! Help me!

JUBAL: Don't play that song.

Melancholy, brokenhearted.

Give me drums, goddammit.

Drums to split my ears.

Drums to march and die.

Don't let me hear nothing but drums.

Drums and blood beating in my ears.

Don't let me think, feel, see, hear.

Just the drums.

Please, God.

Pure, insane, broken, beating,

Louder than my heart,

Louder than fear,

Drums,

Sending us over the top and into the arms of strangers.

They open their arms

Welcome us with red roses

Wash us in blood

Lie down with us in ground made holy

Where we will rise and rise and rise again

Flying into the arms of strangers

Flying into the arms of death

Flying

(As the drums crescendo into madness . . . WE HEAR . . . the famous rebel yell . . . as . . . JIMMY *is shot in the chest.*

LIGHTS SHIFT and FOCUS on . . .

The house.

Upstairs, LIZZIE *rummages through the top drawer of the dresser. She wears a tattered yellow summer dress. She becomes more frantic as WE HEAR boots on the front porch, pounding on the front door. Finally, she finds a small, carved box in the back of the drawer. She opens it, takes out a locket and puts it on. She hears the front door kicked open, then boots on the stairs. She turns with a start, leaving the box on top of the dresser, the drawer hanging open. She picks up the musket lying on the bed and backs to the far wall.*

The door to the room is kicked open and a Union soldier, SAM ENGLISH, *walks into the room. She eyes him warily from behind her gun, but doesn't speak. He stops.)*

SAM ENGLISH: You alone? *(she looks at him with contempt)* What's the matter? Cat got your tongue?

LIZZIE: Get out. This is private property.

SAM ENGLISH: You alone here?

LIZZIE: Why on earth would I tell you that?

SAM ENGLISH: *(sees the box on the dresser, steps towards it)* What's that?

LIZZIE: *(steps in front of the dresser)* Nothin'.

SAM ENGLISH: Get out of the way . . .

LIZZIE: You take one more step you better be prepared to leave this world.

SAM ENGLISH: You sure you want to treat me like this?

LIZZIE: I'm sure I'd like to see you dead. *(He moves quickly towards her, grabs the barrel of the musket and wrestles it from her. In her desperation to hold on, she is dragged several feet across the floor.)*

SAM ENGLISH: You think you're gonna hold back me and all of Sherman's army with this gun?

LIZZIE: Go to hell!

SAM ENGLISH: How old are you?

LIZZIE: None of your business.

SAM ENGLISH: *(she attempts to walk past him, out of the room)* Where do you think you're going?

LIZZIE: Away from you.

SAM ENGLISH: I don't think so.

LIZZIE: I'm going to get my mother.

SAM ENGLISH: She's dead.

LIZZIE: If you know so much how come you don't know if I'm alone or not?

SAM ENGLISH: I know you're alone. All alone.

LIZZIE: You don't know nothin' . . .

SAM ENGLISH: Bring me that box.

LIZZIE: Get it yourself. *(He dumps out the contents of the box, picks it over. Picks up a delicate earring, studies it.)*

LIZZIE: You're gonna rot in hell.

SAM ENGLISH: And you're not? *(He pockets the earrings, button-*

ing them into his vest. She kicks him, hard, in the knee cap, and then scrambles for the door. He lunges for her, tackles her, and brings them both full length on to the floor. She is squirming to get out from under him when we feel the energy in the room change, grow electric with fear and desire.)

Why do you make this so damned difficult?!

LIZZIE: *(she scratches his face)* I hate you!!

SAM ENGLISH: *(he easily pins her arms to the ground)* You're mean as a snake.

LIZZIE: I shoulda killed you when I had the chance.

SAM ENGLISH: Kill me? You think you could do that?

LIZZIE: Watch me. *(He kisses her. She struggles fiercely, then stills.)*

LIZZIE: That's disgusting!

SAM ENGLISH: You like that.

LIZZIE: You don't know what I like . . .

SAM ENGLISH: Yes, I do. *(he kisses her again)*

LIZZIE: Don't . . .

SAM ENGLISH: *(he kisses her neck)* Sshhh . . .

LIZZIE: Stop . . .

SAM ENGLISH: Do you know how sweet you feel to me?

LIZZIE: Don't say that.

SAM ENGLISH: I can take care of you—

LIZZIE: No . . . You can't . . .

SAM ENGLISH: What is it about your face?

(He reaches up to touch her face, then kisses her. It becomes more intense. LIZZIE responds at first, then tries to pull away. As he begins to fumble with her dress. . . . she pulls his revolver from its holster and in one fluid motion, raises it to his neck and fires. The sound of the shot is huge, amplified; it reverberates. She wriggles her way out from underneath him. Her neck, chest and abdomen are soaked in blood. She unbuttons his vest pocket, retrieving the earrings. As she pockets the earrings she realizes that she is covered in blood. She SCREAMS and runs off as . . .

WE HEAR the shouted order: "CLEAR!!" as the house is set on fire. WE HEAR the flames catch, the wood begins to burn, smoke rolls in the air. It is the sound of hell. At the edge of the woods LIZZIE *stops, caught by the sound of her house on fire. She turns, momentarily rooted to the spot, a girl in a blood-soaked dress reflected red in the flames.*

LIGHTS SHIFT and FOCUS ON . . .

The riverbank.

MICAH *is half hidden in a shelter of willows. She is trying to nurse her dead baby. The battle drums and guns continue.*

WE HEAR distant artillery. Smoke and ash drift in the air.)

MICAH: *(pulling her baby tight against her, she tries to sing a lullaby)* "Didn't my Lord deliver Daniel?

Didn't my Lord deliver Daniel?

Didn't my Lord deliver Daniel?

Then why not every one?"

(LIZZIE *ENTERS, covered in blood, panicked.)*

LIZZIE: Micah—we got to go . . . *(no response)* What are you doing? We got to go . . . *(no response)* You hear me? *(pushes her)* What's the matter with you . . . *(No response.* LIZZIE *walks in front of* MICAH, *sees the baby, senses something terribly wrong.)* Oh my Lord, Micah, oh my Lord.

MICAH: She's so cold, Lizzie, so cold . . .

LIZZIE: We got to go, Micah. Now . . .

MICAH: *(putting her shawl around the baby)* No! We got to get her warm. We got to . . .

LIZZIE: You listen to me . . .

MICAH: Why won't she suck? *(brings the baby back to her breast)* *(to Lizzie)* She won't nurse!

LIZZIE: She can't nurse . . .

MICAH: There, there, you don't like my milk. I'll make you a sugar titty. For my sweet girl. You got to nurse, sweet baby. You got to nurse . . .

LIZZIE: She's dead, Micah . . .

MICAH: She's just sleepin' is all. I need some sugar—We got to find some sugar . . .

LIZZIE: She's dead . . .

MICAH: Don't you say that!

LIZZIE: I'm tellin' you the truth.

MICAH: She's breathin'. I can feel her chest rise and fall, like a little bird, like a sweet little bird.

LIZZIE: *(takes* MICAH'S *face in her hands)* Micah! Look at me!

MICAH: *(jerks away)* What's the matter with you? You covered with blood. Don't you put that blood on me . . .

LIZZIE: The soldiers are coming . . .

MICAH: Did you kill my baby?

LIZZIE: You know I didn't. The soldiers . . .

MICAH: She can't be dead. She can't be.

LIZZIE: You come with me now. We got to get away from here.

MICAH: No . . .

   (WE HEAR men marching.)

LIZZIE: You hear that? You hear those soldiers? If we don't get away from here we will all be killed.

MICAH: I can't . . .

   *(*LIZZIE *reaches out to take the baby.* MICAH *recoils.)*

LIZZIE: We got to bury her Micah, and get on out of here.

MICAH: *(moans)* No . . . No . . . ! *(In the soft earth of the riverbank* LIZZIE *quickly digs a grave with her hands.)*

LIZZIE: We can't tote her through these woods.

MICAH: She don't weigh hardly nothin' at all.

LIZZIE: We got to let her rest, Micah. We got to lay her soul to rest, now.

MICAH: What do you think you're doing?

LIZZIE: I'm digging a grave.

MICAH: I can't leave her here.

LIZZIE: I ain't gonna argue with you no more.

MICAH: She's no bother, no bother at all. You see that? She don't even make no sound.

LIZZIE: You've got to do what I'm tellin' you, Micah. *(She rinses the mud from her hands and then reaches to take the baby.* MICAH *jerks away.)*

MICAH: I can't lay her in that ground.

LIZZIE: I'll do it . . .

MICAH: —No!

LIZZIE: Damnation, Micah! That baby is dead . . .

MICAH: It's cold in that ground.

LIZZIE: I know it, but . . .

MICAH: I can't leave my baby, Lizzie, no more'n I could leave you.

LIZZIE: On my honor, Micah, we'll come back.

MICAH: And who's gonna stay with her in the meanwhiles?

LIZZIE: Come on now, you pray with me . . . We consign this baby girl to the earth and pray thee, dear Jesus, to take her into Paradise with thee until the Day of Resurrection when thy faithful shall be united with thee and the heavenly hosts forever and ever. Amen.

MICAH: Whose God is that, Lizzie, treats us like this?

LIZZIE: He's making a feast in heaven for your baby girl.

MICAH: But I want her here—in my arms . . .

LIZZIE: I know you do.

MICAH: Will he raise my baby up?

LIZZIE: She's with your mama now.

MICAH: I'd rather die than bury this child. *(*MICAH *kneels and carefully, reverently, places her baby in the grave. She takes her shawl and covers her.)* This is worse than hell. Worse than anything.

*(*LIZZIE *begins to cover her with earth.)*

MICAH: *(pulling Lizzie away)* No—I can't . . .

LIZZIE: Don't you make me slap you. We got to do this now.

MICAH: *(a cry of anguish)*

LIZZIE: Micah—Please . . .

MICAH: *(gathers herself together and covers her baby with earth)*
You're in God's hands now. Whether I like it or not, no matter . . .
(She turns away from LIZZIE *and, weeping, begins to cover the grave with stones. Let the weeping establish, let* LIZZIE *really hear it, then . . .*

WE HEAR *the sound of* JUBAL'S *cornet drifting on the wind. Its beauty is otherworldly.)*

LIZZIE: Listen to that, Micah. Is it real? . . . *(they both stop to listen)* Who's doin' that? In this place . . .

MICAH: *(putting stones on the grave)*

Fly girl. Fly. Fly to glory. *(the music dies away; pause)*

(still on her knees)

Gimme a sign, Lord.

I pray but I can't hear your voice no more . . .

I hear that river calling me so sweet and low. . .

Calling me to slip away

Gimme a sign, Lord.

Gimme a sign

Let me go or help me stay.

   *(MICAH *begins to wade into the water.)*

LIZZIE: *(feeling her blood-soaked dress she begins to panic)* Help me, Micah! Help me . . . You get over here right now and get this dress clean. Get this blood off me. *(trying to pull her dress over her head)* It's stuck to me, Micah. All this blood . . . Oh! It's stuck to me! I can't stand the smell . . . I can't breathe . . . It ain't never gonna come off . . . Micah . . . Micah! . . . Help me!!

MICAH: C'mon, now. You come into this water. Get it wet, it'll come right off.

   *(LIZZIE *dips into the water. The blood-soaked dress softens and she pulls it over her head. Her chest and arms are still red/brown with blood.)*

LIZZIE: *(seeing the blood on her body)* Oh my God, Micah. Oh my God. Look at me . . . *(she begins rubbing her skin with her hands)* It's not comin' off. I need soap! I need soap—!

MICAH: Well, we ain't got no soap, missy. *(LIZZIE *begins to wail)*

Hush! You want somebody to hear us? Come after us?

LIZZIE: *(scratching at her skin)* What am I gonna do?

MICAH: Here. Use sand. (*she takes a handful of sand from the river bottom, and rubs her arms with it*)

LIZZIE: Ow! That hurts!

MICAH: You keep workin'. It'll come clean.

(JUBAL *emerges silently from the shadows behind them and then disappears.*)

LIZZIE: (*as she works away with the sand*) It's never comin' off … (*then, softly, realizing*) I'm a killer.

MICAH: Don't you say that …

LIZZIE: I'm a killer … You touch me, you die.

MICAH: (*pushing her down on her knees in the water*) You get down on your knees, you beg forgiveness …

LIZZIE: —You touch me … I'll kill you!

MICAH: Stop that! (*she slaps* LIZZIE)

LIZZIE: (*immediately angry*) How dare you!?

MICAH: You got to hold on, Lizzie … You hear me, child?

(*WE SEE a line of torches moving through the distant trees. WE HEAR the sound of men marching.*)

LIZZIE: (*suddenly embracing* MICAH) Don't leave me, Micah. Please. I need you.

(*LIGHTS SHIFT and FOCUS on …*

The edge of the woods, the battlefield. Near dark.

The detritus of war litters the ground: powder packets, discarded ramrods, broken bayonets, pistols, muskets, boots, haversacks, hats, etc. The ground is littered with dead men in blue, grey and homespun. They lie together in the intimate embrace of death. JUBAL *forages among the dead, cuts the strap on a haversack, soaked with blood, struggles to pull it away from the dead soldier.*)

JUBAL: I swear the dead absorb the light. Drink it like the waters of absolution. (*picking the soldier's pocket*) Combs, watches, letters, greenbacks worth somethin'.

I kneel down.

I'm not here to pray.

Kneel beside them

The earth slips soft under my knees

The earth already claiming them

They melt in the darkness

Were these once men? Boys?

 (hears a groan)

 Who's there?!

Don't you go reachin' out to me.

Ghosts of men.

I got work to do here.

No time for you. No time for you.

Don't cry to me, cry to heaven.

I can't hear your voices crying in the dark

I can't hear you.

I can't hear nothing anymore.

(LIGHTS SHIFT and FOCUS on . . .

Another part of the battlefield.

We SEE fires burning on the hillside.

We SEE torches and lanterns moving in the dark and HEAR men calling for their fallen comrades.)

VOICES: *(o.s.)* Byron!

Daniel, for the love of God—are you out there?

Daniel? Daniel, answer me!

Sullivan!

Jeff Hicks!

Wheeler!

Daniel!

 (MICAH *forages among the dead for clothes. She struggles to pull the jacket off a dead soldier.* LIZZIE, *in her wet shift, begins to shiver.)*

MICAH: Help me . . . (LIZZIE *ignores her*) We got to get some clothes . . . *(still not helping)* Help me . . . *(struggling)*

LIZZIE: Does it always look like this? Men thick as leaves.

MICAH: Don't go over there, girl. That ditch is clotted with the dead.

LIZZIE: Some of 'em are still alive, Micah! Can't you hear them groaning and calling out?

MICAH: Don't you go over there! There's too many, Lizzie. Too many to believe.

LIZZIE: How can we still be alive when everything . . . everyone . . .

MICAH: God's done let us live, Lizzie.

LIZZIE: I can't listen to them dying. I can't stand it!

MICAH: We'll get us some clothes and then we'll be movin' on.

LIZZIE: Now, Micah.

VOICES: Mama . . .
Mama . . .
Over here . . .
Over this way.
Over here.
I'm begging you.
Water . . .
Water . . .
Why don't you do somethin'?
Why don't you?
Over here . . .
Over this way.
Over here.
Mama . . .
Mama!
Help me!
Help me!

MICAH: You help me here.

LIZZIE: Oh God, Oh God. They're talkin' to us, Micah. Can't you hear them?

MICAH: In the name of Jesus, you are a trial, girl. You come on and help me . . .

LIZZIE: —You come on and go with me.

MICAH: Soon as we get some clothes.

LIZZIE: I'll get some directly—(points)—over there—where I can't hear these dyin' boys crying for their mamas. Micah, for once will you do what I'm tellin' you?

(They move off, further away from the ditch and the sound of the dying men. Again, MICAH struggles to get a jacket off a dead soldier.)

Is this how my daddy died?

MICAH: No good's gonna come from that kind of talk. Now, lend me a hand . . .

LIZZIE: Where are they now? Are their souls still here?

MICAH: Come over here . . .

LIZZIE: Heaven must be fit to bust.

MICAH: Lizzie . . .

LIZZIE: I bet they ain't all in heaven, either.

MICAH: Help me . . .

LIZZIE: I can't . . .

MICAH: Yes, you can.

LIZZIE: I can't touch him.

MICAH: He's not gonna bite you . . .

LIZZIE: He's dead, Micah!

MICAH: What kinda idiot you take me for? I know that!

(MICAH *gets the jacket off the soldier.* LIZZIE *holds out her hand, expecting* MICAH *to give her the jacket. Instead,* MICAH *slips the jacket on and hugs herself in its warmth.*)

LIZZIE: What are you doing?

MICAH: What's it look like I'm doing? Gettin' me a jacket.

LIZZIE: What about me?

MICAH: Help yourself. There's plenty to go around.

LIZZIE: Gimme yours. You can get another one.

(Micah shakes her head, no)

What're you doin' sayin' no to me like that?

MICAH: Nothin'.

LIZZIE: You think 'cause we're not home anymore you don't have to treat me right?

MICAH: I'm treatin' you fine.

LIZZIE: No, you ain't. You ain't doin' what I tell you.

MICAH: I don't have to do what you tell me no more.

LIZZIE: Yes, you do!

MICAH: I don't have to stand here and argue with you neither.

LIZZIE: Is that right?

MICAH: That's right.

LIZZIE: *(a beat)* Well, you look ridiculous.

MICAH: Thank you.

LIZZIE: Like some hillbilly jackass.

MICAH: Well, you ain't seen yourself lately, little princess.

LIZZIE: You really gonna wear that?

MICAH: Well, I ain't plannin' on travellin' through these woods with two armies stumbling about in my shift, like you.

(LIZZIE *collects her courage, kneels, begins to unbutton the soldier's shirt. As she struggles with his dead weight,* MICAH *stoops to help her. She hands* LIZZIE *the shirt.)*

LIZZIE: *(Pulls the shift over her head, then pulls the shirt on. Amazed:)* It's nearly new . . .

MICAH: *(looking around)* And all these Union boys, they still got boots. *(she pulls his boots off)*

LIZZIE: Everything they got looks like it just come out of a box.

MICAH: Help me with his pants.

LIZZIE: Micah, no . . .

MICAH: What did you think you were gonna wear?

LIZZIE: He'll be naked. *(she giggles)*

MICAH: Nearly.

LIZZIE: I ain't never seen a naked man before.

MICAH: Never?

LIZZIE: Never.

MICAH: Well, here's your chance . . .

LIZZIE: How old you think he is?

MICAH: Seventeen . . . eighteen, maybe.

LIZZIE: *(pulling the pants on, looking at the soldier)* He looks so . . .

MICAH: Here. Use this rope to tie up your pants. We'll find you a jacket by and by. *(pause)*

LIZZIE: Why'd you name your baby Elizabeth?

That's my name.

MICAH: I know that.

LIZZIE: You named her after me?

MICAH: I can't tell if you're glad or takin' offense.

LIZZIE: I can't either.

MICAH: It's a beautiful name, is all. No harm meant. *(a beat)*

LIZZIE: I'm sorry about what happened . . . Oh, Micah. Didn't they tell us the Yankees were devils . . .

MICAH: Wouldn't I like to shoot one of those Yankee sons of bitches; but that won't answer. Won't answer nothin'.

LIZZIE: You think you could do that? Kill somebody?

MICAH: They make killin' look simple as breathin'.

LIZZIE: *(a beat)* You think God's turned his back on us?

MICAH: *(teasing)* On you, maybe . . .

LIZZIE: I ain't foolin'.

MICAH: I believe God's got a plan for us.

LIZZIE: *(skeptical)* Just for us?

MICAH: I believe he's gonna lead his people out of slavery. *(silence)* Which way you think is North?

LIZZIE: I got no idea.

MICAH: Which way you think the army's goin'?

LIZZIE: Don't know.

MICAH: Be nice if one of us knew something . . . *(pause)* In all my life I never once left that farm.

LIZZIE: I've never been further than Brice's Crossroads.

MICAH: I think we need to find a place to hide 'til morning. Then we can get our bearings and figure out what to do.

LIZZIE: We could follow the stars.

(they both look up)

MICAH: Which one?

LIZZIE: How should I know?

MICAH: What do they teach you in that school of yours?

LIZZIE: Not one single thing that applies in this situation, I can tell you that . . . *(sits, suddenly exhausted, a kid again)* I want to go home.

MICAH: There's nothing left . . .

LIZZIE: You don't know that for sure. Maybe we could find . . . Maybe we could find . . .

MICAH: —What?!

LIZZIE: I don't know! I just can't believe . . .

MICAH: You believe it. And you leave it all behind.

LIZZIE: I can't . . .

MICAH: We're gonna get out of here. We're gonna be all right.

LIZZIE: You think so? You think there's still someplace on earth where things are all right?

MICAH: If we can live long enough to get there.

LIZZIE: It don't exist. Every damn thing's broken. Far as the eye can see.

MICAH: —What did he do to you?

LIZZIE: Leave me alone!

(She heads into the woods. MICAH *grabs her, pulls her close.* LIZZIE *lashes out.)*

MICAH: *(shoves Lizzie away; she falls on her butt)* I don't know what you're fighting me for . . .

LIZZIE: *(suddenly fighting tears)* Where were you?

MICAH: I told you . . .

LIZZIE: Worthless! You're worthless . . .

MICAH: *(kneels beside her)* Come on . . . come on . . . I'm here now. I'm here now. You're gonna be all right.

LIZZIE: I'm never gonna be all right. I hurt so bad, Micah.

MICAH: *(rocking her)* I know, baby. I know . . .

LIZZIE: *(fighting tears)* What're we supposed to do? Where are we supposed to go?

MICAH: Shhhh . . . *(a beat)*

LIZZIE: I want to go home. I want to sit in Papa's rocker and pretend he's still alive. I want to eat your cornbread smothered in honey and butter. I want to eat a roast chicken every darn Sunday. I even want to go to church. Back when there were still some boys sittin' in the pews. And we had coats and hats and shoes and gloves. And some of 'em even matched.

MICAH: I want my Luther singin' and dreamin' . . . and promisin' me half a dozen babies . . . And a wooden floor like you got in your house.

LIZZIE: He promised you that?

MICAH: He did.

LIZZIE: We'll go back. We'll go back one day. . . . And I will feel how glad I am it is that day—a new day—and not this day, not this day. *(she closes her eyes)* I'll walk into the yard. And the house—God, Micah, they didn't burn the house after all—nor kill nobody neither—and I'll walk across the yard in the spring sun . . . And there's Mama. Look! There's Mama standing in the yard, watching me come.

MICAH: *(trying to distract her from her grief)* Come on. We got to get you lookin' like a boy. So nobody's gonna touch you. Let me see you, there. Turn around.

(hands her a cap)

Put this on . . .

LIZZIE: No . . .

MICAH: Just do it . . . (LIZZIE *puts the cap on)* Wouldn't your ma have a fit if she could see you now?

LIZZIE: I don't like you bein' so bossy all of a sudden.

MICAH: You might pass. We should cut your hair.

LIZZIE: No! You ain't touchin' one single hair on my head.

MICAH: Tomorrow maybe . . . You look all right.

LIZZIE: Why are you the only one left? Not my mama, not my daddy, not my brothers. You . . .

MICAH: Why are you the only one left? Not my mama, not my Luther, not my baby. You . . .

LIZZIE: You're not allowed to talk to me like that . . .

MICAH: Like what?

LIZZIE: Like you think you're somebody . . .

MICAH: What do you think I am, Lizzie? One step up from a mule?

LIZZIE: I didn't mean that.

MICAH: What did you mean?

LIZZIE: You got your place.

MICAH: And what place is that?

LIZZIE: Same place you've always had.

MICAH: That place is gone, Lizzie. Or ain't you noticed?

LIZZIE: You're not believin' all that Yankee truck? Freedom this, freedom that, freedom to burn my house, freedom to kill your baby? Freedom to be lost, to be hungry? Well, la dee dah, your freedom don't look like much to me.

MICAH: You got no earthly idea what it looks like to me . . .

LIZZIE: —Is that right?

MICAH: You ain't never seen me, Lizzie, for who I am.

LIZZIE: I know who you are.

MICAH: You been walkin' around blind your whole life. Just like your mama before you.

LIZZIE: Don't you drag my mama into this . . .

MICAH: Your daddy such a good man. Your mama such a good woman . . . Well, I ain't your nigger and I ain't your daddy's nigger no more . . .

LIZZIE: Then why are you still here?

MICAH: For a smart girl you work damn hard at being stupid.

LIZZIE: What are you talking about?

MICAH: You honest to God don't know?

LIZZIE: If I knew, why would I be askin' you?

MICAH: I'm your sister, you little fool.

LIZZIE: No, you're not!

MICAH: Suit yourself.

LIZZIE: I don't believe you.

MICAH: You think I don't know what you've been through?

LIZZIE: I am not your sister!

MICAH: I heard you the first time.

LIZZIE: You're lying.

MICAH: I wish I was.

LIZZIE: My daddy never did that. You are filled with lies and ugliness. I'd rather die than be called kin to you.

MICAH: Your daddy . . .

LIZZIE: *(covers her ears)* Don't!

MICAH: My mama had three children for your daddy . . .

LIZZIE: —No! . . .

MICAH: And when I was 14 . . .

LIZZIE: Stop. Stop . . . !

MICAH: Just about your age . . .

LIZZIE: My daddy . . . Oh, God . . .

MICAH: He'd been waiting on me . . .

LIZZIE: That's my daddy . . .

MICAH: I could feel him waiting . . .

LIZZIE: *(she picks up her musket, begins to back away)*—I'm warning you . . .

MICAH: I was not sorry to see your daddy go to war. *(she levels the musket at* MICAH*)* You gonna shoot me for telling you the truth? I didn't make it happen, Lizzie. He was a grown man. It was his habit. *(a beat)*

What do you think it was like for me as a little girl seein' your daddy come into our cabin for my Mama? And what do you think it was like for my Mama havin' to see your daddy come into our cabin for me?

*(*LIZZIE *tries to pull back the hammer)*

Go ahead and shoot. Maybe killing's the only thing your family ain't already done to mine . . .

LIZZIE: *(she is shaking)* I can't—No, I can't . . .

(she turns and runs away)

MICAH: Lizzie!!! . . . Lizzie!!! Go ahead and get lost in these woods, if that's what you want. I ain't comin' after you. You hear me?! I ain't your keeper, you stubborn little mule. You is on your own. Too bad you don't know nothin' about stayin' alive in these woods . . . Damnation! You are a trial . . .

(MICAH *moves deeper into the woods, looking for food among the dead soldiers. A harvest moon is rising. She shoos away foraging birds. The sound of their wings is ominous.*

WE HEAR a riderless horse picking its way among the dead. The horse shies when the birds take flight. WE HEAR it snort, trot away, empty stirrups jangling.

A hand closes around MICAH *'s ankle. She screams.*)

JACK: Help me.

MICAH: Turn me loose.

JACK: Help me.

MICAH: I can't help you.

JACK: For the love of God.

MICAH: You're gonna die here.

JACK: I am not!

MICAH: Just like everybody else.

JACK: Lift me up.

MICAH: You turn me loose, I'll lift you up. *(He lets go of her leg. She hauls him to a seated position, his back against a tree.)*

JACK: You're gonna help me . . .

MICAH: I don't have time to fool with you. *(she forages through a dead man's haversack)*

JACK: *(hearing her)* What are you doing?

MICAH: *(finds hardtack, begins to eat)* He don't need it no more.

JACK: It's not right.

MICAH: It ain't right I'm hungry either.

JACK: It's disrespectful.

MICAH: So I should show my respect by starving to death?

JACK: I didn't say that.

MICAH: You never relieved a dead boy of his musket or ammunition or hardtack?

JACK: That's different.

MICAH: I don't think so.

JACK: Hand me my canteen.

MICAH: Get it yourself.

JACK: I can't reach it 'cause I can't see it.

MICAH: Why not?

JACK: Blood's gummed up my eyes.

MICAH: Shoot! You been shot in the head? You're not gonna make it for sure.

JACK: Could you—?

MICAH: No.

JACK: I think maybe if I get this blood out of my eyes I'll be able to see.

MICAH: See what?

JACK: See my way out of here. *(pause)*

MICAH: Alright. I'm gonna take care of your eyes. Then I'm goin'. You got that?

JACK: As long as I can see I'll be fine. *(she kneels beside him, opens a canteen, soaks a rag and bathes his eyes)*
Take it easy.

MICAH: Hold still.

JACK: Take it easy!

MICAH: You're makin' this mighty difficult. *(pause)* Lord! You're a blasted mess.

JACK: And you are a comfort and a balm.

MICAH: *(sits back on her heels)* Well, now you can see the horse-man when he comes for you.

JACK: What horseman?

MICAH: You know what horseman.

JACK: I swear I don't.

MICAH: Well, then, maybe it's the Devil comin' for you . . .

JACK: You've seen this horseman?

MICAH: Many a time. Ridin' through these fields.

JACK: Somebody oughta drive that son of a bitch out of here.

MICAH: Well, it ain't gonna be you. That's for sure.

JACK: You are some angel of mercy.

MICAH: I'm no angel.

JACK: That is correct. Are you done?

MICAH: I'm done.

JACK: You sure?

MICAH: I'm sure.

JACK: *(turning his head)* Can you see me?

MICAH: Well, what do you think?

JACK: I mean it's not so dark you can't see me?

MICAH: I can see you pretty clear.

JACK: Because I can't see you. *(pause)* Are you sure you got it all? *(terrified, he grabs the rag, wipes his eyes)*

MICAH: I'm sure. *(pause)* You can't see nothin'? *(he can't speak)* Maybe you just need some time. Maybe by tomorrow morning . . . *(silence)* Maybe you gotta get up, standin' on your feet, movin' around. Get the blood flowin' and then maybe your sight'll come clear. Here. Put your arm around my neck. *(With* MICAH's *help he manages to stand. He is woozy and unsteady.)* Alright. You alright there?

JACK: Just dizzy, that's all.

MICAH: Hold on to me. You think you can take a step?

JACK: I can do it. *(he stumbles, she supports him)*

MICAH: All right . . .

JACK: Hold still!

MICAH: What did you say?

JACK: I said, hold still, damn it!! I am trying to get my balance . . .

MICAH: You ain't my lord and master, mister.

JACK: You'll do what I tell you.

MICAH: *(She steps away from him. Unsteady, he sinks to the ground.)* I ain't your slave.

JACK: You are gonna do what I tell you for whatever reason you want, because I am not gonna die here.

MICAH: Is that right?

JACK: That's right.

MICAH: You think I can't say no to you? You think I ain't got the right to say no to you?

JACK: I could have you put in chains . . .

MICAH: You'd need some help . . .

JACK: Damn it! Will you just do what I'm telling you?

MICAH: I ain't your dog you can kick one minute, caress the next.

JACK: *(he pulls his pistol)* You get over here and take care of my arm . . .

MICAH: Is that supposed to scare me?

JACK: I'm not afraid of hurting you to get what I need.

MICAH: You can't even see me . . .

(She takes a step away. He fires a shot just past her shoulder, startling her.)

JACK: You want to live, you're going to do exactly what I tell you. You hear me? Get busy, girl. You wash this wound. You wash it good. I am not gonna lose my arm. *(pause)* What're you waiting for?

MICAH: There's no more water in this canteen. And I need soap. And some rags.

JACK: Can you see a canteen, or a haversack nearby?

MICAH: *(looks)* Yes.

JACK: How far?

MICAH: A ways.

JACK: Three paces? Five?

MICAH: Three.

JACK: Are there any guns on the ground?

MICAH: *(looks again)* No.

JACK: Are you lying?

MICAH: You're gonna have to take your chances.

JACK: Don't move until I tell you. You take three paces. You reach for whatever canteen and all you can find. Now, listen to me. You take four paces and I'm gonna cripple you. Hurt you bad enough you can't run, not so bad you can't help me. You understand me?

MICAH: I understand you.

JACK: Move slow.

MICAH: *(she moves three paces, reaches a canteen and haversack)* If you let me take one more step I can reach another canteen.

JACK: Go ahead. Now come on back slow. *(she does)* Is there water?

MICAH: Some.

JACK: Rags?

MICAH: Yes.

JACK: Soap?

MICAH: No.

JACK: Whiskey?

MICAH: No.

JACK: Shit.

MICAH: You thirsty?

JACK: Cleans better than water. Take a look at my head first.

MICAH: *(probing the wound)* It nicked your eyebrow and made a ridge clear along the side of your head. Looks like maybe there's some shot deep buried. Musta knocked you cold.

JACK: I don't remember.

MICAH: *(she peels back his blood-soaked shirt sleeve; the wound is appalling)* Well, mister, you are forevermore a mess.

JACK: How bad is it?

MICAH: You got a hole in your arm. Looks like the ball went straight through.

JACK: The bone must've shattered. You feel any splinters?

MICAH: *(probing the wound)* I don't like puttin' my hands inside your body. Don't seem right.

JACK: Take a rag and make a tourniquet to stop the bleeding while you clean it. *(she tears a piece of cloth)* Tie it tight.

MICAH: All right.

JACK: Tight. *(she ties the knot with vigor)* Ow!

MICAH: How's that?

JACK: Get on with it.

MICAH: Some light would be nice. My mind pictures this hole in you big as a silo. *(she begins to clean the wound; he winces and pulls away)* Hold still!

JACK: Jesus!

MICAH: Hurts?

JACK: *(through clenched teeth)* Some.

MICAH: Don't hold your breath. That makes it worse. *(pause)*

JACK: What's your name?

MICAH: What's yours?

JACK: Jack. Jack Walker. You gonna tell me your name?

MICAH: I ain't givin' you nothin' I don't have to.

JACK: You about done, Miss No-Name?

MICAH: Almost.

JACK: *(in pain)* God damn it!

MICAH: That's as clean as I can get it. Maybe come mornin', they'll come lookin' for you. Bring you to a surgeon to tend this right. *(she unties the tourniquet)*

JACK: They're not coming back. Sherman's moving too fast for the dead and the wounded.

MICAH: They can't just . . .

JACK: They wouldn't stop for Christ himself . . . *(he nudges her with the gun)* Get me some water.

(She stands, as if to obey, then grabs the barrel of the gun and yanks it out of his hand.)

Shit . . .

MICAH: I got a hard time decidin' how many places to shoot you. In the face for my Luther. In the chest for my Mama. Shoot off both your hands for my baby . . .

JACK: —Go ahead and pull that trigger; Shoot me in the head, though. Make it quick.

MICAH: Are you the Devil himself tempting me to this sin?

JACK: That's right. I'm the Devil himself. Do the world a favor . . . *(a beat)* You can't do it, can you? When it comes right down to it, you're as good for nothing as they say you are . . .

(she squeezes the trigger, the chamber is empty)

MICAH: *(she steps away from him, staggered by what she's almost done)* Oh, my God . . . *(a beat)*—You knew—!

JACK: Of course I knew . . . (MICAH *picks up a canteen and a haversack)* What are you doing?

(she turns to leave)

JACK: *(cont)* Wait . . . Wait !! I've got money. You want money? I'll give you everything I've got . . . *(frantically searches his pockets)*

MICAH: I don't want your money.

JACK: I'm asking you . . . I'm begging you . . . *(a beat)*

You won't last the night in these woods. You'll be strung up before daylight . . .

(Without warning, she swings the butt of the pistol, hard, against his head. WE HEAR the thunk of wood on bone and JACK *collapses. She puts the gun in her waistband and walks off. At the edge of the clearing she stops to look back at* JACK. *He is unmoving.*

SHE EXITS

FADE TO BLACK)

END OF ACT I

ACT II

(Deep in another part of the woods. The light is ghostly. Shadows are menacing; they move, contort, dissolve. The trees are so dense you can't see the sky. A low ground fog drifts and swirls. This was the scene of a grisly battle. It is a charnel house. Dead men dot the ground. Tree trunks are blasted. An owl hoots. Crows caw. Birds grow bold and feed on the dead. The sound of their wings is menacing. LIZZIE, *lost, enters. As the fog shifts, more and more horrors are revealed to her. She begins to cross the battlefield, sees a dead man, turns quickly, slips in blood-soaked grass, falls, groans, gets up as quickly as she can.)*

LIZZIE: No ... Oh ... God! ... darn ... damn! ... Damn! *(She hears a sound. Stops. Listens intently. The owl hoots again.)* Who's there? Who's there?! *(She picks up her musket, turns, peering into the dark. WE HEAR her frightened, ragged breathing. She moves toward a tree, looking for cover.*

JUBAL *appears out of the mist. He is barefoot, ragged. His uniform—or what's left of it—is homespun. He wears the results of his foraging—an officer's long gray coat with two bars on the collar. The coat is stiff and crusted with blood and has a big ragged hole in the back. A pair of shoes are slung over his shoulder by the laces. He carries a soldier's haversack with a cornet tied to the side.)*

JUBAL: You lost?

LIZZIE: *(raising the gun)* You touch me, you're dead.

JUBAL: Everybody's dead. Everybody.

LIZZIE: Turn around and git back to where you come from.

JUBAL: You lost?

LIZZIE: I ain't lost.

JUBAL: Then what're you doin' here?

LIZZIE: None of your business. *(points the gun)* Git!

JUBAL: I can track anything. Deer. Possum. Bear. You.

LIZZIE: So?

JUBAL: You stink.

LIZZIE: *(she sniffs inside her shirt)* You don't smell so sweet yourself.

JUBAL: Some animals don't leave no tracks. Just a scent. You I found 'cause you stink.

LIZZIE: Would you quit that?

JUBAL: There's a living man in here.

LIZZIE: I don't think so.

JUBAL: And I'm gonna find him. Same way I found you. *(he taps his nose)*

LIZZIE: I saw a body out there—draped over a fence, missin' his whole left side and so blood-soaked I couldn't say whether he's Union or Confederate or a butchered hog.

JUBAL: I seen it.

LIZZIE: And boys everywhere dyin' and callin' out and some of 'em reachin' out to me. I saw a man just strollin' along through those boys like it's a summer's day, shootin' anything that moved. *(reaches down, picks up a haversack)* I'll give you this you get me out of here.

JUBAL: What do I want with that?

LIZZIE: There's food inside. Maybe money.

JUBAL: *(points to her neck)* Gimme that . . .

LIZZIE: *(touches the locket at her throat)* No.

JUBAL: *(steps forward)* Pretty.

LIZZIE: *(raises gun)* Turn around and start walkin'.

JUBAL: You think I can't find you again?

LIZZIE: You come near me again, I'll kill you.

JUBAL: Maybe. Maybe not. *(he reaches toward her)*

LIZZIE: *(levels the gun at his chest)* Back off.

JUBAL: Yellow dress.

LIZZIE: What?

JUBAL: You got a yellow dress and raven hair and you walk like a cat with too many toes. I had a cat like that once.

LIZZIE: I don't have a yellow dress.

JUBAL: I can see it. Your hair floats out like wings around your head. Your feet leave tracks that fill with water. The soft earth holds a girl like you.

LIZZIE: What are you talking about?

JUBAL: I'm talking about who you are.

LIZZIE: Sure. You're some kind of expert. Sniff me out. Know who I am.

JUBAL: You got blood on you.

LIZZIE: *(startled, looks at her hands)* I do not!

JUBAL: Suit yourself.

LIZZIE: Can you get me out of here? Please, mister. I'm scared.

JUBAL: The dead are everywhere.

LIZZIE: I'm not dead. And you're not dead.

JUBAL: *(shouts)* Mister!

LIZZIE: Quit that!

JUBAL: Mister!!

LIZZIE: What are you doing?

JUBAL: Mister . . . !!

LIZZIE: *(an intense whisper)* Are you crazy? Quit that hollerin' . . . You want somebody to come after us??

JUBAL: Saved my life. I'm gonna find him . . .

LIZZIE: You get me out of here, I'll help you find him.

JUBAL: You don't know him.

LIZZIE: You help me, I'll help you. . . You know the way. We'll get to the river. I'll make us a fire. In the morning we'll find your friend.

JUBAL: Not my friend. Not yet.

LIZZIE: What's your name?

JUBAL: He's still breathing. I can't leave him out here—alive . . .

LIZZIE: There's nobody left alive out here.

JUBAL: Don't you say that! He may be waitin' to die, but he ain't dead yet. I can feel it.

LIZZIE: I'll take you to my house. It's a nice house. When's the last time you slept in a real bed?

JUBAL: I'm not leavin' him alone out here.

LIZZIE: When's the last time?

JUBAL: About never.

LIZZIE: There's quilts on the beds. Candles by the bedside. You come outta these woods with me.

JUBAL: You ain't got no house.

LIZZIE: I do, too!

JUBAL: Burned down around your ears today. That's part of your smell.

LIZZIE: How do you do that?

JUBAL: I'm just awake is all. Awake in my mind. You got a mama?

LIZZIE: Did have.

JUBAL: Papa?

LIZZIE: Died at Petersburg.

JUBAL: So you got nobody.

LIZZIE: I got me a slave woman. But according to Mister Lincoln she don't belong to me no more neither.

JUBAL: You know Mister Lincoln?

LIZZIE: What do you think? Mister Lincoln's sneaking down to Georgia to meet me, Miss Lizzie Peake? Bypasses Jeff Davis, General Lee and Stonewall Jackson to come straight to me?

JUBAL: Jackson's dead.

LIZZIE: I know that.

JUBAL: So what's Lincoln like? Is he as tall as they say?

LIZZIE: I never met him.

JUBAL: But you said . . .

LIZZIE: It was a joke.

JUBAL: But it wasn't funny.

LIZZIE: Says you.

JUBAL: How can you say it's funny? You weren't laughin' either.

LIZZIE: I was trying to be funny.

JUBAL: So you've never met him.

LIZZIE: No.

JUBAL: I thought you was tellin' the truth. I thought you was a truthful, you can count on me girl.

LIZZIE: I am.

JUBAL: Maybe not.

LIZZIE: I am.

JUBAL: Prove it.

LIZZIE: How?

JUBAL: You help me find Mister . . .

LIZZIE: —Mister Lincoln ain't here.

JUBAL: I know that. Another mister. You help me. He needs our help . . .

LIZZIE: What's your name?

JUBAL: I give you that maybe you know too much about me.

LIZZIE: It's just your name.

JUBAL: It's who I am, Miss Lizzie Peak.

LIZZIE: I'm gonna tell you something I never told another living soul.

JUBAL: Don't.

LIZZIE: So you can trust me again.

JUBAL: Gimme that locket.

LIZZIE: No!

JUBAL: Then tell me somethin' as pretty as that gold on your throat.

LIZZIE: What I got to tell you ain't pretty.

JUBAL: Then don't tell me. I don't want to carry your troubles.

LIZZIE: You are makin' this impossible.

JUBAL: I'll tell you what . . . *(untying the cornet)* You let me wear that gold—just for awhile—and I'll let you carry my music. Then we'll swap.

LIZZIE: I don't know.

JUBAL: Then we'll go find Mister.

LIZZIE: How do I know you ain't gonna take my mama's locket and run off on me?

JUBAL: You got my music.

LIZZIE: Maybe it don't really mean nothin' to you . . .

JUBAL: You look at me . . .

LIZZIE: So?

JUBAL: Now you look at that cornet. *(she looks)* Don't fit, does it? Looks like it comes from a whole other world.

LIZZIE: Where'd you get it?

JUBAL: Found it. Only stroke of good luck I ever had.

LIZZIE: If we swap it's just for awhile.

JUBAL: I swear it. Just for awhile.

(She takes off the locket, hands it to JUBAL. *He fumbles with the*

clasp. She fastens it around his neck. He touches the gold with delight. Then, with ceremony, he hands her the cornet. She holds it in both her hands.)

LIZZIE: Can you play this thing?

JUBAL: That's my gift.

LIZZIE: What're you talking about?

JUBAL: You think I'm stupid. Backwoods, barefoot stupid.

LIZZIE: I never said that.

JUBAL: I can see it in your eyes.

LIZZIE: I never thought that.

JUBAL: Now you're lyin' again.

LIZZIE: When are you gonna tell me your name?

JUBAL: What's your gift, Miss Lizzie Peake?

LIZZIE: I don't have one.

JUBAL: Everybody's got one. God don't stint.

LIZZIE: Then I ain't found it yet.

JUBAL: You been lookin'?

LIZZIE: *(holds out the cornet)* Let me hear you play.

JUBAL: *(doesn't take it)* You trust me to wear the gold and hold the music?

LIZZIE: I trust you.

JUBAL: Is that smart?

LIZZIE: I think so. *(he takes the cornet)* And I know you're not stupid. Strange, maybe, but not stupid.

JUBAL: I'm beginning to see that yellow dress again.

LIZZIE: There is no yellow dress.

JUBAL: When I start to like you I can see that yellow dress.

LIZZIE: Play.

JUBAL: I play for you. And then we find Mister. Deal? *(he spits on the ground)*

LIZZIE: Deal. *(she spits on the ground, takes her heel rubs the spit together)*

(JUBAL plays. It's so beautiful it's otherworldly. Transporting.

LIZZIE *closes her eyes, hugs herself and sways to the music. She lifts her arms, as though she has a partner, and begins to dance.* JUBAL *responds by playing faster, a jig or a reel.* LIZZIE *dances on, in a moment of pure joy, until she stops, suddenly shy, breathless.)*

LIZZIE: That's . . .

JUBAL: —Don't name it, girl. Let it live a bit before you tie it down. *(he gives her back the cornet)*

LIZZIE: How do you do that?

JUBAL: I don't know. Maybe I play all the things I got no words for.

LIZZIE: *(touching it with new feeling now that she's experienced its magic)* Can you teach me?

JUBAL: Can you learn?

LIZZIE: I'm pretty quick.

JUBAL: It ain't easy.

LIZZIE: I'm pretty stubborn.

JUBAL: Maybe.

LIZZIE: Who taught you?

JUBAL: I ain't been properly taught. I just picked it up.

LIZZIE: Just like that?

JUBAL: It took some time. You wanna try it?

LIZZIE: Can I? *(she takes the cornet, blows into it: nothing)*

JUBAL: A little more air. *(blows again, with all her might: a SPLAT of sound)* See what I mean?

LIZZIE: *(handing it back to him)* I could do it. If you give me a chance, and some time, I could do it.

JUBAL: Maybe you could.

LIZZIE: You gonna tell me your name now?

JUBAL: Jubal Haley.

LIZZIE: *(they shake hands)* Pleased to meet you.

JUBAL: You really never met Mister Lincoln?

LIZZIE: Never.

JUBAL: You made it sound like you did.

LIZZIE: I like stories. I make things up sometimes.

JUBAL: Next time you make one up for me, you tell me, so I know.

LIZZIE: All right.

JUBAL: Don't make a fool outta me, Miss Lizzie Peake. I don't like it.

LIZZIE: Will you accept my humble apology, Mr. Jubal Haley?

JUBAL: *(nods)* Accepted.

LIZZIE: Now who's Mister?

JUBAL: He saved my life.

LIZZIE: How?

JUBAL: Looked me straight in the face and didn't pull the trigger. I'm out of ammunition. He sees that. I'm a dead man looking down the barrel of Mister Yankee's gun. Lookin' straight in my eyes, no smell of fear on him, and he don't shoot. The boy behind me shot him. I saw the ball rip right through his arm and then we were over their works. They're in retreat. Rebels swarming everywhere. Picking up Yankee guns, picking up Yankee ammunition. And he's lying there, near to dead, or close enough to look it.

LIZZIE: Wait a minute. You are lookin' for some Yankee?

JUBAL: That's right.

LIZZIE: *(still can't believe it)* You want to help some Yankee.

JUBAL: That's right.

LIZZIE: You been shaken up once too often, Jubal Haley. You've gone plumb crazy.

JUBAL: He saved my life.

LIZZIE: And took how many others?

JUBAL: You don't understand . . .

LIZZIE: Why does everybody always say that to me? I understand plenty.

JUBAL: I'm gonna find him.

LIZZIE: He's probably dead.

JUBAL: No. He's crawled off somewheres to die. Into the trees, into the dark. *(taps his nose)* We're gonna find him.

(He moves into the woods. LIZZIE *hesitates, then follows.*
LIGHTS SHIFT and come up on . . .
MICAH, *crouching by the unmoving* JACK. *She watches him for a moment, then reaches out and touches him.)*

MICAH: Is you still alive, Mister? Or have I killed you for sure? *(pause)* I went lookin' for my Lizzie. In less than half a mile I am lost. And I'm seein' things I don't want to see, don't want to remember, don't want to believe are even possible. And I'm thinkin'—she is lost—my God, lost forever . . . Some crazy renegade gonna take her up—terrify her—leave her for dead . . . I let her go. How could I let her go? She's a child alone in these woods. There are crows everywhere. Feedin' on the dead. Bold as brass.

And I come across a man—a slave man—tied to a fence. Beaten beyond sense and left to die. Flies feasting on his blood. I wanted to untie him, lay him down, lay him to rest, close his staring eyes. His skin is gray in the moonlight. Gray where there's no blood. His head tipped forward—like he's under a yoke—or like his neck's been snapped on its stem. I want to be brave enough to touch him, untie him, lay him down. But I'm shakin' and cryin' and ready to wail in the night air . . .

When I hear somethin' movin' in the dark. Slow and steady. Who's out there in that darkness? Is somebody followin' me? Will they snap my neck and tie me to a tree to die?

And then I hear the soldiers. Marchin'. They canteens bangin' with every step. I run off. I run off to hide. I ain't found my Lizzie. That child . . . if she dies it's my fault. I should of . . . should of . . . And you . . . what I done to you . . . how am I any different, any different at all . . . *(pause)*

JACK: You come back to finish me off?

MICAH: Jesus, Lord, I thought you . . .

JACK: —No such luck. *(a beat)* Is there any water?

MICAH: *(hands him a canteen)* Not much . . .

JACK: *(drinks with intense thirst)* Can you get more?

MICAH: That crick is clotted with the dead. The water's red. Even in the moonlight.

JACK: We'll find some. By and by. *(a beat)* You still there?

MICAH: I'm right here.

JACK: Jesus, my head . . .

MICAH: I am sorry I struck you.

JACK: No, you're not.

MICAH: I . . .

JACK: Don't let me fall asleep. I think if I fall asleep, I'll never wake up again.

MICAH: You need your rest . . .

JACK: Promise me . . .

MICAH: You're not bleedin' no more. You'll get your strength back.

JACK: I have nightmares about losing my hands. I swear I'd rather die. How do I know you're not going to leave me again?

MICAH: You don't. *(a beat)*

JACK: Do you believe God is watching us?

MICAH: Don't ask me that this night . . .

JACK: I haven't been on my knees to God in two years. But I've been on my knees to kill more times than I can count.

MICAH: Mister . . .

JACK: —I wanted to die in this battle rather than live to fight and kill again. I swore I'd never kill another man. Sumner—Jesus. We've been together since the beginning. Survived Fredericksburg, goddamnit! Chancellorsville, Gettysburg, Cold Harbor. Kept rising from the dead. And I quit on him, gave him up. Left him wide open. *(pause)* I should have covered him. I just froze. Looking this Confederate boy straight in the face. And me choosing not to shoot. You can't do that. Sumner's behind me, counting on me, and I'm playing God, sparing this boy's life. Well, you don't get to choose like that. You don't get to choose. *(a beat)* You've got to get me up. I've got to bury him. *(he struggles to get up)*

MICAH: You ain't goin' anywheres tonight. *(she tries to cover him with his coat)*

JACK: *(pushing the coat away)* Don't!! I can't close my eyes. Don't you understand? Help me find him. Will you do that?

MICAH: It's the middle of the night, Mister . . .

JACK: —I can't stand the idea of him alone out there . . .

MICAH: There's so many boys, his soul is in the company of legions.

JACK: —I can't stand it—! I wish I believed in something; anything, anymore.

MICAH: Oh, Lord, yes.

JACK: Something to get me through this night.

MICAH: It's all over now.

JACK: Is it? All over? Jesus.

MICAH: Truth is, we are gonna carry this night forevermore. Won't nobody ever want to talk about it neither. What we saw tonight, what we did tonight, what we buried tonight. Don't I wish I could pray.

(WE HEAR a lone coyote howl and then several others join in. The chorus swells, then falls silent.)

JACK: I've been afraid before. You're terrified before a fight. You'd be an idiot not to be. The more you see, the longer you survive, the worse it gets. Your mind plays tricks on you to get you through. You fix your eye on the belt of the man in front of you—you curse the drummer behind you . . . And then you just go. In this burst of motion. Screaming and running. You just go. There's so many men, so much life all around you. It's like a wave. But this . . . this is different . . . quiet like and steady. Like the deepest shadows will open up and pull me down . . . I wish that damned sun would come up.

MICAH: I ain't afraid of the dark. I like the softness of it. I like the way the night air feels heavy in your hands, on your face, in your mouth. You can taste the moisture in it.

JACK: Maybe you'll let me touch your face . . .

MICAH: —Maybe I won't.

JACK: I won't hurt you . . . *(a beat)* I never . . .

MICAH: What?

JACK: Talked to or touched a nig . . . a negro . . . a . . . colored person . . .

MICAH: —Where on earth are you from?

JACK: Maine.

MICAH: Ain't that North?

JACK: Yes.

MICAH: Well, where are all the freedmen goin' then?

JACK: The big cities: Philadelphia, New York, Boston.

MICAH: There are no colored people in the entire state of Maine?

JACK: I never met one.

MICAH: God have mercy. Are you tellin' me the truth?

JACK: Yes.

MICAH: Is Maine some little itty bitty state?

JACK: Hardly.

MICAH: Does nothin' grow there?

JACK: Potatoes. Apples. Hardwood. Fish.

MICAH: And . . .

JACK: There are shipbuilders, ironmongers, quarrymen.

MICAH: And white men do the work?

JACK: Of course.

MICAH: If you hate the colored man so much why are you fightin' for Mister Lincoln?

JACK: I do not hate . . .

MICAH: —A whole entire state that's nothin' but white . . . ? Is that what it's like up North? They don't want us neither?

JACK: —Some people . . . Abolitionists—

MICAH: —How many of them you got in Maine?

JACK: You're getting the wrong idea . . .

MICAH: Am I? What's gonna happen to us, Mister?

JACK: I don't know. I'd be lying if I said I did know. *(a beat)* Let me touch your face . . .

MICAH: No . . . !

JACK: Then tell me your name.

MICAH: I don't think so.

JACK: Come on. I am trying to get to know you.

MICAH: Why?

JACK: Why not?

MICAH: That's a pretty sorry reason.

JACK: Because you're here and you're alive and in the midst of this open grave that seems like some kind of miracle.

MICAH: *(she takes his hand and puts it on her face)* Go on, then.

(WE HEAR a shot.)

JACK: *(pulling away)* What was that?

(WE HEAR another shot, then several more, in quick succession.)

We've got to get away from here . . .

MICAH: *(she helps him to his feet)* Take it easy. You're startin' to bleed again.

JACK: *(puts his hand to his head, it comes away bloody)* Shit.

MICAH: *(reaching for a rag)* Let me . . .

JACK: Leave it!

MICAH: Lord, you've got fever . . .

JACK: I'm fine. Let's go . . .

(They EXIT as . . .

LIGHTS SHIFT and FOCUS on . . .

JUBAL and LIZZIE, walking along the edge of the battlefield.

WE HEAR distant desultory drums, men marching.)

LIZZIE: What's that?

JUBAL: Another regiment.

LIZZIE: They've been movin' all night.

JUBAL: They say Sherman's got so many men they form a column 60 miles wide. Ain't nothin' left behind.

LIZZIE: I don't like hearing them movin' in the dark like that. Can't tell if they're dead or alive.

JUBAL: You hungry?

LIZZIE: You know somebody who isn't?

JUBAL: You got anything to eat?

LIZZIE: What do you think?

JUBAL: Not likely. *(indicates battlefield)* Those boys in there. They're ripe for the picking.

LIZZIE: I'm not goin' back in there.

JUBAL: I found me a few things. *(opens his haversack)*

LIZZIE: What've you got? *(Jubal spreads food out on top of his haversack)* There's blood on there.

(He breaks off the piece that's bloodied and throws it aside. Hands the rest to her.

She refuses.)

What else have you got?

JUBAL: You're too picky, girl. *(holds it out to her again)*

LIZZIE: *(takes the food)* Some dying boy bled all over this.

(tries to eat it) I can't eat this.

JUBAL: Then you're gonna starve. *(She takes a bite, chews, then gags when she tries to swallow. JUBAL thumps her on the back—way too hard—)*

LIZZIE: Quit that! *(He hands her his canteen. She drinks, chokes, coughs. The cough brings on her tears. She turns away, ashamed, trying to stop crying.)*

JUBAL: You all right?

LIZZIE: *(wiping her nose on her sleeve)* I'm fine. *(he looks at her)* It's nothing.

JUBAL: *(He digs a wizened apple out of his pack and hands it to her.)* Here. I've been saving this. You have it. *(She takes the apple, deftly splits it in two, handing half to JUBAL. They eat.)*

LIZZIE: Is it true the Yanks burned Atlanta?

JUBAL: Looked like the gates of hell.

LIZZIE: Were you there?

JUBAL: I never seen a city before in my life. And there it was. So big and so beautiful. Even in the fire. It's like the whole world was burning . . . the earth, the streets, the trees, even the sky. I know I shouldn't say it was beautiful. But it was something unearthly. You know how the preachers talk about the conflagration in Revelations and they make it sound so scary, like the

Devil's work is gonna be ugly. It's like they don't want us to know that the Devil's work has the power and the glory of God in it, too.

LIZZIE: We're gonna lose this war, aren't we?

JUBAL: There ain't nothing left to fight with.

LIZZIE: Everything I ever loved is buried in the ground or burned to the ground.

JUBAL: Everything?

LIZZIE: I got these . . . *(digs the earrings from her pocket)* And my locket. They were my mama's.

JUBAL: Nothing else?

LIZZIE: Not one damn thing.

JUBAL: Don't you have diamonds and such sewn in your skirts?

LIZZIE: Not even a skirt . . .

JUBAL: Sewn in your underdrawers then . . . *(he reaches for her waist, she recoils violently)*

LIZZIE: Don't touch me . . .

JUBAL: *(reaching for her again, playful)* Well, they gots to be someplace . . .

LIZZIE: DON'T . . .

JUBAL: I was only playing . . .

LIZZIE: I got nothing.

JUBAL: What about your slave woman?

LIZZIE: She's gone.

JUBAL: For good?

LIZZIE: For good.

JUBAL: Lizzie . . .

LIZZIE: She's nothing to me.

(LIGHTS SHIFT and FOCUS on . . .

JACK *and* MICAH. JACK'S *fever is getting worse.)*

JACK: Touch me . . .

MICAH: You're burning with fever . . .

JACK: Here. Put your hand inside my shirt.

MICAH: You're sick. I can't . . .

JACK: *(taking her hand)* Touch me . . . *(she puts her hand inside his shirt)* When you touch me I know I'm still alive. Don't you let me slip away.

MICAH: You're gonna be fine . . .

JACK: Don't lie to me! Can I have some water? *(she pulls the canteen close, shakes it)*

MICAH: It's empty . . .

JACK: I'm thirsty !

MICAH: I know.

JACK: You've got to find me some water.

MICAH: *(she picks up the other nearby canteens; they're all empty)* There's no water, Mister . . .

JACK: Damn it! You get to that crick . . .

MICAH: That water is foul . . .

JACK: I don't care—! Don't you understand?!

MICAH: It's the fever makin' you thirsty . . .

JACK: Find me some water. Please . . .

MICAH: There ain't no water. Close your eyes, take a breath.

JACK: *(closing his eyes)* I can't see a thing unless I close my eyes. I close my eyes and I see stars. I'm not making sense, am I? I'm raving like some damned idiot—

MICAH: You're fine.

JACK: *(scared)* I'm not fine!

MICAH: Ssshhh. I'm right here. Just close your eyes again. What do you see now?

JACK: *(laughs)* Dinner.

MICAH: I close my eyes and I see . . . I see my baby.

JACK: You got a baby?

MICAH: Baby girl.

JACK: Where is she?

MICAH: She died this morning.

JACK: My God . . .

MICAH: We were buried in the root cellar. I had my hand over her mouth to keep her quiet. Soldiers were stabbing the straw with their bayonets. And when that steel came flashing through the straw I lay on top of her. I thought I could shelter her with my body.

JACK: Tell me your name . . .

MICAH: I wish you could see my hands. I always thought my hands could keep my baby safe.

JACK: Put your hands on my head. Everything's spinning.

MICAH: *(holding his head, speaking to herself as much as to Jack)* These hands . . . These hands . . . Lord.

I was all alone when she was born.

I caught her with these hands

Held her with these hands

Buried her with these hands

And I buried my grief. Buried it deep

Cause I'm still gonna use these hands

You hear me, God? You hear me?!

God don't just take. No sir!

There's somethin' comin'

And I'm gonna hold on with these hands

I'm gonna hold on til it comes . . .

JACK: Please. Get me some water . . . I need some water . . .

(He starts to shiver with chills and fever. She pulls him to her as he shakes with fever. She rocks him, wipes his sweat-soaked face. Pause. She unbuttons her shirt, and pulls him to her breast. He drinks. Pause)

MICAH: Micah . . . My name is Micah.

(LIGHTS SHIFT and FOCUS on . . .

JUBAL *and* LIZZIE*)*

LIZZIE: Have you killed people?

JUBAL: I ain't proud of it.

LIZZIE: How many?

JUBAL: My share, I suppose.

LIZZIE: Up close?

JUBAL: Some.

LIZZIE: Could you see their faces?

JUBAL: Why are you asking me this?

LIZZIE: I killed a man today.

JUBAL: Why?

LIZZIE: He was in my house, stealing my mama's earrings and then . . .

JUBAL: Did he hurt you?

LIZZIE: He kissed me.

JUBAL: You killed him for kissing you?

LIZZIE: No . . . I . . . He smelled like fire and horses and leather and he seemed so lonely . . . He was touching my face and my neck and really looking at me like I was somebody, you know? And then . . . *(pause)* I took his pistol and shot him . . . I shot him in the neck, Jubal.

JUBAL: He hurt you.

LIZZIE: There was my pick of boys I was maybe supposed to marry. Even if they ain't already dead, not a one of 'em would ever want me now.

JUBAL: You don't know that for sure.

LIZZIE: There's nobody to take me in or take me up ever again. Nobody.

JUBAL: You got your land.

LIZZIE: No, I don't.

JUBAL: You the only one left?

LIZZIE: Yes.

JUBAL: Then it's yours.

LIZZIE: And how am I gonna prove that?

JUBAL: At least you got something to fight for, something to go back for, something to build on.

LIZZIE: I can't do that. I don't know the first thing about . . .

JUBAL: But you can learn.

LIZZIE: I don't think . . .

JUBAL: They're maybe deep buried now, but your family, girl, they're in that ground. You tend it, just a bit, they gonna rise up. You watch. Your mama's roses, they'll come back.

LIZZIE: Am I supposed to live on roses?

JUBAL: You never planted nothin' in your life?

LIZZIE: I never had to do that.

JUBAL: There's no shame in it. *(a beat)* If I kissed you right now would you shoot me?

LIZZIE: Don't try me.

JUBAL: I ain't never kissed a girl.

LIZZIE: In your life?

JUBAL: Never.

LIZZIE: I'd hate to die never having had the chance to love somebody. You ever think about that when you're fighting? All the things you might never get to do if you die?

JUBAL: You really can't think of anything at all. It's as though you become something else. Not really a man. Something else.

LIZZIE: I killed that boy. It could have been you. I killed him for my mama's earrings, I killed him for my daddy and my brothers dead in this war, for my house, for being hungry, for being scared, for touching me . . . I don't think he would've killed me. *(she kneels down)* I need you to say the words. *(she pulls on his hand to make him kneel)*

JUBAL: What words?

LIZZIE: Somethin' from the Bible. You pick.

JUBAL: I don't know . . .

LIZZIE: I need you to say a prayer and lay your hands on me and make me whole again. Can you do that?

JUBAL: You gonna let me touch you?

LIZZIE: I'm asking you to touch me, yes. *(he reaches out to caress her hair)* Not like that!

JUBAL: *(startled)* What other way is there?

LIZZIE: With a prayer.

JUBAL: *(shy, uncomfortable, he kneels in front of her)* I'm no preacher.

LIZZIE: You're all I've got, Jubal. *(she closes her eyes)*

JUBAL: I'm a little rusty.

LIZZIE: *(opens her eyes)* That's all right. *(closes her eyes again; pause)* Do you know one?

JUBAL: Of course I know one! *(takes a deep breath)* Our father . . .

LIZZIE: *(prompts)* Who art in heaven . . .

JUBAL: Gimme a minute! I know this! . . . Hallowed be this ground . . .

LIZZIE: —Thy name.

JUBAL: —Thy name . . . Thy kingdom come, thy will be done. On earth as it is in heaven.

LIZZIE: That's it . . .

JUBAL: Give us this day our daily bread, And forgive us our trespasses as we forgive those who trespass against us. Lead us not into . . .

LIZZIE: Temptation . . .

JUBAL: —I know it! . . . Temptation. But deliver us from evil. For thine is the kingdom and the power and the glory. Forever and ever. Amen.

LIZZIE: Amen. *(She opens her eyes. They are nearly nose to nose.)*

JUBAL: Now can I kiss you?

LIZZIE: No!

JUBAL: Why not?

LIZZIE: I don't feel any different.

JUBAL: Maybe words can't make you feel any different.

LIZZIE: You be him. And tell me you forgive me.

JUBAL: That ain't gonna work!

LIZZIE: Well, something has to work . . .

JUBAL: Maybe a kiss would work.

LIZZIE: A kiss is what got me into this mess.

JUBAL: I could die tomorrow . . .

LIZZIE: Fine! *(She offers him her cheek and closes her eyes. He sits back on his heels, doesn't kiss her. She opens her eyes.)* What's the matter, now?

JUBAL: I never knew my mama. I ain't never touched nor been touched by a girl or a woman in my life . . .

LIZZIE: *(very skeptical)* Didn't your daddy ever kiss you?

JUBAL: No!

LIZZIE: And you don't have a sister neither?

JUBAL: No.

LIZZIE: No aunts, no grandma, no kissing cousins?

JUBAL: Nobody. *(pause)*

LIZZIE: So I guess it's up to me.

JUBAL: I guess it is.

LIZZIE: You're unlucky in love. You should've got somebody who knew what she was doing.

JUBAL: I don't mind that it's you.

LIZZIE: Close your eyes, Jubal Haley, I'm gonna give you the kiss of peace. *(she moves toward him; he pulls back)*

JUBAL: If this is the only kiss I'm gonna get, I'd kinda like to see it.

LIZZIE: You are making this mighty difficult! What do you think you're gonna see, anyways?

JUBAL: I don't know. Maybe I just like lookin' at you.

LIZZIE: You hush or I'm not gonna do this.

JUBAL: I'm ready.

LIZZIE: All right. *(pause)*

JUBAL: I'm ready.

LIZZIE: *(she leans towards him, then pulls back)* I think maybe we need to stand up. *(they stand)* You put your arms like this . . . *(She places his hands on her waist. She puts her hands on his shoulders . . . he's looking straight in her eyes, waiting. A beat.)* If you don't mind, I think I'm gonna close my eyes.

JUBAL: I don't mind. *(she closes her eyes and kisses him on the lips*
(LIGHTS SHIFT and FOCUS on . . .
JACK *and* MICAH)

MICAH: I want so many children I can't hold 'em all. I got an ache in me the size of Georgia. My body don't know my baby's dead. You know what kind of hunger I'm talkin' about? In my chest, in my gut. I got hunger in the soles of my feet. I feel your hands on me and I think, child, child, give me a child. All the life in my body. All of it that I can feel so strong inside me. Did God set me free just to die here? Just when the sadness is like to drown me, when I want to crawl inside that ground beside my baby girl, I got this hunger, this hunger for touch like I never felt before. Like every sound, every breath, every smell, everything I see around me . . . Like I've never seen it before, like I've never felt anything before. Nothing like this, like this. I look at you. It would be so easy to hate you. But who are you? Who are you, that God should put you in my path? *(pause)*

JACK: It's different to what I thought . . . quieter . . . *(a beat)* It was always leading to this, wasn't it? No matter what we call it or how we laugh in death's teeth. Oh the lies we tell: We will survive. Our lives will mean something. We will go home. Fish on the banks of our rivers, court, marry, have children, work hard, grow old. It seems so simple, all of that, all of that . . . Just wanting to live . . .

(LIGHTS fade on JACK *and* MICAH *as . . .*

WE HEAR another regiment moving; the sound of hundreds of marching feet.

LIGHTS SHIFT and come up on . . .

The gray light of near dawn. JUBAL *and* LIZZIE *come upon* MICAH *and* JACK. *An owl flies overhead.)*

LIZZIE: That's her—!

JUBAL: Hush! You think I don't know that? *(*JUBAL *claps his hand over her mouth, silencing her, then pulls her away.)*

LIZZIE: Is that the man?

JUBAL: Will you hush?! *(he pulls her further away)*

LIZZIE: What do you suppose they're doing?

JUBAL: He's sick.

LIZZIE: How do you know?

JUBAL: *(turns her to face them)* Breathe.

LIZZIE: *(she breathes)* All right.

JUBAL: What do you smell?

LIZZIE: Something terrible.

JUBAL: That's them bodies. Breathe again.

LIZZIE: I don't want to do this . . .

JUBAL: Breathe the next layer. Can you smell the trees? The dew on the grass?

LIZZIE: Not too strong.

JUBAL: But it's there.

LIZZIE: It's there.

JUBAL: See if you can smell something sweet . . . too sweet. *(she nods her head)* That's his flesh gone bad.

LIZZIE: *(hitting him, scared)* I don't like this!

JUBAL: *(he licks his hands, then tries to smooth his hair)* How do I look?

LIZZIE: You look the same as always.

JUBAL: Do I look crazy? I don't want him to think I'm crazy.

LIZZIE: What are you talking about?

JUBAL: When he sees me . . . What can I give him, Lizzie? What can I give him that'll make a damned bit of difference now? You think he'll recognize me when he sees me? You think he'll believe me? Or you think he'll want to kill me—?

LIZZIE: How should I know? What's wrong with you all of a sudden?

JUBAL: I didn't think he'd have to die . . . I thought . . . I thought we'd sit awhile and talk . . . I thought I'd play for him . . . That's the only gift I've got . . . He saved my life and I got no gift for him. No gift that's big enough. Through all this death . . . Death in my eyes, in my mouth, under my feet . . . Through all this death, this never-ending death . . . He stopped. And right then I knew . . . It can stop, it can end. We can make it stop. We can make it stop. *(pause)*

I'm not goin' back. Will you still talk to me if I don't go back?

LIZZIE: Why wouldn't I? You afraid I'll think you're a coward?

JUBAL: It's not the honorable thing to do.

LIZZIE: I don't see much honor in killing people.

JUBAL: What if every soldier just up and walked away?

LIZZIE: Then this damned war would be over.

JUBAL: But the good men aren't walking away.

LIZZIE: You're a good man, Jubal.

JUBAL: I got ideas I never told nobody. I got dreams, even.

LIZZIE: Me, too.

JUBAL: Dreams of living on the river. Maybe build me a little houseboat. Plant kitchen crops right near the banks. And fish and track. Ride that river. Walk that land. Just my own square mile. Come to know it like I know my cornet. I got a hankering in me to play music. Maybe make things up. Drown out the sound of this war. Drifting on the river, dragging a line, and playing my cornet.

LIZZIE: Take me with you . . .

JUBAL: It's just a dream.

LIZZIE: I don't care. I can work. I can dig. I can plant. I can help you.

JUBAL: I don't even have me a half acre. Nor a hoe nor a mule. I ain't got nothing to make a life with, except for my two hands.

LIZZIE: What do you think I've got?

JUBAL: Some relation somewhere to take you in. Send you to school.

LIZZIE: I got nobody! And I don't want to go to school!—Why are you doing this?

JUBAL: What?

LIZZIE: You are getting ready to say goodbye to me.

JUBAL: *(looking at* MICAH *)* That's who you belong with.

LIZZIE: I do not! She's no kin to me!

JUBAL: Think about your daddy. And your mama. You think they'd like to see you setting out with me?

LIZZIE: What are you saying?

JUBAL: They built you a house, girl, and brought you up in it.

They taught you how to read and write, how to look at pictures, tell stories. They didn't bring you up to meet no backwoods conscript turned deserter. Did they? If they was here right now they'd have you running the other way.

LIZZIE: But they're not here . . . *(the sun begins to rise)*

JUBAL: Lizzie, everything is gonna change when that sun comes up.

LIZZIE: No, it's not!

JUBAL: There's not a soul on earth who'd let you come with me. Look at me, girl . . .

LIZZIE: They don't know you like I do.

JUBAL: That don't matter. Facts is facts.

LIZZIE: It's because I kissed that Yankee.

JUBAL: That's got nothing to do with it.

LIZZIE: It's because I don't know enough about kissing.

JUBAL: For God's sake, Lizzie . . .

LIZZIE: You think I'm worthless. Good for nothing.

JUBAL: Stop it. None of that is true. None of it. Don't you believe it. *(pause)*

LIZZIE: You're gonna leave me, aren't you?

JUBAL: I'm gonna do what's right. Insofar as I am able.

LIZZIE: So I got nothing.

JUBAL: You got your own self . . .

LIZZIE: That's all?

JUBAL: Look around you, girl. You got your own self.

(pause; in the silence, WE HEAR a hammer cocked back)

MICAH: Who's there? Show yourself . . .

LIZZIE: *(stepping into the clearing)* It's me, Micah. Put your gun down.

MICAH: Lizzie—Thank God. Are you all right, child? I thought for sure you were gone forever. *(*JUBAL *steps forward. If anything he looks more hungry and ragged in the dawn light.)* Who's that with you?

JUBAL: Jubal Haley.

MICAH: *(points the gun at* JUBAL*)* Stop right there. What are you? Renegade? Deserter?

LIZZIE: Put your gun down, Micah. Jubal's not gonna hurt nobody.

MICAH: Can I have your word?

JUBAL: Yes, ma'am.

MICAH: It's a miracle, Lizzie . . .

LIZZIE: —We weren't looking for you, we were looking for him.

JUBAL: Is he bad?

MICAH: He's burning up. And he can't stay awake . . .

JUBAL: Can I look at his arm? *(*MICAH *nods, shifts* JACK, *he groans.* JUBAL *kneels beside* JACK, *undoes the bandage, rips his sleeve and pulls it back. Red streaks run clear to* JACK*'s shoulder. His arm is puffy, the color of blackberries.)* He's gonna lose that arm.

MICAH: Oh, God.

LIZZIE: What's wrong with him?

JUBAL: Blood poison.

MICAH: We have to help him.

JUBAL: I can't . . . I don't know anything about taking off a man's arm. We need a surgeon.

JACK: *(waking)* Who's that?

JUBAL: Jubal Haley, sir.

JACK: Do I know you, soldier?

JUBAL: You saved my life.

JACK: *(drifting)* No . . . No . . .

LIZZIE: Is he gonna die?

MICAH: Hush!

JUBAL: We breached your works, I was out of ammunition, I was close enough to touch you with my hands . . . and then . . .

JACK: *(reaches up blindly, grabs* JUBAL *by the collar)* Get out of here before I kill you now.

JUBAL: I seen what you did for me. I come to tell you thank you.

JACK: My men are dead because I was stupid enough to spare your life. And you come here to say thank you . . .

JUBAL: It's my life, sir. I ain't ashamed to prize it.

JACK: I remember you.

JUBAL: I know you do.

JACK: You are gonna dig my grave.

JUBAL: No, sir.

JACK: And then you are gonna find my friend Sumner. And when you dig our grave you will make it ample for two soldiers from Maine who died in Georgia.

LIZZIE: He can't make you, Jubal . . .

JACK: Who's that?

MICAH: It's Lizzie. The girl I told you about.

LIZZIE: I'm with Jubal now.

MICAH: A no count deserter?!

LIZZIE: He's not a deserter.

MICAH: If he's alive and he's still here, he's a deserter.

LIZZIE: If he's so no count how come he could find you? And you! You weren't even looking for me! Instead you're lying with some Yankee! You're a traitor, Micah. Pure and simple.

JUBAL: He saved my life.

LIZZIE: I don't care what he did. How do you know he didn't shoot my papa or my brothers? How do you know he isn't planning to shoot all of us now?

MICAH: He's just a boy. A dying boy.

LIZZIE: Good.

MICAH: You don't mean that.

LIZZIE: Oh, yes, I do. Let 'em all die. Let God rain destruction on their land, their houses, their women and their children. Let them reap the harvest they have sown.

JUBAL: *(to* MICAH*)* What's his name?

MICAH: Jack. Jack Walker.

JUBAL: *(to* JACK*)* Mister Jack Walker, I am gonna open this ground for you. And I will find your friend Sumner and lay him beside you.

(JUBAL *turns away from her and walks to a nearby clearing. He begins to dig* JACK's *grave.*)

JACK: Micah . . .

LIZZIE: I'm gonna help Jubal dig your grave, Mister. *(she crosses to* JUBAL, *digs beside him)*

JUBAL: He's dying . . .

LIZZIE: So?

JUBAL: Don't you think he's scared?

LIZZIE: It's what he deserves.

JUBAL: Nobody deserves to die like that.

JACK: Micah? Are you there?

MICAH: I'm right here.

JUBAL: Maybe what's coming, Lizzie, is gonna be good.

LIZZIE: No, it's not . . .

JUBAL: Maybe it's gonna be better.

LIZZIE: Whatever it is, it's gonna be lonely.

JACK: You've got to follow this army.

MICAH: What are you talking about?

JACK: There are thousands of freedmen and women following Sherman's army.

MICAH: I can't leave Lizzie.

JACK: If you stay here, you're gonna starve. Both of you. *(reaching in his breast pocket for his wallet)* You take this money. You sew it inside your clothes, someplace safe.

MICAH: I can't take that . . .

JACK: Take it! *(he hands her his commonplace book)* Now get me a piece of paper out of there. *(finding a pencil in his shirt)* You write this down.

MICAH: I can't read nor write, Mister.

JACK: Put the paper here. I'll do it. *(She puts the paper on his lap. He writes.)* Hold it still. This is the name of my commanding officer. And my signature. General Joshua Hall. You find him. You give him this paper. He'll help you get North.

MICAH: But Georgia's my home.

JACK: Not anymore.

MICAH: Don't say that! My baby's buried here . . . my mama . . . my . . .

JACK: —You could be kidnapped and sold again. Take it . . . *(holding out the paper)* Please.

MICAH: These soldiers gonna give me a crust of bread? A scrap of firewood? In charity? In Christian kindness?

JACK: There are good men in this army.

MICAH: And how am I supposed to know who's who?

JACK: You'll take your chances, like you did with me.

MICAH: *(not taking it)* What's it say on there?

JACK: General Joshua Hall: Please give any and all assistance to Miss Micah Lee, a freedwoman. She did everything in her power to try to save my life. Jack Walker, 17th Maine. You think about it. *(she takes the paper and puts it in her pocket; pause)*

MICAH: —Maybe this boy could get you a surgeon. Maybe we could . . .

JACK: We don't have time.

MICAH: It doesn't quite reach your shoulder . . .

JACK: The poison's moving all through me. You've seen it . . .

MICAH: I wish . . .

JACK: *(struggling to stay conscious)* God, how does it happen so fast? *(a beat)* Sing to me.

MICAH: *(she tries, can't)* I can't. . . . Jubal! *(points to his cornet)* Can you play that thing?

JUBAL: Yes, ma'am. *(he pushes* LIZZIE*)* You go to her.

LIZZIE: No.

JUBAL: Get on . . .

LIZZIE: I'm not goin'.

JUBAL: You make your peace with this woman who loves you.

LIZZIE: You don't know what you're talkin' about.

JUBAL: You can't afford to be foolish and blind, Lizzie Peake.

LIZZIE: I'm no fool!

JUBAL: Then what are you so afraid of? (*He reaches for his cornet, and, standing in the grave, begins to play.*

LIZZIE *hauls herself up and sits on the edge of the grave, stubborn, watching* MICAH *and* JACK.)

JACK: *(hearing the music)* Listen! Listen there to the boys . . . Oh God, it would be snowing at home . . .

MICAH: *(he begins to shiver; she covers him)* I keep thinkin' about my Luther dyin' alone, without a blanket or a cup or a human voice to slake his misery. I think that's the death too many boys been asked to die. I don't want to think my Luther died unshriven and alone. I don't want to think that the crows devoured his beautiful eyes. I want to think there was another woman somewheres, come onto the battlefield with a bucket and a dipper and a prayer book. I want to think that somewhere, someone took pity on my Luther, laid her hands on him, give him a drink, said a prayer. Maybe she's a white woman, a Quaker woman. Maybe she's a girl. A young girl and she ain't been taught to hate, she ain't been trapped yet in this world of color. Maybe she's awake and alive and curious in her mind. And she will comfort my Luther. She will not pass him by like he's a dog. She will not give comfort to the white boy beside him, pretending she can't see him. She will see that my Luther is a man. A living, breathing man. *(he drifts away again)*

LIZZIE: *(crossing slowly to* MICAH*)* Micah . . . ?

MICAH: Come sit by me. (LIZZIE *sits,* MICAH *takes her hand,* LIZZIE *withdraws it)*

LIZZIE: When you look at him, what do you see . . . ?

MICAH: I see a man.

LIZZIE: Not a Yankee? Not a killer? Not a white man?

MICAH: Oh, Lizzie . . . What does it matter anymore?

LIZZIE: It matters to me.

MICAH: When a baby's born, or when someone dies, it's like the heavens open, just for a moment, and you see how vast it is— God's hand . . .

LIZZIE: If these are the gates of heaven, I say to hell with it.

MICAH: Beyond this, Lizzie. There's something beyond this.

LIZZIE: I don't believe that anymore.

MICAH: We were brought here to find something in these ashes, something of life . . .

LIZZIE: I'm scared, Micah.

MICAH: I know, baby.

LIZZIE: Why didn't you come after me?

MICAH: I thought you was gonna shoot me.

LIZZIE: I could never do that.

MICAH: That's good to know. *(she reaches out to* LIZZIE *again,* LIZZIE *doesn't withdraw)*

LIZZIE: What do you see when you see me?

MICAH: I see you like I've always seen you; like my child and my sister all rolled into one.

LIZZIE: Don't say that . . .

MICAH: Why not?

LIZZIE: I don't know how to live in this skin, in this world, and be your sister.

MICAH: Maybe you don't want to know, Lizzie. But I think you see pretty clear. *(a beat)* Maybe I'm gonna follow this army. You think you might come along with me?

LIZZIE: Leave Georgia?

MICAH: You thinkin' of makin' a life with that boy—? You're dreamin'.

LIZZIE: Dreamin'?! Well, you've gone plumb crazy if you're thinkin' of following this army. Ain't those the same Yankees who killed your baby? You think that little piece of paper is gonna protect you or me?

MICAH: We got to start somewhere.

LIZZIE: Start what?

MICAH: Start livin'.

LIZZIE: I can't leave this place, Micah. It's in me too deep.

MICAH: You sure about that?

LIZZIE: I'm goin' home. And I wish you'd come with me.

MICAH: To do your work?

LIZZIE: We could work together.

MICAH: You think so?

LIZZIE: I know it. *(a beat)*

MICAH: If I stay with you, it's as your sister, not . . .

LIZZIE: —I know.

MICAH: Do you?

LIZZIE: You're all I've got, Micah.

MICAH: Ain't we come to a pretty pass. Nothin' but each other.

LIZZIE: And a piece of land.

MICAH: Good land.

LIZZIE: That it is. *(pause; realizing JACK has died)* Oh my God, Micah . . .

MICAH: No . . . God . . . No . . . To slip away like that all alone.

LIZZIE: He's not alone.

MICAH: Yesterday he was quick and whole and I didn't know him at all, and now . . . Oh, Lizzie, to be buried so far from home. *(She runs her hands over his face, closes his eyes.*

JUBAL, realizing that something has happened, stops playing, leaves the grave.)

JUBAL: I didn't think he'd have to die. *(bends to JACK, finds his pocket watch, snapping it open)* Look at that. Not a scratch. To have come through all this . . .

MICAH: Don't you take that . . .

JUBAL: I wouldn't take it. I just wanted to touch it. *(he closes the watch, puts it in JACK's hands, stooping to pick him up)* Can you help me carry him to the grave?

MICAH: Wait! *(she folds his hands, touches his face)* All right . . .

(MICAH and JUBAL carry JACK to the grave. The sun begins to arc in bright rays. They lay him in the grave.)

MICAH: *(indicating JACK's commonplace book)* Is there a blank page in that book, Lizzie? You take that pencil and write a letter to his mama . . . You tell her . . . You tell her . . . *(to JUBAL)* What about Sumner?

JUBAL: I will find him and bury him here. Just like I promised.

LIZZIE: *(writing)* Dear Mrs. Walker, Your son Jack died just north of Brice's Crossroads, Georgia. He was severely wounded while saving another boy's life. We buried him at dawn on November 15th beside his comrade Sumner, with his pocket watch in his hands. He was . . . he was among friends when he died.

JUBAL: That's a good letter.

LIZZIE: She's gonna weep no matter. Just like my mama. *(pause)* *(*JUBAL *begins to fill in the grave)*

MICAH: Oh, what this earth has been asked to hold.

JUBAL: How far away is that Maine?

LIZZIE: About as far away as you can get.

MICAH: Look at that sun comin' up. Gonna light his way. *(a beat)* It don't seem finished somehow. I wish we had a preacher.

JUBAL: You could sing for him. Like he asked you.

MICAH: I can't . . .

LIZZIE: Yes, you can, Micah. That's your gift.

MICAH: *(singing/speaking brokenly)*

"Steal away, steal away to Jesus. Steal away, steal away home. I ain't got long to stay here.

*(*JUBAL *picks up his cornet, begins to play under* MICAH*)*

My Lord he calls me

He calls me by the thunder

The trumpet sounds within my soul

I ain't got long to stay here

Steal away, steal away to Jesus,

Steal away, steal away home

I ain't got long to stay here."

(pause)

LIZZIE: God forgive us. Forgive us all.

(As JUBAL*'s music transforms into the suggestion of "Taps," WE HEAR hundreds of horses' hooves beating on soft earth, as though all the armies, dead and alive, are passing in the dawn.*

As the sound of marching men increases, JUBAL *turns and melts away into the woods.)*

TABLEAUX

END OF PLAY

APOCALYPSO!

BY WILLIAM DONNELLY

for HDM

BIOGRAPHY

William Donnelly is the resident playwright for the Massachusetts-based Industrial Theater. Productions include *Painted Alice, Motel Stories, Apocalypso!, Host,* and *Best Man. Apocalypso!* was named a Clauder Competition finalist for 2000 and was included as part of Portland Stage Company's Little Festival of the Unexpected. His plays have appeared at the annual Boston Theater Marathon and are published in Bakers Play's anthologies of the event. He has been the recipient of a Massachusetts Cultural Council grant and is a member of the Dramatists Guild.

CHARACTERS

DORA—late teens, early 20s
GUS—40s
BOONE—20s
SHERRY—40s
WALT—20s
GIN—20s
CAL—30s
DWIGHT—20s

TIME & PLACE

A small town.
Next Christmas.

APOCALYPSO!

ACT I

1. A BAR, CHRISTMAS NIGHT

(GUS *and* BOONE *are seated.* DORA *enters.*)

DORA: I have a message. (*No response.*) I have a message. (*Pause. She turns and exits.*)

GUS: What is with this world?

BOONE: I dunno.

GUS: People walkin' around . . .

BOONE: You're tellin' me . . .

GUS: Comin' into places . . .

BOONE: Bargin' in . . .

GUS: Talkin' some sorta nonsense . . .

BOONE: "I have a message?"

GUS: It's all gone t'hell.

BOONE: Straight to.

GUS: Hell in a thing with a handle.

BOONE: And there you are. (*They drink.*)

GUS: Wanna know part of the problem? It's the holidays.

BOONE: Yeah?

GUS: Well, people get crazy 'round the holidays.

BOONE: I've remarked that.

GUS: I've seen guys . . . Christmas Eve . . . they're so crazy with pressures . . . they're ready to jump off a bridge.

BOONE: *It's a Wonderful Life.*

GUS: It is. But on occasion—

BOONE: No, I'm saying, that's what happens in *It's a Wonderful Life.*

GUS: Does it?

BOONE: Jimmy Stewart. He's on a bridge. That's what they're addressing.

GUS: No, but what I'm sayin' . . . I've seen guys in the world . . . Christmas Eve . . .

BOONE: It's a tough time for people.

GUS: 'Cause there's so many concerns. Relatives. Presents. "Who Believes What."

BOONE: Who believes what?

GUS: Do I wanna say Merry Christmas, Happy Chanukah? People on the street. You wanna be friendly. But there's a sense of danger.

BOONE: What are you?

GUS: Whadayou mean?

BOONE: Whadayou believe?

GUS: Oh, I don't believe nothin'.

BOONE: Hah.

GUS: I believe Man Is Doomed.

BOONE: Right.

GUS: And you wanna know why?

BOONE: Tell me in a minute. I gotta make a deposit.

(BOONE *exits to bathroom.* GUS *notices* BOONE *has left his wallet. He looks around. He picks it up. He opens it.* SHERRY *enters unnoticed.* GUS *pockets the wallet.*)

SHERRY: You boys all set?

GUS: Guy's got trouble you read about.

SHERRY: Y'don't say.

GUS: He was tellin' me. Separated. Sleepin' on a couch.

SHERRY: Sounds tough.

GUS: It is tough. It's very tough. My heart goes out. Give us a couple more, will ya?

SHERRY: On who's tab?

GUS: Well . . .

SHERRY: 'Cause you're about done.

GUS: Sherry . . .

SHERRY: No . . .

GUS: C'mon. We're here. We're having fun . . .

SHERRY: I'm working. I thought we had an agreement?

GUS: Just bring us a couple more. *(Beat.)* Bring us a couple more and I'll do your feet when we get home. *(She starts to exit.)* Don't draw 'em too quick, right?

(BOONE enters. SHERRY passes. They nearly collide.)

SHERRY: 'Scuse me.

BOONE: Jeez.

GUS: HEY, THAT'S MY FRIEND, THERE! Sorry 'bout that.

BOONE: I'm only walking.

GUS: It's not you. It's women. Women are an angry race.

BOONE: Guess so.

GUS: Angry and haughty. There're certain people . . . they can only operate in rudeness. It's a function, I think, of their fear.

BOONE: Fear?

GUS: 'Cause the world's gonna end.

BOONE: Someday.

GUS: Oh, no. *No* no. And don't think I don't know what you're thinkin'. "Every year another crackpot." Sure. I'm prone to think it myself. But I'll tell ya somethin': I seen things. And the Time Is Now. Get past the layers of, whatever . . . insensitivity, human stupidness . . . there's an animal knowledge there. And the animal part of you knows.

BOONE: That the world's gonna end?

GUS: I'll tellin' ya. I got these dogs.

(SHERRY puts down a couple beers and exits. BOONE reaches for his wallet.)

I got it.

BOONE: Sure?

GUS: My tab.

(SHERRY exits.)

BOONE: Thank you.

GUS: Please. So my dogs. Big dog little dog. I've had 'em . . . I don't know . . . dogs live a while nowdays. Little one's been sick as of late.

BOONE: What's the problem?

GUS: Got a illness. Thing's been—not to be disgusting, but—she's been throwin' up everywhere. She eats. Can't keep nothin' down. You know the scenario.

BOONE: She's a her?

GUS: Female.

BOONE: I knew it.

GUS: Anyway, God bless her, she looks a wreck. Sluggish. Matted. She looks like a fat kid on a train. So the other day I can't take it anymore. I break down. I decide to bring her to the vet.

BOONE: She hadn't been to the vet?

GUS: No.

BOONE: Ever?

GUS: I got her free I'm gonna pay for a vet? You're missin' the crux of my point. I was gonna take her to the vet. I'm on my way to takin' her to the vet. I turn around to put the leash on her. She vomits. All over my nice convertible sofa.

BOONE: Yours?

GUS: Well. I use it.

BOONE: Right.

GUS: So now I got a sick dog; vomit; and a healthy dog who's all of a sudden very interested in the problems of my life.

BOONE: There was another dog?

GUS: I told you that.

BOONE: When?

GUS: Big dog little dog I said.

BOONE: Oh, right. I'm there.

GUS: Okay. So. Two dogs. I go to the other room t'get a cloth.

BOONE: Somethin' to mop up the spill.

GUS: Can't just let it sit there.

BOONE: It'll soak through the foam.

GUS: Exactly my concern. So I'm tryin' to restore order. I'm hollerin' at Smiley.

BOONE: The sick dog.

GUS: The other dog. I'm comforting the sick dog.

BOONE: Of course you would.

GUS: "There there."

BOONE: She don't know.

GUS: So I go in the kitchen. Sponge. Dishrag. I come back. They're both standin' there.

BOONE: Near the spill?

GUS: The sick . . .

BOONE: I know what's next.

GUS: See, you think you would know.

BOONE: No, the healthy dog's eating it, right?

GUS: Mm-hm.

BOONE: Or they both are. Am I right?

GUS: Right. *(Beat.)* That's what you'd think. But the healthy dog? He's urinating on the sick.

BOONE: Christ!

GUS: Leg up. Peeing on the other dog's puke.

BOONE: That is bedlam!

GUS: You should try living it.

BOONE: *(Pause.)* I wouldn't have considered urinating on it.

GUS: Who would? But that's what I'm sayin'. It's a sign. *(Beat.)* Look at it for its essence. Big dog sees little dog vomit on the sofa. The weight of the End is approaching. He knows. The animal knowledge in him . . .

BOONE: . . . the instinct . . .

GUS: . . . Precisely what I'm sayin' . . . the instink in him triggers a response. "Dog's puking on the sofa. All bets are off."

BOONE: Anarchy.

GUS: Anarchy I'm sayin'. It's the end of the line, he's thinkin'. "Consequences do not apply."

BOONE: And you think he thought that?

GUS: I could see it in him. I could read it on his face. He knows what's what. He's a dog, but he's tuned into his animal side.

BOONE: Well that's all he's got.

GUS: Yeah, but he's workin' it.

BOONE: *(Pause.)* So what happened?

GUS: Hm?

BOONE: What happened the dog?

GUS: Oh, I cleaned it up.

BOONE: No, I mean what happened with the vet?

GUS: I didn't take her to the vet.

BOONE: Why not?

GUS: The world's gonna end. What's the point?

2. WALT'S APARTMENT

(WALT is seated at a kitchen table eating cereal, reading a letter. In time he stops and pulls a hair out of his mouth. He pauses. He looks at the bowl. He stirs the contents. He grabs the cereal box. He looks inside. He puts his hand in and fishes around. BOONE *enters.)*

BOONE: I already took it.

WALT: What.

BOONE: The prize.

WALT: There was hair.

BOONE: Where?

WALT: In my cereal.

BOONE: You should write a letter.

WALT: *(Pause.)* What time you get in last night?

BOONE: Late. Wallet got stolen.

WALT: At the Nickel?

BOONE: Didn't even know 'til I got home.

WALT: Sure you didn't just lose it?

BOONE: Whadid I do? Leave it somewhere? Leave it on the bar?

WALT: Well, you never know . . .

BOONE: Is that what you think of me? I'm tellin' ya. There are people out there. They're out there. And this is at Christmas.

WALT: What was in it?

BOONE: Oh, I had some things.

WALT: Uh-huh.

BOONE: Had my license. People's phone numbers.

WALT: But as far as money . . .

BOONE: Oh, there was money.

WALT: There was.

BOONE: Yeah. 'Cause that's where I carry it. So I don't have to take off my shoe.

WALT: Right. But what I'm asking . . . As far as rent . . . ? *(Beat.)* It's been three weeks Boone.

BOONE: Can I eat my breakfast? Can I do that? I got robbed. I'm kinda traumatized.

WALT: I'm sorry.

BOONE: It's a violation you know.

WALT: Forget I brought it up.

BOONE: I'd like to . . .

WALT: Seriously. Forget it. I got you covered.

BOONE: You sure?

WALT: I got you covered.

BOONE: Thank you, Walt. *(Pause.)* Any mail?

WALT: *(Reading letter.)* No.

BOONE: What's that?

WALT: Oh. My sister's coming.

BOONE: When?

WALT: Doesn't say.

BOONE: Didn't know you had a sister. Never mentioned it.

WALT: You forget sometimes. *(Pulling another hair out of his mouth.)* What is the story here?

BOONE: You should definitely write a letter.

WALT: It's not from them.

BOONE: Who?

WALT: The cereal people. *(He looks at* BOONE.*)* Is your hair coming out?

BOONE: What?

WALT: Are you losing hair?

BOONE: Well . . . yeah, obviously I don't still have all my hair, but—

WALT: Check.

BOONE: What?

WALT: Check.

BOONE: No.

WALT: DO IT.

BOONE: Walt.

WALT: DO IT.

BOONE: NO.

WALT: 'Kay. *(Pause. He lunges at* BOONE*'s head.)*

BOONE: ALRIGHT IT'S MINE. It's all mine. I'm losing hair like a sick cat.

WALT: God . . .

BOONE: Sleeping on a couch. Rapidly balding. This is the state of my life.

WALT: Didn't mean to lay into you like that.

BOONE: No, hey, you're protecting the sanitary condition of your home, I understand. I'd do the same thing if I had a home. . .

WALT: Boone . . .

BOONE: No, I'm just saying. If I was in your position, I'd be like you. But since I'm not. Since I'm homeless. Since I knit my soul to El Diablo . . .

WALT: Maybe this will help—

BOONE: Do you know that she called me last night? I got home the Nickel, phone's ringin'. "Oh, hi," she says. "I didn't think you'd be there." You didn't think I'd be here why'd you call?

WALT: Where was I?

BOONE: I don't know. But then she's on the other end sayin'

nothin'. Did you call to not talk? Finally. "What do you want, Gin?" And I said it real nonchalant so as to irritate her. Not nonchalant, but put-upon, you know what I'm sayin'?

WALT: Haughty.

BOONE: Yeah. *Yeah.* And you know what she ends up sayin'? "You have my Blondie."

WALT: What?

BOONE: She says I have her Blondie album.

WALT: You still got albums?

BOONE: I'm sayin' CDs but I don't like to say CDs. You're missing the thing. Two in the morning. Why's a wife gotta call you two in the morning to tell you she wants her album?

WALT: I don't know.

BOONE: Because she *doesn't* want her album. She could care about the album. She's got a bunch of my albums, am I calling her? Blondie's just a device.

WALT: You think so?

BOONE: Blondie's just a pretense.

WALT: So whadid you tell her?

BOONE: I told her what she wanted to hear. "You'll get your Blondie." And I said it real knowingly. So she'd know.

WALT: Sounds like you caught her off guard.

BOONE: Oh, I did. I definitely did. You could hear it in the way she hung up.

WALT: *(Pause.)* So you're gonna bring her her album.

BOONE: Absolutely.

WALT: And you think that's a good idea?

BOONE: I don't even listen to Blondie.

WALT: Right. But . . .

BOONE: What?

WALT: I don't wanna involve myself if I shouldn't.

BOONE: Walter. Please. I'm involving you.

WALT: *(Pause.)* Maybe you shouldn't keep jumping for her.

BOONE: When you say "jump" . . .

WALT: Look. Who am I, right? Last time I had a girl, I was going forty-five minutes outta my way to be tortured. Least you're over the phone . . .

BOONE: Who's this?

WALT: The one from Woonsocket.

BOONE: That clam.

WALT: Right. So what do I know? But seems to me when she's always lookin' for you to jump, and then you do, she knows she has you. And when she knows she has you, if you'll pardon my sayin', she doesn't respect you. And you've not come any farther.

BOONE: You don't think she respects me?

WALT: I don't know what goes on, Boone . . .

BOONE: No, but that's what you think from what you've seen.

WALT: I think respect is an issue.

BOONE: *(Pause.)* Thank you.

WALT: It's just an opinion.

BOONE: No, that's the thing. You're right. And I need to hear it. She's always doing this to me. Soon as I make progress, who's on the phone? Why wouldn't it be? Jerk. I knew I should've killed her with a rock. Do you know how ashamed I am I'm like this?

WALT: You don't have to be ashamed.

BOONE: The girl is all treachery. She thinks she's cute, but I see. Calling me up. And I'm supposed to, what? Hop on my bike? Bring her a fresh pan of brownies? Screw her. Every time she calls, you know what that tells me? *(Beat.)* I'm still on her mind.

WALT: Boone . . .

BOONE: No, I know she's Evil, but I do kinda feel bad.

WALT: About what?

BOONE: Well. It is her album.

WALT: Let's do this . . .

BOONE: What? It's clearly a favorite.

WALT: Let's do this. Give me the CD. And I'll deliver it.

BOONE: Really?

WALT: That way, you don't have to feel bad. And you don't have to stay in these "patterns."

BOONE: You don't mind?

WALT: I'd be honored.

BOONE: You're a Great Man.

WALT: Stop it.

BOONE: Seriously. You take me in . . .

WALT: C'mon . . .

BOONE: No, you take me into your home . . . You're a Friend.

WALT: I do what I can.

BOONE: . . . and then you do some more. And I thank you. *(Pause.)* I don't know, Walter. I try to put her out of my mind. But I can't stop thinking.

WALT: It takes time.

BOONE: I guess. But it's weird. I get these . . . visions.

(Lights change. Music. GIN *enters and acts out the scene* BOONE *describes.)*

She's standing there. And it's night.

On a street I've never seen.

And she's wearing this dress. Which I've also never seen.

She's waiting for somebody.

And it feels like the past or something.

Like the movies.

And she looks so confident.

That's what kills me. She doesn't even care.

Then up comes this figure.

(The MAN *enters wearing a raincoat, fedora and full-face black mask.)*

He's faceless.

He takes her by the hips.

He whispers in her ear:

BOONE & MAN: Excuse me . . . are you married?

BOONE: And she looks at him and she says:

BOONE & GIN: Not very. Not now.

(The lights fade on GIN *and the* MAN. *The* MAN *exits.* GIN *remains.)*

WALT: Then what?

BOONE: That's it.

WALT: That's all?

BOONE: To think she's off somewhere saying those things.

WALT: It'll pass.

BOONE: I know that. Intellectually. I know. But . . . Your sister . . . when she comes? You should try and explain to her.

WALT: Explain what?

BOONE: If she starts to feel I want to wound her . . . make it known it's not her personally. But what she represents.

WALT: I'll brief her.

3. A PARKING LOT

*(*GIN *is waiting, trying to light a cigarette. Her lighter won't work.* WALT *enters.)*

GIN: Was there trouble?

WALT: Hi . . . no . . . I just . . .

GIN: . . . hello . . .

WALT: I had some difficulty. Finding the street.

GIN: Really?

WALT: Yeah, when we talked, I thought, "Oh, right, that's the one," but when I got down here— *(Beat.)* I thought you were talking about the street by the dog track. The one on the side, that runs parallel where the, what is it . . . where that bait store is, I think. Or it used to be a bait store. You know where I'm talking about. You take a left at those lights, and it's on the right-hand side, NO it's a chainsaw place or something. I think I think of it as a bait store because I'm picturing the other place near the lake, 'cause you wouldn't put a bait store—But the river does run out there, doesn't it? Doesn't it cross the highway, underneath, and . . . yeah, I think it does, and it forms one of the hazards on the golf course maybe? Not the . . . obviously . . . it's not a wide point where it hits the course, but I'm pretty sure because I thought I used to see guys fishing up there. Off the highway. But maybe not. Now that I think about it I don't know where I am. But that's the street I thought we were talking about. And that's where I got turned around, so, you look nice.

GIN: I'm having dinner.

WALT: Oh. I didn't know. Am I keeping you?

GIN: No. *(Beat.)* But we did say "six."

WALT: Where you going?

GIN: Sheridan's.

WALT: Oh yeah? We used to go there all the time, my family. Steak joint, right?

GIN: Yes.

WALT: We used to love it there. They had this bread they served with everything. Toast, really. Extra thick slices. I almost wanna say it was grilled.

GIN: Texas Toast.

WALT: Hm?

GIN: They call it Texas Toast.

WALT: Do they?

GIN: Yes. It's on the menu.

WALT: I used to love that stuff. I'd steal my dad's. Or he'd steal mine. It's hard to remember. Such a long time ago. *(Beat.)* I remember that toast, though. It was buttered. *(Pause.)* Do you like toast?

GIN: I'm sorry I snapped at you.

WALT: No . . . did you?

GIN: I'm just . . . my mind is . . .

WALT: I understand. *(Beat.)* I have the disc.

GIN: What?

WALT: The disc you called for. The Blondie.

GIN: Oh. Right.

WALT: He said you called pretty late.

GIN: I didn't think he'd pick up.

WALT: Guess he was just getting in. Somebody took his wallet.

GIN: Did they.

WALT: He thinks at the bar.

GIN: Made off with a two dollar bill and a Blockbuster card. Quite a score. Has he looked for a place of his own yet?

WALT: Well . . . he's not really in a position . . .

GIN: Is that what he said?

WALT: Not in those words.

GIN: But at least he's out making an effort.

WALT: He's doing the best he can.

GIN: And the tragic part is, I know that that's true. The Best He Can. Seriously. At what point do you say: "You know what? I've shamed myself enough"?

WALT: I don't know.

GIN: Whatever. I don't care. You're the one that has to live with him.

WALT: Yeah.

GIN: You took him in.

WALT: It's just a favor.

GIN: We'd all be happier now if I'd've smothered him in his sleep.

WALT: What time are you meeting for dinner?

GIN: Around seven.

WALT: Should probably get going. *(Pause.)* Anyone I know?

GIN: I don't think so.

WALT: Somebody from Work?

GIN: No.

WALT: Oh. Somebody from Life . . . I understand. Of course, you have no obligation to tell me.

GIN: I realize that.

WALT: *(Pause.)* Would you tell me?

GIN: It's my sister.

WALT: Oh. Oh, God. I'm sorry.

GIN: It's alright.

WALT: No. God. What a jerk. As if it's my business, right? As if I have a say in . . . Please. You'll have to forgive me. I don't quite know . . . how this works yet.

GIN: It's alright. It's nice that you're jealous. It shows that you care. *(They kiss.)* If he answers next time I'll hang up.

WALT: Thank you.

GIN: Or I'll tell him to give back my blender.

4. A RESTAURANT

(CAL is seated. GIN enters.)

CAL: I ordered toast.

GIN: I'm not eating toast.

CAL: You're not?

GIN: I'm off bread.

CAL: Altogether?

GIN: As much as possible.

CAL: When did this happen?

GIN: I don't know.

CAL: Huh. Off bread. *(Pause.)* Is the window alright?

GIN: Sure.

CAL: It's not too drafty . . .

GIN: No.

CAL: We could switch if you like . . .

GIN: I'm fine. *(She takes out her cigarettes. CAL gives her a look. She puts the cigarettes away.)* Been here long?

CAL: Not really. *(Pause.)* Your hair's different.

GIN: Yeah.

CAL: It looks good.

GIN: Thanks.

CAL: *(Pause.)* We missed you at Christmas. I know we said we weren't going to exchange this year, but . . .

(She reaches into her purse and takes out a small gift box.)

GIN: What's this?

CAL: It's for you.

GIN: I thought we said we weren't exchanging?

CAL: No, I know.

GIN: So what are you doing?

CAL: It's just—It's nothing.

GIN: I don't have anything for you.

CAL: I didn't expect you would.

GIN: No, but had I known . . .

CAL: It's just a little something I saw. I thought of you . . .

GIN: But I've got nothing. I don't want to have to sit here in a public . . . Really, Callie. That's a pretty hostile gesture.

CAL: I didn't mean anything by it.

GIN: No you didn't mean it, but c'mon . . . As far as I knew we weren't exchanging, and now I have to sit here, I have to open it, and you're getting nothing.

CAL: You don't have to open it. Open it at home. I don't care. It's just earrings.

GIN: You got me earrings? *(Beat.)* From where?

CAL: Open them.

GIN: No. *(Beat.)* Are they gold?

CAL: Gin . . .

GIN: I'm only asking because I won't wear gold and you know that.

CAL: They're not gold.

GIN: Good. *(Beat.)* I'll get you something tomorrow.

CAL: You don't have to get me anything.

GIN: That's what you said before.

CAL: When it's Christmas, and I see something, I can't help myself. And since you weren't there—

GIN: Did you get my message?

CAL: Yes. Yes, I got your *message*, but we were expecting you. *(Pause.)* It was a very nice time. *(Pause.)* We were wondering what you're doing for New Year's.

GIN: Haven't decided.

CAL: We were thinking of having a little get-together. Nothing fancy. But Dwight suggested we stay in. Considering how crazy it can be.

(DORA enters.)

DORA: I have a message.

(No response.)

I have a message.

(Pause. She exits.)

CAL: Poor thing.

GIN: You shouldn't have taken the window seat.

CAL: Sorry.

GIN: I just hate it when they look at you.

CAL: I was reading in my Book: despite their hardships, the displaced are usually very spiritual. More so than people the same age from more comfortable backgrounds.

GIN: Because they need to believe. Look at their lives.

CAL: No, but it goes much further than that. It said: in a random poll, something like sixty-five percent of homeless answered yes when asked if angels walk among them.

GIN: I could go out now, get seventy-five percent to say rain is dry. What does that prove but their bewilderment?

CAL: I'm just telling you what the book said.

GIN: What book?

CAL: *The "Yes" Doctrine.*

GIN: Ugh.

CAL: What . . . ?

GIN: Every month with you . . .

CAL: What?

GIN: Every other month, it's a Process or a Prophecy or some other bullshit new religion that's gonna change you.

CAL: I like to stay open.

GIN: I swear t'God. You're the type liquidates their house so some yahoo can build him a theme park. *(Pause.)* What are you getting?

CAL: I don't know.

GIN: It's all meat . . .

CAL: No meat now either?

GIN: Not really.

CAL: Well, it's good that we talk. I was going to get you shrimp for the party.

GIN: Why?

CAL: Because you like it.

GIN: No.

CAL: Yes you do. That's the only reason I'd get it, years past. For you and Boone.

GIN: That was him.

CAL: *(Pause.)* Have you seen Boone?

GIN: Why would I?

CAL: I don't know. Whatever reason.

GIN: There's no reason. So no.

CAL: Oh. Because I thought I saw you. The other day.

GIN: Where?

CAL: Picking up Dwight. Something let go on his truck. Some belt. So I was looking for his building in the industrial park—I always get lost in there because it all looks the same—and as I passed one of the abandoned places, one of the older places, I saw in the parking lot, this car—

GIN: It wasn't me.

CAL: I didn't finish.

GIN: No, I know, but it wasn't me.

CAL: Well, whomever I saw, even if it wasn't you, there was a resemblance . . .

GIN: Are you saying it was me?

CAL: No . . .

GIN: Why would I be there? With him? In a parking lot? It makes no sense.

CAL: That's why I bring it up.

GIN: If it makes no sense, why is it in your mind at all?

CAL: I'm just telling you what I saw. (GIN *picks up her menu. Pause.*) Do you know what you want?

GIN: I don't want anything. *(She prepares to leave.)*

CAL: What are you doing?

GIN: It was wrong of me to agree to this place. I can't eat anything.

CAL: I thought you liked it here.

GIN: Well . . .

CAL: You used to like it.

GIN: Why do you do that? Why do you insist that you know me? I don't like it here. I was dragged here as a child because I had no choice, and now that I have a choice, I've chosen not to like it.

CAL: So we'll go someplace else.

GIN: What are you doing hanging around parking lots anyway?

CAL: Gin.

GIN: *(Pause.)* I'm not running out on you. I just . . . I can't. You know that I love you. I just don't have your compulsion to "share." What do you want me to say?

CAL: I want you there for New Year's.

(GIN *lingers for a moment then exits. Her gift remains on the table.* CAL *picks up the box.*)

5. CAL & DWIGHT'S HOME

(DWIGHT *is trying to coil a string of Christmas lights.*)

DWIGHT: *(On phone.)* Yah. No. I'm not . . . Luther? I'm not mad. It's your life. You have to do—Right. Well, I'm disappointed. I'm—This is not my decision. You wanna play, you gotta do your bit, now—Listen. Players play. 'f you're a player, you come to practice, you come to the games, you work. 'f you're not, you show up now'n again, you wear the jersey, and you sit, it's nothing per—That's Just the Way It Works. I'm not gonna get in the middle, tell you how to live your life. Luther. If your mom says you've got a previous engagement, who am I to tell her no?

(CAL enters.)

DWIGHT: *(cont)* Alls I'm sayin'... you miss a practice, come next game, how can I guarantee you'll play? Because there's rules, Luther. Look. We'll have to see. Well. When we see then we'll know. Alright? Alright. *(He hangs up.)* Damn kid... *(To CAL.)* I took down the tree.

CAL: I see that. Any particular reason?

DWIGHT: Christmas is done.

CAL: It's still the holiday season.

DWIGHT: Yeah, I don't really buy into that, though.

CAL: You might not buy into it, but it's true.

DWIGHT: Yeah, the people who believe that usually have tree fires. You hear that on the phone?

CAL: I was coming in.

DWIGHT: I'm losing a guard. I got a practice Saturday, I got no point guard.

CAL: Can't somebody else guard?

DWIGHT: Sweetie... I appreciate your input, but—No offense.

CAL: Pardon me.

DWIGHT: No. I'm just saying. I don't know where their minds are sometimes—

CAL: You scheduled a practice this Saturday?

DWIGHT: Yeah.

CAL: It's New Year's.

DWIGHT: It's Saturday. Saturday we practice.

CAL: Isn't that asking a lot?

DWIGHT: They made a commitment to the Team.

CAL: They're ten-year-old kids! What do you want from them?

DWIGHT: *(Quietly.)* Why are you yelling at me?

CAL: I'm not, I'm just asking.

DWIGHT: *(Pause.)* Want a little dedication.

CAL: You . . . are an adorable man. *(She embraces him.)*

DWIGHT: Callie . . . c'mon . . . I'm all tangled here. *(Beat.)* Oh, so, Baer called. We are playing tonight, so.

CAL: You're playing cards tonight?

DWIGHT: Why?

CAL: Kinda late isn't it?

DWIGHT: What time is it?

CAL: After eight.

DWIGHT: Where's your shawl, Granny?

CAL: Okay . . .

DWIGHT: Why you home so early? She didn't show?

CAL: No, she showed. She just couldn't stay.

DWIGHT: That— *(He picks up the phone.)* You want me to call her?

CAL: Honey . . .

DWIGHT: I'll call her right now.

CAL: And what will you say?

DWIGHT: I'll say she's not yours anymore, she's mine . . .

CAL: . . . your property . . . ?

DWIGHT: . . . and I'm the only one can treat her bad, yes.

CAL: Maybe if you sent a nasty note.

DWIGHT: I just wanna know where she gets off.

CAL: Wish I knew.

DWIGHT: Treating you like that. And you tried to help her.

CAL: I'd like to help.

DWIGHT: But what does she say?

CAL: I don't want your help.

DWIGHT: I think I will call her. No one upsets my girl.

CAL: Aw, puppa.

DWIGHT: So, what, she just left you there?

CAL: She came in. I get The Routine. She tells me she's off bread

whatever that means. Before I know it, she's out the door, I
don't even get a meal.

DWIGHT: You haven't eaten?

CAL: I had a soda.

DWIGHT: Did you say something to upset her?

CAL: These days, anything I say . . .

DWIGHT: . . . as long as I've known her . . .

CAL: Yes, but that's misleading.

DWIGHT: Yeah, you say that . . .

CAL: No. You don't know. She would always come to me. We
could always talk. But now whenever I try . . . *(Pause.)* Maybe I
disgust her.

DWIGHT: What?

CAL: Not in a "disgusting" way. Because I'm happy. She can see
we're doing well. When you're forced to face someone's—I
don't mean to sound like a jerk, but—success against your own
failures—

DWIGHT: It's not like you were taunting her with it.

CAL: No.

DWIGHT: *(Beat.)* Were you?

CAL: No, but if she felt it. If that's something she feels, how can I
convince her otherwise?

DWIGHT: You're taking too much on yourself. If things were different, would she be any less miserable? Could be she's supposed to be miserable. Could be it's her natural state.

CAL: C'mon . . .

DWIGHT: No, I just don't know what more you can do. She's the
one who's gonna wake up one day. . .

CAL: Maybe . . .

DWIGHT: She's the one who's gonna realize . . .

CAL: *(Pause.)* Don't even know why I bother . . .

DWIGHT: What am I always saying?

CAL: . . . give her a gift, I'm the bad guy.

DWIGHT: You need to cut yourself loose.

CAL: I would if I could. Extract myself from the whole situation . . .

DWIGHT: . . . there you go . . .

CAL: . . . shut her off cold. No birthdays. No Christmas. No access to nieces and nephews. Someday they'll dig up a picture: "Who's Auntie Gin?" Or maybe it's best they know nothing. Maybe I'll tell them I was born in the woods.

DWIGHT: That you could do. *(Smiling.)* Maybe we just won't have kids. *(He embraces her.)*

CAL: Don't you have a game to get to?

DWIGHT: Callie . . .

CAL: No . . .

DWIGHT: I'm only kidding with you . . .

CAL: If you were kidding it would be a joke.

DWIGHT: *(Pause.)* What do you want me to say? Every time you mention kids . . . All these books you got. All these tapes. What do they say? The Planet Is Dying. God is not Catholic. You really wanna bring up a child in that? I don't think you know what it is to bring life into this shitty world. And I know kids. I coach kids. They're not sane. You don't want that sorta thing running loose in your house. They'll screw up everything. Turn you all ugly.

CAL: What does that mean?

DWIGHT: Nothing, I— Nothing. *(Beat.)* I didn't mean "ugly."

CAL: We don't have to talk about this now.

DWIGHT: Callie, all I'm saying . . .

CAL: Why don't you go to your game.

DWIGHT: *(Pause. He starts to pick up Christmas lights; he stops.)* I'll take care of that stuff tomorrow.

6. SPLIT

SCENE A — BAR

(GUS *talking to* SHERRY *at the bar.*)

GUS: . . . and that's my point. Sure. Something's gonna happen. But something's always gonna happen. What's got me is the new potentialities. You wanna talk about normal life: there are horrible things—which is most things—and then horrendous things —which is everything worse. Now, when you come to this idea of The End . . . that's gotta be something like we never seen before. Won't be no meltdown. —crash. This is gonna be an inward kind of a thing. A rebellion of the animal self. You watch. Guys'll be walking down the street: "Why am I wearing this suit?" Epiphany. They'll strip down, pound their chests, go tearing up the infrastructure. That's what I'm looking for anyways.

SHERRY: TV says you gotta worry about asteroids.

GUS: Yeah, I'm more worried about our animals coming back out.

SHERRY: Saw something else that said the Bible's coming true.

GUS: TV and the Bible been tellin' us stuff for years. When have they ever been right?

SHERRY: I'm just telling you what I saw. It was kinda eerie. Something about earthquakes and a red cow in Jerusalem and extremists trying to rebuild a temple—something like that. Whatever it was, it's all in the Bible, and they're saying that it's right here upon us.

GUS: Oh, I got no doubt that it's right here upon us, but if you think it'll play out like it does in some book—

SHERRY: Who are you to say?

GUS: Who are they?

SHERRY: Thousands of years of human belief and you're gonna bet on a rebellion of the animal self over plain Biblical judgment?

GUS: Judgment? What's that gonna be? Guy comes out of the sky? Lines us all up? "You, go there, you're bad." Nah. Think of the logistics. People hidin'. Sayin' they're someone else.

SHERRY: If it's God he'll know.

GUS: God . . . if it's God it'd be done already. Guy like that wouldn't wait. I think it's a con. I think if it was really gonna happen . . .

SHERRY: . . . you'd have a lot to answer for.

GUS: Whadayou sayin'?

SHERRY: If it comes down to sin and bad deeds, you're gonna run up against a fair deal of resistance.

GUS: Who are you— No. I'm a good guy.

SHERRY: When?

GUS: When? I did your feet for you. Like I said.

SHERRY: And you took twenty bucks for it.

GUS: But the gesture, Sherry . . . I coulda took the money, done nothin' at all.

SHERRY: Like with that wallet.

GUS: I . . . *(Short pause.)* You're sayin' things make no kinda sense to me.

SHERRY: On Christmas. On Christmas, Gus. I saw you take that boy's wallet. And you never said a word. That's a bad thing.

GUS: Don't let's judge each other.

SHERRY: I want you to return it.

GUS: What?

SHERRY: I want you to start the year in decency.

GUS: Fine, but I didn't do nothin' . . .

SHERRY: If this is the Judgment, you wanna face it with a stolen wallet in your pants?

GUS: *(Pause.)* No.

SHERRY: Then Return it. First thing tomorrow.

GUS: *(Pause.)* You think I'm bad? I know not on the surface, but when you're sittin' around thinkin' of me . . . Is that what you think? (SHERRY *says nothing. She exits. Pause.* DWIGHT *enters.)*

DWIGHT: How's it going?

GUS: It goes. (DWIGHT *sits.)* Bartender's out the back. *(Calling after her.)* BUT SHE CAN'T HIDE FOREVER.

SCENE B—WALT'S CAR

WALT: Did you like me before?

GIN: When?

WALT: Before you knew me. When you only knew me through Boone.

GIN: Oh yeah . . .

WALT: Really . . . ?

GIN: Yeah. I've always liked you. Did you like me?

WALT: You know I did.

GIN: I didn't know that . . .

WALT: Since I met you.

GIN: No.

WALT: Since he first introduced us. That whole time. I'd always be in these "relationships," which I wouldn't even call anything, but all the while I was thinking of you.

GIN: But you were involved with those girls, it wasn't like it was nothing.

WALT: No, it wasn't "nothing," it just wasn't really "anything."

GIN: What about that one girl . . . you seemed to really like her.

WALT: Which?

GIN: The girl from Woonsocket.

WALT: I thought you didn't like her.

GIN: I never said that.

WALT: Oh. 'Cause we all went out that time and you said, "I wouldn't expect a big girl to be that unfunny."

GIN: That doesn't mean I didn't like her . . .

WALT: But I shouldn't have even bothered, is my point. No matter how much I liked her, no matter how good a person . . .

GIN: Because she wasn't right for you.

WALT: Well . . .

GIN: Those girls were never right.

WALT: Some were alright.

GIN: No, they were all wrong. Especially that girl. Big hair. Fat ass.

WALT: She wasn't a bad person.

GIN: No, but— *(Smiles.)* Look at you . . . She wasn't a bad person. She was just wrong.

WALT: It was never really anything anyway. *(Pause.)* I'm just glad to be . . . y'know . . . here. Not that I'm glad you guys stopped. 'Cause I wouldn't wish that on anybody. But between that and this, I'd definitely take this. Well. Minus the guilt. Obviously. But that's probably the same for you. Unless I'm completely off.

GIN: Are you asking me something?

WALT: Don't you ever feel guilty?

GIN: About what?

WALT: You don't?

GIN: It's not that I don't, I just . . . *(Beat.)* I've thought a lot about it . . .

WALT: And what do you think?

GIN: Well . . . I could feel guilty . . .

WALT: . . . uh-huh . . .

GIN: . . . but what would that prove?

WALT: *(Pause.)* That's a really good point.

BAR

(GUS has been staring at DWIGHT.)

DWIGHT: There a problem?

GUS: How do I know you?

DWIGHT: I don't know.

GUS: You work somewhere?

DWIGHT: Yeah.

GUS: Where?

DWIGHT: Industrial park.

GUS: Nah, I don't go there. What else you do?

DWIGHT: I coach.

GUS: Yeah?

DWIGHT: Saturday mornings. Junior basketball.

GUS: Basketball . . . *(Pause.)* You used to play!

DWIGHT: A little.

GUS: You used to play for the high school!

DWIGHT: I did.

GUS: You were on that championship team!

DWIGHT: I was.

GUS: Aw. You were a player.

DWIGHT: Well . . .

GUS: Yeah, I saw a bunch of those games. I used to work there. At the school.

DWIGHT: Didya?

GUS: Janitor. Yeah. You guys took it all one year.

DWIGHT: We sure did.

GUS: I remember one game. Against Durfee. They had this huge kid. I don't recall his name. He looked like a safe except with bigger legs. Anyway, time's runnin' out. They're down one. They dish it to him in the post. And you come, I think, from Worcester or somethin', strip 'im from behind. AAANNNTT. *(Beat.)* You know that was a long ride home. For them I'm sayin'.

DWIGHT: I don't remember that.

GUS: Aw, it was unbelievable. Then you had that tournament game. Eleven for twelve from the floor.

DWIGHT: No . . .

GUS: Or ten for eleven, either way. Very impressive. And that year you guys won? You especially . . . I'm tellin' ya. It was like watchin' some kinda Art.

DWIGHT: Well, thank you. Really. It's nice to hear from someone who appreciates . . . who was there. Most people, you try and tell 'em . . . to adequately convey what went on, but they don't really get it, y'know? But this . . . guy's like you. It's really gratifying.

GUS: Hey, don't thank me. You were the one out there. *(Beat.)* You were the best high school guard I ever seen.

DWIGHT: I didn't play guard.

GUS: Didn't ya?

DWIGHT: No.

GUS: *(Pause.)* Tommy Davis.

DWIGHT: Dwight. Tommy's my brother.

GUS: Oh. *(Pause.)* Your brother could play.

SCENE C — WALT'S APARTMENT

BOONE: *(Drunk, wearing a hat.)* It was Christmas. In our first apartment. Our presents were wrapped. But we couldn't afford a tree. So we decorated a coat rack. And it was just the two of us. We wanted to open our presents. So she said, "We'll go to bed now, and pretend it's tomorrow." So we went in the room. We got under the covers. We closed our eyes. And after a minute she said, "Wake up, sweetie . . . , it's Christmas." And we jumped outta bed. Opened our gifts. And she got me this hat.

CAR

WALT: But it's hard. I'm happy. When I'm with you. Even though it's Bad it's not— It works. And no, it's not like I want it to be a nightmare, but it's kinda tough to tell if just feeling that it's okay, still makes it actually okay, y'know? Because, I'll tell ya, when I'm here, there's no question about it: It's good and it's clicking and . . . yeah. But when I'm with Boone . . . and I see him sitting there . . . I can't decide what should be more important.

GIN: I'll ask you this . . . If right now . . . this very night . . . I went back to him . . . would he feel bad for you?

WALT: No.

GIN: He'd have nothing to say . . . no concern at all for your feelings?

WALT: Probably not.

GIN: So where's the conflict?

WALT: *(Pause.)* Again . . . solid point.

BAR

GUS: No idea what's keepin' her. You in a hurry at all?

DWIGHT: . . . got a card game waitin' on me.

GUS: You're playin' cards?

DWIGHT: I was thinkin' about it.

GUS: Now there's a Man. Here we are. Livin' in the shadow of Judgment. This one's out playin' cards.

DWIGHT: It's just cards. *(Beat.)* Where you get "judgment"?

GUS: Just a thought going around. It's a weighty one though. *(Beat.)* Whadayou believe?

DWIGHT: About what?

GUS: . . . faith, fate, iniquity . . .

DWIGHT: Well . . .

GUS: 'Cause I believe you live, you die . . . but I don't know . . . if you're Bad . . . *(Pause.)* If a person does wrong . . . does it hurt to cover his bases? This is just me thinkin', but— We've all done wrong. And we none of us know. When that curtain falls— We don't know. *(Pause.)* I'm sorry I thought you were your brother.

DWIGHT: It's okay.

GUS: And I'm not just sayin' it 'cause we all could die.

SCENE D—CAL & DWIGHT'S HOME

CAL: *(Reading)* ". . . the notion of a God who punishes His creations for what is in their Nature is ludicrous. Attempting to control the behavior of a spouse is like attempting to control the wind or the mystical Alaskan salmon. Our purpose in relationships is not to bend others to our will, but to embrace their will and, in so doing, create harmony."

WALT: 'Cause when it comes right down to it . . .

GIN: Yes?

WALT: What we're doing? In my heart . . . I don't feel it's wrong.

GIN: No. Of course not. *(Pause.)* But it is.

SCENE E — A STREET

DORA: I have a message.

The end will come like a channel changing;

like a dream switching;

like a drop from a height

into blackness.

The floods,

tornadoes,

earthquakes,

and comets—

these are but diversions.

Cruel jokes.

There are strings on our lives,

and we feel but cannot see,

as our heads jerk toward the fire

to keep us heedless of the smoke.

The end will come during the commercial.

Not in a blaze, but a hiccup.

Not in a blur, but a breath.

In fact, some say, if you look closely,

you will notice that the end has come.

That it's already come and gone.

And we, as we're equipped,

are the lingering crowd—

watching the credits;

wondering what the Best Boy does.

My name is Heliodora. I am a messenger of the Supreme Council of Fate and Determination.

If for some reason you are not completely satisfied, cancel at any time.

GUS: Sherry! Come pour my buddy here a drink!

CAL: *(Reading.)* ". . . say Yes to the fact we are all wounded children."

BOONE: A faceless man.

CAL: "Say Yes to all things because Yes is the key."

GUS: Sherry!

BOONE: Comes up behind her.

CAL: "Yes is the medicine."

BOONE: Hands on her hips.

CAL: "Yes Is the Way."

(SHERRY *enters.*)

BOONE: And he whispers in her ear.

(CAL*'s phone rings.*)

WALT: I'm afraid I might love you.

(SHERRY *stares at* DWIGHT. *He turns away from her.*)

GUS: Whatsa matter?

CAL: *(Answering phone.)* Hello?

SHERRY: *(To* GUS, *of* DWIGHT.*)* Him I don't serve.

DORA: *(To* WALT *and* GIN.*)* I have a message.

WALT: Oh my God.

GIN: What?

WALT: My sister.

ACT II

1. WALT'S APARTMENT

(DORA *is eating cereal.* WALT *is watching her.*)

WALT: Is it good?

DORA: *(She pulls a hair out of her mouth.)* No.

WALT: I got your letter. *(Pause.)* I didn't understand it.

DORA: I'm not surprised.

WALT: I got the part about you wanting to visit . . .

DORA: Which I'm doing . . .

WALT: . . . but I'm a little hazy on the Supreme Council of Fate and Determination stuff.

DORA: *(Pause.)* Do you have a job?

WALT: Yeah.

DORA: That's my job.

WALT: You're a messenger?

DORA: Yes.

WALT: For the Supreme Council . . .

DORA: Yes.

WALT: And what is that? *(She looks at him.)* If you don't mind my asking.

DORA: Some. Who are less informed than others. Would refer to the whole of the Council as an individual. And the word they would use to describe that individual is most often some form of the word "god." But, in actuality, the council, being that it's not an individual, but a Group . . . are you with me? . . . is called the Supreme Council of Fate and Determination. And that's who I work for.

WALT: So you haven't been taking your medication. *(Pause.)* Does mom know where you are?

(DORA shrugs.)

WALT: *(cont)* Do you think maybe you should call her?

DORA: She doesn't care where I am. She doesn't understand my work.

WALT: I think it would be good though . . . to let mom know you're safe.

DORA: I don't have time for that.

WALT: It'll only take a minute.

DORA: There is. No. Time. We are four days away from the End.

I told mom that. She doesn't want to face it? Fine. But that is the truth. I came here as a favor. Because you are my brother. And because I thought you might like to know. I have been instructed. By my employers. To alert the world that we are about to enter a period which will significantly alter the manner in which people like you . . . i.e. the Unenlightened . . . will continue to exist. Now, you can either prepare yourself as you deem necessary, or remain ignorant. That's your call. But be forewarned. If you do ignore me, and we do meet again in the context of an Afterlife or some other semblance of Eternity; I will say "I told you so." You shouldn't eat that cereal, by the way, it contains pesticides.

WALT: Where are you going?

DORA: To the bathroom. Can I not do that around here?

(She exits as BOONE *enters.)*

BOONE: Your sister? She's cute.

WALT: She's a messenger of God.

BOONE: Is she nice?

2. CAL & DWIGHT'S HOME

(CAL *is seated drinking coffee.* DWIGHT *enters, preparing for work.)*

CAL: You got in late.

DWIGHT: Yeah. We went late.

CAL: Did you have fun?

DWIGHT: It was alright.

CAL: Who was there?

DWIGHT: Just . . . the guys. You know . . .

CAL: Which guys? I mean to say, who?

DWIGHT: The guys. The regular . . . Davey. Carver. Baer . . .

CAL: Really?

DWIGHT: Yeah.

CAL: Baer was there?

DWIGHT: Did I not just say . . . ?

CAL: No, yeah, you did. I'm just trying to get it straight because Baer called. He called here. Last night. Wondering where you were.

DWIGHT: *(Pause.)* Musta been . . . It was probably early. Before I showed. And then I showed. And then we got in the game . . .

CAL: You got in the game . . .

DWIGHT: And then he forgot . . . To let you know. That was probably it. He just forgot.

CAL: Yeah. That was probably it.

3. WALT'S APARTMENT

(BOONE at the table. DORA enters. Pause. She sits across from him.)

DORA: Are you bothered by dangerous chemicals?

BOONE: Why, do you have some?

DORA: That cereal. It's poison.

BOONE: Oh. I was gonna have waffles.

DORA: You have waffles?

BOONE: No. We did, but. They got eaten.

DORA: It's tough to keep waffles.

BOONE: No. They were the frozen kind. They keep for awhile.

DORA: Right. But I meant because they're good . . . they're tough to keep.

BOONE: Oh, you mean because they taste so good . . .

DORA: Don't you find that?

BOONE: That's precisely what I find.

DORA: *(Pause.)* So you live here.

BOONE: Yeah. Got separated.

DORA: From your wife?

BOONE: My "estranged wife."

DORA: Do you work?

BOONE: I'm in-between things just now.

DORA: I'm a messenger of the Supreme Council of Fate and Determination.

BOONE: Yeah, Walt said. *(Beat.)* I lost my wallet Christmas night . . .

DORA: I don't deal with that sort of thing. So Walt left, huh?

BOONE: I think he did.

DORA: Probably to see his girl.

BOONE: He doesn't have a girl.

DORA: Doesn't he?

BOONE: Not that I know of.

DORA: I saw him with a girl. When I was out spreading the word.

BOONE: The word?

DORA: That the end is near.

BOONE: Oh.

DORA: That's my message.

BOONE: Oh. I saw you! At the bar! That's right. You came in and then you left. You look different cleaned up. And when I'm not drunk.

DORA: I don't remember seeing you.

BOONE: Well, you were working. *(Beat.)* So that's your message? That the end is near?

DORA: That's it.

BOONE: And this is a lock or just something you think?

DORA: Oh, it's a lock.

BOONE: Huh. Well, you know what I say, then? Bring It On. I welcome the End.

DORA: That's the spirit.

BOONE: What could be worse? The ghetto of my own life . . .

DORA: Things have been bad?

BOONE: My luck, the world would keep going. *(Beat.)* You know when you're alone? And you can't rid yourself of your own stupidity?

DORA: I do.

BOONE: My whole life is: "What went wrong? Why won't she love me?"

DORA: Your ex . . .

BOONE: And I was crazy for this girl. I was. I'd do anything for her. Then outta the blue. "I'm smothering," she says—I'm . . . I don't know . . . that she felt castrated . . .

DORA: And this was a girl?

BOONE: How can someone one day . . . maybe you can say . . . when you think that everything's fine— How can they just level you like that?

DORA: You know what they say about boxers . . . ? They say a boxer can only get knocked out by the punch he didn't see.

BOONE: They say that?

DORA: . . . and I don't box, but . . .

BOONE: But you believe it's true.

DORA: It's like with most things: if you hear it, and it feels true . . .

BOONE: . . . then it probably is.

DORA: . . . that's what I think anyway. There's a lot of things . . . they happen . . . and you didn't see them coming . . . but when you look back . . .

BOONE: In hindsight . . .

DORA: They suddenly make sense.

BOONE: Like with childhood.

DORA: Or some mystery you may have solved.

BOONE: And it's all a mystery. This whole life. *(Beat.)* So why would a person . . . who was loved. When it's just so clear that you care . . . why would they have to pull away like that?

DORA: There are people . . . and they can be quite nice . . . but they run from those who love them.

BOONE: But "why?" Do you see what I mean? WHY DO THEY DO THIS?

DORA: Perhaps they feel unworthy.

BOONE: Yeah?

DORA: Either that or they're mean.

BOONE: Yes. Thank you. Unworthy. This is good. I finally have a name for her treating me like a jerk.

DORA: Glad I could help.

BOONE: You're really sharp on these things.

DORA: Oh, I'm a genius.

BOONE: Maybe now I can get free of her. Now that I've identified her illness.

DORA: I don't see why not.

BOONE: 'Cause I mean, when you look at it: What does she really have?

DORA: She has her self-loathing.

BOONE: And she can keep that.

DORA: You don't need it.

BOONE: I'm beyond it.

DORA: You're so beyond it.

BOONE: I'm up the road . . . she's like a dot.

DORA: You're so beyond it, if you were to call it, you'd need the area code.

BOONE: Yeah. Thank you. Really. *(Beat.)* Wonder if this new-found clarity will help take care of my visions.

DORA: You have visions?

BOONE: All the time.

DORA: Me too!

BOONE: What are yours about?

DORA: Are you familiar with the concept of post-millennial molecular re-sequencing?

BOONE: No.

DORA: *(Short pause.)* What are yours about?

BOONE: It's just one really. And it's about her. I was telling Walt.
(Lights change. Music as before. GIN *enters.)*

BOONE: *(cont)* She's standing there. I don't know where. She's waiting.

(A MAN *enters; masked, as before, carrying a blender.)*
And up comes this figure.
A faceless man.
He pulls her to him.
And they speak.
GIN: Do you think Boone knows? *(The* MAN *takes off his mask. It is* WALT.)
WALT: He hasn't a clue.
BOONE: *(Standing.)* Oh, man . . .
DORA: What's the matter?
BOONE: That prick.

4. A PARKING LOT

(In the car. WALT *is holding a blender.)*
GIN: You don't think he's suspicious . . .
WALT: No, but if you keep calling . . .
GIN: I didn't think he'd be there.
WALT: Where else would he be?
GIN: Sorry.
WALT: I don't even care about that now. I'm worried about my sister.
GIN: Why, what happened?
WALT: Nothing. It's just what she says.
GIN: What'd she say?
WALT: She's just always had these tendencies . . .
GIN: Tendencies?
WALT: She's always had a very active fantasy life. When we were young, she used to make up all these people and situations to surround herself with.
GIN: For instance . . . ?
WALT: She had imaginary friends she would refer to as "disciples."

And for a while, in junior high, she pretended she was a sheep. We went along with it. Seemed harmless. But after a few months—

GIN: She was allowed to be a sheep for a period of months?

WALT: It was discouraged after a period of months. She kept up with it for about a year.

GIN: And no one stopped her.

WALT: It's what she did. She wasn't crazy.

GIN: But she is now.

WALT: I don't know what she is now. She has problems.

GIN: And now they're yours.

WALT: Well. Yes. Well. I feel I have an obligation . . .

GIN: Yes, of course you do. But what about the things in your own life which demand your immediate attention?

WALT: Like what?

GIN: Like this. Whatever this is.

WALT: You know what this is.

GIN: No. See. You tell me what it is. I don't know if that makes it so.

WALT: I told you the other night.

GIN: What did you tell me?

WALT: Don't make me say it.

GIN: Well, Walter . . . how can we talk?

WALT: I told you in the car.

GIN: And that's another thing. Am I a cheerleader? When are you gonna take me someplace that doesn't have bucket seats?

WALT: What else can we do?

GIN: We could get a room somewhere. We could go to your house —it's not even an American car—

WALT: What about your place?

GIN: I have a cat.

WALT: And . . . ?

GIN: You're not allergic?

WALT: No.

GIN: Well . . . she can't be disturbed, don't—

WALT: Gin—

GIN: Don't try and divert me—

WALT: Gin, you know we can't go to my house.

GIN: Well, maybe that should change, Walter. Maybe that's one of the things which demand your immediate attention.

WALT: What do you want me to do? You want me to kick him out? If that's what we're saying let's say it. Take him by the neck. Throw him in the street. That's something you'd like to see?

GIN: I wouldn't object to that. *(Beat.)* I'm not telling you what to do . . .

WALT: No . . .

GIN: I just think it's best.

WALT: It's what you think.

GIN: Listen. *(She places* WALT*'s hand between her legs.)* It means a lot to me. At this point in time. To have someone. Who's there for me. If you're not that person, that's my problem. But I don't think that's the case. What do you think?

WALT: You'll have it. He's out.

GIN: Thank you. *(She returns his hand.)* Now about your sister . . .

5. SHERRY'S APARTMENT

(GUS enters with key in hand. DWIGHT *is behind him carrying a gift.)*

GUS: . . . it's one of those things. Certain people . . . you know the type . . . they can only operate in rudeness.

DWIGHT: I understand.

GUS: I'm sure she didn't mean to offend you last night. A lot of people she won't serve. SWEETIE? She works all these hours . . . there's pressures there . . . SHERRY? I know she's here 'cause the kid's here.

DWIGHT: Who?

GUS: Not hers. Her daughter's. They're down for the holidays. She's off with friends this mornin'...

DWIGHT: There's a kid here now?

GUS: Wanna know the truth ... it's sorta drivin' me nuts. But I'm fighting my natural urge to complain.

DWIGHT: Maybe I should come back ...

GUS: Whadayou talkin' about? You're all the way down here.

DWIGHT: I didn't know you had guests ...

GUS: It's just the kid. You don't like kids? *(SHERRY enters from bedroom.)* There she is. Hey, honey. Look who I run into. My buddy Tommy here wanted to see—

SHERRY: *(Interrupting after "Tommy.")* Dwight.

GUS: Right. My buddy Dwight ... I run into him this morning. Said he wanted to come over and talk about last night. So I brung him here. To talk. *(Beat.)* And I did so rather selflessly.

SHERRY: You return that wallet?

GUS: I was out to breakfast. You know what I did, though? I tried a grapefruit.

SHERRY: So your answer is no.

GUS: It's on the list. I think you're missing the important element ...

SHERRY: I don't think I am.

GUS: Awright. *(Pause.)* So what do we have to talk about?

SHERRY: Would you go buy me some cigarettes, please.

GUS: I think I got a half a pack in my—

SHERRY: Go for a walk so you won't be here for a while, please.

GUS: *(He begins to exit. Stops.)* I hope you take into account that I did this thing and I didn't even ask for a gratuity.

SHERRY: Noted. *(GUS exits.)*

DWIGHT: I brought a ... something for the tree ... for underneath ...

SHERRY: Tree's gone.

DWIGHT: Right ... but ... nevertheless ...

SHERRY: Just— Right there is— Put it down.

DWIGHT: Sorry. I'm a little ... Well. As you can imagine. *(Pause.)* Your husband ... he's very nice.

SHERRY: He's not my husband.

DWIGHT: He's not.

SHERRY: No. We're livin' in sin.

DWIGHT: Oh ...

SHERRY: Actually, he's livin' in sin and I'm payin' for it.

DWIGHT: Either way. Seems like a nice guy. *(Pause.)* I uh ... don't really know where to start.

SHERRY: She's not here.

DWIGHT: I didn't think she'd be.

SHERRY: No ... ?

DWIGHT: That's not why I came. How, ah ... how are you?

SHERRY: I'm fine.

DWIGHT: Yeah? Good. Me too. Things've been . . . Well. I'm coachin' now. Married.

SHERRY: Are ya.

DWIGHT: Yeah, she's ... I don't think you'd know her. She didn't go to school with Pattie and me.

SHERRY: Ah ... *don't.* Okay?

DWIGHT: What did I do?

SHERRY: To hear my daughter's name come outta your mouth ... Just don't.

DWIGHT: Sorry. *(Pause.)* How is she? *(Long pause.)* You'd rather I leave. . .

SHERRY: No ...

DWIGHT: It's okay if you do ... it wouldn't be wrong ...

SHERRY: If I wanted you to leave ... Believe me.

DWIGHT: I believe you. *(Pause.)* So.

SHERRY: Lookit, why don't you just sit tight a minute, I got a coupla things I gotta take care of.

DWIGHT: Can I help?

SHERRY: You wanna help with the *kid?*

DWIGHT: Uh . . .

SHERRY: Why start now?

6. CAL & DWIGHT'S HOME

(BOONE, DORA, *and* CAL *drinking coffee.*)

BOONE: I miss this.

CAL: Do you?

BOONE: I missed it on the holiday.

CAL: What did you do this year?

BOONE: Got some Chinese. Then at night I went to the Nickel . . . got robbed.

CAL: That's no way to celebrate.

DORA: I slept under a bridge in a discarded oil drum.

CAL: Oh, my.

DORA: Found a tin of butter cookies, though.

CAL: That . . . sounds nice.

DORA: I enjoyed them. *(Pause.)*

BOONE: I meant to send you guys a card.

CAL: That's okay.

BOONE: No, I wanted to. Just because things didn't work out with your sister . . .

CAL: Don't even, Boone. Anytime. Anything you need. We're still here for you.

BOONE: Thank you. Really. *(Pause.)* So what I was wondering . . .

DORA: . . . what do you know about the deviltry?

CAL: The what now . . . ?

DORA: Between your kin and mine. You know.

CAL: I have to say . . . she tells me nothing.

DORA: She's cold to you.

CAL: Well, she's not quite . . . forthcoming.

DORA: She's a dodger. An island.

CAL: Those things . . . she can be.

BOONE: I'd say so, too.

DORA: And on the Walt front . . .

BOONE: That pud.

CAL: You're sure they're together?

BOONE: I'm pretty . . . well . . . Dora?

DORA: We're sure.

CAL: You saw them?

DORA: I saw. And I know.

CAL: *(To* BOONE.*)* What is with these people?

BOONE: *(To* DORA.*)* Weren't we just saying?

CAL: You give yourself over. You say, "There. Now I trust you."

BOONE: And that's an easy thing?

CAL: Oh, yeah, it's so easy.

BOONE: No wonder we're guarded. Well. Not to speak for you.

CAL: No, we all are. And of course we are. The way they treat us. Making up card games. Lying to our faces . . .

BOONE: Uh-oh.

CAL: . . . just don't blatantly lie, you know? Don't lie when you don't know the truth.

BOONE: Whadid he do?

CAL: I don't even know. I'm not certain of anything.

BOONE: But you suspect? You have suspicions?

CAL: I think . . . Well. I can't really say for sure . . .

DORA: You think he's screwing around? *(Pause.)* Pretend you know me.

CAL: Yes. That's what I think.

BOONE: I'm so sorry.

CAL: But, no. It's okay. Because my book says . . . and as far as—

DORA: *(Cutting her off after "book".)* Your book? (CAL *hands her the book.) The "Yes" Doctrine.*

CAL: It says we are all individual people. Independent and controlling of our own destinies. And when we try and capture each other . . .

DORA: Capture . . . ?

CAL: In Prisons of Demand. In "relationships."

DORA: Right . . .

CAL: . . . we are asking of our partners not "devotion" but "compliance."

DORA: *(Beat.)* And you believe this crap?

CAL: Well . . . believe?

DORA: This is something you read, and accept, and adhere to?

CAL: I . . .

DORA: If your man is fucking around, he needs to know.

BOONE: Dora . . .

DORA: No. I'm sorry, I don't mean to insult your taste, but let's be honest. You don't feel At Ease about this. You don't feel Adult and Reasonable and Rational about this. You probably feel betrayed. So be betrayed. This is not a flaw . . . to feel what you feel. Tear into this boy. He made you a promise. Remind him. This life is yours people. Settle up now because we're just about done. *(Beat.)* Put it to you this way. Do you respect him?

CAL: Yes. I do.

DORA: Then talk to him.

BOONE: *(Long pause.)* She's pretty forward, yeah?

7. SHERRY'S APARTMENT

(SHERRY re-enters.)

DWIGHT: Look. I don't mean to upset your whole . . . You got a life, I know that.

SHERRY: You don't upset me.

DWIGHT: I just figured— I hadn't run into you when I did, who can say, right? But since it happened. And since I'm here. Not that it would cure anything, but— If there was something I could do.

SHERRY: Do.

DWIGHT: To square things. With you.

SHERRY: Something you could do.

DWIGHT: Yes. What can be done? Is there anything?

SHERRY: Maybe you could shovel my driveway.

DWIGHT: Is that something you'd like?

SHERRY: What are you asking me?

DWIGHT: I know it seems strange . . .

SHERRY: But it doesn't, is the thing. There's nothing strange about it. I'm sure you got a lotta guilt on your head. His birthday comes up, you feel that emptiness. I recognize you're human. But you're gonna have to realize: You did what you did, and we're over it. Pattie especially. And believe me, I can understand why you'd worry. Back then? She was a terror. No argument. But to see her now—up there, her place in the city—she is the strongest person I know. And she is magic with that kid. I got no interest in letting you off. Out of anybody, I'm the one would like to see you swing. But it's all done now. If you're lookin' for peace, you're lookin' in the wrong place. Go to your own life. Do right there. Beyond that . . .

DWIGHT: *(Pause.)* Does he ask about me?

SHERRY: Not when he's here.

DWIGHT: But he knows?

SHERRY: Who knows what kids know? I'm just "Nana."

DWIGHT: But they're good, though?

SHERRY: They're perfect. Let 'em stay that way.

DWIGHT: *(Long pause.)* Thank you.

SHERRY: No, I'm not after—

DWIGHT: No. Really. Thank you.

SHERRY: It's okay. I'm actually proud. I always said, I ever saw you again, I'd hit you with a rolling pin.

DWIGHT: But you held back.

SHERRY: Well, I don't actually own one. *(Beat.)* So this box here, what is it, somethin' for me?

DWIGHT: I, no, I got him a truck. Thought maybe he could . . . I dunno . . . take it out, push it around in the dirt. I used to like doing that. Figured he might, too.

SHERRY: I'm sure he'll love it. *(Pause.)* You wanna see him?

DWIGHT: *(Pause.)* No. I don't wanna cause a disturbance or anything.

SHERRY: He's sleeping. If you're quiet . . .

DWIGHT: *(Pause.)* Are you sure?

SHERRY: Go look at your son.

DWIGHT: Thank you. Thank you, Mrs. . . .

SHERRY: Shhh . . .

(The stage dims. DWIGHT moves into an isolated pool of light. He looks at the boy.)

DWIGHT: Whatever you do, don't wake up or your nana's gonna kill me. Jesus, look at you. You probably don't know this yet, but people always say that kids take on the features of the family. Like the looks. But, I swear, I never thought you'd actually have my . . . face, you know? I tried to picture it, but . . . my nose. My eyebrows. You're a good lookin' kid.

I don't know if they got you involved in any sort of hoops program up there, but you should really consider it. You're never too young and if there's anything to this genetics business, there's bound to be some talent there.

So, listen, I didn't come here just to rattle on. I'm not too good at talkin' t'little guys like you. I just thought . . . I just felt . . . that maybe it'd be a good thing if I was to, ah, I dunno, apologize. For bein' stupid. For bein' young. For bein' too afraid to meet you before now. It's nice to meet you. I'll, ah . . . get outta your way now. Let you get back to the business at hand.

You grow up good, okay? Grow up right.

Where'd you learn to sleep like that, it's fucken beautiful.

Good night, son. 'Night.

8. WALT'S APARTMENT

(WALT *is waiting with a duffel bag beside him.* BOONE *and* DORA *enter.*)

BOONE: Where you going?

WALT: Nowhere. It's your bag.

BOONE: That's why I'm askin'.

WALT: We need to talk.

BOONE: *(To* DORA.*)* He's got my bag.

DORA: I see that.

WALT: We have some things we need to discuss.

BOONE: *(To* DORA.*)* It's probably packed with my stuff.

DORA: Probably.

WALT: You haven't paid me rent.

BOONE: Thought you had me covered.

WALT: I did, but . . . I can't keep carrying you.

BOONE: If I'd known it was a problem . . .

WALT: It's just too much, y'know. It's too much to ask. Not only the money, but— I took you in.

BOONE: How many people have to say that?

WALT: I understand if you're upset, but this isn't just about you. I've got some things which demand my immediate attention, and I really I think I need to . . .

BOONE: *(Overlapping. To* DORA.*)* This is all her.

DORA: Yeah?

BOONE: Classic.

WALT: You don't have to take everything now.

BOONE: This is her thing, right?

WALT: Who?

BOONE: She put it to you. "Kick him out, I want you to myself." Somethin' like that?

WALT: If I knew who you were talking about.

BOONE: Look. You gotta realize it's a swindle. She'll test her grip.

She'll toss you aside. I don't know why. Maybe she likes to hurt. Maybe the challenge. Some people— Whatever. I'm not gonna stand around and advise you. *(He picks up his bag, starts for the door.)*

WALT: *(Pause.)* How did you know?

BOONE: Kinda came to me.

WALT: I didn't mean for it to happen.

BOONE: She approached you, right?

WALT: How do you mean?

BOONE: I asked to move in. She approached you . . . "I've had these feelings"? Now why would she do that? *(To DORA.)* Are you coming?

DORA: Oh, yeah.

BOONE: Do you need anything?

DORA: I'm fine. *(She goes to BOONE.)*

WALT: What's this supposed to be?

DORA: *(She takes BOONE's arm.)* We're an item.

WALT: When did this happened?

DORA: Before we were born.

WALT: So you're not staying?

DORA: I gotta go with my old man.

BOONE: You don't have to call me that.

DORA: Sorry.

WALT: *(To BOONE.)* You are aware that she's crazy.

DORA: I'm not crazy.

WALT: You said you were a sheep.

DORA: I said I was The Lamb. *(To BOONE.)* He has never understood me.

WALT: So this is it, then?

BOONE: I'll get you your money.

DORA: I'll see that he does.

WALT: Okay.

BOONE: So, I'll see ya around.

WALT: Yeah.

DORA: Bye.

WALT: Bye. *(To* BOONE *as they're exiting.)* She does care for me.

BOONE: *(Off.)* Awright . . .

DORA: *(After a pause, returning.)* Can we borrow your car?

9. CAL & DWIGHT'S HOME

(CAL *is reading a new book.* DWIGHT *enters.)*

DWIGHT: Hey.

CAL: Hi.

DWIGHT: What'cha got?

CAL: Book.

DWIGHT: *The "Yes" Doctrine?*

CAL: Novel.

DWIGHT: Ah . . . *(Pause.)* So I've decided to cancel practice. The practice Saturday? I figure it's New Year's . . . they're just kids. I don't want to . . . overtax their—

CAL: Are we gonna talk?

DWIGHT: I'd like to.

CAL: Because if yes, I'm not gonna "ease" into it.

DWIGHT: No . . .

CAL: I'm sick of easing into everything.

DWIGHT: That's fine.

CAL: What?

DWIGHT: I . . . yes. I said "That's fine."

CAL: So, okay. So let's get into it.

DWIGHT: Alright.

CAL: I don't want to guess.

DWIGHT: No.

CAL: I'm just gonna go from the assumption you've done some-thing and you're sorry. You screwed up. It happens. I can see you're contrite. But you know what? That's a by-product. What has to happen first is the confession. And I don't want to waste time getting sweet-talked while you cushion the blow. I'm not some weakling. If you've got a girl on the side—a boy—you've killed somebody, just say it to me straight and let it hit and be a man.

DWIGHT: Yes.

CAL: And don't try and pull back from it. Don't try and dress it up with that, "It meant nothing," nonsense. If you did it, it has meaning, otherwise, what does that say? It's not some empty— I'm only interested in the deed. You confess your wrong, and from there, it's my decision how we proceed.

DWIGHT: Okay.

CAL: But, you know what? I don't even think I wanna know. If you give me details, all I'm gonna see is you and some tramp holding hands down the soda fountain. No. Forget it. I'm not prepared to be haunted. *(Beat.)* Lookit, don't tell me anything. Whatever it is, I don't care. I'm not gonna leave you. Just tell me it's settled and you're sorry and we'll both move on. 'Cause that's all I want to hear. Alright? Done. *(She sits and begins to read.)*

DWIGHT: *(Pause.)* . . . *what* is it you wanna hear?

CAL: Nothing. I want to hear nothing. Forget all words. We're fine.

DWIGHT: Okay. *(Long pause.)* You *know* I'm gonna tell you.

CAL: Goddam right you are. Now go out there and make me tea.

10. WALT'S APARTMENT

(GIN enters. WALT shows the place off as this is the first time she's seen it.)

WALT: Hah . . . ? So . . . ?

GIN: Yeah . . .

WALT: Whadaya think?

GIN: It's small. Ever crack a window?

WALT: It's winter.

GIN: It's like a hamper. *(Beat.)* So he didn't put up a fight?

WALT: No. He knew.

GIN: You told him?

WALT: He knew.

GIN: And what did he say?

WALT: Nothing. He seemed resolved.

GIN: Really. *(Beat.)* Resolved . . .

WALT: But whadayou think, though.

GIN: Yeah, I said.

WALT: It's not the car.

GIN: That is true.

WALT: *(Stretching out in front of her.)* So . . . Whadaya feel like doing?

GIN: He didn't say anything?

WALT: No. He sorta seemed different.

GIN: How so?

WALT: He didn't care. I think it had something to do with my sister.

GIN: Where is your sister?

WALT: With him. They took the car.

GIN: They stole your car?

WALT: It's a loaner. I felt bad.

GIN: Why are they together?

WALT: I think something happened between them.

GIN: Between your sister and Boone?

WALT: I think they're an item.

GIN: What makes you say that?

WALT: She said so.

GIN: She said they're an item?

WALT: That's what I got from it. *(Beat.)* So . . .

   (There is a knock. GUS *enters.)*

Can I help you?

GUS: H'yadoin'. I'm lookin' for a James Boone . . . Jimmy Boone . . . any . . . ?

WALT: He doesn't live here anymore.

GUS: No? Ah. Well. Any idea how a person would get in touch with him?

WALT: Is there a problem?

GUS: No, nothin' like that. I, ah . . . found his wallet, is all. I was hopin' to give it back to him. *(Beat.)* Could I sit down a minute? I got this spur in my heel and I been . . . No. You're absolutely right. I sit down. Next thing, you're off'rin' me a cold one . . . *(Beat.)* Awright, the truth of it is I took his wallet. Not on purpose. That is to say, not maliciously. There was twenty-four bucks and I only used three and I only got eggs no bacon and nothin' illegal, so. —Little bit of grapefruit, which is a start. And I left him an I.O.U. so he can contact me for reimbursement anytime he wants and I swear I'll pay him if I'm in better financial standing. I'd just like to say at this point that if the notion of involving law enforcement has crossed either of your minds I hope this show of good faith will dissuade you. From callin' the cops I'm sayin'. Nice place, by the way. Very homey.

GIN: Give it here, I'll get it to him.

GUS: *(Hesitating.)* Aw-right . . . are you, uh . . . close . . . to Mr. Boone?

GIN: He'll get it, okay, so let me see it.

GUS: I'm not trying to be combative, I just wanna make sure it reaches him without incident.

GIN: You already stole it, I can't steal it again.

GUS: *(Beat.)* Aren't you the pleasant sort.

GIN: Just give me the wallet, will you please? We're in the middle of something here.

GUS: Look, lady, I'm only tryin' to do right . . .

GIN: Great . . .

GUS: . . . tryin' to be a Nice Guy . . .

GIN: . . . thank you . . .

GUS: . . . no need for you to make me out The Dick.

WALT: Hey now . . .

GUS: No.

GIN: Are we finished here? Are we done?

(GUS *purposefully hands the wallet to* WALT.)

GUS: Thanks for your time. Really. Maybe someday soon we'll get together, you can pee on me again. *(He exits.)*

WALT: Anyway . . .

GIN: When did all this happen?

WALT: What?

GIN: With your sister.

WALT: What are you talking about?

GIN: Your sister and Boone. When did it happen? You were saying before . . .

WALT: Oh. I'm not sure. Guess they just hit it off.

GIN: And what exactly does that mean?

WALT: I don't know. They spent some time . . . something clicked . . .

GIN: WHAT CLICKED?

WALT: Why are you so concerned with this?

GIN: Because Boone is my husband . . .

WALT: Your ex—

GIN: . . . and I don't particularly like the idea of some tart-whore . . .

WALT: . . . hey . . .

GIN: . . . in less than twenty-four hours time . . . what kind of nonsense is that? *(She takes a pack of cigarettes from her purse. Again, her lighter won't work.)*

WALT: Maybe it was meant to be.

GIN: Could you not insult me with remarks like that? You said yourself the girl was crazy.

WALT: I never said—

GIN: You said she was a sheep.

WALT: She was a lamb. I had it wrong.

GIN: . . . well . . .

WALT: That girl . . . is my sister. And I really don't think it's right for you . . .

GIN: I don't care what you think. Can you understand that? Your thoughts are not what interest me. It's probably gonna work out best for both of us if from now on whenever the phrase "I think" pops into your head, you just ignore it and say instead: "Thinking is not my strong suit."

WALT: *(Pause.)* I thought you cared for me.

GIN: Well, clearly, you were wrong. Do you have some matches for me or what?

(WALT *calmly grabs* GIN *and escorts her to the door.*)

Hey. Don't . . . You don't handle me . . .

WALT: He should've killed you when he had the chance.

11. A PARKING LOT

(BOONE *and* DORA *in* WALT*'s car.*)

BOONE: . . . and how will it happen?

DORA: You really want to know?

BOONE: I think so.

DORA: You don't want to be surprised?

BOONE: I don't react well to surprises.

DORA: What do you do?

BOONE: I scream . . .

DORA: . . . uh-huh . . .

BOONE: And then I wet myself.

DORA: I see.

BOONE: So will you tell me?

DORA: Alright. *(Beat.)* At midnight. Everything will freeze. But you won't feel frozen. You'll just feel still.

BOONE: You won't be scared?

DORA: Just still. Then all the things around us. Clothes. Furniture. Pavement. Buildings. They'll all simultaneously shut off like television sets.

BOONE: Shut off?

DORA: Because they're not here. We see them. And we believe them. But they're just assumptions. And when it's time, they'll shut off and we'll stand as we're meant to—side by side—naked—suspended over blackness—silent. And we'll feel a warmth envelop us. A sensation like a warm bath. And in an instant we will melt into the void, separating back into the individual molecules that first joined together to form us.

BOONE: And that'll be it?

DORA: As far as I know.

BOONE: Doesn't sound too bad.

DORA: It's not. Considering.

BOONE: But why will this happen?

DORA: Well, they rejected my idea.

BOONE: Which was?

DORA: A big Caribbean dance-a-thon.

BOONE: That breaks us into molecules?

DORA: That just goes on and on.

BOONE: I like that idea.

DORA: Yeah, but . . . you know . . . politics . . .

BOONE: But I guess what I'm really asking is . . . why now?

DORA: Guess it's just time. You didn't think it would last forever.

BOONE: *(Pause.)* Less than three days.

DORA: Yeah.

BOONE: Glad I met you when I did.

   (GIN *enters.*)

GIN: Boone! I found you. I have your wallet. I thought I should get it to you as soon as possible. Hi, I'm Gin. Boone's wife. Well . . . mostly. And you are . . . ? You guys didn't break down or anything did ya? 'Cause I'm parked right up the way if you need a lift. Boone, I was hoping we could talk over a few things. Just to talk. It shouldn't take too long. It's freezing out here. Can we talk? In private? Okay. You're mad. I deserve that. But if you would just hear me out. Can't you please just do this one thing for me?

BOONE: Goodnight, Gin.

GIN: Can't we ...

BOONE: Go home. It's cold.

12. SPLIT, NEW YEAR'S EVE

SCENE A—BAR

GUS: Six minutes 'til ...

SHERRY: Isn't that something.

GUS: Do we say Happy New Year's yet?

SHERRY: I'm not gonna.

GUS: *(Beat.)* That's a lot of years.

SHERRY: Got that right.

GUS: Seems they just keep on comin'.

SHERRY: 'Bout every twelve months.

GUS: I'm not even nervous anymore. I know what I been sayin' but— If this is the end, irregardless how it comes, what can they say? I didn't try? I took my shot. And I got derided for it. "Go do Right," you said. Well. This is what I found: You have to be what you are. Innovators. Losers. It's all just a place on the food chain. Who are we to dispute that? You take sharks. All they do: They eat ... they act surly. This is the extent of their contribution. Why are we so arrogant to say it's not alright for people, too?

SHERRY: What is it you're saying to me?

GUS: This is the whole megillah: It is not in my nature to do Good. And I can say this now with perspective.

SHERRY: That's some line of thinkin'.

GUS: Yeah, I come up with it myself.

SHERRY: Y'know what's fascinating . . . I can see your lips move, but I'd swear you were talking outta the other end.

SCENE B — CAL & DWIGHT'S HOME

CAL: You hear that?

DWIGHT: What?

CAL: It's quiet.

DWIGHT: Maybe everyone's out.

CAL: Maybe.

DWIGHT: Do you think it means anything?

CAL: What would it mean?

DWIGHT: I don't know.

CAL: So what about resolutions?

DWIGHT: Haven't thought about it.

CAL: I've been trying to come up with one that means something. A little more substantial than, "I'm gonna lose weight, quit swearing . . ." *(Beat.)* What do you suppose they used to do?

DWIGHT: When?

CAL: Way back. Probably didn't have time for resolutions . . .

DWIGHT: Probably.

CAL: Probably said, this year I'm gonna avoid rickets . . .

DWIGHT: There you go . . .

CAL: . . . not lose my thumb down the Mill.

DWIGHT: That's a thing to resolve.

CAL: *(Long pause.)* I'm glad we stayed in.

DWIGHT: Me too. *(Beat.)* So you still love me, then?
   (GIN enters.)

GIN: I, ah, don't mean to interrupt . . .

CAL: No. Not at all.

GIN: Door was open . . . I wasn't sure if you were still . . . *(To DWIGHT.)* Hi.

DWIGHT: Hello.

GIN: Hi. I just, ah . . . *(Pause.)* I didn't want to be alone.

CAL: Well, you're always welcome here.

GIN: Thank you, Cal. Thank you.

SCENE C — WALT'S APARTMENT

(WALT, BOONE, *and* DORA *are watching the clock.* DORA *doesn't look away.)*

WALT: *(Drunk, wearing* BOONE*'s hat.)* So, this is it?

BOONE: That's what they say.

WALT: You'd think you'd feel something.

BOONE: Apparently not.

WALT: I don't know. It's all a little tidy, don't ya think? I mean, why now? Why tonight? Am I really supposed to believe that the movements of the universe coincide with your standard insurance company calendar?

BOONE: —shaping up that way.

WALT: I can't see time doing that. Okay, yeah, they say it's year *blank*, but what does that mean? Some White Guy says so? Some Greek with a sundial? Only reason we're sitting here in the first place is 'cause the pagans lost. Time . . .

BOONE: Yes?

WALT: . . . is relative. *(Beat.)* Nothing's gonna happen. It didn't happen before, it won't happen again.

BOONE: Maybe so.

WALT: Maybe? No. That is the fact.

BOONE: Yeah. *(He looks at* DORA. *Looks back at* WALT.*)* But "what if," though?

WALT: "What if?"

BOONE: What if . . . the clock strikes . . .

WALT: Right . . .

BOONE: And that's it. That's all. How would *that* be? That

moment before . . . *(Beat.)* The things you wanted to do.

DWIGHT: The things you'll miss.

GUS: The things you regret.

CAL: The things you'll remember.

GIN: The things you'll forget.

SHERRY: The things you wanted to fix.

BOONE: What if this is it?

(Clock strikes twelve.)

(Silence.)

WALT: Nothing.

CAL: Another year.

SHERRY: Another day.

(All is still. DORA *walks center. She is enveloped in a soft, white light. Her shadow appears on the back wall of the stage. From out of the shadow grows a pair of wings. She smiles.)*

END OF PLAY

THE BATHTUB DIARIES

BY LAURA HARRINGTON

CHARACTERS

Napoleon—46, wears white breeches, black boots, (occasionally slippers), and a shirt

Joan of Arc—18, wears black jeans, a T-shirt and some chain mail

Dr. Barry O'Meara—40s, the doctor assigned to Napoleon on St Helena, also plays Walt Whitman, 40s, and Dr. Staubling, 50s, a Civil War surgeon

Captain Hudson Lowe—40s, also plays Ulysses S. Grant, 60s, and Dr. Desgenettes, 30s, Napoleon's army surgeon in Egypt

Wiley Faulkner—20s, a Confederate foot soldier, also plays Count Charles Tristan de Montholon, 30s (a fop of his time), J. Robert Oppenheimer, 50s, and the Bloody Soldier

Empress Josephine—50, also plays Marsha, 50, a suburban housewife from the 1950s, Clara Barton, 40s, and Albine de Montholon, 30s

Three Rats—(wearing half masks or using hand puppets) also play Peter, 12, and Simon, 8, sons of Napoleon's groom, Town Crier, Very Young Soldier, Stretcher-Bearers, and Maisy and Daisy, cleaning women in their 60s

Puppets

(In general, characters wear clothing appropriate to their time in history.)

TIME & PLACE

1815-1821.

The island of St Helena during Napoleon's final exile.

NOTES

The play moves fluidly and quickly between the actual island of St Helena and Napoleon's dreams and nightmares during the last days of his exile.

SFX = Sound Effects
Sound effects are made by the actors, occasionally augmented by amplified sound.

This is a work of fiction. Liberties have been taken with the actual historical record.

"I don't know why, but the little bastard scares me."

THE BATHTUB DIARIES
ACT I

(An English soldier raises the Union Jack on a prominent flagpole. Lights come on one by one in the sentry boxes and watch towers which dot the horizon.)

(SFX: A ROAR of CANNON announces Napoleon's arrival on the island of St Helena, site of his final exile.)

RATS: 12 October 1815. The Island of St Helena. The exile begins

TOWN CRIER: Hear ye! Hear ye! By the order of His Majesty, King George the III of England! As the island of St Helena is now the official gaol of Napoleon Bonaparte, the inhabitants of said island shall henceforth obey the following rules and regulations:

No ship may approach the harbor of Jamestown without official permission. Local fishermen may go out in their boats only at certain hours of the day, to be posted by the governor, and must carry a dated license with them at all times. A curfew is now in effect and anyone found wandering out of doors after 9 o'clock at night will be arrested.

As to the prisoner himself . . .

(LIGHT SHIFTS and we see . . .

NAPOLEON, *pacing off the dimensions of the land surrounding Longwood House, the limits of his prison.* CAPTAIN HUDSON LOWE *is in attendance.)*

NAPOLEON: 46, 47, 48 . . .

MONTHOLON: *(he follows exactly three paces behind* NAPOLEON, *balancing a silver tea tray)* Your tea, sire.

NAPOLEON: *(to* MONTHOLON*)* Later. *(to* LOWE*)* Remove your hat, sir.

LOWE: I beg your pardon?

NAPOLEON: You are in the presence of the Emperor. *(LOWE hesitates)* Your HAT! *(LOWE removes his hat)* Do not speak unless spoken to. Do not sit unless given a command. Really, you are a man of the world. You should not require instruction. *(Lowe bites his tongue)* However, if you have never been at court, you may consult Count Montholon. He is an expert in all matters of protocol. *(NAPOLEON turns the corner, continues pacing)* 49, 50, 51 . . . *(looks up, taking in the vast plain)* This is it?! This . . . this . . . wasteland?

RATS: Welcome to Deadwood Plain.

LOWE: Mister Bonaparte—

NAPOLEON: Mister? MISTER?!! Do you dare insult me?

LOWE: The renovations are proceeding well.

NAPOLEON: Try not to remind me that you are my jailer. I have been promised the utmost civility by the joint nations responsible for my exile.

LOWE: You may occupy half of Longwood while the remainder of the construction is completed.

NAPOLEON: Did I invite you to speak?

LOWE: You are no longer an emperor, sir. You are a common prisoner receiving uncommon concessions from the English government.

NAPOLEON: Uncommon concessions?! You are renovating a chicken shack.

LOWE: A summer retreat built by a prominent citizen.

NAPOLEON: A shack I say! And where are the trees? The gardens, the kitchen gardens, the roses . . . Does nothing grow on this vast ROCK!?

LOWE: We have men working round the clock.

NAPOLEON: Are they bringing me earth? And trees? And planting a windbreak? *(no answer)* Typical of English incompetence: to imprison me and then make me wait for my prison!

RATS: On a clear day it is possible to see Blue Hill, Lemon Valley, Rupert's Bay. Of course, we don't have very many clear days.

LOWE: The papers, fabrics, rugs, are all being imported.

NAPOLEON: English, I suppose?

LOWE: French.

NAPOLEON: They are the best.

LOWE: Yes.

RATS: Sounds delicious. Something new to chew!

NAPOLEON: Well, that's something.

LOWE: Yes, it is.

NAPOLEON: Not enough, of course. *(gestures)* We need a stream—here—And a pond—there—And an allée of plane trees—there—When can you get them? Two thousand trees should suffice. Here—we will make a hill. And there—a walkway beneath rose-covered pergolas. Sixty dozen roses. Josephine has hundreds at Malmaison. And lemons, and limes, and grapes, and pear trees; cherry, apple, persimmon. Are you getting this down? This can all be transformed—as I transformed Paris, Versailles, all of France . . .

(SFX: The pounding of stakes)

(SFX: Wind)

NAPOLEON: What is that noise?

LOWE: They are erecting the perimeter fence.

NAPOLEON: A fence.

LOWE: Yes.

NAPOLEON: You will enclose me.

LOWE: Four square miles with watch boxes and sentry towers every fifty feet.

NAPOLEON: Four square miles of unprepossessing dirt lying beneath an everpresent, maddening wind.

LOWE: Exactly.

NAPOLEON: Write this down! We will need a ballroom. And silkworms. For the ladies' dresses. We must do it all. We must start from scratch. And build a new world.

LOWE: No.

NAPOLEON: Did I ask you a question?

LOWE: No.

NAPOLEON: I issued an order.

LOWE: And I am issuing my answer: No to everything you have asked for. Yes to the shack, the dirt, the vast empty plain, the fence, the everpresent guards, and the mocking winds.

(SFX: More wind)

RATS: And rats! Don't forget the rats! Unlimited rats!

NAPOLEON: You look like a hyena caught in a trap. You have the face of a debt collector, an imbecile, a man only fit to hire assassins, a creature so soaked in evil one glance from your malignant eye could poison a cup of coffee. I have seen Prussians, Tartars, Cossacks, Kalmucks, but never before in my life have I seen so ill favored and forbidding a countenance.

LOWE: As as enemy and a disturber of the world, you have been placed beyond the pale of civil and social relations. We cast you out, we cut you off . . .

NAPOLEON: Montholon! Your pistol! *(takes pistol from* MONTHOLON *and hands it to* LOWE*)* Kill me now, Lowe. Save us both alot of time and trouble. Save the English government millions of pounds per annum. Have I provoked you enough to pull the trigger? Not yet?? We shall see.

(SFX: Howling wind)

(As the WIND begins to HOWL, NAPOLEON *turns his back on* LOWE *and steps into a spotlight. On another part of the stage lights come up on* DR. STAUBLING, *a Civil War surgeon, and* DR. DESGENETTES, *a surgeon from* NAPOLEON*'s Egyptian campaign. They each wear blood-spattered aprons, and smoke cigars. They are each standing in a pool of blood.)*

NAPOLEON: What is death and how do you define death? Have you examined men after their death? What is their appearance?

When does the soul quit the body? When do you suppose the soul enters the body? Is it possible to observe this phenomenon?

Have you seen it? Have you seen it, doctor, with your own eyes?

Did you know it for what it was or did you laugh it away? For I can imagine nothing more terrifying to our sense of responsibility—as doctors—as generals—than to admit that the soul is real.

(Lights expand on the surgeons and come up on . . .

MAISY *and* DAISY, *mopping up the blood)*

MAISY: I'm ready to retire.

DAISY: Me too.

MAISY: My feet hurt.

DAISY: You're telling me. Look here. I've got bunions.

MAISY: Bunions. That's nothing. My toes don't bend anymore.

DAISY: How long you been workin'?

MAISY: What are you asking me for? Same as you. Forever.

DAISY: Seems like it.

MAISY: Not seems like. Is.

DAISY: You ever find anything?

MAISY: Like what?

DAISY: Letters, buttons . . . money . . .

MAISY: Nothin'. How 'bout you?

DAISY: You'd think—

MAISY: What?

DAISY: With so much life, so much blood leaking into the ground . . . I don't know—

MAISY: What?

DAISY: You'd think there'd be something left behind.

MAISY: Death don't leave nothin' behind.

DAISY: Nothin' to hang on to, you mean?

MAISY: Nothin'.

> (MAISY *and* DAISY *continue mopping blood as LIGHTS SHIFT and we see . . .*
>
> WILEY FAULKNER, *a 16-year-old Confederate soldier, propped in a corner, his shirt front covered in blood.*)
>
> *(SFX: A distant harmonica)*
>
> *(Two* STRETCHER-BEARER*s arrive.)*

STRETCHER-BEARER #1: There's another one.

STRETCHER-BEARER #2: All right there, buddy. We'll get you to the hospital.

WILEY: Leave me be.

STRETCHER-BEARER #1: C'mon, son.

WILEY: I can't bear to lie down The pain's like to kill me.

STRETCHER-BEARER #2: We got to get you to the hospital.

WILEY: I ain't moving.

STRETCHER-BEARER #2: I don't have time to argue with you. We got thousands of boys to move.

WILEY: —So move 'em! *(he coughs up blood)*

STRETCHER-BEARER #2: Son—

WILEY: If you move me, I swear I'll die. Just leave me some water.

STRETCHER-BEARER #1: There's to be a meeting in here.

WILEY: Let's meet.

STRETCHER-BEARER #2: Our orders are to move you.

WILEY: You think I'm too young to look my own death in the face? You want me to have any chance at all, you leave me be. I ain't gonna disturb no meeting.

STRETCHER-BEARER #1: All right then.

WILEY: They won't even notice me.

(STRETCHER-BEARER*s exit*)

(JOAN OF ARC *steps through the wall*)

JOAN: I noticed you.

WILEY: Who are you?

JOAN: You don't recognize me?

WILEY: Am I dreaming? Shit! I'm dead—

JOAN: No, no. *(she places her hand over his wound)* There, now. Try a deep breath. Is that better?

WILEY: Who are you?

JOAN: *(uncovers her shoulder, reveals a scar)* I was supposed to die from this. I didn't.

WILEY: You remind me of someone.

JOAN: Are you here for the meeting?

WILEY: What meeting?

JOAN: We've been summoned. *(extends her hand)* My name's Joan.

WILEY: *(shakes it)* Wiley Faulkner.

JOAN: Pleased to meet you.

WILEY: Summoned for what?

JOAN: To end the war.

WILEY: Good luck.

(NAPOLEON *enters*)

JOAN: Oh, good heavens, there's Napoleon. What does he know about ending wars?

NAPOLEON: A chair! I need a chair!

WILEY: Did you say Napoleon?

JOAN: He's not one to get his own chair now, is he? Poor boy. He's got to find someone to go fetch it for him. What a handicap not being able to do anything for yourself.

NAPOLEON: A chair, I say!

JOAN: I always stuck with the common soldier. Didn't raise myself up. Didn't preen. Not too much, that is. Some of the clothes were lovely. And I did have a special weakness for my flag.

(SFX: *Battle flags snapping in the wind.*)

JOAN: *(cont)* I was vain, you know? Didn't think so at the time, but winning battles, crowning the King and hearing God's voice . . . well, it's hard work to stay humble.

WILEY: I don't understand. Aren't you dead? And if you're dead, does that mean I'm dead?

JOAN: No, no, no. You're not dead. We've got some special dispensation. Like I said, we've been summoned.

WILEY: By who?

JOAN: I'm not at liberty to reveal that. *(spotting* WALT WHITMAN, *offstage)* Oh, look, there's Walt Whitman. He's your era, isn't he?

WILEY: Never heard of him.

JOAN: Oh, the fate of poets. I believe I'm to be the only woman. Clara Barton's been invited, but says she's too busy to come. And Florence Nightingale could not be found. Although what they think I could possibly know about ending wars is beyond me. I landed somewhere near the end of the Hundred Years War—and I did help to unite France—but really, what I did was fight. I would have kept on fighting 'til I'd driven every English soldier into the sea. Getting captured put an end to that ambition. But I must say, I still wanted to fight them. The rush of animals and men, the battle cries, the screams of the wounded, the horses, the ringing bells ... all of it ... all of it ... And inside my head this clear bright light; a stillness so profound ... the stillness of God ... of madness ... I had never felt so intensely alive.

(SFX: Bells)

(GRANT *and* OPPENHEIMER *step into individual spotlights)*

GRANT: We rolled through Georgia like locusts, like the plague.

OPPENHEIMER: We lit the stars.

GRANT: Atlanta in flames. Indiscriminate.

OPPENHEIMER: We had stopped hitting certain tragets in Japan—to more clearly test the bomb's efficacy.

GRANT: A revolution in strategy.

OPPENHEIMER: The irresistible glitter of technology.

GRANT: And then, repeating rifles. More deaths per minute.

OPPENHEIMER: Madness.

GRANT: Total war. *(the spots blink out)*

(SFX: Bells)

JOAN: Do you like fighting, Wiley?

WILEY: No, ma'am. No, I don't. (WHITMAN *enters and approaches* WILEY. *He does not see* JOAN.)

WHITMAN: Do you need a surgeon?

WILEY: No. I seem to have been ... healed. *(He looks at* JOAN. *She exits quietly.)*

WHITMAN: Remarkable. *(he takes an orange from his pocket)* Would you care for an orange?

WILEY: Yes. No ...

WHITMAN: I'll peel it for you. You decide.

WILEY: What are you doing here?

WHITMAN: Meaning ... shouldn't I be giving this orange to a boy in blue?

WILEY: Yes.

WHITMAN: I hate war. I don't hate the boys who suffer war. How long have you been fighting?

WILEY: Fourteen months.

WHITMAN: You consider yourself a lucky man?

WILEY: No, sir.

WHITMAN: But you have survived.

WILEY: More or less.

WHITMAN: Is there anyone you'd like to write to? I have paper. And stamps. I can write for you, if you like.

WILEY: What would you say?

WHITMAN: No. You tell me what to say. I write it down.

WILEY: I will live through this—

WHITMAN: Perhaps.

WILEY: Did you pay someone to take your place?

WHITMAN: No.

WILEY: What, then?

WHITMAN: I volunteered to nurse.

WILEY: *(contemptuous)* How heroic.

WHITMAN: *(he stands to leave)* Is there anything I can get you?

WILEY: Don't go.

WHITMAN: Why not?

WILEY: I feel like the dark could swallow me.

WHITMAN: I'll write for you, shall I? *(takes out paper, sits)* After a battle, the fields are littered with men and muskets and horses and, believe it or not, paper. Hundreds of letters. Dear Mother, Dear Sally, Dear Dad, Beloved, My Darling . . . and they all say the same thing. Remember me. Boys covered with blood, with flies, boys sinking into the earth. Oh, if they could stand up, stand up and sing, what a song would fill the air, tear the sky, tear the earth. Remember me. God have mercy. If there is a God. And if there is mercy. Remember me.

(SFX: Paper/ leaves blowing in the wind)

(LIGHTS FADE on WILEY *and* WHITMAN *and . . .*

FOCUS ON . . . NAPOLEON)

NAPOLEON: Remember me?! Remember me?! They will remember me forever!!!!

RATS: If they have not already forgotten you. Time marches on, old man. Without you.

NAPOLEON: No! They will remember me. All of me. As a schoolboy. Commanding the cannons. As a General. A husband. A lover. At the pyramids. Leipzig. Versailles.

RATS: Out of sight! Out of MIND!!

NAPOLEON: I remember my first boots, my first pistol. White flesh, bare arms, nipples. I remember the first horse who died between my knees. I remember standing among the dead and dying on the bridge of Arcola. I remember the pastry cook. I remember the soldier who carried parsley in his helmet to garnish my chicken. All through the Russian winter. Imagine. Parsley in a helmet. Imagine the Emperor feasting on chicken while his men . . . his men . . .

(SFX: A body falling through space)

(LIGHTS SHIFT and . . .

COUNT MONTHOLON *enters and approaches* NAPOLEON.*)*

(SFX: A body landing on rocks)

MONTHOLON: Another soldier has been blown off the cliff, your Majesty.

NAPOLEON: Only one?

MONTHOLON: Yes, sire.

NAPOLEON: *(blows nose, hands handkerchief to Montholon)* Here. Add this to your collection of relics: beds the great man slept in, chairs he sat in, hankies he blew his nose in.

MONTHOLON: You told me to fetch you if another one blew away, sire. Are you coming?

NAPOLEON: Why can't they blow away in groups of five or six? Or fifty or sixty?

MONTHOLON: They don't post that many guards at that end of the island, sire?

NAPOLEON: What do they think they're keeping me from doing?

Flying away with the birds? Swimming away with the whales? Two thousand English soldiers to guard one French Emperor. They are still afraid of me.

MONTHOLON: Yes, sire.

NAPOLEON: You're boring.

MONTHOLON: I did not follow you into exile to be insulted.

NAPOLEON: Then stop being so dull. Show a little spirit. Fake it if you have to. Did you see the body?

MONTHOLON: No, sire. Sampson came to report. I came to fetch you.

NAPOLEON: Do you want to see the body?

MONTHOLON: Not particularly. Sire.

NAPOLEON: Death doesn't interest you? What about your own death? Does that interest you?

MONTHOLON: Shall I take you there now, sire?

NAPOLEON: By all means.

(LIGHTS SHIFT . . .

and we are on the cliff's edge. Two British soldiers labor to haul the dead soldier up over the edge of the cliff.)

(SFX: Wind)

NAPOLEON: Is he heavy?

SOLDIER: (struggling) No, sir.

NAPOLEON: What's his name?

SOLDIER: Peckham. Sir.

NAPOLEON: First name?

SOLDIER: Jonathan.

NAPOLEON: Rank?

SOLDIER: Private.

NAPOLEON: Careful you don't blow away, Sergeant.

SOLDIER: Yes, sir.

NAPOLEON: Did he like this tour of duty? Did he like St Helena?

(SFX: BIRDS)

SOLDIER: (Hauling the body up over the edge. The dead soldier is *shockingly young.)* He loved the birds here.

NAPOLEON: What?

SOLDIER: Loved the birds. Interesting species here, sir. That's what Peckham said. And the migratory path . . . ? Seems we're a major stop off. For the birds, that is.

NAPOLEON: Maybe he was trying to fly.

SOLDIER: He was a sensible boy, sir.

NAPOLEON: But don't we all go a bit mad here on St Helena?

SOLDIER: *(finding Peckham's notebook in his jacket pocket)* Here, sir. Take a look at this. He sketched them. Quite good, aren't they? *(the two men bend their heads over the sketchbook)*

NAPOLEON: Where do you think I'm going to go, Sergeant?

SOLDIER: Sir?

NAPOLEON: The way you post men to guard these cliffs. As though I can fly—

SOLDIER: Well, sir—

NAPOLEON: You're a rational man. It must be clear to you I cannot fly—

SOLDIER: But your supporters, sir. They could mount an attack at any time. Surely the great French army is capable of orchestrating your escape?

NAPOLEON: No one wants me any longer. The French least of all. Until I die, that is, when they will memorialize me to the last button, to the last strand of hair. How old are you, Sergeant?

SOLDIER: Twenty-nine.

NAPOLEON: And this boy here?

SOLDIER: Eighteen.

NAPOLEON: I am 46. You will not be on this godforsaken island much longer. How I envy you your return trip home. *(looking at the dead boy)* Will they bury him here? Or send him home?

SOLDIER: He'll be buried at sea, sir. The family notified. His effects returned.

NAPOLEON: *(writing his name in the notebook)*

Send them this. One day it will be worth a fortune. I should hate to be buried at sea. So inconclusive. Nothing to visit. I will be remembered. How strange that is. When you bring your grand-children to visit my tomb in Paris, Sergeant, what will you remember? Will you remember Peckham? And the birds? And a man, already old at 46? A man you believed could fly. What a crazy idea. They're going to take my horse away, aren't they? Don't let them, Sergeant. My legs aren't good for much any-more. Riding. And bathing. My only pleasures.

(LIGHTS SHIFT)

RATS: In which the great man gets wet and begins to dream. *(singing)* Bathing, bathing, over the open sea—

(SFX: Water pouring into the tub)

(A large, claw-footed lead bathtub is wheeled on stage.

NAPOLEON, *fully dressed, gets into the tub.* JOAN OF ARC *falls through the ceiling.)*

NAPOLEON: *(startled)* Who the hell are you!?

JOAN: *(scrambling to her feet)* Get up! Get up!! You are turning into a prune—

NAPOLEON: Get out—

JOAN: Not 'til you do.

NAPOLEON: Montholon!

JOAN: He's asleep.

NAPOLEON: Where is your modesty, madame?

JOAN: I'm dead. We don't have to be modest anymore.

NAPOLEON: Is that right?

JOAN: That's right.

NAPOLEON: Well, I'm not dead.

JOAN: Not yet.

NAPOLEON: And I still have a shred of modesty. If you don't mind— *(indicates door)*

JOAN: I won't look—

NAPOLEON: Won't look?! Hell, you will publish your observa-tions: The great man. Naked.

JOAN: I can't publish.

NAPOLEON: Right.

JOAN: Aside from the mortality issue, I can't read or write.

NAPOLEON: Still?

JOAN: What do you mean?

NAPOLEON: Four hundred years in heaven? Don't you think you could spare a few decades to learn to read and write?

JOAN: We're busier than you think.

NAPOLEON: Nice costume. Get out.

JOAN: You don't believe me?

NAPOLEON: I believe you've been sent here to make me think I'm mad. Well, I'm not. I won't be. I see clearly. Much too clearly. It is enough to drive any man mad—yet I refuse. Do you hear me? I refuse. I may be dying but I am not losing my mind!! Now GO—

JOAN: Don't you even want to know why I'm here?

NAPOLEON: I know why you're here.

JOAN: No, you don't.

NAPOLEON: You dare to contradict me? The Emperor of all of Europe?!?

JOAN: Not anymore.

NAPOLEON: GET OUT!!!!!

JOAN: Has it occurred to you I might be able to help you?

NAPOLEON: MONTHOLON!!!

JOAN: He can't hear you. *(with a ROAR—intending to frighten her—*NAPOLEON *stands up in his bath.* JOAN *bursts out laughing.)* Oh, we're going to have a great time together. Could you possibly ROAR again? *(he sinks back into the bath; pause)*

NAPOLEON: Prove it.

JOAN: Prove what?

NAPOLEON: Prove to me you're Joan of Arc.

JOAN: Do you know what I said to the Dauphin to make him believe me—and give me an army?

NAPOLEON: No . . . There's been a great deal of speculation. Absolutely no proof.

JOAN: *(she crosses to the bath, whispers in his ear, then)* Would you have given me an army?

NAPOLEON: He was desperate.

JOAN: And you are not?

NAPOLEON: I don't have an army to give you. Ask the English.

JOAN: I hate the English. Just like you do. I wanted to drive them into the sea. But the English are very good on the sea. You underestimated them. More than once. Kind of your downfall, wasn't it? Don't underestimate me, General.

(she exits)

NAPOLEON: *(bellows)* More hot water! Goddamnit! I want it HOT!!! Hot, do you hear me? Hot!

(LIGHTS FLASH ON AND OFF)

(SFX: Water splashing)

RATS: In which the good doctor begins his bathtub visits.

(SFX: Knocking on the door)

NAPOLEON: Entrez!

O'MEARA: *(entering the bathroom)* Oh, my goodness. I beg your pardon. I had no idea . . . Another day. I'll come back another day, shall I? A more convenient time.

NAPOLEON: Who are you?

O'MEARA: *(doesn't know where to look, can't turn his back on the emperor, in an agony of discomfort and embarrassment)* Dr. Barry O'Meara, sir. Begging your pardon, sir. I was misinformed. I was told you wished to see me and brought here. Please forgive me for intruding on your private . . . in your private . . . I never intended to disturb you at your bath.

NAPOLEON: Look at me when you speak to me!

O'MEARA: *(really seeing the bathtub for the first time, startled)* My God—

NAPOLEON: Yes?

O'MEARA: It looks . . . No . . . I beg your pardon.

NAPOLEON: It looks like a coffin.

O'MEARA: Yes.

NAPOLEON: I am encouraged to practice my death. Who do you work for?

O'MEARA: His royal majesty—

NAPOLEON: —Yes, yes. Who do you answer to?

O'MEARA: Sir Hudson Lowe is my commanding officer.

NAPOLEON: But you are not English.

O'MEARA: Irish.

NAPOLEON: What is it that causes you to serve the English? Surely the good people of Ireland need their doctors.

O'MEARA: It is a royal commission, sir. An honor. A tradition.

NAPOLEON: You will never achieve equal status with the English. To them you are a dog. A useful dog, but a dog nonetheless. You must rise up. You must crush them. You must take their sense of status and shove it down their throats. Let them choke on status, choke until they die.

O'MEARA: Sir. I am a loyal servant.

NAPOLEON: Does that make you blind? And deaf? And stupid???

O'MEARA: No sir.

NAPOLEON: Show a little backbone! A little fire!

O'MEARA: I am finding it difficult—

NAPOLEON: —Yes . . . ?

O'MEARA: I fear . . . I am unable to strike the right tone.

NAPOLEON: I am not a bell to be sounded and struck—

O'MEARA: No, sir.

NAPOLEON: No, sir, yes, sir. Is that how you reached your exalted position on this coveted island??? This most desirable of posts, of assignments . . . ?

O'MEARA: I requested this posting, sir.

NAPOLEON: *(a belly laugh)* Then you are the greatest fool alive.

O'MEARA: I'm sorry you feel that way, sir.

NAPOLEON: So! The English have given me an Irish doctor. Do you not relish the irony? Are you not amused?

O'MEARA: No, sir.

NAPOLEON: You are boring!

O'MEARA: Begging your pardon.

NAPOLEON: Stiff. Humorless.

O'MEARA: Perhaps—

NAPOLEON: —Get out! Get OUT!! Send me someone who can laugh, for god's sake. Someone who can laugh!!!

(SPOTLIGHT on . . . the RATS *who fall down laughing and roll around on the floor.)*

(SFX: Raucous laughter crescendoes then snaps off)

NAPOLEON: *(cont)* No woman could laugh like Josephine. First these little yipping, honeyed barks, rising in pitch. And then the laughter. I swear it began in her toes and missed not one single inch of her flesh. Ahhh, she was masterful. Imagine riding a woman like Josephine on the wave of her laughter.

*(*MONTHOLON *enters)*

MONTHOLON: Your Majesty, the Comtesse de Montholon requests permission to see you.

NAPOLEON: Your wife.

MONTHOLON: Yes, sire.

NAPOLEON: Comes to her Emperor.

MONTHOLON: Yes, sire.

NAPOLEON: Alone . . . ?

MONTHOLON: You know how fond she is of you, your Majesty.

NAPOLEON: She is quite a beauty.

MONTHOLON: Yes, she is.

NAPOLEON: Beautiful enough for three husbands.

MONTHOLON: Yes, sire.

NAPOLEON: Does that not bother you?

MONTHOLON: I am the most fortunate of men, your Majesty.

NAPOLEON: Still, she shines, does she not?

MONTHOLON: Brighter than ever.

NAPOLEON: And you would allow her to shine with me?

MONTHOLON: We are here to serve you—

NAPOLEON: —Adultery is all a matter of a sofa.

MONTHOLON: Will that be all, your Majesty?

NAPOLEON: Show her to the map room. And dismiss the servants.

MONTHOLON: As you wish, sire.

(He bows and exits.)

(SFX: A globe spinning on its axis.)

(Lights come up on NAPOLEON's *map room with a globe of the world and a globe of the heavens flanking the door.* ALBINE DE MONTHOLON *enters, carrying a book. She removes a small, leather-bound journal from her pocket and writes:)*

ALBINE: Wednesday, the 26th: Ennui. Ennui! Thursday, the 27th: The same. Friday, the 28th: The same. Saturday, the 29th: The same. Sunday, the 30th: Grand ennui. Monday, the 31st . . .

*(*NAPOLEON *enters. She quickly stuffs the journal into her pocket and spins the globe.)*

NAPOLEON: Time travelling?

ALBINE: If only we could, your Majesty.

NAPOLEON: Where would you go?

ALBINE: Paris. Of course.

NAPOLEON: Of course. *(takes the book from her)* What are you reading?

ALBINE: A murder mystery. Very popular in France right now. Based on the true story of Madame de Brinvilliers.

NAPOLEON: Not about us?

ALBINE: Alas, sire, no. It tells of a subtle form of poisoning.

NAPOLEON: Ahhh. You study poison.

ALBINE: No, sire, I simply read to pass the time.

NAPOLEON: Who would you poison, my dear? Your husband or your lover?

ALBINE: *(with sangfroid)* Why not both?

NAPOLEON: Clever woman. Have you learned to laugh?

ALBINE: I am determined to be your favorite pupil.

NAPOLEON: Why do I always feel that you are lying?

ALBINE: Your Majesty—

NAPOLEON: Go on, then: Laugh.

ALBINE: *(a hearty belly laugh—forced and phony)* HA! HA! HA!

NAPOLEON: No, no, no! Not like that!

You must manipulate the uvula in your throat.

Open your mouth. *(she does)*

Wider. *(she does)*

(placing his hand on her throat)

Now relax the jaw. *(she does)*

Relax the tongue.

Let it pool in the bottom of your mouth.

Like a puddle!

That's it—

It is the throat that is erotic.

Let it vibrate, my dear.

Let it sing. Go on . . . Go on— *(she attempts a sound)*

Higher. Higher.

(NAPOLEON moves to stand behind her, pressed against her, his fingers lightly on her throat. Whispering in her ear)

Are you Lady Macbeth? Plotting to kill your King?

ALBINE: *(breathless)* Never. Sire.

NAPOLEON: Go on, then—laugh. *(she begins to "yip," encouraging her)* That's it. Like a dog. Like a pup. Yip. Yip. Yip. *(together they bark—an odd chorus—half pleasure, half pain, ridiculous, and full of yearning)*

NAPOLEON/ALBINE: Yip. Yip. Yip.

NAPOLEON: Yes, my dear, yesssss . . . . . .

NAPOLEON/ALBINE: Yip. Yip. Yip.

(as LIGHTS FADE, WE HEAR . . .)

(SFX: Dogs howling and growling, crescendoes, then snaps off)

(LIGHTS SHIFT and FOCUS on . . .)

RATS: *(they play ukuleles and sing)*

Transition music, boys . . .

One and two and . . .

Way down upon the Swanee River . . .

Far, far from home . . .

That's where my heart is yearning ever . . .

Far from the old folks at home . . . .

(LIGHTS SHIFT and come up on . . . Ulysses S. Grant's porch. Grant sits in a rocker, bundled in blankets, writing his memoir. The throat cancer that is killing him makes speaking difficult.)

(NAPOLEON enters)

NAPOLEON: What's the matter with you?

GRANT: Throat cancer.

NAPOLEON: It's killing you?

GRANT: Too many cigars. Etc.

NAPOLEON: Does it hurt? Does it bleed? Why are you here? In the middle of nowhere, on a borrowed porch? What are you writing? Will anyone care? Don't you have servants to write for you?

GRANT: No.

NAPOLEON: No servants?

GRANT: None.

NAPOLEON: Everyone in my employ is writing. They cannot wait to get back to their rooms to write everything down. Every last scrap. My four principal servants? The four apostles. Each convinced that the misery of exile will be transformed into fame. And fortune. Didn't they call you "The Butcher"?

GRANT: We restored the Union.

NAPOLEON: How many men killed?

GRANT: A drop in the bucket compared to your numbers.

NAPOLEON: But my campaigns spanned decades. And continents. Match us up for any four-year period and I believe you win, hands down. And then, of course, there's the question of your Native population. Near genocide I believe.

GRANT: You can't lay that at my door.

NAPOLEON: No? You were secretly opposed to the Western expansion? In your heart of hearts you never wanted to break a treaty?

GRANT: You were a dictator—

NAPOLEON: —Emperor—

GRANT: I was a president. You squandered millions.

NAPOLEON: And made Paris into the City of Light.

GRANT: I studied you. Your tactics, your speed, your brilliance, your arrogance—

NAPOLEON: —I studied you. Your Revolution. Your Constitution. Your House, your Senate. Your Electoral College doesn't quite make sense, however—

GRANT: —your corruption, your mistakes—

NAPOLEON: —Mistakes?! You haven't been reading my version. In my version—

GRANT: There is no VERSION!! There is history. There are facts. Troops killed. Territory gained and lost.

NAPOLEON: So serious, you Americans. So blind to your own empire-building. One vision of the world triumphs over another, that's all. Do you deny the cost in human lives? I'd wager more lives were spent on your empire than on mine.

GRANT: This is not an empire, it's a democracy.

NAPOLEON: Is that right?

GRANT: What do you want?

NAPOLEON: I came to see how much of me is in you.

GRANT: What are you talking about?

NAPOLEON: My military legacy.

GRANT: Is over—

NAPOLEON: Don't kid yourself. William Tecumseh Sherman and his "total war" made me look like a schoolboy.

GRANT: We did what we had to do.

NAPOLEON: Can a nation founded on the revolutionary principles of equality survive the practice of traffic in human flesh? *(a beat)* I retired the guillotine.

(SFX: Guillotine)

You retired the auction block.

(SFX: Gavel on a block)

Shall we call it a draw?

GRANT: We are not equals, sir.

NAPOLEON: The death we have each unleashed rolls like thunder—through the trenches, through the decades—on into the next century and the next and the next. I am living still. And so are you. You know who I'd like to talk to?

GRANT: Who?

NAPOLEON: God.

GRANT: Good luck.

NAPOLEON: Not in my power, not in my purview.

GRANT: I should think not.

NAPOLEON: Too bad, though, isn't it?

GRANT: No, no, it isn't.

NAPOLEON: If you believe in God, that is. *(looks off)* Oh my, here she comes now.

GRANT: Who?

NAPOLEON: *(in awe)* Josephine—

GRANT: Josephine—?

NAPOLEON: Look at her—

GRANT: She's nearly naked.

NAPOLEON: The Directoire style, my friend. Inspired by the Greeks. No one wore it quite so well as Josephine—and that great Amazonian beauty—Therese Tallien. Best friends. They shocked the world. Hard to stay calm in their presence, if you know what I mean?

GRANT: You're not beyond all that?

NAPOLEON: I'm not beyond anything. Look at her. She looks so young. How do I look? Still old and fat?

GRANT: Yes.

NAPOLEON: But I am still Napoleon. The great explorer of the Black Forest—

GRANT: The what?!

NAPOLEON: Metaphor. You Americans never understand metaphor.

JOSEPHINE: *(laughs)* Is this really the republic we all admired so much? It seems so primitive—

NAPOLEON: *(fondling her breasts)* Kiss me— *(she does)* You're more beautiful than ever. Exquisite . . . exquisite . . . *(Grant coughs) (remembering his manners)* Josephine, this is Ulysses S. Grant. A great general of the American Civil War. Nineteenth century.

JOSEPHINE: How remarkable. Lovely to meet you, General. Here we all are. The living, the dead, the dying. And I've brought food from Paris. Let's live a bit, shall we? Champagne, gentlemen!! Champagne! *(as Josephine pours champagne, Napoleon boldly puts his hands up her skirts) (raising her glass)* Let's drink to life, shall we?

NAPOLEON: How did you manage to grow younger?

JOSPEHINE: Wonderful, isn't it? I even got new teeth—Look— *(she bares her new white teeth)*

NAPOLEON: To life—

JOSEPHINE: To life—

GRANT: To life— *(They all drink. JOSEPHINE and NAPOLEON throw their glasses against a rock, smashing them.)*

(NAPOLEON grabs JOSEPHINE and fondles her with abandon.

(LIGHTS FOCUS on . . . NAPOLEON and JOSEPHINE.)

NAPOLEON: You are as young and plump as a chicken, *mon petit chou.*

JOSEPHINE: And I know how much you love chicken . . .

NAPOLEON: *(he begins to lick her knees)* Tasty . . . so tasty . . . Just a little trace of salt . . . *(lick, lick)* . . . and musk . . . *(lick, lick)* . . . and sex . . . *(lick, lick)* How is it you have the flesh of a girl, a child, a maiden?

JOSEPHINE: While you've grown fat.

NAPOLEON: Yes.

JOSEPHINE: And doughy.

NAPOLEON: Yes.

JOSEPHINE: And so pale, my darling boy, so pale.

NAPOLEON: Yes.

JOSEPHINE: But your hair—

NAPOLEON: What's left of it—

JOSEPHINE: —Still so fine . . . baby fine . . .

RATS: Baby bottom!!

NAPOLEON: How could you bear to leave Paris?

JOSEPHINE: I haven't left Paris.

NAPOLEON: How could they let you go?

JOSEPHINE: Who?

NAPOLEON: Did they seal your coffin with lead? Shave the hair from your head to braid into bracelets for your loved ones?

JOSEPHINE: I am with you always, darling, always.

NAPOLEON: Don't leave me. Give me your word. Never leave me.

JOSEPHINE: Leave you? How could I ever leave you?

I am the blood in your boots, the tongue in your mouth,
the bright star in the heavens above you.

I am the soft flannel wrapping your feet.

I am your favorite tricorn hat—you must wear your hat, darling; it is the symbol of your greatness, the image of your power—

I am your sauceboat.

I am the loaf of bread and jug of wine they tuck beside you in your coffin, in case you grow hungry and thirsty on your journey from one world to another.

I am the hole they lay your coffin in,

I am the flagstones covering the lid.

I am the earth, I am the shovel.

I am the rain falling and the willows weeping.

I am the Vale of Geranium in the Valley of the Tomb.

I am your hope and your sorrow,
your wishes and your deep, dreamless sleep.

In your endless days and your sleepless nights,

I am your Paris, I am your Versailles, your Arc de Triomphe.

I am your looted treasures in the Louvre.

I am the ermine mantle covering your shoulders,

I am the crown you take from the Pope and place on your own head.

I am the trumpets and the choir.

I am the Cathedral of Notre Dame.

I open my doors to you.

I am the red velvet laid down on the flagstones.

I am the jewel-encrusted kid slippers on your feet.

I am the Cloak of Marengo.

I am your victories and your defeats.

I am your Empress.

I am your Queen.

RATS: LIGHTS! *(lights blink out on* NAPOLEON *and* JOSEPHINE*)* No, no, no. You don't get to watch. Some dreams are private. But we can tell you this . . . it is a very satisfying encounter.

(LIGHTS SHIFT)

(SFX: Water splashing into the tub.)

(The bathtub is wheeled on stage. NAPOLEON *climbs into the tub. Steam rises.* O'MEARA *enters.)*

O'MEARA: How are you today?

NAPOLEON: How do you think?

O'MEARA: Any complaints?

NAPOLEON: Too numerous to list.

O'MEARA: Something that I, as your physician, might address?

NAPOLEON: The quality of the food, the quality of the air, the light, the water, the wind.

O'MEARA: You imagine I have more power than God.

NAPOLEON: Could you . . . ?

O'MEARA: Yes?

NAPOLEON: Wash my back.

O'MEARA: Wouldn't your valet . . . ?

NAPOLEON: You hesitate to touch me?

O'MEARA: No—

NAPOLEON: Even at my invitation?

O'MEARA: No, it's not—

NAPOLEON: Too menial a task for a physician?

O'MEARA: Hand me the soap—

NAPOLEON: Don't bother.

O'MEARA: General Bonaparte—

NAPOLEON: You are not accustomed to bathe your patients?

O'MEARA: No, I'm not.

NAPOLEON: And yet you are responsible for the health of this body which you are afraid to touch.

O'MEARA: It is a matter of privacy, sir.

NAPOLEON: I have no privacy. I am watched as I walk, followed as I ride, interviewed in my bath—

O'MEARA: At your suggestion, sir—

NAPOLEON: You are so squeamish.

O'MEARA: No, sir.

NAPOLEON: I do not like a squeamish physician.

O'MEARA: You have set me a test and I have failed it.

NAPOLEON: Yes.

O'MEARA: Set me another.

NAPOLEON: Give me something.

O'MEARA: Yes. What is it? What can I get you?

NAPOLEON: Let it end. Let this exile be over.

O'MEARA: You can't be serious—

NAPOLEON: Ahh, the little Irish doctor is shocked. Catholic I suppose. And squeamish. Just my luck.

O'MEARA: You don't mean it.

NAPOLEON: Don't patronize me.

O'MEARA: You are still young.

NAPOLEON: No, I was never young.

O'MEARA: Ah.

NAPOLEON: I have never been afraid of dying. It takes more courage to suffer than to die. They say I took foolish chances in battle. I simply went where I was needed, where my men needed me. My men died for me, for France, for glory. What will I die for?

O'MEARA: We cannot all die in the heat of battle.

NAPOLEON: Spare me your platitudes. Why do you allow this diminishment? This death by inches? Do you fancy yourself a humanitarian, doctor? Do you call this kindness? Montholon! Show the good doctor out—

RATS: More battles!

More life!

More death!

More men! More men!

(LIGHTS SHIFT. NAPOLEON *gets out of the bathtub. Individual spotlights come up on the following characters:* DR. STAUBLING, *a Civil War surgeon;* DR. DESGENETTES, NAPOLEON'*s army surgeon in Egypt;* CLARA BARTON; J. ROBERT OPPENHEIMER; NAPOLEON.)*

(SFX: The nightmare sound of horses in battle: charging, snorting, rearing, dying, underscores the following:)

NAPOLEON: More men! I need more men!!

OPPENHEIMER: We had no idea.

STAUBLING: Morphine! I need morphine!

DESGENETTES: *(to* NAPOLEON*)* They are dying like flies, General.

CLARA BARTON: *(sitting on a box of medical supplies, speaking to an unseen senator)* Well, I know you think a battlefield is no place for a woman, Senator, but I have a warehouse full of supplies.

STAUBLING: We have no bandages, no blankets, food, tents, pans to cook with, utensils to eat with.

DESGENETTES: It is the plague, sir.

OPPENHEIMER: We had no idea.

CLARA BARTON: Do you mean to keep these supplies from our wounded soldiers at the front? Don't tell me the government suppliers are doing their job—the wounded lie on wet ground without a blanket, a cup, with nothing to alleviate their suffering.

DESGENETTES: No, I will not desert these men. No, I will not administer adequate amounts of laudanum to end their lives. I am a doctor! Do you mock me, sir?

NAPOLEON: If they can't cross the desert on their own two feet . . .

DESGENETTES: These men were wounded in your service, sir. And now you talk of deserting them—?!

NAPOLEON: Shall we all die here, Doctor? Is that your solution?

CLARA BARTON: Send me to Gettysburg with these supplies, sir. There is a surgeon there, Dr. Staubling, who is willing to overcome his scruples, who is willing to work with a woman, who is willing to work with anyone who brings supplies and might help him and his men.

STAUBLING: We are drowning in blood.

NAPOLEON: More men! I need more men!

CLARA BARTON: Men are dying as we sit here talking, Senator. Will you not write an order for me to go, give me a pass that we might empty this warehouse and take these supplies where they are needed—

DESGENETTES: You brought these men into the desert; it is your duty to bring them out—

OPPENHEIMER: We had no idea.

NAPOLEON: Shall we bring the plague to Europe, sir? At what port will our ship of mercy be allowed to unload?

STAUBLING: I'm drunk. Too drunk to see another soldier, too drunk to amputate another leg, hand, arm, foot . . .

NAPOLEON: Perhaps in the next war they will invent a better way to deal with the wounded.

OPPENHEIMER: We had no idea.

DESGENETTES: Driving them into the sea to drown—as you did with the Turks?

NAPOLEON: Prisoners of war, doctor.

DESGENETTES: Three thousand men, women and children . . .

OPPENHEIMER: Sooner or later the blood of our victims will destroy us.

DESGENETTES: Bayonetting them to save ammunition?

NAPOLEON: Are you going to build me a foundry and forge bullets?

DESGENETTES: And now the plague.

OPPENHEIMER: The suffering. The endless suffering.

DESGENETTES: It is the wrath of God.

NAPOLEON: More men! More men! I need more men!!

RATS: More men!

More men!

More men!

AIDE-DE-CAMP: *(to* NAPOLEON*)* Sire, your army exists no more.

CLARA BARTON: We are dancing on graves.

DESGENETTES: How many more? How many more?!?

OPPENHEIMER: We had no idea.

(SFX: The atom bomb)

RATS: No idea?!?

A likely excuse!

A poor excuse!

No excuse at all!

Woulda, coulda, shoulda, Bobby.

HA! HA! HA!

(LIGHTS SHIFT and come UP on . . .

MAISY *and* DAISY, *mopping up.)*

MAISY: Mop up operations. That's what they call them now.

DAISY: Who are they kidding?

MAISY: That's what we do.

DAISY: Mop up. Huh. Such a homey image. Housecoat. Hairnet. Mop.

MAISY: As if a mop has anything to do with it.

DAISY: Women and children: collateral damage.

MAISY: Surgical strikes.

DAISY: Carpet bombing.

MAISY: Yes, sir! Roll out that red carpet!

DAISY: What if we quit?

MAISY: Honey, we can't quit. We're eternal.

DAISY: Let's you and me get into that earth, Maisy. And take our mops with us. We've done enough.

MAISY: You think?

DAISY: Teach those boys a lesson.

MAISY: Oh, honey, as if anyone pays attention to us—

DAISY: They will when we're not here.

MAISY: They'd have to be wading in blood before they'd notice.

DAISY: Swimming in it.

MAISY: Let 'em swim.

DAISY: Let 'em drown.

MAISY: No, honey, let 'em stop.

(LIGHTS SHIFT)

(ALBINE DE MONTHOLON stands center stage, NAPOLEON *to one side of her,* COUNT MONTHOLON *to the other.)*

ALBINE: *(to* MONTHOLON*)* Darling, he means nothing to me. *(to* NAPOLEON*)* Sire, you are everything to me. The sun and the moon, the sky and the sea. *(to* MONTHOLON*)* He is ridiculous in bed. I choke on my laughter. *(to* NAPOLEON*)* Never have I been touched like this. Never. Never. *(to* MONTHOLON*)* No one can satisfy me as you can. *(to* NAPOLEON*)* No one can satisfy me as you can. So large. So grand. *(to* MONTHOLON*)* Small. Puny. Miniscule. Laughable. *(to* NAPOLEON*)* You make me laugh, Sire! Laugh! *(to* MONTHOLON*)* No I have never . . . Not like that . . . Never felt . . . no . . . never . . . never . . .

(LIGHTS SHIFT)

(SFX: Knocking)

*(*NAPOLEON *lies down on a table.* COUNT MONTHOLON *rubs him down.)*

NAPOLEON: Rub harder! Rub as if you were scrubbing a donkey.

(MONTHOLON *rubs with renewed energy, even violence*)

(*SFX: More knocking.*)

NAPOLEON: Entrez!

(O'MEARA *enters*)

O'MEARA: Good afternoon, General. Count Montholon.
(MONTHOLON *nods*)

NAPOLEON: Ah, the good doctor.

O'MEARA: How are you today?

NAPOLEON: Who wants to know? You? Or that son of a bitch Lowe?

O'MEARA: As your physician, I am interested in your health.

NAPOLEON: You are a spy.

O'MEARA: You insult me, sir.

NAPOLEON: I have insulted you and yet you call me sir. That is a particular Britishism, communicating disdain. You show your superiority by being unafraid to ape the conventions of inferiority. Speak plainly, man!

O'MEARA: I am not a spy. I believe you know me better than that.

NAPOLEON: And yet they ask you for reports, do they not?

O'MEARA: Which I give them, in my official capacity. I do not give them more than they ask for, or even as much as they would like to know. I can tell you this: They are tired of your little game of cat and mouse.

NAPOLEON: It drives them mad when they cannot see me, when they cannot ascertain if the prisoner is, in fact, still in prison or even still alive. Delicious irony. Let them stew in it. And how are you today? Have you been riding, and walking, and conversing and generally enjoying the pleasures of your freedom, limited, as it is, by this island? What would make you feel truly free, doctor? Do you think about it? Does it occupy your thoughts, your musings, your mind?

(LOWE *Enters*)

LOWE: Good day to you, sir. O'Meara.

NAPOLEON: You were not invited.

LOWE: I do not have eternity to wait for an invitation.

NAPOLEON: *(to* O'MEARA*)* You are responsible for this!

O'MEARA: No, sir, I am not.

NAPOLEON: MONTHOLON!!! Show him OUT!!!

O'MEARA: *(getting up to leave)* General, if I might—

NAPOLEON: Sit *down,* doctor.

O'MEARA: I believe exercise would improve your pallor and your appetite and your general sense of malaise.

NAPOLEON: The island is too small for me.

RATS: But just right for us!

O'MEARA: It is large enough to provide exercise—even within the confines of—

NAPOLEON: *(to* LOWE*)* The climate is not like ours, it is not our sun, nor does it have our seasons. Everything breathes a mortal boredom. Even the good doctor concurs: The situation is disagreeable, unhealthy. It is a desert. It is uninhabitable.

LOWE: I am only obeying instructions and doing what is required of me.

NAPOLEON: That is the line taken by executioners, sir.

LOWE: For your amusement, the British Government has made you a miniature wooden palace. It is at this moment in your front yard. It is a vast, extraordinary toy. Come and see it—

NAPOLEON: I have not the slightest interest in your folly.

LOWE: It is a gesture, sir. Made in good faith.

NAPOLEON: A gesture?!? How about this for a gesture: I want newspapers that are not three months old, news of my family, my wife, my son, more books to read, the freedom to write a private, sealed letter, the freedom to ride where I wish, when I wish—

LOWE: The finest cabinet makers have devised furniture for the palace; there are table linens, fine china.

RATS: It will be our house. We will drink tea. Like the English.

NAPOLEON: I don't need a house filled with furniture. Send me an executioner. And a coffin. GO!!!

LOWE: Don't you even want to see it?

NAPOLEON: If you like dollhouses so much, why don't you go play with it?

LOWE: You're not even curious?

RATS: We're VERY curious! Will there be gilt? velvet hangings? crystal chandeliers? feather beds? satin sheets? Will there be food in all the cupboards?

LOWE: The detail is astonishing. It is a complete miniature world.

NAPOLEON: You are diabolical. You have imprisoned me in a world the size of a teacup and now you want me to clap my hands and marvel at a miniature palace? Am I to imagine being small enough to walk its corridors, sleep in its beds, bathe in its tub, rule its tiny kingdom? To sport so with a captured being is beneath you. The palace belongs to you, Lowe. You are the master of a miniature universe; an obscure, insignificant, irrelevant world. And rather than rising to greatness, you sink and shrink. You are a bone-handled snuffbox. You are a yapping, vicious dog. There is not a scrap of greatness in you; no large ideas, no generous spirit, no human feeling, no questing mind, no mercy. Your palace awaits you, little man. It is the little palace of little bureaucrats. Be sure to wipe your feet at the door.

(LOWE *turns to exit, then pauses at the door*)

LOWE: By the way, you are using table salt much too freely. Our orders from London are to economize. You must dismiss four of your servants at once. Your choice, of course.

(LOWE *exits*)

NAPOLEON: I'd like to blow up this bloody island.

RATS: Sink it in the ocean.

NAPOLEON: Obliterate every last scrap of rock.

RATS: Every gum tree.

NAPOLEON: I wouldn't even mind drowning to do it.

O'MEARA: Impossible, of course.

NAPOLEON: For now.

O'MEARA: What do you mean?

NAPOLEON: Someday they will invent an explosive powerful enough—

O'MEARA: No—

NAPOLEON: Oh, the things we cannot imagine which will come into being—Someday they will blow holes in the ocean.

RATS: Why?

NAPOLEON: Obliterate whole cities.

RATS: Why??

O'MEARA: Where do you get these ideas?

NAPOLEON: And every living being for miles around.

O'MEARA: No, we will never—

NAPOLEON: —Destroy ourselves? HA!!

(LIGHTS SHIFT and FOCUS on . . . J. ROBERT OPPEN-HEIMER. OPPENHEIMER *puts on a pair of "safety glasses" as* NAPOLEON *watches.)*

OPPENHEIMER: These were designed by Jacob Palmer. German engineer. Regulation shatterproof glass. Multilayered lenses. Six, I believe. Tinted. The challenge was to make it possible to see— Observation. The key. Observation . . . from the Latin . . . "observatio" . . . To look. To see. To witness. The primary task of the scientist.

(NAPOLEON puts on his own pair of safety glasses)

How close can we get without melting our eyeballs? How big will it be, as far as it is possible for us to predict? But what about the unpredictable? The unknown . . . the unknowable. Taking this step into the unknown. If we can conceive it . . . Ah . . . to conceive . . . to create . . . The first lie five miles. We have decided to feel safe at five miles. And clap these Coke-bottle glasses onto our faces. Have any of us the capacity to imagine melting flesh? Or the damage we cannot see with the naked eye? It is possible we will explode the atmosphere. In which case the world will disappear.

In the rush to end the war . . . Did any of us doubt, speak our dissent, our fear? What were the lies we told ourselves, told each other? All of them obliterated in that first astonishing mushroom cloud. The colors. The sound. Elation. Elation. How vast. How incomprehensible. How lovely. How lovely in its first flower. It is God's work to end the war. Oh, the lies we tell. The lies we all tell. These lies eat my throat. I will die of cancer at 62, all my questions silenced.

We were in love with the possibility of power, the pure science of pure exploration. And for a cause, oh, what a cause.

These glasses will not protect us from melting flesh, mutated organs, the legions of disappeared. The shadows. I walk with the shadows. Every day. Put on these glasses. And walk. As if I could walk into the epicenter of the blast. As if I could become energy, spirit, split, divine. As if, somehow, I could begin to see.

(Shadows loom up and engulf OPPENHEIMER *and* NAPOLEON.)

(Out of the darkness we see a single candle. NAPOLEON *appears, wearing a nightshirt and a nightcap, carrying a candle. It is the middle of the night.)*

(SFX: Low, throaty, feminine laughter)

NAPOLEON: Who's there? Josephine . . . ? Who's there . . . ? Jo . . . ?

MONTHOLON: *(rising from the couch where he sleeps outside* NAPOLEON*'s door)* Count Montholon, your Majesty.

NAPOLEON: I heard something.

MONTHOLON: I was sleeping.

NAPOLEON: Did you hear anything?

MONTHOLON: No, sire.

NAPOLEON: It sounded like . . . . It sounded like . . . .

MONTHOLON: Would you care for a tisane, your Majesty? Or a brandy?

NAPOLEON: Laughter. Josephine's laughter. So low in her throat. Sweeter than a tune. Do you remember?

MONTHOLON: The Empress did not find me amusing; therefore, I rarely heard her laugh.

NAPOLEON: Were you laughing?

MONTHOLON: No, sire, I was sleeping.

NAPOLEON: You may go.

*(*MONTHOLON *bows and exits.)*

(holding his candle aloft, NAPOLEON *crosses to the window, opens the curtains, throws up the sash, listens to the night sounds)*

(SFX: Night sounds.)

The RATS *pop up and stick their heads through the window.* NAPOLEON *feeds them bits of cheese he keeps in his pockets.)*

NAPOLEON: The soldiers?

RATS: Asleep.

NAPOLEON: All of them?

RATS: We counted, your Majesty. Fifty-two sleeping soldiers. They grow lazy.

NAPOLEON: Look at that moon.

RATS: Ahh. The moon. You grow romantic.

NAPOLEON: I thought I heard Josephine.

RATS: You're dreaming.

NAPOLEON: Have you seen her?

RATS: No, we have not seen her.

NAPOLEON: Her voice . . . remarkable.

RATS: Only the soldiers. Snoring and grunting.

NAPOLEON: Look! There she is.

RATS: Where?

*(*JOSEPHINE *does not appear—only in his imagination.)*

NAPOLEON: And the music. Do you hear the music?

RATS: Snoring. And grunting. And farting. This is not music, your Majesty.

(SFX: A minuet, heard faintly, as though from a passing ship.)

NAPOLEON: No, you are mistaken. Look! There— There she is . . . Oh, how lovely . . . .

*(*NAPOLEON *climbs out the window, walks into the moonlight, and takes the phantom* JOSEPHINE *into his arms. He dances in the moonlight, alone.)*

MUSIC CRESCENDOES, THEN FADES

LIGHTS FADE

ACT II

(SFX: Wind, crashing waves)
(LIGHTS come up on . . . JOAN, WILEY, and NAPOLEON, at the cliff edge.)
(SFX: Birds crying and wheeling in the wind)
(They drop the miniature palace over the edge and watch as it floats down and sinks into the sea.)

JOAN: There it goes—

WILEY: Look! It's floating on the wind!

NAPOLEON: Not for long.

JOAN: Ahhhh . . .

WILEY: Will it float, do you think? Sail away—

NAPOLEON: No, it will sink as surely as . . .

WILEY: As surely as what?

NAPOLEON: As surely as we will all die.

JOAN: Look! The birds are attacking it!

WILEY: There it goes—

JOAN: There it goes . . .

WILEY: Ahhhh.

JOAN: I can't see it anymore! Oh, I wish we could stand inside one of its tiny rooms and ride to the bottom of the ocean floor.

NAPOLEON: Why?

JOAN: I'm curious. What if we could see beneath the earth's skin?

NAPOLEON: A river of blood.

WILEY: Why would you want to?

NAPOLEON: Acres of bones.

JOAN: I want to know the story.

NAPOLEON: The dead . . . the dead are nothing.

JOAN: The dead are everywhere . . . and everything . . .

WILEY: What story?

JOAN: The true story.

NAPOLEON: That presupposes there is a true story.

JOAN: In the beginning . . .

WILEY: —there was peace.

JOAN: —there was the word.

NAPOLEON: There has never been peace. Ever. Not even in the Garden of Eden.

WILEY: Why do they start with words instead of peace?

NAPOLEON: There is no peace!

JOAN: If you could see with the eyes of God—

NAPOLEON: If God has eyes—

JOAN: Could you see beneath my skin, the earth's skin—and if you could, what would you know?

WILEY: How should I know? I'm a private for God's sake!

NAPOLEON: No one knows anything. We make everything up. To suit ourselves, mostly.

WILEY: All this death. You're obsessed.

JOAN: When you think about it, everything we touch, everything we breathe, eat, smell, see, has touched the dead.

WILEY: That's so horrible.

JOAN: The dead are in us, Wiley. In our minds, in our hearts, in our muscles, in our bones.

WILEY: You are in the habit of saying the strangest things.

JOAN: In the beginning was the word. Do you know what that means?

NAPOLEON: Does anyone know what that means?

JOAN: I am trying to talk to Wiley.

NAPOLEON: Well, he's the wrong man for theology.

JOAN: Would you let him speak for himself?

WILEY: He's right. I'm no good with this . . . theology.

JOAN: Do you think God speaks only to scholars?! And priests?!?

WILEY: Honestly, miss, in my era, God doesn't do much speaking at all. Do you still hear voices, Joan?

NAPOLEON: She's in His presence, isn't that right? *(pause)* You mean. You're not? In His presence? In heaven at all? I mean I know I'm not there, but if I thought anyone might be in the presence—if there is a presence—then surely that would be you.

JOAN: It's not what you think—

WILEY: What?

JOAN: I'm not allowed to talk about it.

NAPOLEON: Oh, come on.

WILEY: Why not?

JOAN: I'll tell you later.

NAPOLEON: Later—when?

WILEY: You promise?

NAPOLEON: You mean when we're all dead.

JOAN: It's really not important.

NAPOLEON: So tell us!

JOAN: *(a beat)* Nothing is . . . static.

NAPOLEON: So?

JOAN: Everything . . . changes.

WILEY: What do you mean?

JOAN: All the time.

NAPOLEON: Isn't God the ever constant, unchanging one?

JOAN: Even God.

WILEY: Even God what?

JOAN: Changes. All the time.

WILEY: Like a shape shifter?

JOAN: Like a river. Like time. Like breath.

NAPOLEON: I don't get it.

RATS: I don't get it! I don't get it! I don't get it!

NAPOLEON: *Basta! (he stalks off)*

RATS: We are eternal. We are everlasting. We . . . are . . . God!

JOAN: No, you're not.

RATS: In the beginning, the very beginning . . . there were . . . RATS! Peace comes and goes. Words are forgotten. But rats . . . go on forever.

(SFX: The minuet, again)

NAPOLEON: *(stops in his tracks)* Will no one tell me what I can feel in my heart? Has Josephine died? Where was she? Who was with her? Was she alone? What were her last words?

RATS: She died while you were on Elba. Don't you remember?

NAPOLEON: No!

RATS: During your first exile, Josephine was seen dancing with the Tsar. She was even seen bedding the Tsar. He said he preferred her company to all others in France. Alexander . . . such a large, handsome, lively man. What is it they say about Russian men?

NAPOLEON: Why are you torturing me?

RATS: Josephine was a genius at attracting powerful men.

Of course, this required compromising her principles. Looking back, would you say she had any principles? A genius for survival. Even the reign of terror. Ahhh, Josephine.

NAPOLEON: Did she ask for me?

RATS: You divorced her, remember? To marry a womb?

NAPOLEON: Did she ask for me?

RATS: Of course, sire. She was, after all, first and last, your Queen.

NAPOLEON: She loved me.

RATS: Not much in the beginning. Some say never at all. You were such a funny little man. Unkempt, ill-spoken, so little grace or charm.

(JOSEPHINE appears in her own light)

JOSEPHINE: I was convinced he would wear his boots to bed.

RATS: You needed to ally yourself with the *ancien regime.* You needed her aristocratic pedigree. And titles.

NAPOLEON: I needed—

JOSEPHINE: Darling . . . So quick. No preamble. Could we talk a bit?

NAPOLEON: —a soft voice. A refuge, a confidante; her breasts, her hands, her legs, her lips. Where is she?!

RATS: Your Majesty—

JOSEPHINE: Such a funny little man. I grew to love you. Who

could have predicted that? And then you broke my heart.

(The light blinks out on JOSEPHINE.*)*

NAPOLEON: She really has gone . . . She really has gone . . . *(he sits)* There is no more blood in my body. The devil has eaten the muscles in my legs. A knife twists and turns in my gut. My feet are cold, my legs are cold, my hands are cold. I am dizzy and deaf. Lifting my eyelids exhausts me. Josephine . . . My Josephine . . . Take me home.

(NAPOLEON, *exhausted, near defeat, lies down on the ground, unmoving. The rats prowl around his body; sniffing, licking their lips.)*

RAT 1: I want the green jacket.

RAT 2: I want the embroidered waistcoat.

RAT 1: I want the white breeches.

RAT 2: Can they save his eyes? His tongue?

RAT 1: His tiny ears?

RAT 2: I want the boots!

RAT 1: I want, I want, I want . . . Why???

RAT 2: To be great—

RAT 1: His greatness is past.

RAT 2: To be large—

RAT 1: He is small.

RAT 2: To rule—

RAT 1: He is in prison.

RAT 2: To ride—

RAT 1: He can barely walk—

RAT 2: To live among kings—

RAT 1: He lives among rats.

RAT 2: To do battle—

RAT 1: He will not defeat death.

RAT 2: To be EMPEROR—

RAT 1: Of no one. And nothing.

RAT 2: Why can't I have just a little?

RAT 1: You cannot possess a man's spirit anymore than you can enter his body.

RAT 2: But that's exactly what I want.

RAT 1: You can, however, ingest him.

RAT 2: What?

RAT 1: Eat him.

RAT 2: Now?!?

RAT 1: After he's dead.

(SFX: Chewing)

(LIGHTS SHIFT and focus on WILEY *and* JOAN, *still at the cliff's edge.* NAPOLEON *and the rats remain visible.)*

WILEY: Ah!! *(he recoils in pain, puts his hand to his chest, his hand comes away bloody)* What's happening to me? Can you help me? *(he sinks to his knees as the pain hits him and he has trouble breathing again)* Shit—

JOAN: *(helps him into a seated position)* Is that better? Can you breathe a little easier?

WILEY: *(grabbing her hands, pressing them to his wound)* Do it again—

JOAN: I don't know if I can—

WILEY: What do you mean you don't know if you can? Some saint—!

JOAN: I'll try, Wiley.

WILEY: I should've asked for a money-back guarantee.

JOAN: No such thing.

WILEY: Am I gonna die?

JOAN: You actually survive this battle.

WILEY: But not the war?

JOAN: I can't say.

WILEY: Won't say, more likely. *(she lays her cheek against his chest, listens)* What are you doing?

JOAN: Hush! *(She places her hands beside her face, covering his chest. She lifts her head, her face is bloody, begins to unbutton his shirt.)*

WILEY: What are you doing?

JOAN: I need to get closer.

WILEY: Stop that—

JOAN: Wiley. Trust me. *(She lays her face and hands against his bare chest. Pause)*

WILEY: I don't think you should be doing this—

JOAN: Shhhh— *(pause)* There.

WILEY: There what?

JOAN: *(she lifts her head)* Take a deep breath.

WILEY: *(breathing deep)* Is this gonna last?

JOAN: I hope so. *(she rubs her face with her sleeve, trying to wipe the blood away)*

WILEY: *(pulls out a dirty handkerchief)* Here. Let me do that—*(he cleans her face; looks at her sharply)* What's the matter? *(mist begins to rise from the ground)*

(SFX: Music: choral, ghostly)

JOAN: I don't know. I feel kind of funny.

WILEY: You look different.

JOAN: Different, how?

WILEY: You're white as a sheet.

JOAN: I feel like I'm fading away. (NAPOLEON *suddenly sits up)*

NAPOLEON: Joan . . . ?

WILEY: *(takes her hands)* What's happening to you? You're cold as ice—

JOAN: I'm having trouble hearing you.

WILEY: I'm talking just like always.

JOAN: What?

WILEY: I'M TALKING—

JOAN: *(lays her head against his shoulder)* I'm just going to close my eyes—

WILEY: *(panicked)* NO!!

JOAN: Why not?

WILEY: You're dying, aren't you?

JOAN: I'm dead, Wiley.

WILEY: Well, you're dying away from me— Is it my fault? Do they give you just a limited amount of life and you spent it on me—? *(shakes her)* Joan!—

JOAN: *(slipping away, peaceful)* Mmmmmmmmm . . .

WILEY: Don't go—No—You can't—I don't know what to do— *(he tenderly smoothes her hair, wipes the last trace of blood from her cheek)* Joan . . . ? *(pause)*

(She is really and truly gone. WILEY *is stunned with overwhelming sadness. He lays her down, closes her eyes, then bends to kiss her. Pause. He sits back on his heels, dissolves in tears.)*

*(*NAPOLEON *stands, picks* JOAN *up in his arms and carries her upstage, his head bent in sorrow.* WILEY *disappears in the mist. We HEAR his inchoate cry of anguish; it grows and grows, the grief of thousands, then snaps off.)*

(LIGHTS SHIFT and come up on . . . THE BATHTUB. NAPOLEON *steps into the tub.* O'MEARA *stands beside him, feeling for a pulse.)*

O'MEARA: How odd! I can't find your pulse.

NAPOLEON: Patience, doctor, patience.

O'MEARA: How can this be?

NAPOLEON: I have never felt my own heartbeat. Never. Under any circumstances.

O'MEARA: (relieved) Ah. There it is.

(SFX: Heartbeat)

NAPOLEON: The pounding heart. The sweating palms. The dry mouth. Never.

O'MEARA: So faint. So unusually . . . unaccountably slow. We must get you up. And out.

NAPOLEON: Sssshhhhh!

O'MEARA: *(whispers)* What?

NAPOLEON: *(listens)* There—

O'MEARA: What?

NAPOLEON: Poppleton. That son of a bitch. Spying again.

O'MEARA: He is ordered to report seeing you twice a day.

NAPOLEON: Spying. I do not wish to be seen.

O'MEARA: It is not a game.

NAPOLEON: Why not put a bell around my neck and report its ringing—*(he picks up a nearby bell, rings it viciously)* (MONTHOLON *appears*)

MONTHOLON: *(carrying a glass of wine on a silver tray)* Your wine, sire?

NAPOLEON: *(takes the glass)* Is Poppleton skulking about again?

MONTHOLON: Yes.

NAPOLEON: Shoot him!

O'MEARA: General—

MONTHOLON: That would be murder, sire.

NAPOLEON: Thank you for the ethics lesson, Montholon. You're worthless. *(drinks the wine)*

MONTHOLON: *(smiles)* Will there be anything else, sire?

NAPOLEON: Why did you come into exile with me?

MONTHOLON: My sense of duty, sire. Honor binds me—

NAPOLEON: *(throws bell at him)* Spineless! Jellyfish! Liar! Get out—!!

MONTHOLON: More wine, sire?

NAPOLEON: OUT!! (MONTHOLON *exits*)

O'MEARA: *(takes his wrist again)* Ah! That's a bit better. Thump-thump . . . thump-thump . . . A little spike there, in all the excitement.

NAPOLEON: How large is your penis?

O'MEARA: I beg your pardon—

NAPOLEON: My servants copulate constantly. There is nothing else to do. Is that how you spend your free time, doctor?

O'MEARA: General Bonaparte—

NAPOLEON: What? Irish Catholics aren't allowed to admit they have a penis?

O'MEARA: And how are you feeling?

NAPOLEON: Are you married?

O'MEARA: No, I'm not.

NAPOLEON: Engaged?

O'MEARA: No.

NAPOLEON: Why not, man?!

O'MEARA: As you may have noticed—

NAPOLEON: —You're not that bad looking.

O'MEARA: There are few, if any, suitable young women here on St Helena.

NAPOLEON: Ah. We come to the crux of the matter. No one at home?

O'MEARA: No.

NAPOLEON: Do you go to the whores?

O'MEARA: General—I—

NAPOLEON: You are a man, are you not?

O'MEARA: Have you seen the whores on St Helena?

NAPOLEON: I have not had that pleasure.

O'MEARA: They don't last long here.

NAPOLEON: Why not?

O'MEARA: There are too many soldiers. It is physically overwhelming.

NAPOLEON: Sounds inhuman.

O'MEARA: It is.

NAPOLEON: Then why don't you stop it?

O'MEARA: Do you imagine that I have power and influence?

NAPOLEON: Can you not save their lives, Doctor? What do these girls go home to? Can they possibly marry? Have children? You must put a stop to this. It is the basest slavery—

O'MEARA: Do you think the English will grow tired of St Helena more quickly if we deprive them of their whores?

NAPOLEON: I have no such illusions. They are an invading army.

O'MEARA: The whores are paid.

NAPOLEON: Paid to die at twenty-five? Paid to be childless? How much do you pay them for that?

O'MEARA: No one prepared me for this side of you, General.

NAPOLEON: No one prepared me for anything.

(SFX: Wind. LIGHTS SHIFT).

(SFX: Barking, yipping)

(ALBINE *enters.*)

ALBINE: Will you release me, your Majesty? Allow us to return to France?

NAPOLEON: Are you serious?

ALBINE: I want to go home.

NAPOLEON: Most fortunate of women: to have that choice.

ALBINE: Yes, I am fortunate.

NAPOLEON: So you will desert me—

ALBINE: I need to be careful. I need the best French doctors.

NAPOLEON: Are you unwell?

ALBINE: I am pregnant.

NAPOLEON: Ah . . .

ALBINE: With your child, your Majesty. (NAPOLEON *laughs heartily*) You don't believe me—

NAPOLEON: You don't imagine you are the first woman to claim this honor?

ALBINE: Sire—

NAPOLEON: Dozens.

ALBINE: I am certain—

NAPOLEON: —I am certain you are a clever woman, and a beautiful woman who often pleases her husband.

ALBINE: There is only you, your Majesty.

NAPOLEON: Do you think I am so besotted by you, Madame, as to lose my powers of reason? You are not Josephine and I am not a schoolboy—

(ALBINE *cries prettily*)

NAPOLEON: Did you think to flatter me to win your freedom? Take your freedom, take your leave! You have only to ask—

ALBINE: I wanted to carry your son to France—

NAPOLEON: My son is the King of Rome.

ALBINE: This child—

NAPOLEON: —Madame—

ALBINE: —Your child—

NAPOLEON: Stop this! I am not a fool— *(crosses to his desk, writes swiftly, hands her a piece of paper with the Imperial Seal)*

ALBINE: What is this?

NAPOLEON: Your freedom.

(ALBINE reads)

NAPOLEON: *(cont)* You may leave on the next boat.

ALBINE: What about my husband?

NAPOLEON: You are dispensable, Madame. He is not.

ALBINE: Now you are teasing me.

NAPOLEON: No, I am not.

ALBINE: I beg you—

NAPOLEON: Take your freedom and your husband's child back to France. May you prosper.

ALBINE: *(falls to her knees)* Your Majesty—

NAPOLEON: Do you have a pretty speech planned? A lock of hair loosened to fall—just so—across your face. Your robe, dishevelled, revealing the white globe of your breast. Do you think to conquer me, Madame, with your pretty charms?

ALBINE: You are unfair. You know that I—

NAPOLEON: —love me? It is not love, Madame. It is yipping and boredom and the stimulation of flesh against flesh. We are like the rats. Responding to hunger, lust, smell. We grope in the dark, rut where we can. Unthinking, unfeeling. We pretend passion hoping that our quickened breathing will make us—for a sweet, sweet moment—feel alive. So, my dear, we have aped the living. Go home. Give birth. And remember the dead.

(ALBINE exits)

(SFX: A door slams)

(O'MEARA enters.)

O'MEARA: Stick out your tongue.

NAPOLEON: No.

O'MEARA: A simple request.

NAPOLEON: Why should I?

O'MEARA: The tongue reveals much—

NAPOLEON: What?

O'MEARA: —about the body, the general state of health, defi-ciencies, over-indulgences. Yours, I would guess, reveals your passion for licorice.

NAPOLEON: My teeth could tell you that.

O'MEARA: Your tongue, sir—

NAPOLEON: *(sticks his tongue out, withdraws it quickly)* So?

O'MEARA: I need to examine it. *(produces two metal tongue depressors)* Now—

NAPOLEON: What are those?

O'MEARA: With gentle pressure I will be able to manipulate the tongue.

NAPOLEON: I don't want my tongue manipulated. Looking is one thing. Manipulating something else altogether.

O'MEARA: You have been unwell. You have been in pain.

NAPOLEON: I am in pain.

O'MEARA: Quite constant, I hear. I would like to help you, if I can.

NAPOLEON: Then cure me of this island.

O'MEARA: Let me discover the root of the problem, then we may be able to devise a cure.

NAPOLEON: In the next century and the next will physicians still be manipulating tongues in their search for answers, their search for clues to the body's secrets? I shall have to ask Dr. Oppenheimer.

O'MEARA: Who is Dr. Oppenheimer?

NAPOLEON: You are more like the priests of old, diviners, mys-tics. Would you care to read my tea leaves, doctor?

O'MEARA: You enjoy sporting at my expense.

NAPOLEON: Let me see your tongue.

O'MEARA: I don't think—

NAPOLEON: *(grabs two tongue depressors)* Come, come, doctor. What's good for the goose . . . ?

(O'MEARA hesitates, then sticks out tongue. NAPOLEON traps it, leans in close, examines it minutely)

You had leeks for lunch. Try chewing parsley to clear your breath— And look at that—the map of England in little white dots—even your tongue is unpatriotic— I see a tendency toward self . . . self . . . discovery—

(O'MEARA jerks back, NAPOLEON holds on tight)

Look at that, you can read the tongue. I've struck a nerve. So this is how you deal with the lack of females.

(O'MEARA begins to struggle, clearly uncomfortable) What's the problem? *(begins gasping for air)*

What?

(Takes hold of NAPOLEON's hands. NAPOLEON finally releases him. O'MEARA pants, takes in great gulps of air, frantically moistens his lips.)

Ah, so you yourself don't like this "little nothing," this "little tongue examination" . . . Physician, examine thyself—

O'MEARA: I had not thought you cruel. Or barbarous.

NAPOLEON: You had not thought to enter my body before today, doctor.

O'MEARA: I am trying—

NAPOLEON: Yes, you are very trying—

O'MEARA: *(an explosion of frustrated sound!!!)*

NAPOLEON: Do you not realize, Dr. O'Meara, that we like you? That we enjoy your company? That we have grown fond of your person?

O'MEARA: I . . . I— *(mopping his brow)* May I have something to drink?

NAPOLEON: Montholon! (MONTHOLON *appears)* Brandy for the doctor! (MONTHOLON *pours and serves brandy, exits)* Drink, man. Drink—

(O'MEARA drinks)

The Emperor's favor . . . His regard. His affection, even. Perhaps, one day, his respect—

O'MEARA: *(deeply touched)* Sir—I am honored.

(pause)

NAPOLEON: I have bizarre dreams, O'Meara . . . And yet they seem much more than dreams. Dancing with Josephine. Sporting and arguing with Joan of Arc. Interviewing Ulysses S. Grant.

O'MEARA: Who?

NAPOLEON: American General. And President. Second half of this century.

O'MEARA: What?

NAPOLEON: I have met surgeons and soldiers from the American Civil War. I have bedded Josephine, ridden horses into exhaustion, seen the dead of centuries . . . . There are rats who talk to me, sing to me, spy for me, laugh at me, common soldiers who burn their standards and eat the ash as though it were the host, the body of Christ; this, out of respect for me, and the dead who fell for those flags.

I am leaving this world, am I not? I believe my spirit—remarkable, isn't it, that a man such as I should claim a spirit—my spirit is already journeying.

(he sticks his tongue out)

Can you read that on my tongue?

(he throws his head back and laughs) (all characters join him.)

(SFX: Raucous laughter)

(LIGHTS SHIFT)

(LOWE detains O'MEARA as he is leaving Longwood.)

LOWE: Dr. O'Meara, your presence is no longer required on St Helena. You have been recalled to London. They will have news of your next posting.

O'MEARA: But, sir—

LOWE: The *Anglia* is sailing at dawn. That should give you enough time to put your affairs in order.

O'MEARA: I cannot leave my patient.

LOWE: Dr. Antommarchi is perfectly competent.

O'MEARA: A charlatan, sir. And you know it.

LOWE: *(handing him a sealed envelope)* Here are your orders.

O'MEARA: I will not leave my patient.

LOWE: Do you dare contradict me?

NAPOLEON: *(o.s)* *(calling him)* Dr. O'Meara—

O'MEARA: You know he is attached to me.

LOWE: Do not flatter yourself, sir.

NAPOLEON: *(o.s.)* Dr. O'Meara—

O'MEARA: You know he is failing.

LOWE: Come, come. He could live for decades yet.

O'MEARA: Weeks. Possibly months.

NAPOLEON: *(o.s)* Dr. O'Meara . . . I am growing impatient!
Will you be black or white?

LOWE: Chess, is it? I hear he cheats.

O'MEARA: Captain Lowe, if I might beg you to reconsider—

LOWE: Do not cross me, O'Meara. Or your career will be over.

O'MEARA: Allow me to say goodbye to him.

LOWE: I'm afraid you don't have time.

(O'MEARA, *furious, exits, as* NAPOLEON *enters)*

NAPOLEON: Dr. O'Meara—

LOWE: *(gloating)* Has been dismissed.

(LOWE *turns on his heel and EXITS as . . .*
NAPOLEON *turns and bellows:)*

NAPOLEON: My horse! . . . My horse!! . . . Bring me my goddamned horse!

(no answer)

RATS: A horse! A horse! My kingdom for a horse!

NAPOLEON: Groom!—What is his name?—Charles! . . . Raoul!
Damn it! Where's my groom? Where's my horse? Where is
everybody? There are twenty people in my service—and two
thousand soldiers guarding me—and not one can hear me??
Not ONE??? *(a very young groom, Peter, is shoved onstage by
unseen hands)*

PETER: Sir!

NAPOLEON: Where's my horse?

PETER: Sir?

NAPOLEON: My horse—

PETER: Yes, sir!

NAPOLEON: Go get it—

PETER: No, sir.

NAPOLEON: Shall I cut off your head?

   (SFX: *The blade of a guillotine falls.*)

PETER: No, sir!

NAPOLEON: Who are you?

PETER: Peter, sir.

NAPOLEON: I've never seen you before.

PETER: I'm Raoul's son.

NAPOLEON: Ah—

PETER: His only son.

NAPOLEON: Where's my horse?

PETER: Gone, sir.

NAPOLEON: What do you mean, gone?

PETER: Taken to the other end of the island.

NAPOLEON: Why?

PETER: Captain Lowe—

NAPOLEON: That son of a bitch! I'll kill him!

PETER: . . . ordered the horse removed.

NAPOLEON: So bring me another horse.

PETER: I can't.

NAPOLEON: Why not?

PETER: Captain Lowe—

NAPOLEON: Do you want to die today?

PETER: No, sir.

NAPOLEON: Then GET ME MY HORSE!!!

PETER: Sir—

NAPOLEON: *(advancing on him, slapping his face, cuffing his ears)*
You DARE DEFY YOUR EMPEROR!?

PETER: There are no horses, sir.

NAPOLEON: On this entire godforsaken island, there are no
horses? IDIOT!!

PETER: None for you.

NAPOLEON: None for me?

PETER: No, sir.

NAPOLEON: Son of a bitch.

PETER: Yes, sir.

NAPOLEON: Why?

PETER: He didn't say, sir.

NAPOLEON: There are few pleasures here.

PETER: The girls are nice.

NAPOLEON: What?!

PETER: The girls are nice.

NAPOLEON: You think so.

PETER: They're very . . . warm.

NAPOLEON: There are few pleasures for an old man like me.

PETER: I could bring you a girl, sir.

NAPOLEON: Really?

PETER: They ask about you—

NAPOLEON: And what do you tell them?

PETER: They dream of gracing your bed.

NAPOLEON: You are a clever boy.

PETER: Bearing your child.

NAPOLEON: No. They want to know if I am shrivelled. And old.
If I still have balls.

PETER: No, sir—

NAPOLEON:"Have you seen him in his bath? Is it true that
Napoleon—?"

PETER: No sir. We are loyal—

NAPOLEON: Bullshit. You would sell my piss to the Pope for holy
water if you could.

PETER: Don't know the Pope, sir. But I do know some girls. If you change your mind.

NAPOLEON: A HORSE is what I want. Do you understand?

PETER: I'm sorry, sir.

NAPOLEON: This is part of his plan, that son of a bitch! Lowe! Goddamn you! Everything is rotting. I am rotting. The mold climbs the walls, the rats dance beneath the floors, the paper in my books disintegrates. I am surrounded by the English—the English for god's sake— I am in exile from my country, from my family, from my people, from my food! And the one thing I love, have always loved, but especially here—is riding. In the midst of my prison I have the illusion of movement, speed, freedom. This is only an illusion, Raoul's son, but we all have illusions, illusions we cherish, nurture, rock like little babies in our arms. My illusions have been keeping me alive. *(a beat)* Get down on your hands and knees.

PETER: What?!

NAPOLEON: Down, I say.

PETER: Sir—

NAPOLEON: Down. *(shoves him to his knees)* I'm going to ride you.

PETER: Oh, no—

NAPOLEON: *(steps over him, trapping him with his knees)* Giddy up!

PETER: Sir. I can't move—

NAPOLEON: What's wrong with you?

PETER: I'm 12!

NAPOLEON: A poor excuse.

PETER: *(collapsing flat on the floor)* Oooomph!

NAPOLEON: *(using his crop)* Get up, I say! Up!!

PETER: I can't—

NAPOLEON: Can't? Won't? Can't? Won't? What do I care? I WILL RIDE—*(lifts the groom's head by his hair)* If you do not bring me a horse, I will drive you till you collapse. *(pulls him to his feet, shoves him offstage)* Tell your father that—*(bellowing)*

Lowe! You son of a bitch, LOWE! *(another, even younger, boy,* SIMON, *is shoved onstage)*

SIMON: Lowe is not here, sir.

NAPOLEON: Not here?!

SIMON: He's in Jamestown, sir, where he always is.

NAPOLEON: Summon him! Let him wait several hours in the anteroom to my chamber, and then, then, I shall deign to speak to him, scream at him, I shall turn the air blue.

SIMON: Lowe has refused to return to Longwood.

NAPOLEON: Refused?

SIMON: Since you last kept him waiting eleven and a half hours and then spat at him.

NAPOLEON: He is a petty man to hold a grudge.

SIMON: Shall you go to him, sir?

NAPOLEON: Never!

SIMON: Why not?

NAPOLEON: And appear to beg, to need him, to be some overweening sycophant asking for favors . . . from the English?!?!? I am the Emperor of all France, all Europe, all—

SIMON: —Not anymore, sir. Now you don't even have a horse.

NAPOLEON: Why aren't you afraid of me?

SIMON: I'm too young to be taken seriously.

NAPOLEON: Ahh . . .

SIMON: And I don't believe you'd stoop to killing an eight-year-old.

NAPOLEON: Smart boy.

SIMON: Very.

NAPOLEON: Modest, too.

SIMON: If I'm smart, isn't denying it false modesty?

NAPOLEON: Maybe they'd give you a horse.

SIMON: Maybe they would.

NAPOLEON: And then you could give your horse to me—

SIMON: Why would I do that?

NAPOLEON: For love of your Emperor.

SIMON: I'm supposed to love you?

NAPOLEON: Yes!

SIMON: I hardly know you.

NAPOLEON: You are French. Therefore you love me.

SIMON: No one told me.

NAPOLEON: Ah.

SIMON: Is this an actual feeling I'm supposed to have—or is it a form of patriotic duty which imitates the feeling of love?

NAPOLEON: Love of your Emperor . . . there is no higher calling, no higher duty. It resides in your heart, in your soul, in your mind; it courses through your blood, it is the very air you breathe.

SIMON: What about God?

NAPOLEON: What about him?

SIMON: You have placed yourself at His level.

NAPOLEON: Exactly.

SIMON: But you are nothing but a man—human, fallible, mortal.

NAPOLEON: You think I am mortal?

SIMON: We are all mortal.

NAPOLEON: I will live forever.

SIMON: Your body will defeat you. They say you are dying even now—

NAPOLEON: I will never die. In one thousand years, in two thousand years, people will still know my name, still marvel at my deeds, still base their laws on my Civil code.

SIMON: But your body, sir—

NAPOLEON: Will rest in state in Paris. I will be visited by thousands every single day.

SIMON: Not you, sir. Your tomb.

NAPOLEON: Is it not me within that tomb? My essence, my self, my—

SIMON : —Your ashes, sir—

NAPOLEON: Angels will guard my tomb. Splendor such as you have never seen.

(Two men enter wearing a horse costume.)

SIMON: Ah . . . here is your horse now, sir—

NAPOLEON: Do you think me mad? Do you think me daft?

SIMON: Shall I give you a leg up, sir?

NAPOLEON: *(viciously kicking the horse's "rump")* Go! You fools— *(The "horse" falls apart in front of our eyes; the sky begins to "rain" pieces of dead horses: heads, legs, hooves, etc.* SIMON, *terrified, tries to hide behind* NAPOLEON.*)* Don't touch me!

SIMON: But, sir—

NAPOLEON: *(beating him away)* Get away from me—*(a horse's head falls, knocking* NAPOLEON *over)* Shit! *(*SIMON *cowers on the ground, his hands over his head)*

SIMON: Make it stop!

NAPOLEON: I can't.

SIMON: Some big deal Emperor!

NAPOLEON: This is a natural phenomenon.

SIMON: Natural?!?

NAPOLEON: Nature has never bent to my will. *(the "rain" stops)*

SIMON: This is disgusting.

NAPOLEON: Yes.

SIMON: It stinks.

NAPOLEON: It does.

SIMON: This is no ordinary rainstorm.

NAPOLEON: No, it's not.

SIMON : This is more like some horrible explosion, some bomb.

NAPOLEON: These are all the horses who died in my service.

SIMON: Someone collected them and found a way to drop them from the sky?

NAPOLEON: Who knows? *(pointing)* We called that one King Henry. *(*NAPOLEON *begins to crawl around, pulling pieces of horses together, as though he's going to reassemble them)* Let's see if we can put old Henry back together. Got any glue?

SIMON: Are you mad?

NAPOLEON: Look: King Henry died on the Egyptian campaign.

That's twenty years and 16,000 kilometers from here. If he can fall from the sky, still bloody and with his hide still on—why can't we put him back together?

SIMON: How can you touch that?

NAPOLEON: Feel it—

SIMON: NO!

NAPOLEON: Still warm. What does that mean? *(Simon begins to crawl off, away from* NAPOLEON*)* Resurrection! King Henry will live again. And I will ride again. Ride off this island, ride through the sky, ride to Egypt. And begin again. This time there will be no plague, no desertion, no abandonment. This time my Josephine will not be left behind. King Henry will be the most magnificent horse who ever lived. He will share my tent. No, he will have his own tent, his own ship. He will live forever. Forever. Forever. *(putting his hands on the horse's head)* Come back to life and I will build you a palace, a pyramid, your own tomb in Paris. Magnificent . . . Magnificent . . . *(he stands)* Magnificent animals fell to their knees and could not get up. They were eaten. Some men drank their blood. For my men were also starving. And dying of thirst. What did we know of Egypt? Of the desert? Of the sun? And the sun's power to blind, to scour the soul, to drive men mad?

(A young SOLDIER, *wearing the uniform of the Egyptian campaign, enters.)*

SOLDIER: *(saluting)* Reporting on the Bay of Jaffa, sir.

NAPOLEON: Yes?

SOLDIER: Prisoners dispatched, sir.

NAPOLEON: How many?

SOLDIER: Three thousand, sir.

NAPOLEON: Ammunition used?

SOLDIER: None, sir. As per your instructions.

NAPOLEON: Alternative methods?

SOLDIER: Bayonets. Clubs. The sea was our ally, sir.

NAPOLEON: How so?

SOLDIER: Drowning. Sir.

NAPOLEON: Burial details?

SOLDIER: No, sir.

NAPOLEON: No, sir?!?

SOLDIER: Again, sir, the sea was our ally. We were timed for the outgoing tide.

(SPOTLIGHT on a second very young soldier. As he speaks, blood drips from his uniform, from his hair, from the tips of his fingers, from the cuffs of his pants, and pools at his feet.)

BLOODY SOLDIER: Three thousand men, women and children surrendered to us when we took the town of Jaffa. It soon became clear that marching these prisoners along with us to Acre was impracticable. We had no rations to spare. Impossible to supply fresh water. The humanitarian notion we all adopted was that we were saving them from certain suffering and ultimately, death. This "detail" fell to my unit. Fresh recruits: 16, 17 years old. If it feels like murder, is it? What is murder when serving your Emperor? Whose murder is it? His or mine? I like to think that these thoughts are in our heads as we bayonet women and children. These thoughts. Or any thoughts. Anything that might make us human, or recall us to our humanity. Or is this murder calculated? Calculated to call us to our own deaths with greater ease, greater surrender. When we crossed that line and murdered for the Emperor, we became monsters . . . and perfect. Perfect soldiers. Hungry for death. Even our own.

(MARSHA enters, wheeling a cart with sandwich fixings. MARSHA wears a cocktail dress and a cocktail hat and a fluffy hostess apron á là 1950s USA.)

MARSHA: *(sings out, full of good cheer)* Lunchtime! . . . How many are we today? One, two, three, four—will the boys in the horse costume be having lunch?

NAPOLEON: Who are you?

MARSHA: Don't you love dining al fresco? *(She kicks some horse's heads out of the way and spreads a picnic blanket on the ground. She tosses throw pillows onto the blanket. Approaching NAPOLEON, she attempts to take him by the arm, purring.)* Emperor . . . ? Perhaps you'd like to—

NAPOLEON: Don't touch me!

MARSHA: *(whispers to him)* It's hard not to touch you. Have other women told you that? *(He backs away from her. She looks inside the cart)* Now! Let's see what we have today? Pâté de foie gras— Yummy!

(holds up a tin of foie gras)

Imagine the journey this little tin has been on!

(laughs, opens another compartment)

We've got ham . . . "jambon" to you, right Boney? Now what's this? *(holds up a very large cow's tongue)*

Why, I think that's a tongue. My goodness— What do you do with it? Slap it on a piece of bread with some mustard? Garnish with cor-ni-chons? You'd need an awfully big pickle to stand up to that tongue— *(laughs gaily)*

Of course, we're not just making lunch, here, we're building sandwiches for an Emperor. Larger than life is the order of the day. *(walking right up to NAPOLEON)* How do you like my hat?

NAPOLEON: *(recoils)* Madame—

MARSHA: Yes, yes. Lunch first. I get distracted so easily. How about something to drink? *(opens another compartment, pulls out bottles)* Let's see . . . We've got Coke . . . and . . . Puligny Montrachet. What'll it be?

NAPOLEON: Wine.

MARSHA: And the soldiers?

NAPOLEON: Do not drink.

MARSHA: *(conspiratorially)* Why not? If they had too much to drink and fell asleep and left us to our own devices, who would be the wiser? Don't you long to be free of them? To breathe, to think, to taste, to laugh, to love . . . without them?

NAPOLEON: Madame, I am fat.

MARSHA: Yes.

NAPOLEON: And gray.

MARSHA: Yes.

NAPOLEON: I am not . . . what I once was.

MARSHA: How can you be sure?

NAPOLEON: Are you a phantom?

MARSHA: *(takes his hand, places it on her breast)* This is the heart, sir, of a warm-blooded, red-blooded, wildly repressed American adult female of the 1950s. We are outrageously unpredictable. We long for something more, some indefinable, unattainable . . . "more." The modern, suburban counterpart to your Waterloo, your Egypt, your . . . Dare I say it? We have so much in common.

NAPOLEON: Wine all around!

MARSHA: *(pours)* That's the ticket. *(passes tray with glasses)* Can the children have wine?

NAPOLEON: Yes! Yes! Wine for everyone! Now. Leave us! *(the children and soldiers retreat a few steps, stop)*

MARSHA: But what about our picnic?

NAPOLEON: I do not break bread with my jailers. Leave us! *(they take one more step back)*

MARSHA: *(stabbing the tongue with a long fork, it jumps on the cutting board)* Let's see if I can carve this—*(wields knife)* It's supposed to be quite a delicacy. I've never tried it myself. *(she begins to carve; blood spurts from the tongue, splattering her face and neck)* Oooohhhh! *(she leaps back)* Oh! That's disgusting! My God! It's moving! How can that be?

(She stabs the tongue with the knife repeatedly. WE HEAR an enormous GROAN, then a SIGH from the tongue. She stabs the knife through the tongue and holds it aloft in victory.)

Take that! *(she grins excitedly as blood streams down her arm)* Oh, Boney! Oh, Boney! Lunch is never this exciting in America!

(she stabs the knife and tongue back onto the carving board and advances on NAPOLEON)

NAPOLEON: Madame. You need a bath.

MARSHA: *(grabs his glass of wine, downs it, throws off her cocktail hat)* Let's get elemental, shall we? *(her tongue flicks rapidly in and out of her mouth as . . . the tongue flops on the carving board, then stills)*

NAPOLEON: In some cultures cutting the tongue from the mouth is the prescribed punishment for certain crimes. Tell me: Does the root of the tongue ever heal? Or do you drown swallowing your own blood? How do you lick your lips? Push food to the back of your throat to swallow? How do you taste your food? Pleasure a woman? The tongue is full of blood, sensations. So private. So sexual as it hides in the cave of your mouth. Flicker, flicker: like a light, like a snake.

MARSHA: Don't cry, don't cry.

NAPOLEON: *(raging)* Did you think you could contain me? Silence me? In the darkest recesses of my mouth . . . In the darkest recesses of my mind . . .

MARSHA: *(as though she is speaking to a child)* I will lick your tears, sire. Come with me. *(she touches his face)* There now . . . there now, the face of the Emperor, the warrior, the murderer of millions. *(painting his face with blood)* A bloody badge of honor. Kiss me. *(she leans into him; he opens his mouth to scream and blood rushes out of his mouth)* OOHHHHH!!!

(He collapses to his knees. the tongue on the cutting board flops. She kneels beside him, brings his head to her breast, his blood runs down her chest.)

(She sings a lullaby:)

"IT'S THE BLOOD OF AGES

THE BLOOD OF LIFE

THE BLOOD OF OUR SONS AND HUSBANDS

I AM EVERY MOTHER AND EVERY WIFE

WE HAVE DRUNK THE BLOOD OF MILLIONS

A CONSECRATION

THE SACRAMENT OF LIFE."

(Dead soldiers rise up from the ground and sing the kyrie from Mozart's Mass in C Major:)

SOLDIERS: "LORD HAVE MERCY UPON US

CHRIST HAVE MERCY UPON US

LORD HAVE MERCY UPON US."

NAPOLEON: *(holding a puppet of himself in full military regalia; speaking through the puppet:)* I like to think that was written for me. Of course, Mozart was long dead. Died young. Short.

Brilliant. Childish. Unpredictable. We had so much in common. *(to* MARSHA*)* Come, woman. *(he pulls her to him with one hand)* Let me touch you. *(reaching under her skirt, pulls her panties off, flings them aside)*

(The RATS *appear, sticking their heads up from under the floor.)*

RATS: In which they do the deed. Do the deed. Do the deed!

NAPOLEON: *(grabs an apple from the lunch cart, throws it at them)* Shut up!

(the RATS *giggle)*

MARSHA: My name is—

NAPOLEON: *(pulling her down onto the ground)*

RATS: The nasty! The nasty! The nasty!

MARSHA: My name is—

NAPOLEON: *(stroking her thigh with one hand, bends the puppet's head to kiss her)*

RATS: Ménage à trois! Ha! Ha! Ha!

MARSHA: My name is—

NAPOLEON: *(the puppet speaks)* Let me forget . . . let me forget everything and everyone. *(*NAPOLEON *lies beside her and lays the puppet on top of her)* Even you. Even your name. Even your smell, your sex, your tongue. *(*NAPOLEON *opens his mouth in a silent cry)* Everything . . . everything . . . everything.

(LIGHTS SHIFT)

*(*JOAN *enters)*

RATS: In which Joan of Arc leads the Generals in an impromptu tap dance. They've all been practicing so hard. Be nice to them. Ready boys?

*(*NAPOLEON, GRANT, O'MEARA, JOAN, *and the* NAPOLEON *puppet enter and take their places)*

And one and two and three and . . . .

(The Generals and JOAN *all dance—quite well. The* NAPOLEON *puppet dances front and center, and takes over leading them. The tapping is amplified and augmented with drums, crescendoing as . . . dozens of puppets appear from under the floor—the dead from these several wars—wounded, bandaged, missing arms, legs, eyes,*

ears, heads, chests, stomachs . . . And they dance. A macabre dance which becomes perfectly synchronized so that the tapping—now in unison—is the sound of madness, the sound of war.)

(MAISY *and* DAISY *enter, begin mopping up as the dancers fade away)*

MAISY: It never ends.

DAISY: Finish one place, wring out your mop, and voilá, you're starting over.

MAISY: The music was nice.

DAISY: Since when do dead men sing?

MAISY: Who knows? I kind of like it.

DAISY: Their mouths are all bloody.

MAISY: I wonder how the air moves in and out of their lungs?

DAISY: Well, yes. And I wonder how dead men stand up out of their graves.

MAISY: And dance.

DAISY: Now I've seen everything.

MAISY: More cleanup.

DAISY: What?

MAISY: If we have to repeatedly put them in their graves—

DAISY: Well, that's what happens . . . war by war.

MAISY: No, I mean the same men over and over—

DAISY: Once used to be enough.

MAISY: Maybe the earth is full.

DAISY: What?

MAISY: Maybe there's no more room.

DAISY: No more room for the dead?

MAISY: Why else would they get out of their graves?

DAISY: To sing, no less.

(LIGHTS SHIFT and come up on . . .)

(NAPOLEON, *sitting alone, the puppet in his lap.)*

(He is dishevelled, bloody.)

NAPOLEON: The Age of Reason? This was not the Age of Reason.

Reason. What is that? Define it! This is the Age of Passion, of Passion I say! Unbridled lust—lust for gold, lust for power, lust for land, art, avenues, gilt, silk, sable, pâté de foie gras. You think I am talking of myself? Ha! I am talking of you, of nations, of governments. Yes, we fight for dominance, for spoils, but more, much more, we fight for trade, to control trade, what is traded, the means of trading, the trade routes. If you control sugar! coffee! spice! oil! You control the world.

RATS: We control the crumbs!

(SFX: Chewing)

NAPOLEON: You control nothing.

RATS: We control the books.

NAPOLEON: My books.

RATS: Today the spines, tomorrow the appendices.

NAPOLEON: Between you and the mold—

RATS: We control the wallpaper!

NAPOLEON: Take it! Take it!

RATS: We control the walls!

NAPOLEON: You think I care?

RATS: We control the floors, the floorboards, the joists, the—

NAPOLEON: —Take it all! Let this whole prison ring down around my ears.

RATS: We control the kitchen!

NAPOLEON: More! More! Control it all! Eat it all— Brick by brick, board by board, stone by stone, wall by wall. Let this pathetic house of cards fall. You are my allies, my armies, my generals. I will direct you, organize you, set your strategy!

RATS: We are anarchists! We don't want a ruler! Besides, hasn't anyone told you? You're dead. Tra la!

NAPOLEON: What do you mean? Dead?

(JOAN appears)

JOAN: Didn't we dream the same dream? The fleur de lis, the Imperial Bee, the ermine mantle, the horses, the battle flags, the devotion of men, of armies, the Union of all France.

NAPOLEON: Did the boat bring any limes? any almonds? pomegranates? ginger? wine? On the whole, one could say it brought nothing. What is the weather like? Is there any sun? What time is it? What has happened to the Russian aide-de-camp? Where is Dr. O'Meara? Is he here or did they send him away because he was too fond of us?

JOAN: I am France.

NAPOLEON: No, I am France.

RATS: You're dead.

JOAN/ NAPOLEON: Never. Never. We will never die.

(They exit. LIGHTS SHIFT)

(SFX: Trumpet flourish)

MONTHOLON: The Emperor is dead! Long live the Emperor! The Emperor is dead! Long live the Emperor!

(LOWE, basking in his moment of triumph, wheels NAPOLEON's body onstage. He lies in state in a tin coffin lined with white satin, which rests on a velvet draped bier.)

(LOWE stands at the head of the coffin, MONTHOLON at the foot. JOSEPHINE, PETER, SIMON, and WALT WHITMAN file past. WALT WHITMAN places coins on the dead man's eyes. PETER tucks a loaf of bread under his arm, SIMON, a bottle of wine. JOSEPHINE lays the tricorn hat on his chest, kisses him.)

(SFX: Trumpet flourish)

(Count MONTHOLON unrolls an official document, carrying the Imperial Seal.)

MONTHOLON: The last will and testament of Napoleon Bonaparte: A necklace of gold and diamonds for my manservant, Marchand. A sum of two million francs for Count Montholon. A silver alarm clock for my mother, Letizia Ramolino Bonaparte. Lace for my wife, Marie Louise de Hapsbourg-Lorraine. A medal cabinet for my sister Pauline. A silver and gold candlestick for my sister Caroline. A ringlet made from my hair for each member of my family. My heart in a silver casket to my wife, Marie Louise. To my son, my link to immortality, all of my prized possessions: the silver washstand, the Sèvres plates, and the medals and fine costumes brought into exile with me.

(fade out on MONTHOLON *as . . .)*

(ALL exit)

(SFX: The coffin lid SLAMS shut.)

(SFX: Nails are hammered to secure the lid.)

COMMANDER: *(from o.s.)* Ready! Fire!

(SFX: Musket shot, the beginning of a 21-gun salute)

*(*JOAN *and* JOSEPHINE *step into individual spotlights and address the audience. The closed coffin, in a pale ghostly light, shrouded in mist, appears upstage of* JOAN *and* JOSEPHINE, *and rolls very slowly towards them.)*

JOAN: They have brought the coffin to the grave in the Vale of Geranium. There are four of them, one inside the other, like Russian dolls.

(SFX: Musket shot)

JOSEPHINE: The first, a tin coffin, lined in white satin, contains the body. The Emperor's body.

(SFX: Musket shot)

JOAN: The lid is soldered in place and the tin coffin is lowered into the mahogany coffin, which is secured and then fit into the lead coffin, and soldered again.

(SFX: Musket shot)

JOSEPHINE: It is said that with the air excluded, the body will be preserved for centuries.

(SFX: Musket shot)

JOAN: These three coffins are fitted into the fourth and final coffin made from the dining room table of one of the island's residents.

(SFX: Musket shot)

JOSEPHINE: The whole is then draped in purple velvet and the Cloak of Marengo.

(SFX: Musket shot)

(LIGHTS EXPAND as every character enters, marching in unison, each wearing the full costume of their rank, their heads bare in honour of the dead.)

(SFX: Cannon; from the coast, from the harbor; it is a booming salute, so intense and prolonged it feels more like a battle than a burial.)

JOSEPHINE: They heave the coffin into the stone-lined hole in the ground. Another slab of stone is lowered on top of it, and then cement is poured over the cracks to seal this, the fifth and final container.

(SFX: Dirt shovelled into the grave)

JOAN: Now the red earth and finally, planks covered with black cloth placed on top of the raw soil. There are no speeches. And no inscription.

(All characters exit in unison. The coffin is now front and center.

Three young soldiers enter to stand guard.)

JOSEPHINE: A guard of three soldiers keep watch over the tomb day and night. As if he could still, somehow, escape. The Vale of Geranium has become the Valley of the Tomb. The Emperor breathes no more.

(SFX: Cannon: a final, tumultuous roar.)

(JOAN and JOSEPHINE exit)

(LIGHTS SHIFT)

(NAPOLEON enters, exquisitely costumed.)

NAPOLEON: Nineteen years later, is it a word or a kiss that finally breaks the spell of this exile and this island? Pah! It is nothing but politics. The Cult of Napoleon triumphs. I am resurrected and brought home to Paris in the fullest of pomp and circumstance. The Prince de Joinville, third son of King Louis Philippe, heads the French retinue. *La Belle Poule* and *La Favorite*, their sails and rigging swathed in black, lie at anchor in Jamestown harbor. The stateroom walls are hung with black velvet studded with golden stars and silver tassels, and thousands of Imperial Bees. A polished ebony coffin shaped like a stone sarcophagus stands ready for the Emperor's body. My body. Inside the coffin are these words:

RATS: Napoleon. Emperor and King. Died at St Helena 5 May 1821.

NAPOLEON: They lift me out of my grave on 12 October 1840, exactly twenty-five years since my arrival on St Helena. It takes 18 English soldiers nine hours to pry off the covering stones, dig through six feet of wet, slippery clay, break through the layers of cement reinforced with bands of metal, and, finally, reach the coffins. Someone announces:

RATS: We are now but six inches from the Emperor.

NAPOLEON: They cut through the screws and lift off one lid, through a layer of lead, a layer of wood, until they reach the fourth and final coffin. They cut through the soldered edges and pause before they open the lid. Prayers are said.

RATS: "Out of the depths have I cried unto thee, O Lord." *(Psalm 130)*

(SFX: Coffin lid opening)

NAPOLEON: There, in the center of it all, like the heart nestling in the chest, is my body. The black riding boots have split open revealing white toes. The hands: white, hard and perfect. The jacket of the Chasseur du Gard, still green with a bright red lining. The medals and buttons tarnished, the face pale, three teeth showing where the lip has pulled back, the skin gray where the stubble of a new beard first started to grow. The eyelids hard and firmly closed with no chance of seeing a flicker of movement. No chance at all. They look on me as if . . . as if . . .

RATS: Now can we eat him?

NAPOLEON: You are incorrigible.

RATS: We have waited a long time, your Majesty.

NAPOLEON: They want to lift me out, probe the secrets of my body, but the Corsican priest stops them. They seal the coffin before the action of the air can destroy the impression of immortality.

(SFX: Gunshot)

NAPOLEON: With gunshot and cannon shot, with drums rolling and the sun setting into a red sea, the coffin is carried to the upper deck of *La Belle Poule.*

(SFX: Drum roll)

NAPOLEON: There, by the light of lanterns, the priest recites the prayers for the dead. Does he say the words "*sursum corda*"? Lift

up your hearts ...? or even "In the midst of life we are in death"
...? Does he speak of Resurrection and the sure and certain
hope of life everlasting? Perhaps. Perhaps not.

(SFX: The minuet)

NAPOLEON: The priest—

RATS: —and the rats! Don't forget the rats!

NAPOLEON: Are you returning to Paris with me?

RATS: Of course, your Majesty.

NAPOLEON: The priest and the rats sit together, keeping watch
over the corpse until the dawn.

RATS: We will keep watch forever, your Majesty. Forever.

(NAPOLEON bows and exits)

*(As lights begin to fade, Maisy and Daisy enter, pushing their
mops.)*

FADE TO BLACK

CURTAIN

END OF PLAY

DR. SAM IS UNDER
YOUR BED

BY PRUDENCE WRIGHT HOLMES

BIOGRAPHY

Prudence Wright Holmes is an actor who has appeared in the films *Sister Act I* and *II* with Whoopi Goldberg, *Kingpin* with Woody Harrelson, and *In Dreams* with Annette Bening. She has appeared on Broadway with Meryl Streep in *Happy End*, with Maggie Smith in *Lettice And Lovage*, and with George C. Scott in *Inherit The Wind*. She was in the original cast of *Godspell* and *Sister Mary Ignatius Explains It All for You*. She has appeared in many regional theaters, including The Long Wharf, The Guthrie, Syracuse Stage, and Portland Stage. She has appeared in many roles on TV. She has also done over one hundred television commercials. As a writer, she has read her work at KGB Red Room, The Living Room, and The Cornelia Street Café. *Dr. Sam Is Under Your Bed* will be produced at The New York Theater Workshop in the winter of 2003.

Dr. Sam Is Under Your Bed is a solo piece performed by one actress playing all the parts.

To Coree Spencer, Kent Paul, Doug Moser, Ralph Sevush, John Weidman, and all my friends at Dramatist's Guild

DR. SAM IS UNDER YOUR BED

"MOM, LOCK THE DOORS, THERE'S A KILLER ON THE LOOSE!" My father rushes into the living room, waving a newspaper. "Wife of this rich doctor outside of Cleveland was murdered last night. Everyone thinks her husband did her in. No sign of forced entry, no murder weapon found, and the guy's an osteopath, and everybody knows they're just a bunch of quacks."

He shoves the paper in my mother's face. On the front page, there's a picture of a hacked-up dead body. My mother takes the paper. "The neighbors say he was a high roller—smoking, drinking. Ooh, he drove a Jaguar!"

"See, Mom, that proves it."

My father doesn't smoke. As for drinking, he tells me, "It'll kill you more surely than a pistol shot." And he always drives his El Dorado Cadillac five miles under the speed limit.

But today, July 5, 1954, my father might have broken that law for the first time in his life. He has just returned from The Million Dollar Round Table, near Cleveland. With a killer on the loose, he wants to get out of Northern Ohio as fast as he can.

The Million Dollar Round Table is this convention for insurance agents who sell over a million dollars worth of insurance. My father goes every year.

He snatches the paper from my mother. Sweat is pouring off his bald head. "Thirty-five blows to the head. And her pajamas were pulled off."

"Burt, shh! Little pitchers have big ears!"

I look up from changing the diapers on my Betsy-Wetsy doll.

"Sleepy time," my mother says.

Betsy-Wetsy and I head up stairs.

"Watch out, Dr. Sam could be under your bed."

"Who's Dr. Sam, Daddy?"

"The guy who killed his wife. Dr. Sam Sheppard."

Bay Village is the Cleveland suburb where Dr. Sam's wife, Marilyn, was murdered. We live south of there in a town called Bexley, near Columbus, but it's still too close for comfort.

Headline, July 7, 1954: "GET THAT KILLER."

July 14: "GETTING AWAY WITH MURDER."

July 16: "WHEN WILL THE REAL KILLER BE ARRESTED?"

July 17: My father's friend Stu Tuttle calls.

"Did you know yours truly made the front page of the Cleveland *Plain Dealer*, commander?" My father and Stu are old navy buddies.

"How come?"

"I went over to the scene of the crime to see if I could lend a hand. Reporter snapped my picture. The place was a three-ring circus. The whole neighborhood running around hunting up evidence."

"They find anything?"

"I found a trowel in the garden. Thought it might be the murder weapon. So, I turned it over to the police. But first I used it to dig up some grass from the front lawn."

"What'd you want with that?"

"Are you kidding? That grass could be worth a fortune some day. Oh, and Burt one more thing. I hear Dr. Sam's middle name is Holmes. Any relation? . . . Burt, Burt are you there?" *(Click)*

Headline, July 23: "WHO WILL SPEAK FOR MARILYN?"

"I will." He runs into the front yard. He spots some neighbors.

"Bob, Jack, Homer, can I bend your ears for a minute!" I watch from my bedroom window as a group of men gather on our lawn.

"Men, there's a killer in our midst. And he isn't like those coloreds down on Long Street that don't know any better. This guy's one of our kind gone bad. This is too close to home, boys. Our loved ones gotta be protected. What we oughtta do is start writing letters to the governor demanding the immediate arrest of Dr. Sam."

Stu Tuttle ambles in. "Governor Lausche's already gotten hundreds, and he's settin' on his hands."

"Just like a Democrat." My father turns to his neighbors. "We need a battle plan! Tomorrow, let's march up to Bay Village and mount an offensive."

Stu says to my father, "Commander, you're the highest-ranking officer here. I think you should spearhead this mission." The men cheer.

My father mounts the front porch. Other neighbors come into our yard.

"Thanks for your faith in me boys, I'd be honored to serve. Now here's the strategy: We'll have a three-pronged offensive. First, we'll keep pouring the heat on the governor; second, we'll deploy a unit to Sheppard's inquest, to make sure justice is served. And third: We've got to surround the enemy, force him out into the open. Now, this weekend at oh six hundred hours, men whose names begin with A through M—you take the land offensive. Drive up to Bay Village and camp out in Sheppard's front yard. N through Z—you're the amphibious unit. Sheppard lives on Lake Erie. We'll establish a beachhead in his back yard. We'll bring 'Dr. Poke in the Back' to his knees just like we did in Italy with those lousy Krauts." Stu Tuttle steps forward.

"Commander, my boat's up in Buckeye Lake. I'll get it tonight."

"But Stuie, isn't tonight the Y-Teen father-daughter dinner at the country club?"

"Yes, sir, it is, but sacrifices have to be made."

"I knew I could count on you, buddy. All right, go home and rest. Tomorrow, D day in Bay Village."

The next morning Stu comes to our door.

"Mission accomplished, sir. My boat's up on a trailer and ready to go."

He hands my father a bag. My father opens it.

"What's this?"

"A hermetically sealed jar of Dr. Sam's grass. Like I told you, someday it's going to be worth a bundle."

My father places the jar on our mantel under the picture of his distant cousin, Oliver Wendell Holmes.

July 26: My mother and I turn on the radio.

"Good morning, friends and neighbors. This is the Early Worm, coming to you from WBNS radio here in the heart of the Buckeye State. Today we're up in Bay Village, for the third day of the inquest into the brutal murder of Marilyn Sheppard. Her husband, Dr. Sam Sheppard, is the prime suspect. We're here with Mr. Burton Holmes, whose Citizens for Justice group kept a vigil at Sheppard's house this weekend. So, Mr. Holmes, what do you think of the inquest so far?"

"My favorite moment was when the coroner frisked Dr. Sam and threw out his lawyer. What does he need a lawyer for if he's innocent?"

"So you think he's guilty?"

"No doubt about it. There's a rumor that Doctor Sam had a lady friend. Even if he didn't kill the wife, adultery is a felony in this state."

"Oh, excuse me, Mr. Holmes, Dr. Sam has returned to the stand. Let's listen in."

Coroner: "Dr. Sheppard, did you attend a striptease party with a Susan Hayes?"

Sheppard: "No."

"Did you sleep in the same bedroom as Susan Hayes?"

"No."

"Did you have 'sexyul' relations with Miss Hayes?"

"No."

My mother and I hear a familiar voice shout, "Tell the truth. Liar, skirt chaser, killer!"

July 30: "DR. SAM SHEPPARD ARRESTED FOR THE FIRST DEGREE MURDER OF MARILYN SHEPPARD."

Now that justice has been done, my father can return to his civic duties in Bexley. Not only is he general manager of the Aetna Life Insurance Company, he is also is the chairman of the vestry at St. Alban's Episcopal Church, the president of the Humane Society, and he gives more blood to the Red Cross than anyone in town. Like everyone else around here, my father likes Ike, but he feels a special kinship with Vice President of the United States Richard Nixon. He tells me how Nixon saved America from Alger Hiss, this Ivy League snob who was a Communist spy. But what my father likes best about Nixon is that they were both commanders in the navy during World War II. Actually, my father was in both the army and the navy during the war. But his days in the navy were the happiest time of his life, that is, until he became the president of Citizens for Justice.

All that summer Dr. Sam is the talk of the town. I watch the news every night, but they never tell me what I want to know most: "Daddy, why were Marilyn's pajamas pulled off?"

"Uh . . . would you like Daddy to read you a bedtime story?"

My father has this insurance book. He reads it every night, so I think it must have some good stories.

"Yes, yes. *Risk Appraisal,* please."

I soon find out it tells the symptoms of various diseases and gives statistics about how likely certain age groups are to die from them. There's one illness I like best.

"Read me Lion's Head Disease, read me Lion's Head Disease!"

"Facial bones enlarge, and hair covers the entire body, teeth grow into fangs."

I run to the mirror and check my teeth.

"Don't worry, honey, it only strikes one in five million."

Headline, October 28: "DR. SAM'S TRIAL BEGINS TODAY."

My father shows me the headline with pictures of two famous reporters—Dorothy Kilgallen and Walter Winchell—who are right here in Ohio, telling the whole country about something that's happening in our very own state. We see people we know on television. Old friends from faraway call wanting to know the inside scoop. When my father tucks me in at night, we talk about what's coming up at the trial the next day. I can't wait to get up in the morning.

When it comes to choosing a jury, my father explains that we want people who will do the right thing. The first person called tells the judge he made a point of reading everything he could about the murder. He's elected foreman. When it's over, we're off to a great start. All of the jurors except one have read articles about Dr. Sam.

A few days later, the Cleveland *Plain Dealer* helps things along. It prints the names and addresses of the jurors on the front page. In case anyone wants to talk to them.

"That lying louse will never see the light of day again." I dream of my father bringing home Dr. Sam's head on a pole.

The trial begins. My mother tells me, "They can't really prove he did it, so they're going to try to poke holes in his story about being happily married." One of the first witnesses is Dr. Sam's neighbor. She tells the court that Marilyn told her that a friend told Marilyn that Dr. Sam told a friend that he was considering divorce.

It turns out that when Dr. Sam said he didn't have a girlfriend, he wasn't exactly telling the truth. The police find Susan Hayes in California and fly her back to Ohio to spill the beans.

My father tells me, "Any man who has a floozy and lies about it is capable of killing his wife." My father knows only too well how much trouble floozies can cause. In fact, he has a deep dark secret that I'm not supposed to talk about: His sister was a floozy. She was the Elizabeth Taylor of their hometown, Brandon, Vermont. She ran off with the local Episcopal priest, who was married. After that, nobody in town would talk to my father, let alone buy insurance from him. So he left Brandon for Providence, Rhode Island.

There he tries to put his sordid past behind him. He gets a job selling insurance for the Aetna Life Insurance Company. A few months later, he has a blind date with a schoolteacher from Boston. She is thirty-three years old and has not managed to hook a man. Now she is practically ready for the glue factory. By this time, my father is up for a job as the general manager of Aetna's office in Columbus, Ohio. But the boss wants a married man.

My parents are married three weeks later.

They go to Columbus to look for a place to live. My father wants to live in Upper Arlington because it's restricted.

My mother likes Bexley because it's safe. There's a policeman at every party. It's the law. But my father has heard there are a lot of Jews there. My mother tells him they're okay because they're rich. Then she tells him how Bexley was founded by a bunch of millionaires who wanted to get away from sinful city life and all the bad people in Columbus. It has no Italians, Irish, or other foreigners who belong to the Catholic church. My father is glad to hear it because he knows that Catholics multiply like rabbits. It's all part of a plot by the Pope to take over the world.

The Pope is someone my father fears as much as Stalin or Mao Tse-tung. But he's still not convinced that he can live side by side with people who killed Jesus Christ. Then my mother tells him something that changes his mind.

"Burt, Bexley's a dry town."

And that's why I'm from Bexley.

After living in Bexley a few years, my parents find out that some people in Bexley do drink. But if they get out of hand, they are carted away to Harding Sanitarium late at night and nobody ever talks about them again. Harding is a large stone building surrounded by an iron fence with spikes run by Seventh Day Adventists.

One morning, we're having breakfast when Tommy, the neighbor's boy, comes to the door. I answer it. "I'm Dr. Sam and you're Marilyn. Bang, you're dead," he says and squirts me with his water pistol.

"Tommy, you dumbbell. Everybody knows Dr. Sam didn't shoot Marilyn. He beat her till she died. Thirty-five blows to the head. And he pulled off her p.j.'s, right, Daddy?"

"That's right, honey."

"Okay, I'll beat you up."

"Son, you leave her pajamas on."

My fun and games with Tommy come to an end. He gets his arm cut off by a motor boat in Buckeye Lake, and now he wears a hook. I've heard those scary stories about the man with the hook who goes crazy and kills everyone in sight. So, one day when I'm supposed to come over, I call Tommy. "I can't." He wants to know why. I think fast. "I have Lion's Head disease."

Headline, December 21: "DR. SAM IS GUILTY. GETS LIFE."

"Ho, ho, ho, Santa's coming early." My father bounds in and hands my mother a big box. Inside is a mink coat. She puts it on, and then we all dash off to a victory party at the Army Depot.

My father takes the stage and raises his glass to toast the crowd.

"Here's to a job well done, boys." He downs his Verner's ginger ale in one gulp and hands me his cherry. "Dr. Sam's family's gonna appeal. We've got to be vigilant. Just like Nixon's been with Alger Hiss. Every time Sheppard comes up for parole, the Citizens for Justice oughtta be right there, making sure that he goes to meet his Maker in a striped suit."

The men cheer. My father scoops me up in his arms and whirls me around. His blubbery belly heaves as he gasps for breath and his face is as red as the cherry I just ate. Thank God we have insurance.

Headline, 1955: "DR. SAM MOVED TO THE OHIO STATE PENITENTIARY IN COLUMBUS."

This year, I start taking ballet lessons. My teacher always has the windows open wide, even when it's snowing, and still she's drenched with sweat. We beg her to close them. She says she can't because she has a disease called menopause. I look it up in *Risk Appraisal.* It's not there. My mother finally explains, "It's a sickness ladies get that makes them so hot they sometimes go insane."

I hope I never catch it.

So this one day, I'm in my room practicing for our next recital, "I'm Tina the Ballerina"—when my father runs in.

"We're going on a family outing."

We all pile in the El Dorado and head downtown.

My father pulls up in front of a big old black building with barbed-wire fence around it. He runs over to the fence and rolls his newspaper into a megaphone.

"Hey Sheppard, hey jailbird. How do you like making license plates, you bone cruncher?"

I call out, "Hey, you quack."

"Get moving," a man shouts from the guardhouse.

My father jumps in the car. He rolls down the windows and yells at the top of his lungs, "Bye, Dr. Sam. Don't eat too much bread and water." Then he revs the motor and lays on the horn and tears out of there. We laugh all the way home.

The next weekend, we go again. But when he wants to go on the third weekend, I throw a fit.

"Daddy, it's the hottest day of the summer. I want to go swimming."

He drags me along anyway. I scream the entire way there and back. My father steps on the gas. He goes thirty-five in a twenty-five mile an hour zone. A cop pulls him over and gives him a ticket. My father glares at me, "This is all your fault." I wail even louder. "Pipe down, Or you'll get me another ticket for disturbing the peace."

He creeps toward home.

I spot a gas station.

"I have to go to the bathroom."

My father doesn't seem to hear me. I see another one.

"Daddy. Stop there. Please."

He keeps right on driving.

I kick the seat. "I have to go. I have to go. I have to go."

He grabs my arm. "Hold it till you get home."

"I can't. You're the meanest Daddy that ever was." I let go and wet the front seat of his El Dorado.

My father drags me in the house by my hair and gets out his paddle.

Then he sends me to my room. A few hours later, I go downstairs and find my father collapsed on the chaise lounge on the front porch. He's drenched with sweat. He looks at me.

"You learn your lesson?"

I don't answer.

"You're as stubborn as a mule. Go get me some lemonade."

I look at him.

"You sure sweat a lot. Maybe you have menopause."

"You watch your language, young lady . . . " He swats at me. "Now go and get me a drink."

I take the pitcher and pour it over his head. He starts sobbing. He crawls on all fours to my mother in the kitchen.

"Mom, she's a bad girl, spank her."

My mother grabs me by the arm.

"Go upstairs to your room."

I go upstairs—to my parent's room. I find my mother's fingernail scissors. I spend the rest of the afternoon cutting every necktie in my father's closet into little bitty pieces. I'm just about done when my mother finds me.

"What have you done, you naughty little girl? I'm going to send you up to the children's division of Harding Sanitarium where they keep kids in kennels like dogs and they don't even let them out to go to the bathroom."

"I don't care."

"And you know what you'll be eating for dinner? Soy bean pork chops."

"No, mother, please. I'll starve."

In Bexley, to be without our meat is a fate worse than death.

"Good morning, neighbors. This is the Early Worm. Today the Chamber of Commerce announced its choice for the 1959 Man of the Year. He is Mr. Burton C. Holmes, general manager of the Aetna Life Insurance Company. He was recognized for his outstanding acts of citizenship."

Partially because of my father's Citizens for Justice group, Dr. Sam has been kept in jail for over five years. His appeals have been rejected by every court, including the state Supreme Court. The fifties end in a blaze of glory for my father. The sixties won't.

But they do begin with a bang. It's an election year. Bexley is the epicenter of Nixon territory in Ohio. We go to $1,000 a plate dinners and rallies all over the state. When Nixon loses, my father and many others in Bexley wear black armbands. There is talk of secession.

In 1963, a song by Bob Dylan goes to the top of the hit parade. (*"The Times They Are A-Changin'"* *plays.*) We hear it on the way to school one day.

My father says, "Honey, why would anyone want to listen to that guy? He can't carry a tune in a bucket."

"It's not about his voice, Daddy, it's his message."

"Well, his message isn't good for a girl your age to listen to."

"Don't worry, I don't like Bob Dylan. *(turns off radio)* I'm beyond that silly kid's stuff. I'm an existentialist."

"What's that?"

"It's a club. Some friends and I started it at school. Our motto is 'existence precedes essence.'"

"You kids today sure are different from when I was growing up. All we wanted was to get a date for the prom."

"The prom. Oh, Daddy, please. I don't have time for anything so superficial."

The truth is, I can't get a date. That's why I become an existentialist. There is a secret sorority at our school called The Webbers. These girls know how to web boys—like spiders. They get all the cute boys and existentialists like me might just as well forget it.

But even though I'm not a Bob Dylan fan, it is clear he is on to something about how the times are changing. They're changing around our house, too.

My father catches our cleaning girl drinking paregoric and fires her on the spot. Now my mother has to break in the new girl, Minnie Jones. Minnie is not easily broken.

One day my mother is rushing out to an emergency meeting of the African Violet Society. As she leaves, she hands Minnie a list of chores.

Minnie hands it back to her. "Miz Holmes, washing and ironing will be an extra three dollars."

"I pay you a good salary."

"You pay me to clean the house, you want more, you pay more."

My mother hesitates. She has to get there in ten minutes.

"Oh, all right, just remember to separate the darks from the whites." Minnie stares at my mother for a minute, then she takes the basket without a word.

That summer, I'm a sophomore at Bexley High. I want to spend my summer vacation discussing Kierkegaard across town at that hotbed of free thinkers—Ohio State University. But my father has noticed my inability to web boys. So he decides to groom me to be his heir at Aetna. He takes me to lunch at the Toddle House and makes his pitch.

"Insurance is a great way to make a living, honey. If John Smith buys a $50,000 policy in the year 1963 and pays into it every month, by the year 1983 he'll have $120,000."

"Who's John Smith?"

"I'd pay you a good salary. You'll be sitting in air conditioning."

"No."

"You can have your own charge-a-plate at the Bexley Book Nook."

That's how I meet my first bunch of career girls.

My job is pulling out dead people's cards from the files. My father's secretary, Jewel Flitz, instructs me on the fine points of this difficult operation.

"We have to keep our files up to date. Here's a list of new dead people. Pull 'em out. Then, stamp 'deceased' on them. Send them to claims and when they come back, tear them into four equal pieces, and throw them away."

I come up with my own version of the system. I create a huge mound of torn-up cards on my desk. I hide behind it and immerse myself in one of the great works of literature like *To the Lighthouse* by Virginia Woolf. The only human contact I have is when the phone rings and Jewel calls out to me with an update:

"Four-car pileup, I-70, Artabelle Quigley, decapitated."

Even though, I don't know Artabelle, I burst into tears. "We are doomed. Come pain, bury your fangs in my flesh."

No one in the office recognizes the quote from Virginia Woolf. I think it perfectly captures the moment, but everyone stares at me in silence. Then, Jewel comes over and puts her arm around me. "Don't take it so hard, hon. I can guarantee you, Artabelle didn't feel a thing."

The next day she posts a clipping about the accident on the office bulletin board. It reflects all of my father's interests: his clients' deaths and misfortunes, my father's activities and honors, Richard Nixon, and of course, Dr. Sam.

Headline: "BAILEY HOPES FOR REVERSAL OF SHEPPARD'S GUILTY VERDICT."

My father says Dr. Sam's new lawyer, some young kid named F. Lee Bailey, has filed a writ of habeas corpus seeking to overturn Dr. Sam's conviction. He is sure the judge will send Dr. Sam and his upstart lawyer packing.

Jewel tries to help me fit in at the office. She introduces me to the other girls. Methyl Murdock, a woman with yellow teeth, tells me, "Dumb old me. I'm lucky to work for your father. He is a great man."

I wonder how long she'll think so. Jewel is pushing my father to fire Methyl because she doesn't wear deodorant.

"Mr. Holmes, her blouses all have big stains under the arms. And that's bad for business."

Not that Jewel hasn't tried to help Methyl. She has. She even gave her a bottle of her favorite perfume—Evening in Paris. But Methyl gives it back to her "I'm sorry. Dumb old me. I can't wear perfume. It gives me a headache."

Headline: "DR. SAM SAVES LIFE OF FELLOW INMATE."

My father comes in late that afternoon from Steubenville. He's humming as he hands Jewel some cards.

"I got five new prospects at Juddy Johnson's viewing."

Then he sees the headlines and stops in his tracks.

"Who put up this article on Sheppard?"

Everyone looks at the floor.

"Looks to me like this came from that rag, the *Columbus Star.* I'm going to take it down. But I want to know who did this."

No one speaks.

"All right, you can all stay till someone owns up to this."

We all sit in silence. I stare at the clock. It is 5:22. The office closes at 5:30. Tonight my friend Linda and I are planning to sneak into the 7 o'clock show of this art movie—*The Garden of Eden* at the Bexley Theater. If this drags on, I won't make it. If I get in, for the first time in my life, I'll get to see a real penis.

Quitting time comes and goes. My father walks down the aisle, waiting for someone to crack. A new girl is sniffling, "I'm diabetic. I can't miss my supper." Jewel hands her a package of saltines. "Dismissed," my father tells her. Jewel says to my father, "That was so nice of you, Mr. Holmes. A lot nicer than Dr. Sam was to poor Marilyn."

My father smiles. "I'm ordering a new Dictaphone for you tomorrow, Jewel. And you can leave, too."

By now it's 6:15. Even though I had nothing to do with the clipping, I stand up.

"I did it, Daddy."

My father stares at me—like the man on that old TV show *I Led Three Lives* who finds out his wife is a Communist.

"You?"

"I'm sorry. But Dr. Sam has been doing good—"

"Hush up, NOW. If you ever do anything like this again—"

The other girls lean forward in their seats. They want to see what he is going to do to me. My father notices. "You girls can go." They gather up their things, trying not to stare.

When we are alone, my father lets loose. "Every article favorable to Dr. Sam makes it easier for him to get out of jail. And then none of us will be safe."

"Oh Daddy, please—"

"No. Sheppard is the lowest form of humanity there is and don't you ever forget it."

I look at the clock. It's 6:35. "You're right, Daddy. Dr. Sam is the scum of the earth. Now can we go?"

My father wipes his brow. "You've learned a valuable lesson today, haven't you?" I smile and head for the car. On the way home, I tell him I have to visit a sick friend. I have him drop me off a block from the theater.

I doze off as the movie grinds through scenes about a young woman leaving home. Then she goes to a nudist colony. Linda elbows me, "Penis." I've never seen anything so ugly. But other audience members don't seem to think so. There, leaning forward in their seats, I see several members of the African Violet Society.

The next day my father walks in the office with a big smile on his face. Jewel is always the first to greet him.

"Good morning, Mr. Holmes. Do you need me for anything?"

"Come take dictation." Dictation lasts two hours. When my father takes me to lunch at the Toddle House, even though we eat on the patio, all I can smell is Evening in Paris. Suddenly, I flash on that grotesque thing I saw last night at The Bexley Theater. I picture my father and Jewel frolicking naked in *The Garden of Eden*. I can't eat a bite of my poor boy. I tell my father I've got a stack of dead people waiting for me and hurry back to the office.

At 3:00 P.M. it's time for a coffee break. All the girls grab their purses and cigarettes and head for the ladies lounge. There, amidst mirrors and Kotex machines, Jewel takes center stage. She pulls out a Winston and stares at my bushy eyebrows.

"You have such pretty eyes. You should highlight them. You know what I do with my eyebrows? I put Nair on them. Then I just draw them in the way I want them. I can have different eyebrows every day of the week. Watch." *(She puts down her Winston and starts to wipe off her eyebrows.)*

Methyl leans over Jewel with a plate of brownies. Her armpit is even with Jewel's nose. "Want one?"

(Jewel rolls her eyes and turns her head away). "No thanks." She pulls out her bottle of Evening in Paris perfume and squirts it into the air. Then, she wipes off her sloping eyebrows and replaces them with two inverted V's.

"My fourth husband flipped for the horseshoes. But my new husband says the teepees make me look younger."

"Beautiful. Dumb old me tried it once. But it just made the bags under my eyes look bigger."

(Jewel lowers her voice. Smokes.) "A little Preparation H would do the trick."

"Ohhh!"

I seize the opportunity to move as far away from Jewel and her eyebrows as I can. Methyl follows me with her brownies, "Want one?"

I take the least burned one and put it in my purse.

"Thanks."

"No. Thank you."

"What for?"

"The clippings. I did it. Dumb old me. I should have spoken

up, but I was just so scared your father would fire me. I hope he wasn't too hard on you."

"No."

Methyl reaches in her purse and flashes a paperback at me. The title is *The Sheppard Murder Case*. "The man who wrote it has all sorts of proof that Dr. Sam didn't do it."

"Oh, I don't know, Methyl. My father says there was no sign of forced entry."

"They didn't lock their doors."

"Wasn't the murder weapon a surgical instrument?"

"Now they think the weapon was a flashlight."

"Well, it still could have been Dr. Sam."

"And another thing, the police never did tests to find out why poor Marilyn's pajamas were pulled off."

"Why were they?"

"Someone had his way with her."

"Methyl, could I borrow that book?"

She transfers the goods to my purse.

"You won't tell your father, will you?"

"My lips are sealed."

 Headline: "CONVICTED WIFE-SLAYER ENGAGED."

Apparently Ariane Tebbenjohans doesn't share my feelings about penises. It says in the paper that she's become Dr. Sam's fiancée. Ariane is a German woman who used to be Joseph Goebbel's sister-in-law. She writes Dr. Sam a letter and they become pen pals. Now she's bankrolling his case.

Dr. Sam isn't the only one receiving letters. My father writes one to the judge.

"It has been more than two months since your court received a writ of habeas corpus, seeking to overturn the conviction of Dr. Sam Sheppard. We, the undersigned citizens of Ohio, are alarmed at the prospect of this murderer being unleashed in our midst. We urge you to keep this menace to society kept under lock and key for the rest of his unnatural life."

(Clap) "Oh, that's wonderful, Mr. Holmes." Jewel's been taking dictation. My father grabs the petition and signs it with an exclamation point after his name. Then he stands up and announces:

"We're going to pass this around, and everybody will add their

John Hancocks! Not to mention the names of any competitors."

(laugh) "Oh, Mr. Holmes, you're a card." Jewel always loves a good insurance joke.

One girl after another signs, and then the letter reaches Methyl. She stares at it. She picks up the pen. She puts it down.

"Could you come back to me?"

My father comes up behind her. "Why don't you sign it now?"

"I want to think about it."

"You want the Butcher of Bay Village roaming the streets again, Methyl?"

"Dumb old me, I know I shouldn't say this, but I feel kinda sorry for him. I always kinda felt that maybe, I mean, the trial just didn't seem fair and all the evidence was really just circumstantial . . . Oh, Mr. Holmes. I think he's innocent."

"Methyl, go home."

"I'm sorry, Mr. Holmes, dumb old me, I can come back, can't I?"

"We'll see."

I put down my dead people's cards and go up to my father. "Daddy, leave her alone. She didn't do anything wrong."

"You're too young to understand this."

"I understand that you're trying to turn this office into some kind of police state, and anybody who doesn't agree with you is sent to Siberia."

"Go back to your desk, now."

"If she goes, I go."

"That's it. I'm canceling your charge account at the Bexley Book Nook."

"Go ahead, you dictator."

Methyl tries to intervene. "You're right Mr. Holmes, Dr. Sam probably did kill Marilyn—"

I come up between them. "He did not, Methyl, and you know it. It's a scientific fact that the killer was left-handed, and Dr. Sam's not. He didn't even have any blood on his pants—how could he have killed anybody? And besides, it's practically certain that Marilyn was raped—"

"SHUT YOUR FILTHY MOUTH!" My father throws my purse and my book bag at me and drags me to the door and flings it open. "Don't ever darken this door again. You're a disgrace."

I get in his face, "I wish you were dead in the grave with maggots eating your eyeballs."

I walk out, slam the door and burst into tears. But thank God, my career in insurance is over.

Every morning, I wait till my father leaves, and then I come downstairs and hang around the house talking to our maid Minnie. I've never had a talk with a black person before, and Minnie seems very exotic. In the afternoon, I head up to the No Exit Coffee House at Ohio State. My mother fears I'm heading to hell in a hand basket. Finally, she tells my father.

A few days later I'm up at the No Exit. During a rap session on *The Second Sex*, I look up and see Minnie standing in the back. When we take an espresso break, I go up to her.

"Minnie, what are you doing here?"

"I always did like a good cup of coffee. How about introducing me to those liberation gals?"

Minnie joins our group. After the meeting, she offers to buy me another cup of coffee.

"This is an espresso."

"What's that?"

"A special coffee that artists and great thinkers drink."

Minnie orders one. We sip our espresso. Minnie suddenly puts down her cup.

"I gotta tell the truth and shame the devil. Your father sent me here. He's afraid you're hanging out with the wrong kinda folks."

"You're spying on me?"

"Well, just kinda checking up on you. But after tonight's meeting, I ain't gonna do it no more."

"Is he paying you?"

Minnie doesn't answer.

"You keep that money. We'll make up some story that'll calm him down, but worry him enough to keep paying you."

Minnie reports back to my father.

"All they do is talk about how women can make their lives better."

"Oh, well, that doesn't sound too bad."

"But, Mr. Holmes, I swear to God some of those women ain't wearing bras and—"

"Minnie, please! Here's ten dollars, go back again."

I let Minnie spy on me for the rest of the summer. She hits it off with some of the regulars at the coffee house. She stops pressing her hair and starts talking about things like the oppression of the masses and Mahatma Gandhi. Then, she joins the NAACP's fight for integration. She kicks off the fundraising drive by donating some of the money my father's paying her for checking up on me.

"My, that David Janssen is a nice-looking man." My parents and I have just seen a new TV show called *The Fugitive*. It's loosely based on the Sheppard case. It portrays the Dr. Sam character as an innocent man. After the first episode, my father gets on the phone with Stu Tuttle.

"Who did Sheppard pay off to write this garbage? Now what we ought to do, Stuie, is get in touch with ABC."

"I don't have time for that whole Sheppard mess anymore, Burt. I've just been chosen to head up the Ohio chapter of the Goldwater for President campaign."

"Haven't you heard about his Jewish grandfather?"

"Oh Burt, that was a long time ago. Barry's become a Methodist."

One night I come into the kitchen and I see my father showing some insurance charts to Minnie. Minnie points to one.

"Well, ain't that somethin', Mr. Holmes. You mean to tell me that if John Smith buys a $50,000 policy in the year 1963, and he pays into it every month, by 1983 he'll have $120,000?"

"That's right."

"Well, shoot, that life insurance is some good stuff."

This happens night after night. Finally Minnie tells my father she wants to learn the insurance business. He offers to help her apply for a loan to go to Ohio State. Now when I go to the No Exit, I see Minnie in a corner pouring over actuarial tables.

Headline, July 16, 1964: "DR. SAM RELEASED FROM THE OHIO STATE PENITENTIARY. JUDGE SAYS HE GOT AN UNFAIR TRIAL."

Soon after, Dr. Sam marries Ariane Tebbenjohans.

That night, I come downstairs in an old bathrobe and find my father sitting in his favorite chair, staring into space.

"Daddy, hear the good news about Dr. Sam?"

He doesn't even look at me.

"Want a scotch?"

Still nothing.

"Supper!" My mother calls from the kitchen.

"I made your favorite, Burt, City Chicken." Cubes of mutton, rolled in cornflakes, stuck on a skewer, and then my mother fries the hell out of it. And a delicious Henny Penny salad, which involves apples, potato chips, and mayonnaise, and of course, the dreaded lima bean, which I wouldn't eat if my life depended on it. I know what'll get my father.

I take a bite of the City Chicken and spit it out. My father comes to life. "Where are your manners?"

"I'm not eating this crap."

"You talk worse than any man I ever met in the army or the navy."

"I'll say whatever I damn please."

"Oh no you won't." My father leans over and bites me on the arm. "Ouch!" He throws some money on the table.

"Here's five dollars. Go eat at the Toddle House."

"Give me twenty. I'll go to Arlington Arms and celebrate with Dr. Sam and Ariane."

My father rises up like Godzilla about to destroy Tokyo. He grabs a fistful of Henny Penny salad and throws it in my face. I grab a fistful of lima beans and fling them at him. My father ducks under the table. Then he pops back up. He has a bottle of Verner's ginger ale in his hand, and he's shaking it. Now he yanks off the top and sprays me with it. SHHHHHH! I take my plate and throw it in his face. He lunges at me and rips off my robe. I am completely naked. My mother cowers in the corner. Just then, our cat comes racing through the room. My father trips over her. All 250 pounds of him topple on me.

We're rolling around on the floor, smearing food on each other. My father punches me again and again. Just then the phone rings. My mother runs for it.

"Old lady Delker drowned in the bathtub." My father staggers up. Duty calls. I bolt out of the house stark naked. I throw on an old bedspread I find in the garage. Then I run three blocks to

Linda's house. Her father is in jail for check forgery and her mother has just had the first lobotomy in town, so things are calmer there.

I spend the night in the emergency room. I go home and lock myself in my room. The next evening my father knocks on my bedroom door. "You're not mad at your, old dad, are you?" I slam the door in his face. I keep my distance my whole senior year. And, in the fall, my dream comes true. I finally escape Bexley.

I go to Pittsburgh to college.

But at the end of my freshman year, I head home to Bexley.

Headline, June 6, 1966: "U.S. SUPREME COURT BACKS DR. SAM. SAYS HE GOT UNFAIR TRIAL."

I expect my father to come in loaded for bear. Instead, he throws himself into my mother's arms, "Mom, I can't breathe, I'm going to die." It's the only time I've ever seen my parents embrace. By the end of the evening, he's in the hospital with pleurisy.

Headline, June 24: "PROSECUTOR ORDERS DR. SAM RETRIED."

My father bounces back from pleurisy and heads off to the Million Dollar Round Table.

Headline, November 16: "DR. SAM ACQUITTED IN SECOND TRIAL. WILL RESUME MEDICAL CAREER."

That night my phone in my dorm room rings at midnight. "Your father didn't come home tonight. I've called his office, every funeral home in town, even the highway patrol, and no one has seen him."

"Oh, Mother, I'm sure you'll hear from him." She does.

My father comes in the next day. "Mom, I'm leaving."

Then he packs up his clothes and moves out.

Jewel Flitz.

My mother moves to our summerhouse on Cape Cod. My father never calls. My mother hears through the grapevine that he and Jewel are making wedding plans. He builds her a dream house out by the country club.

The day before the wedding, my father gets a visit from a process server. Jewel's fifth husband is suing him for alienation of affection. He's asking for half a million dollars. My father calls him. Before he can get a word out, Number Five shouts, "Go to hell, ya goddamn skirt chaser." My father tosses and turns all night.

Wedding day. I'm not invited, and of course, neither is my mother. But her spies are everywhere. She calls to give me the inside scoop.

"You'll never guess the mess your father has gotten himself into now. He's at the church about to walk down the aisle. That woman and her eyebrows are waiting for him at the altar. Suddenly he feels his heart pounding like a jackhammer. The room starts to spin. So he turns around and walks out the back door. He runs to the nearest pay phone and calls me and says, 'Mom, I've made a big mistake. Take me back. Please.'"

"What did you do?"

"I hung up on him."

My father is not deterred. He calls her every day for the rest of his life.

Headline: "BROKEN-HEARTED BRIDE VOWS TO GET EVEN WITH LYING LOVER BOY."

Underneath is a tearful picture of Jewel. She must be upset. She has forgotten to draw in any eyebrows. The paper says Jewel is suing for breach of promise . . . Number Five won't drop his lawsuit either, even though he takes Jewel back . . . My father tries to take possession of the dream house. But he's put it in Jewel's name as a wedding present. Now she's changed all the locks and it's up for sale. When the brass at Aetna find out about this scandal, they give my father the sack. He tells my mother,

"Aetna's not going to have Burt Holmes to kick around, I'm going to open up my own shop." He does. But since he's using most of his liquid assets for his new business, he decides to live somewhere cheap. He picks the Forty Winks Motel. But he still has time to send me clippings about Dr. Sam.

Headline: "DIVORCE! DR. SAM TAKES POT SHOTS AT ARIANE."

Headline: "DR. SAM SUED FOR MALPRACTICE. KILLS TWO ON OPERATING TABLE."

One day my father is going out the door of the Forty Winks, when a motorcycle comes roaring down Main Street. A teenage girl and an older man get off and go into the building across the street. My father stares. That man looks familiar. Then it hits him. "Sheppard!"

Against his better judgment, my father buys another copy of the *Columbus Star*. He finds an article about Dr. Sam's new career.

"Tonight Killer Sheppard, AKA Dr. Sam Sheppard, the convicted wife-slayer, is beginning a new career as a professional wrestler. He is challenging the Boston Bruiser at the Fairgrounds." The *Star* says Dr. Sam's a newlywed. The third Mrs. Sheppard is the teenage daughter of his wrestling manager. Dr. Sam has given her an ocelot as a wedding present.

My father buys a ticket to the fight. He plans to wait outside for Dr. Sam and give him a piece of his mind. But after only two rounds the Boston Bruiser gets Dr. Sam in a hammerlock hold. Then he flips him onto the mat. "Killer Sheppard" is out cold.

My father is not deterred. He keeps tabs on Dr. Sam after he gets out of the hospital. He sees him sitting on the porch downing fifths of vodka.

Finally, my father can't stand it anymore. He is determined to let Dr. Sam have it. He is halfway across the street, when an ambulance comes speeding by. It stops in front of Dr. Sam's building. My father watches as they carry a body out on a stretcher covered with a sheet.

Headline, April 6, 1970: "DR. SAM IS DEAD AT 46."

The coroner suspects drug and alcohol poisoning.

After Dr. Sam dies, my father tries to find a reason to go on. At least his business is booming. He decides he can't run his office by himself. He places an ad in the paper. One day, he gets a call. "If you give me a job, we'll drop the lawsuits."

My father agrees. On her first day back, Jewel waits for my father to go to lunch. She writes herself a check for $10,000 "severance pay," cashes it, and she and Number Five skip town.

I'm living in New York by now and I still don't know how to web boys, so I go to New Age workshops. They all say the same thing: Heal your relationship with your father.

When I drive across country that summer, I decide to stop off in Columbus.

I pull up in front of my father's apartment in my beat-up

Datsun. The grass is unmowed, and the front door is banging in the wind. My father has taped the names of the former tenants on the door so no one will know he lives there. When I finally find him, he ushers me in and shows me his new prized possession: a Richard Nixon commemorative coin, which is on the mantel next to Dr. Sam's grass.

"Someday they'll get rid of that Kennedy half-dollar and put Nixon's face on one instead."

I get down to business. I suggest doing an exercise I learned at one of my workshops.

"I am going to tell you things I like about you for a few minutes. All you have to do is say thank you. Then we'll switch."

"Oh, I don't know—"

I forge ahead.

"Something I like about you is you dress well."

My father doesn't answer.

"Daddy, you're supposed to say thank you."

He doesn't look up.

"Thank you."

"Something I like about you is you have nice eyes, something I like about you is you're successful. Something I like about you is you're generous. Something I like about you is you took good care of us. Something I like about you is I love you."

"Want some Verner's ginger ale?"

"No, Daddy, it's your turn."

My father gets up and heads to the kitchen.

He sits back down. A couple of minutes pass. He crunches the ice in his glass.

"Daddy, just say 'Something I like about you is', and fill in the blank."

A few more minutes pass. He shifts in his seat, stares at the ceiling. Finally, he mutters, "Something I like about you is . . . you have nice friends."

"Daddy, you don't know any of my friends."

Beads of sweat line his forehead. He looks out the window. "That jalopy of yours doesn't look like it'll make it to California. How about if I buy you another one?"

I leave Columbus in a brand-new Ford Falcon.

Headline, August 9, 1974: "NIXON RESIGNS."

I call my father to offer condolences. All he says is "Nixon was framed." He sounds so much older.

A few months later he invites me to meet him at a Million Dollar Round Table in the Poconos.

I wait for him in the banquet hall on the night of the big dinner dance. The place is filled with men in tuxedos and women in formal gowns. Suddenly all conversation ceases, forks drop. Heads turn to the door where my father is making an entrance. On his arm is an aging peroxide blonde in a skintight leopard jumpsuit unzipped almost to her navel. He's wearing a toupee. They spot me and come over to my table.

"Meet your new stepmother," my father says. My new mom has an opinion on everything. She tells me that blacks smell bad because they never bathe, and Jews ruin her Christmas by sending cards saying "Happy Holidays." "It's Christmas, goddamnit."

But she does spruce up my father. She buys him Nehru shirts and love beads. He grows sideburns. She gets him to build another house out by the country club. She buys a new wardrobe so large that half the garage has to be converted to a storage area for her clothes. Then, she moves in every long-lost relative she can dig up.

The next time I hear about my father is when my mother calls.

"Your father's in another pickle. He broke his arm and the doctor botched the operation. He can't drive anymore. His lovely wife won't take him to work. So, rain or shine he has to walk to the bus stop a mile away. One of the African Violet Society ladies saw him standing at one in the pouring rain, with his toupee sliding halfway down his face."

Since he can't get around, business falls off. One day a customer comes in at two in the afternoon and finds him asleep. Finally, he's forced to close the office.

The next day, my stepmother hands him the want ads. He calls a few. When they find out how old he is, they say they'll get back to him. Then he gets a call to go for an interview with a firm downtown. As he sits in the waiting room, he hears a familiar voice

"Mr. Holmes, good to see you again."

My father stares at the black woman in a business suit.

"Minnie, what are you doing here?"

"This is my company, Mr. Holmes, and by the way, call me by my new name—Nkuma. Nkuma Africa."

She invites him into the office.

"Did you know there's a new Mrs. Holmes? We live in a big place out by the Country Club. Her mother and her grandson live with us, and all her people come up from the hills of West Virginia to stay quite often."

"Well, Mr. Holmes, why don't you come down here and work for me? I've gone as far as I can go selling to my brothers and sisters."

"You must have a big family, too."

"I mean the black community. Mr.Holmes. With your contacts and experience, I know we could make this business take off."

"No offense, N-Numa, but about your name. Some people in Bexley wouldn't be able to pronounce . . . "

"My name is not negotiable, Burt. Nkuma, Goddess of the Nigerian Dawn. Now, here's a list of all the top business groups in town. Tell me who you know."

Nkuma's business takes off. Her picture's in the paper all the time now. She's given more blood than anyone in town, including my father.

August 1981. Now I am no longer disgusted by the sight of that grotesque thing I saw at the Bexley Theater. In fact, I'm fond of one in particular. I call my father.

"Daddy, I'm getting married."

"Congratulations. When's the wedding?"

"In a few months."

"I'll send you a check."

I hear a bloodcurdling scream on the other end.

"She can't have our money."

I decide not to invite my stepmother to the wedding.

My wedding is a week away when I get a message on my machine.

"She took away my checkbook, but I'm gonna try to make a break for it."

My wedding day arrives. The ceremony is to be held at two. At 1:55 there is still no sign of my father. Suddenly an El Dorado Cadillac comes screeching into the front yard. My father is pushed out the back door. He runs in. "Let's get this show on the road. I only have an hour." We rush through the ceremony. Just as we are bowing down to Meher Baba and vowing to be physically immortal, we hear a horn honking. My father hands me an envelope, and he dashes out. I open it. Inside is a life insurance policy.

Headline: "DNA TESTS POINT TO THE SHEPPARD'S FORMER WINDOW WASHER AS MARILYN'S REAL KILLER."

Later, my stepmother calls me. "I just found your father dead on the toilet."

I go back to Ohio one last time. I see old friends like Methyl, Stu Tuttle, and of course, Nkuma. After the service I go up to Nkuma and thank her for helping my father.

"He was a big help to me, too. I'm going to the Million Dollar Round Table this year." She hands me a box. "I cleaned out his desk. There are some things in here I thought you might like to have."

In it, I find my father's Richard Nixon coin and some old letters from men in my father's navy unit. Several announce the births of sons. All of the babies are named Burton. There's also a letter from James Forrestal, the Secretary of the Navy, writing on behalf of President Roosevelt. It talks of my father's "brilliant seamanship," "fearless leadership," and "inspiring courage under extremely perilous conditions" during the battle of Anzio. One of my father's superiors wrote about him:

"March 10, 1944. At 1730 on D day, while Lt. Holmes was unloading the *John Banbard*, the ship the *Samuel Huntington* was bombed. He immediately cast off and proceeded to the stricken ship. Lt. Holmes dove into the water repeatedly to rescue the survivors. He personally rendered first aid, treating the burned, bandaging the wounded and administering morphine. A total of 56 men were rescued. Because of his initiative, intrepidity and devotion to duty without regard to his personal safety, and his actions above and beyond the call of duty, it is highly recommended that Lt. Burton Holmes be awarded the Distinguished

Service Cross—one of the highest honors a soldier can receive.

And there was one last thing I found in the box—this jar. *(Holds up jar with Dr. Sam's grass)*

END OF PLAY

KIDDING JANE

A PLAY
IN TWO ACTS

BY AUGUST SCHULENBURG

Thanks to Lisa and Keith, my family, and Heather

BIOGRAPHY

August Schulenburg's play *Carrin Beginning* won the Founder's Award and a staged reading from Riverside Stage Company. It was subsequently produced at the Chelsea Playhouse, where it was nominated by *Newsweek* for Best New Play Premiering Off-Broadway. *Kidding Jane* was a Finalist for the Clauder Competition, the Princess Grace Award, and the Plays for the 21st Century Competition. August Schulenburg writes, directs, and acts for Equalogy, a theater company raising awareness on issues of violence against women.

CHARACTERS

Jane Williams-Dane—37, a woman of means, white
Martin Dane—47, her husband, a wealthy stockbroker, black
Kate Dane—their daughter, a ghost
Kidd Trick—16, a would-be rap artist, black

TIME & PLACE

The play takes place in Martha's Vineyard and Philadelphia, each setting more suggested than created.

The time is now.

A fluid change from one scene to the next.

And by all means, music.

KIDDING JANE

ACT I

SCENE 1

Philadelphia Juvenile Hall. A table with three chairs. MARTIN *and* JANE *stand as* KIDD *enters.*

KIDD: All right, suckers, sit down and shut up, 'cause I'm only gonna say this shit once.

JANE: Hi, I'm—

KIDD: Rule the first, don't interrupt me, bitch.

MARTIN: I'd prefer if you didn't—

KIDD: *(Overlapping)* Rule the second, shut up.

MARTIN: *(Overlapping)* —speak to my wife that way, young man.

KIDD: Did you hear what I just said?

MARTIN: Did you hear me?

KIDD: You didn't, proving why rule two exists in the first place.

MARTIN: Excuse me, Robert, I think—

KIDD: Rule the fucking third, don't call me Robert, that ain't my name.

JANE: Kidd Trick?

KIDD: Yeah, brothers call me Kidd.

JANE: All right, Kidd—

KIDD: Didn't say you could.

MARTIN: Young man, I want you to understand something—

KIDD: Rule four, I ain't no young man, I'm a fucking thug, which ain't even rule four, that shit rule seven, see now you fucked up the whole order on account of you didn't hear rule two, I can't fucking work with you people.

JANE: Hi, I'm Jane, this is Martin, and we're really glad to meet you.

KIDD: Aw shit, don't you smile at me like that, bitch.

MARTIN: Call my wife that again, and the whole thing's off.

KIDD: Fine with me! I don't need no fucking do-gooders getting into heaven on my black back, that's rule five and six, no fucking do-gooders, five, no goddamn crusaders, six, which brings us to seven, I'm a fucking thug, which means eight, don't preach me no religion or education, takes me to nine, I ain't shining my fucking teeth for no pussy-ass job, and now we at ten, which I ain't even gonna tell you, cause you bitches ain't ready to hear it.

JANE: What's rule four?

KIDD: What?

JANE: Rule four, you didn't say rule four—

KIDD: Rule four is shut the fuck up, ho.

JANE: I thought that was rule two.

KIDD: No, rule two was shut up, rule four, is shut the fuck up, ho, there is a difference, and don't think you smarter than me, bitch, cause you ain't.

MARTIN: Good, we've got some rules of our own.

KIDD: No you don't get rules, that's rule ten.

MARTIN: Rule one, you'll have to get a job.

KIDD: Man, you don't fucking hear shit, do you? I ain't slanging fries and you ain't slapping me in no suit, I got my work, and you stay outa my way.

JANE: Your work?

MARTIN: Selling drugs, right?

KIDD: Oh fuck you, righteous ass Oreo, I know there was a day when you was kicking it to Mayfield and wishing you was half the pimp I already am, but I'm getting off the motherfucking track, no, I don't deal no crack, I'm a dealer of words, playing poker with the English language and don't ever bluff.

JANE: You're a poet?

KIDD: Uh yeah, we got this new thing, though, probably ain't never heard of it, called rap, see, probably don't know what that is—

MARTIN: What do you see for your future?

KIDD: I'm gonna get a parakeet and teach it to say, "Polly wanna a cracker" every time you step in the room.

MARTIN: You don't have any plans.

KIDD: I got plans, man, I got dreams, shit, I'm breathing, ain't I? Maybe I ain't gonna go to obedience school like you did, but I'm gonna make my buck, don't you worry.

JANE: Rapping?

KIDD: Naw, they gonna need a new word for the shit I bring, gonna stick my dick in the dictionary and knock that ol' bitch up, gonna give Webster a different kind of stroke, know what I'm saying? And I pay you back, too, soon as my shit gets tight, cause I don't want no debt to no motherfucking do-gooders, I pay it all back.

JANE: If you come with us, Kidd, you'll be a part of our family, not—

KIDD: Yeah, you wish I was part of your family, not that you gonna like it when I busting some bitch's ass at three A.M. and my boys are hitting your liquor closet, but one day, I gonna be a bonafide made-man-playa-gangsta-pimp-daddy-shaft-of-light, gonna be tight, gonna buck like a motherfuck, and rap myself right into sound, die into rhyme, just kick it forever up in the air till some brother calls me down like God on the FM and turns me all the way up; you could be a part of that shit, so yeah, hell yeah, better take me now before someone else does.

MARTIN: We'll talk it over.

KIDD: Yeah, I know what that means.

JANE: It was nice talking to you.

KIDD: Bitch, don't waste my motherfucking time. I'm out.

(KIDD *exits.*)

MARTIN: Jane, no.

JANE: What?

MARTIN: Before you even think it, no.

JANE: I already thought it.

MARTIN: Well don't, this kid's bad news.

JANE: All he's ever gotten is bad news, what do you expect?

MARTIN: More of his rules, more of this— (MARTIN *reads from a sheet.*) Possession, dealing, assault and battery, dealing, vandalism—he's the worst one yet.

JANE: Isn't it great?

MARTIN: How about I give another ten thousand to charity and we call it a deal.

JANE: Oh charity, charity, what does that do?

MARTIN: Twenty thousand.

JANE: I want to change someone's life.

MARTIN: You change plenty of lives—

JANE: What, with my book club? My community theater performances?

MARTIN: Fifty thousand.

JANE: I don't want money, I want something to do—

MARTIN: Start a gallery on the Vineyard.

JANE: Something worth doing, Martin.

MARTIN: Fine, then let's build some soup kitchens, how about organic soup kitchens?

JANE: Martin.

MARTIN: We can import some lepers, they can work in the soup kitchen, not with the food, but—

JANE: Martin.

MARTIN: We can import endangered species to be the lepers' pets, leopards for lepers—

JANE: Would you stop? You're not going to change kids like Kidd by throwing money at them.

MARTIN: Kids like Kidd, what do you mean?

JANE: I mean, his nickname, Kidd, Robert, kids like Robert—

MARTIN: Do you see what you're saying?

JANE: I love you so much.

MARTIN: Do you see what this is about?

JANE: You're so perceptive, I love that—

MARTIN: Do you see why I don't want a reminder of him in my house?

JANE: He won't be in your house, he's dead, and I'm fucking elated; so don't tell me this has anything to do with what we don't talk about because it's over, right?

MARTIN: I thought so, but this—

JANE: Martin, I think I'm a good Mom, I think that's something I'm good at—

MARTIN: You're a great wife, and—

JANE: No, I'm not, I haven't been. But if I could be a Mom again, maybe—

MARTIN: If that's what you want, Jane, you're young enough, we could try again—

JANE: I don't want another baby.

MARTIN: Fine.

JANE: What I want is this, him, the worst kid in the bunch—

MARTIN: Jane—

JANE: But when I'm done with him, woh, this kid, Martin, this kid's going to be good—

MARTIN: Jane, baby—

JANE: A stockbroker, like you, you can be his role model—

MARTIN: I don't want to be a role model—

JANE: No, a doctor, he's going to cure cancer, and leprosy, and if he has time, the common cold, but he'll be busy with his presidential duties—

MARTIN: Jane, would you—

JANE: Not to mention his Oscar, Oscars, multiple Oscars, Martin, including one movie where he plays himself that time he ended world hunger—

MARTIN: I just don't want—

JANE: And when he gives, when the first black president Robert the Kidd Williams-Dane gives his first Oscar speech, he's going to say, I owe it all to Martin and Jane, quite possibly the greatest parents that have ever—

MARTIN: Jane would you stop—

JANE: —say yes, say yes, say yes!

MARTIN: Oh, Jane.

JANE: Thank you.

MARTIN: My baby Jane.

JANE: It's going to be great.

MARTIN: You are my Joan of Arc.

JANE: I love you.

(MARTIN *tries to kiss* JANE. JANE *pulls away.*)

MARTIN: What's wrong?

JANE: Nothing. See— (JANE *kisses* MARTIN.) —nothing.

SCENE 2

The Dane's living room. A few days later.

KIDD: You said it was big but this is motherfucking huge—this sucker got its own area code?

JANE: Welcome home.

KIDD: This ain't my home.

JANE: It is for as long as you like.

MARTIN: I'll bring your bags to your room.

KIDD: That's my dog.

MARTIN: I'm not your dog.

KIDD: Sorry, that's my bitch.

MARTIN: If you want to live here, you better treat me with respect.

KIDD: Yeah, all right. Pops.

MARTIN: Thanks. Do you want to see your room? Well?

JANE: Kidd?

MARTIN: Something wrong?

JANE: The view? Is it the view?

KIDD: That ain't no view. That a kingdom.

JANE: It's yours.

KIDD: Can't be.

JANE: The view is, anyway. And we have boats, I'm sure Martin would love to take you out on a boat.

MARTIN: I sure would.

KIDD: You get to look at that whenever you want?

JANE: Never had a view before?

KIDD: Never had a yard before. Had one window facing bricks.

JANE: Welcome home.

KIDD: I get it now, Pops. I'd sell my skin, hell, I'd sell my soul for this.

MARTIN: I didn't sell anything for this.

KIDD: Just stocks, right?

MARTIN: I'm proud of who I am, Robert, I hope one day—

KIDD: Don't call me that name, niggah.

MARTIN: Don't you call me that name, boy, unless you want to be back in Philly juvenile by tonight!

KIDD: Take it easy, brother.

MARTIN: You don't know what that word means.

KIDD: Yeah, I got an idea what—

MARTIN: You didn't grow up when that word meant more than a nickname.

KIDD: Times change, Pops, ain't no need for your freaking out and shit—

MARTIN: Are you listening? You will not call me that word again.

KIDD: Least call you dog?

MARTIN: No.

KIDD: Term of respect!

MARTIN: No.

KIDD: How about Popdog? Little compromise there, I get my dog, you get your pop, Popdog!

MARTIN: Fine. But I won't always answer.

KIDD: All right. Thanks for carrying my bags, Popdog.

MARTIN: Anytime. (MARTIN *exits. Offstage.*) Robert.

KIDD: *(Whispered)* Niggah.

JANE: So you like the view?

KIDD: Love it a little.

JANE: Yeah, it's something, isn't it?

KIDD: Hate it, too.

JANE: Hate it? Why?

KIDD: Same reason I love it.

JANE: I don't understand what you mean.

KIDD: Get used to that feeling.

SCENE 3

The Dane's dining room. Several weeks later.

KIDD: What the fuck is this shit again?

JANE: It's a tofu burger, it's organic, it's all natural.

KIDD: Yeah, cow shit's a natural thing and I ain't eating that. Hey! Popdog thinks I'm funny.

JANE: He shares your feeling about my food.

KIDD: There like a McDonald's or something? My arteries ain't used to all this room.

MARTIN: No McDonald's on the island.

KIDD: Shit, ain't McNothing on this island.

JANE: We'll take you to Tashmoo tomorrow.

KIDD: Bless you.

JANE: Ha, see Martin, he's very funny.

KIDD: See, Martin? What's Tashmoo, another boring-ass beach?

JANE: I thought you liked them.

KIDD: They all right, but they'd be a hell of a lot better if there was a little booty shaking, know what I'm saying?

JANE: No.

KIDD: Some fine young thang with nothing on and a whole lot going on—bam!

MARTIN: Summer's coming soon.

JANE: I'm sure all the girls'll love you.

KIDD: Hell yeah, tell you what, all them parents better lock their daughter's up, cause my libido took aikido and busts through my Speedo—

(KATE *enters, sitting at the table.*)

JANE: Kate.

KIDD: —need another suit just to house my root—

MARTIN: Jane.

KIDD: —ain't no cockblocking cop can stop the flock of chicks to my dick and rocks—

JANE: Leave me alone—

MARTIN: Jane, baby—

JANE: Just leave me alone! (JANE *stumbles off.*)

KIDD: Shit, guess she ain't into freestyle.

MARTIN: Okay, Robert—

KIDD: Kidd Trick.

MARTIN: —whatever, listen up. Don't say the word daughter again, please.

KIDD: Usually it's other aspects of my vocabulary that piss people off—

MARTIN: Just don't say it, all right? Understand?

KIDD: I don't.

MARTIN: Notice something missing from the walls?

KIDD: Nudie pictures?

MARTIN: Family pictures. Notice no family portraits?

KIDD: Been awhile since I had some myself, so—

MARTIN: She took them all down, understand?

KIDD: Making room for my gold records?

MARTIN: Just don't mention the word again.

(MARTIN *begins to exit.*)

KIDD: Cancer?

MARTIN: What?

KIDD: That bad word, the D word, cancer?

MARTIN: Sure, Kidd, cancer. Excuse me.

(MARTIN *exits. Lights.*)

SCENE 4

In MARTIN*'s car, several weeks later.*

KIDD: You saw the Ku-Klux-Klan smile on that brother!

MARTIN: He's my friend, he's not racist.

KIDD: Whatever, I ain't working for Grandmaster Dragon back there, that's all I'm saying.

MARTIN: I think you're racist against work.

KIDD: You can't be racist against no work.

MARTIN: Why not? You hate it. You think all work's bad, even though you never get to know it, that's bigotry against the workplace right there, Robert.

KIDD: Don't call me that name.

MARTIN: Get a job and I'll call you any name you like.

KIDD: You sign a paper to that?

MARTIN: Show me the dotted line.

KIDD: All right. Come end of the week, you gonna be calling me "Kidd Trick, sexy-ass-mother-fucker-gangsta-playa-thug-dealing-crunk-shit-like-God-dealing-fate-yeah"—hope you don't mind calling me that.

MARTIN: No I don't, Mr. "Kidd Trick sexy-ass-mother-fucker-gangsta-playa-dealing-crunk-shit-like-God-dealing-fate-yeah."

KIDD: You missed thug.

MARTIN: You get a job I'll call you something even better.

KIDD: What's that?

MARTIN: Son.

KIDD: Oh zipa-dee-motherfucking-doo-dah, that's the real incentive, go sweat for some bigot so this limp-dicked pussy-whipped chump-ass bitch can call me son, don't play a playa, Popdog, don't kid the Kidd, don't bring that shit in my house.

MARTIN: I won't. You won't get a job, so I won't call you anything.

KIDD: Don't act like you give a shit falling off a cliff about me, Martin. I see how this whole thing went down, puppet-boy, so don't give me half-ass compassion like you trying to be "Lean on Me" and shit.

MARTIN: Puppet-boy?

KIDD: Yeah, you got a hand up your black ass making you talk white, Popdog, so don't son me no sons.

MARTIN: My wife and I have a very loving relationship.

KIDD: Ah, now I got some cheese to go with my cracker.

MARTIN: I'm a very happy man, if that's cheese, then—

KIDD: Boy, the man must love you, "I'm a very happy man, with a very loving wife," you practice that shit?

MARTIN: I am a man, Kidd. Do you know what a man is?

KIDD: A hard-ass niggah who don't take shit, someone steps, a man brings right to their chin—fuck you!—man don't dress nice and talk nice and marry right and turn white.

MARTIN: A man does the best he can for the folks he loves, that's a man.

KIDD: The pussy he loves.

MARTIN: A woman is a lot more than that.

KIDD: Shit, you ain't a white man or a black one, you a blind one.

MARTIN: I wish I were a deaf one.

KIDD: You here the same reason I am, Ray Charles.

MARTIN: You're here because my wife wants to make a difference.

KIDD: Same with you. Why you think she marry you?

MARTIN: I ask myself that all the time.

KIDD: Yeah, you know the answer, just worth your while to forget it. You like some land in winter all covered in snow, can't see nothing but the beautiful white thang on top of you, but that shit ain't real.

MARTIN: Oh, but you know what's real, right?

KIDD: I seen her kind before, brother, we got a name for it in the hood.

MARTIN: And I don't want to hear it.

KIDD: Growing up in a doll's house, she wants to run with something real, sick of the tea party, wants to smoke some tea and party, fishing for a little danger, you know about fishing, right?

MARTIN: I think you should quit while you're ahead.

KIDD: See, spics and black chicks, they run with a brother 'cause he got cash or cars or whatnot, they don't need no danger, they living it. But a white girl, she got bank but no danger, so she gotta go fishing to catch some fly playa. And that's just what we call 'em, just like you stick some fly on the hook to reel them fish in, those pretty little Ritz crackers ain't nothing but niggah-flies.

(MARTIN *stops the car.*)

What you doing, Popdog?

MARTIN: That's the second time you've used that word in front of me. Know what happens the next?

KIDD: Oh, you gonna rub me out, gangsta? Is that it?

MARTIN: I'm gonna send you back to Philly Juvenile. When you get out, if you get out, you're gonna say that word to the wrong man and they're gonna put a bullet in your head, you're gonna die in a pile of pigeon shit, and get buried in a trash can. Get out of the car.

KIDD: What?

MARTIN: Get out of the car.

KIDD: I ain't getting out of—

MARTIN: Get out of the fucking car!

KIDD: All right, all right, shit.

MARTIN: You're walking home.

KIDD: Walking home?

MARTIN: And thinking about what I've said.

KIDD: It's five miles.

MARTIN: Your great granddaddy walked ten times that every day of his life.

KIDD: And look what happened to him, he's dead!

MARTIN: Walk and think about your life before it's gone.

KIDD: I'll tell you what I'm gonna do, and I'm gonna hit town and fuck shit up.

MARTIN: That's what I expect you to do.

KIDD: Don't play these fucking mind games with me, Popdog.

MARTIN: I'll see you back in the house.

KIDD: Maybe you will.

MARTIN: And maybe I won't. And Robert, my wife loves me for who I am, not the color of my skin.

(MARTIN *pulls away.*)

KIDD: Well she sure don't love you for the size of your dick, little inchy one-balled bitch! Shit! Walk home, I'll walk over your dead body after I pissed on it. You think I'm some sort of little kid? You don't know me, you don't know what I done!

(KATE *enters.*)

Shit. Walk home, fucking freezing out here, fucking cold.

(KATE *opens her mouth to scream and a police siren wails, as if* KATE *were screaming it. It grows very loud.*)

Ah, shit, po-po. Is that you, Popdog? You call them on me, bitch? Well they ain't gonna catch me!

(KIDD *runs, exiting.*)

SCENE 5

In a Martha's Vineyard Detention Center cell. A few months later.

KIDD: Like my crib, Janey?

JANE: No, I don't, Kidd.

KIDD: Shit, who needs a view when you can have your bed and toilet in the same room? Convenience!

JANE: Martin doesn't want me to bail you out this time.

KIDD: Tell him to look at it as my allowance.

JANE: He says I make too many allowances for you already. He says you should stay here for a week or two.

KIDD: And you told him to fuck himself, right?

JANE: No, I didn't.

KIDD: You ain't gonna let me stay here, you a do-gooder, it's like against your motherfucking code to let me stay here.

JANE: It's the third time this month, Kidd.

KIDD: What you expect me to do, Janey? These Island girls ain't never met no real gangsta before, no bonafide playa, I can't disappoint.

JANE: Bring them over to the house, they're always invited—

KIDD: Yeah, that'll show 'em how ghetto I am, kicking it back like a Kennedy, gotta keep it real, can't let this beautiful life powder me white.

JANE: And going to jail keeps you black?

KIDD: Switch that shit and you got it, bitch.

JANE: I don't get it, I don't see why—

KIDD: Cause and effect, Janey, if I hang by some wall a second too long my black ass'll be up against it before—

JANE: You're here 'cause you drove a moped through a store window, not 'cause you're black!

KIDD: To prove I ain't ashamed of it! Now sure, I can go camouflaging myself in a suit and smile like motherfucking Martin but that shit ain't real, that ain't—

JANE: Martin is a real black man, Kidd, and—

KIDD: Janey, that brother's a chameleon, turns skin to suit his surroundings, naw, what am I saying, niggah's a snake, shed his skin when he married you.

JANE: So he doesn't get to be black because he married me?

KIDD: No, he married you cause he don't wanna be black, he don't wanna be no niggah, he's ashamed—

JANE: Being black and being the N word are two very different things—

KIDD: Oh yeah? What's the difference?

JANE: I mean, being black doesn't make you that word—

KIDD: Then what does, Janey, I'm curious. Oh that's right, it is being black that makes you "that word," but Martin ain't none of that, and you're his proof, his trophy—

JANE: Kidd, he married me because of who I am, and that's why—

KIDD: Right, white.

JANE: The fact I'm white has nothing to do with who I am.

KIDD: But the fact I'm black's got everything to do with me, and you want me to forget that, course you do, that's the difference between niggaz and crackers, crackers forget history ever happened, niggaz remember where they from, who been there, what they done, and maybe that don't get you no trophy life but at least it's real, maybe it puts your black ass in jail but at least it's real!

JANE: Then I'm staying with you.

KIDD: What?

JANE: Here, in the cell, I'm staying with you.

KIDD: All right, we can kick it in here.

JANE: Good, I wanna keep it real.

KIDD: You even know what that word means?

JANE: I wanna find out.

KIDD: You can't.

JANE: 'Cause I'm not black.

KIDD: That's right, until your skin makes the world cross the street, you can't ever know.

JANE: I won't ever understand you 'cause I'm white.

KIDD: That's what I'm saying.

JANE: Well, you won't ever understand me 'cause I'm a woman.

KIDD: Shit, I never said I understand women.

JANE: Don't you want to?

KIDD: I understand enough to get what I want.

JANE: What's that?

KIDD: You know what it is.

JANE: You get a lot of that?

KIDD: I pimp it, yeah, you know.

JANE: You're lying.

KIDD: You can think what you want, but you go back to the Northeast and ask all them little boys with my eyes who their daddy be and you find out.

JANE: You've never had sex before, have you?

KIDD: I don't have sex, I bust tail, I pimp hard, I'm an ass-stinging, train-running, sperm-slinging, whose-your-daddy, hung-like-a-fire-hose thug of love—

JANE: No, you never have.

KIDD: Fuck you, get out of this jail cell, you pissing me off.

JANE: I know a virgin when I see one.

KIDD: Don't you call me that.

JANE: Virgin.

KIDD: I ain't kidding, bitch.

JANE: Just a big old "V."

KIDD: I ain't playing now, Janey.

JANE: V-boy.

KIDD: Say that again and I'll show you I ain't no virgin.

JANE: V-V-V-V-V-V—

KIDD: Knock that the fuck off—

JANE: V-V-V-V-V-V—

KIDD: All right—

> (KIDD *grabs* JANE *forcefully, covers her mouth and pulls her to him.* JANE *struggles.*)

This what you wanted? Huh? You like this? Think I'm some sort of fucking boy? I show you, I show you right now.

> (JANE *stops struggling.*)

I throw you on the floor right now, bitch. Run my own personal train on you. Show you I ain't no motherfucking virgin.

> (JANE *stands as if unafraid.*)

I'll do it. I ain't kidding. You better try to get away before I give you what I got. I will.

(JANE *mumbles something into* KIDD*'s hand.*)

What?

(KIDD *removes his hand.*)

JANE: Tell me the truth and I'll bail you out.

KIDD: I did.

JANE: Tell me the truth and I'll pay for the whole thing.

KIDD: I told you the truth.

JANE: See you in a few weeks, Kidd. (JANE *starts to exit.*)

KIDD: All right all right all right, I am, I am.

JANE: You're what?

KIDD: You know.

JANE: No I don't.

KIDD: The thing you said, I am.

JANE: A player?

KIDD: Don't play me, I said what you wanted, though I lied just to get the fuck out of here, now get me the fuck out of here.

JANE: You said, "I am, I am." I didn't want you to say, "I am, I am."

KIDD: I admitted I was.

JANE: What?

KIDD: I'm just saying it to get the fuck out of here.

JANE: Then it should be easy to say.

KIDD: It is.

JANE: Then say it.

KIDD: Fine, fucking virgin, virgin, virgin!

JANE: Who is?

KIDD: I am!

JANE: You're what?

KIDD: I am a motherfucking virgin, are you motherfucking satisfied?

(JANE *is laughing.*)

Don't you fucking laugh, bitch! Don't you dare laugh at me.

JANE: I'm laughing at us.

KIDD: At me, don't lie, you laughing at me.

JANE: Maybe a little.

(JANE *tries to hug* KIDD, *who pushes her away.*)

KIDD: What you doing?

JANE: Sorry, sorry.

KIDD: Don't go thinking we're best friends, bitch, you had your laugh, now get me the fuck out here.

JANE: Let's go.

KIDD: Wait.

JANE: What?

KIDD: How did you know?

JANE: When I was growing up, if you weren't sleeping around you weren't liberated. I wanted to be liberated, so I slept around.

KIDD: Yeah?

JANE: No. But if you asked me, I did.

KIDD: That don't make no sense.

JANE: Course not, you can't get it unless you're a girl, you can't understand until your breasts make the world cross the street. Let's go.

(JANE *exits.*)

SCENE 6

The Dane's kitchen. Dinner. A month later.

MARTIN: I'm not sitting down until I hear an apology.

JANE: Martin, it was a protest.

MARTIN: It was a prank.

JANE: It was symbolic, the restaurant's the soup, and—

MARTIN: I understand the symbolism, Jane, he still drowned a raccoon in clam chowder.

KIDD: Drowned nothing, that 'coon was roadkill, Popdog.

JANE: See, he didn't hurt it, and—

MARTIN: *(Exiting)* Excuse me.

JANE: Where are you going?

MARTIN: I've lost my appetite.

JANE: I thought we agreed, no leaving the dinner table while—

MARTIN: Robert also agreed to behave himself at work.

KIDD: But Kidd Trick never did, Kidd Trick remains a badass.

MARTIN: Well, maybe your bad ass would like eating in the garage, because—

JANE: Hey, I remember someone else who used to call himself a badass.

MARTIN: Jane—

JANE: What, Martin, your ass was twice as bad as Kidd's.

KIDD: No.

JANE: Oh yeah, you should've seen him, he gave these speeches—

KIDD: Our Martin was a speaker?

JANE: A shouter, a screamer, he would pound the podium, spit into the fifth row—

KIDD: I bet he had an Afro.

JANE: He did.

KIDD: Was it big?

JANE: Bigger than me.

KIDD: I thought so

MARTIN: *(Overlapping)* Please pass the kale, Jane.

KIDD: *(Overlapping)* —I bet he was a scary-looking motherfucker.

JANE: Oh he was, he was, it was love at first sight.

MARTIN: Jane—

KIDD: *(Overlapping)* Naw, really?

MARTIN: *(Overlapping)* —the kale, please.

JANE: Oh yeah, I'd never seen anyone so passionate, so angry, so badass, so...

MARTIN: Jane?

KIDD: So black? That the word you looking for?

JANE: So much like you, you two are so much alike, I never—
Martin, that's why the two of you don't get along, but—

MARTIN: Would you please just give me some kale?

JANE: Yeah, sure, much as you want. Just had to ask.

KIDD: So, Martin was a gangsta?

MARTIN: No, my anger, my passion, was directed toward social
change, toward creating jobs you're too gangsta to take—

KIDD: Hey, I gotta focus on school, Popdog.

JANE: But you didn't have a job, Martin.

MARTIN: Excuse me?

JANE: Not a real one, I mean, at first, I made the money, because
you had a mission, well, Kidd has a mission—

KIDD: Martin had a mission?

JANE: Oh yeah, he was going to be the first black president!

KIDD: What happened?

JANE: Well, he decided you needed real money to run for office,
so he went to school for—

MARTIN: I had a daughter.

(KATE *enters.* JANE *looks away.*)

KIDD: Damn, this some slamming kale, Janey, all soy saucy and
shit.

JANE: Yeah, there's some soy.

KIDD: I'm tasting it, and some, what, ginger?

JANE: Little bit.

KIDD: Just enough, yeah, I didn't know kale could taste like this,
really, this some award-winning shit.

(KATE *approaches the chair to sit down.*)

JANE: Thanks, Kidd.

KIDD: No, thank you, I got a whole new relationship with vegeta-
bles now, thanks to your cooking, sometimes I catch myself
looking funny at grass and lawns and shit, really—

JANE: (JANE *flings the chair away from* KATE.) Go away, go away,
go away!

KIDD: (KIDD *also flings his chair away.*) Yeah, take that, what the

fuck's up now, chair? You got four legs we still take you down—
(JANE *runs out.* KATE *exits after.*)

Shit. Yo, Popdog, what you do that for? What, you just eating your meal? That shit all right with you?

MARTIN: I know you're skipping school.

KIDD: What you talking about? I wish I was skipping school—

MARTIN: I followed you.

KIDD: I take a day off, here and there—

MARTIN: For a week.

KIDD: Sabbatical, brother, you take those, right?

MARTIN: Lower your voice. I'm not going to tell Jane.

KIDD: Tell Mother Teresa, you know she'd love to hear it, bitch wants me to fuck up, Popdog, every do-gooder needs a badass, and from the sound of it, yours just ain't bad enough no more.

MARTIN: She'll give up on you, Robert.

KIDD: What the fuck do I care?

MARTIN: She'll hate you.

KIDD: Should I repeat my question? What the fuck—

MARTIN: She'll send you to juvenile, I got the papers ready.

KIDD: Good, I'm ready to go.

MARTIN: It's your life.

KIDD: And I'm gonna make something of it.

MARTIN: How you going to do that?

KIDD: The way a black man does, dealing rock, shooting the rock or busting rhymes.

MARTIN: Look where those things got you, how about you try school?

KIDD: Yeah right, so I can end up like you?

MARTIN: Happy? If you're lucky.

KIDD: Oh, yeah, cause you're a fucking joyride, Popdog—

MARTIN: I have everything I ever wanted, call it what you like.

KIDD: All right, I'll call you a sellout, a token black-boy, just keeping your bitch and colleagues affirmative in the eyes of the world—

MARTIN: No, Robert, you're the token black boy, of course you think I've sold out, that's what people in power want you to think, cause then you'll waste your life dealing rock, shooting the rock and busting rhymes.

KIDD: I'm taking the world on my terms.

MARTIN: Robert, that is their terms, they gave you those three choices and told you anything else was selling out.

KIDD: I know what I want, hell of a lot more than I can say for you.

MARTIN: You know what I want?

KIDD: I think you forgot that a long time ago.

MARTIN: My wife to be happy. Go to school, Robert.

KIDD: You need me to wear a name tag, Popdog?

MARTIN: Go to school or get out of my house.

(JANE *enters.*)

JANE: Martin, what're you saying?

MARTIN: Jane, baby, you're all right, I—

JANE: Did you tell Kidd to get out of our house?

MARTIN: No.

JANE: I just heard you. Kidd? Did he say that?

KIDD: Naw, Popdog was telling a story, that's all.

JANE: A story?

KIDD: Oh yeah, a story about getting out of the house.

JANE: My Dad.

KIDD: Yeah, your Daddy, get out of the house, right, Popdog?

JANE: Why tell that story?

KIDD: 'Cause I wanted to know.

JANE: No, you don't, I try to forget he exists, ha, existed.

KIDD: Why? 'Cause he said, get out of the house?

JANE: No, is that what—Martin was being gracious, he said, well, I can't even say what he said.

KIDD: Well, now I gotta know, 'cause if you can't say it—

MARTIN: Jane told him she wanted to marry me. So he said, real polite, "Martin, I like you, I respect you, but I don't want half-nigger grandchildren."

KIDD: Shit. What the fuck did you do?

JANE: This.

(JANE *kisses* MARTIN *while giving the finger as if to her father.*)

KIDD: Yeah, all right, fuck off. *(They continue to kiss.)* Should I go, or—

(MARTIN *breaks away.*)

MARTIN: How much was it you gave up for me? Thirty million?

JANE: Who knows, who cares, he's dead, I'm glad. Let's eat.

MARTIN: Yeah, I'm feeling hungry again.

JANE: Kidd?

SCENE 7

In the Dane's living room. A month later. Schubert's "Unfinished Symphony" plays.

KIDD: Mozart.

JANE: Nope. Schubert.

KIDD: Bitch!

JANE: "The Unfinished Symphony".

KIDD: All these bitches sound the same, Schubert, Schumann, Shostafuckoff; how the hell am I supposed to keep these motherfuckers straight?

JANE: Well, to me, Skinny Pimp, Pimp Daddy, Trick Daddy all sound the same.

KIDD: They sure as hell ain't.

JANE: Not to you.

KIDD: Not to anyone with a fucking brain between their ears! See, if we was appreciating music I could feel, I'd remember the shit.

JANE: Why can't you feel these composers?

KIDD: 'Cause they got nothing to do with me, they ain't heard of slanging or shooting or dying young—

JANE: Half of these composers died young, real young, Mozart and Schubert—

KIDD: Yeah, five hundred years ago they died young—

JANE: Right, it's history.

KIDD: Ain't my history.

JANE: If Beethoven was black—

KIDD: If Beethoven was a brother he wouldn't get to write no music.

JANE: That's true, but he's still your history, you're a human being.

KIDD: Not according to history.

JANE: So that means Sojourner Truth isn't part of my history?

KIDD: Ah, a sister! No, no she can be part of your history. Matter of fact, Janey, why don't you name me some more of your historical brothers and sisters.

JANE: There's plenty of historical important African-Americans.

KIDD: And I wanna hear about 'em, Janey, tell 'em to me.

JANE: Fredrick Douglass, Martin Luther King, Malcolm X, Jackie Robinson, uh, there's that guy—

KIDD: Mmm, right, that guy—

JANE: No, that guy who debated Fredrick Douglass, uh, Buster, Buster Washington—

KIDD: Oh, Buster Washington, yeah, I like him way better than his brother Booker T.

JANE: Right, Booker, this is just off the top of my head—

KIDD: George Washington, John Adams, John Quincy Adams, Thomas Jefferson, Andrew Jackson, Ben Franklin, Benedict Arnold, William Shakespeare, Julius Caesar, Homer, Plato, Socrates, Jesus Christ, Santa Claus, oh, I know Santa ain't real, but I ain't even got to Honest Abe and already I'm doubling your score, Janey, so tell you what; when you can come up with half as many brothers and sisters as I got historical white ancestors, you can tell me about history and why I should feel it.

JANE: Let's study something else. How about English?

KIDD: Ooh, that sounds hard, better start with Ebonics and work my way up.

JANE: What about math? Why don't we work on math?

KIDD: Yeah, all right, what's two plus two?

JANE: I know you know the answer to that.

KIDD: Do you?

JANE: Kidd—

KIDD: Just tell me, Janey, what's two plus two?

JANE: Four, no matter what.

KIDD: If you're black, it's three. Economics.

JANE: My husband makes more than most white people ever do.

KIDD: That's cause he is white, you fucked all the color clean out of the niggah.

JANE: So, I see, if you're rich, you're white, if you're poor, you're black.

KIDD: Put it together, Janey, put it together.

JANE: Is there such a thing as a rich black man?

KIDD: Yeah, rappers who work for black producers. That's it. Every other niggah making money made it through a white man, like the Midas touch, whatever a white man touches, turn white.

(JANE *touches* KIDD.)

JANE: You're white!

KIDD: Fuck you.

(JANE *chases* KIDD, *touching him.*)

JANE: I'm gonna make you whiter! White, white, white, white, white—

KIDD: Knock that shit off, bitch!

JANE: Who wrote the "Ode to Joy"?

KIDD: What?

JANE: Who wrote the "Ode to Joy"?

KIDD: Fuck do I care, Beethoven?

JANE: You're right! It's working.

KIDD: What?

JANE: Soon you'll be playing golf and wearing suits, riding yachts and talking stocks! Mwa-ha-ha-ha!

KIDD: Fuck that, if anything, you gonna catch black from me.

JANE: That right?

KIDD: Hell, yeah, we gonna be kicking back some 40's round about this time next week. We gonna put some meat on that ass, teach it to shake.

JANE: You gonna teach me how?

KIDD: Be like teaching a brick to jump, but—

JANE: Shit, I didn't think you could. Don't waste my time, motherfucker.

KIDD: It's "Don't waste my motherfucking time," get it right.

JANE: I need a real playa, not some pretender to teach me the gangsta ways.

KIDD: You wanna learn the gangsta ways?

JANE: Yeah, teach me what Westcoast means, what crunk means, what bounce is, all that shit.

KIDD: You don't wanna know.

JANE: It's part of my world, I wanna know.

KIDD: You don't want part of this world.

JANE: Look at this way, the more we talk about Puff Daddy, the less we talk about Prokofiev.

KIDD: You want me to teach you?

JANE: Yeah.

KIDD: Make you a bonafide gangsta bitch?

JANE: That's my dream, brother.

KIDD: You got a long way to go before you start calling me brother.

JANE: Then let's get started, bitch.

SCENE 8

In the Dane's living room. Trick Daddy plays.

JANE: Uhh . . . give me a second . . . Eastcoast.

KIDD: Maybe.

JANE: Uh . . . New York?

KIDD: Not even close. Miami. Miami thug style—

JANE: Oh—

KIDD: Which means?

JANE: Trick Daddy?

KIDD: All right, you slow, but you catching on. Maybe in another month, you can get your Gangsta Junior card or something.

JANE: I did some extra credit.

KIDD: Did you now? Fuck Gangsta Junior, you looking at your Doctorate in Dre, keep stepping to it like this.

JANE: You ready for it?

KIDD: For what?

JANE: For the words I be bringing

The pain I be slinging

The bell will be ringing

When I knock you out

Ain't no doubt this is what I'm all about

I'm the sleuth of truth bringing word to rich folk

Making them choke on their caviar

In their fancy car private bar

I say when you gonna give the love

To the people you above

We die to make you shine

Build your towers of power

When will be our time to taste the glory of the flower

Unh unh unh unh

The glory of the flower!

(KIDD *laughs hysterically.*)

What? What's so funny? I went for a bounce flavor.

KIDD: Oh, you bounced, you bounced like a bad check, baby. You bounced like a baby on concrete.

JANE: Oh, that's sick.

KIDD: So was that shit, oh girl, girl, girl, what have I been teaching you?

JANE: What was wrong with it?

KIDD: What was right with it?

JANE: Wasn't there anything good?

KIDD: Yeah, the part where you shut up.

JANE: I worked all night on that.

KIDD: All right, all right, it wasn't that bad, lot of brothers out there bringing rhymes twice that half ass, we make it tight, I make that shit knocking for you.

JANE: You will?

KIDD: Yeah, here's how. You know that beginning part?

JANE: Yeah.

KIDD: Cut it.

JANE: How much?

KIDD: Much as you can.

JANE: I don't know how much—

KIDD: All right, all right, let me see your little paper there.

(KIDD *takes* JANE*'s script.*)
"For the words I be bringing
The pain I be slinging
The bell will be ringing
When I knock you out
Ain't no doubt
This is what I'm all about."
Yeah that whole thing can go.

JANE: I tried to make it sound like real rappers do.

KIDD: Yeah, but you lying. You ain't gonna knock nobody out. That's not what you about. When you ever done sling pain?

JANE: I slung a lot of pain in my day.

KIDD: Yeah, say I'm a rival MC, I come out with some tight shit dissing your weak-ass crap, you gonna sling pain my way?

JANE: Ain't no doubt.

KIDD: There a lot of doubt.

JANE: Go ahead, dis me, find out.

KIDD: You a punk bitch without a rhyme in your white-ass corpse.

JANE: Oh yeah? (JANE *slaps* KIDD *across the arm.*)

KIDD: Oh, you a pain slinger all right.

JANE: See you talk after I pop a cap in your ass.

KIDD: Easy, Janey, look, you can spit these rhymes, just not half-ass. Even if you ain't a pain slinger, you gotta sound like one. Lot of rich niggaz right now ain't slung no pain but they sound like badass motherfuckers.

JANE: For the words I be bringing

The pain I be slinging—

KIDD: You just lowering your voice.

JANE: The pain I be slinging

The bell will be ringing—

KIDD: Now you sound like a pirate.

JANE: How am I supposed to sound?

KIDD: Like a badass motherfucker.

JANE: How do I sound like that?

KIDD: It ain't something you get through a correspondence course, baby. You gotta earn that shit, school of hard knocks, U of crack rocks, of dirty streets, of getting beat—

JANE: I didn't go to that school.

KIDD: No shit.

JANE: But I've been angry before.

KIDD: Hell of a lot deeper than angry.

JANE: I've hated before.

KIDD: Yeah, you a real hater all right.

JANE: Maybe I am.

KIDD: Janey, you just a nice old white chick.

JANE: Old?

KIDD: You know what I mean.

JANE: I'm thirty-seven.

KIDD: I know, I know, that ain't old, sorry I said that shit.

JANE: I feel older. This last year felt like twenty.

KIDD: That shit's good. Whatever you thinking of, keep thinking that shit, it's turning you hard.

JANE: Hard?

KIDD: Yeah, whatever it is fucking with you, let it get into your blood, step up Janey, step up, picture whatever that shit be in your mind's eye—

JANE: It's always there.

KIDD: And it makes you mad?

JANE: No.

KIDD: Yeah it does, I can see it.

JANE: It's out of my control.

KIDD: Still pisses you the fuck off, right?

JANE: It's out of my control.

KIDD: Fuck that, nothing's out of our control, we make our lives, ain't no star makes us what we are—

JANE: I can't think that, I'll go crazy.

KIDD: Go crazy, bitch, ain't no rich niggah got rich without going crazy, get motherfucking crazy and then you gonna be a gangsta, you tell that fucking thing that burns you deep to fuck off—

JANE: Fuck off.

KIDD: Like you mean it, bitch.

JANE: Fuck off.

KIDD: I can't hear you.

JANE: Fuck off.

KIDD: I ain't buying it.

JANE: Fuck off.

KIDD: Don't fucking lie to me!

JANE: Fuck off!

KIDD: Shit, I guess it don't mean nothing to you—

JANE: Fuck you, you fucking fucker Fucking liar fucking faker
How the fuck could you take her

My only fucking girl

My eyes my world

She's gone she's gone

How the fuck do I go on

It's not enough that you're dead

I want a gun to your head

So I can pull the fucking trigger

'Cause you're such a fucking killer

So bring it on death

Take my last fucking breath

Bring your pain and your power

I will fucking devour

Every piece of you till there ain't nothing left of you but life.

KIDD: All right. Okay. Gotta write that one down. That shit tight, buck tight. Got a little gangsta in you after all. You all right?

JANE: Yeah, fine.

KIDD: You don't look fine.

JANE: No, no, I am, I'm glad I could, uh, get it right.

KIDD: It ain't quite right.

JANE: More hate?

KIDD: No, no, you got the hate, yeah, you got that shit covered—

JANE: More craziness?

KIDD: No, you doing all right there, too. Just, the really tight ones, I mean, the Gods of this shit, they got something else.

JANE: More crunk?

KIDD: No, and that ain't the way you use that word anyway, work on that tomorrow. No, there's something else, something better, 2Pac had it, more than anyone.

JANE: What is it?

KIDD: How do you say a sound? What do you call that thing that sounds like up, better places, greener pastures, all that shit?

JANE: I don't know.

KIDD: Sounds like when you run at pigeons and all at once, they're in the air, what's that sound?

JANE: Wings?

KIDD: Yeah, sounds like doing ninety over the interstate, top down, near dawn, and you ain't nowhere near the ground, what's that?

JANE: Dangerous?

KIDD: Yeah, dangerous, cause you want it so bad—that's it, that wanting it so bad, that dreaming it so hard that when it happens, if it happens, it's like the world unlocks for you, that danger, that want, that dream, what is that?

JANE: Hope?

KIDD: That's the word. Yeah, hope, that's it, that's what the real playas got.

JANE: And that's what I'm missing?

KIDD: Yeah, but we work on that tomorrow.

SCENE 9

On the Dane's boat.

JANE: He's getting better.

MARTIN: Maybe.

JANE: What do you mean, maybe? Two months without a single detention or suspension or need I mention an apprehension by, uh, what's, a police word that rhymes with ension?

MARTIN: Jane.

JANE: Oh right, rap is noise, jazz is music, I forgot. But I'm getting off the motherfucking track. He's getting better, and it's thanks to you. Don't laugh, you're like his role model.

MARTIN: I never asked to be—

JANE: Too late, you are, and of course you are, a strong black man who's made it, on his own terms, from hard times, just like Kidd.

MARTIN: Please don't compare us, Jane.

JANE: Fine, I won't, I just want to thank you, that's all.

MARTIN: You can thank me on land, I've got a lot of work tonight.

JANE: No, Martin, I want to thank you.

MARTIN: Oh.

JANE: Turn off the boat.

(MARTIN *turns off the boat.*)

MARTIN: Are you sure, it's chilly out here, and—

(JANE *kisses* MARTIN, *breaks away.*)

JANE: I'm getting better.

MARTIN: I can tell.

JANE: I'm sleeping, I'm eating, yesterday I napped, a nap, Martin, what's that?

MARTIN: You look well rested.

(JANE *kisses* MARTIN, *breaks away.*)

JANE: And when's the last time I had a scream dream?

MARTIN: Two nights ago.

JANE: Three nights.

MARTIN: Okay.

JANE: It was three.

MARTIN: You're right, it was.

JANE: Shut up.

(JANE *kisses* MARTIN, *breaks away.*)

And yesterday I thought about my Dad, and I didn't want to shoot someone.

MARTIN: Really?

JANE: Yeah, no migraine, no bile, just a quick urge to punch, and that was it.

MARTIN: Well, good.

(JANE *kisses* MARTIN, *breaks away.*)

JANE: You know, I think it's 'cause of Kidd.

MARTIN: Kidd?

JANE: Me getting better, he's so funny, he makes awful stuff seem funny.

MARTIN: He does have a sense of humor.

JANE: You don't think so.

MARTIN: No, I do.

JANE: You think he's an asshole.

MARTIN: Assholes are funny things.

JANE: Hey!

(JANE *kisses* MARTIN, *breaks away.*)

But why stop here, you know?

MARTIN: I want to continue.

JANE: I don't mean this, I mean, Kidd, why stop with him?

MARTIN: I don't, I didn't think—

JANE: Why not adopt other kids, once he's gone?

MARTIN: That's an option.

JANE: Oh, that's an option, that's an option, listen to you.

MARTIN: Jane—

JANE: Shut up.

(JANE *kisses* MARTIN, *breaks away.*)

But don't you think about it? If everyone did what we did?

MARTIN: What did we do?

JANE: We changed his life, we saved it, Martin! Where would Kidd be without us?

MARTIN: Far, far away.

JANE: Dead, or at best, in jail, or even worse, out of jail and hurting someone, that's why people hurt people, 'cause they don't have other people to help them.

MARTIN: Very eloquent.

JANE: Stop talking.

(JANE *tries to kiss* MARTIN, *who stops her.*)

MARTIN: Jane.

JANE: What? Does it really sound so bad? Do you really hate Kidd that much?

MARTIN: I don't hate him at all—

JANE: Then why not? Why not adopt more? I'm not saying like

every year, but every other year, and maybe other couples would hear about us, they'd start doing the same thing, and little by little this stupid motherfucking worthless world might turn out all right!

(MARTIN *kisses* JANE, JANE *pulls away.*)

You're a good kisser. You're such a good kisser.

MARTIN: Then let me.

JANE: But what about the idea? Is it really so crazy?

MARTIN: Jane.

JANE: I don't like that look—

MARTIN: We can change some things.

JANE: Stop it—

MARTIN: Other things we can't.

(JANE *starts trying to kiss* MARTIN, *who keeps trying to break away.*)

We can't change what happened. We can't bring her back. No matter how many kids you save, you can't save Kate—

(JANE *finally catches* MARTIN *in a fierce kiss, as* KATE *enters.*)

KATE: Is this my voice, Mother?

(JANE *tries to ignore* KATE*'s voice through kissing* MARTIN.*)

Was this what I sounded like? Do you remember? What did my voice sound like when it happened? What did my voice sound like when I screamed?

(KATE *opens her mouth to scream, but the sound is* JANE*'s voice screaming.*)

MARTIN: Jane!

SCENE 10

(*In* MARTIN*'s car.*)

MARTIN: So you ready for Halloween?

KIDD: Yeah, Popdog, I got a few Trixies I think I'm gonna trick.

MARTIN: Who will be driving?

KIDD: I don't know, one of my dogs, I guess.

MARTIN: Will they be drinking?

KIDD: Only the driver.

MARTIN: You're a wiseass.

KIDD: Better than a dumb ass.

MARTIN: Shame you can't take this car.

KIDD: Yeah, that is a crying shame. I'd open this motherfucker up. She's sick of your light feet, she wants to go.

MARTIN: I could only give her to someone I felt was responsible.

KIDD: How long this lecture gonna be, cause I—

MARTIN: That's why I'm giving it to you.

KIDD: Unh, what?

MARTIN: A C in Botany, don't blame you there, a B- in Math, an A- in Music History, and an A in English, not a single call from cop or dean, I'm proud of you, Robert.

KIDD: Don't call me that.

MARTIN: I was wrong about you. You might make something of yourself after all.

KIDD: Just maybe.

MARTIN: I'm sorry, you will, and I'm sorry I didn't believe in you.

KIDD: Why should you?

MARTIN: I do now. You've got a great future ahead of you. You may not like the way I made my money, but my money can make you any kind of life you want. Rap? You want to be a rap star? Fine, I've got friends in the industry. But why not a teacher?

KIDD: 'Cause I don't like school.

MARTIN: Oh, enough of that bullshit gangsta crap. You do too like school, you're good at it, I bet you could do any damn thing you wanted with that head on your shoulders.

KIDD: Thanks.

MARTIN: I mean it, like a politician! You don't like society, change it.

KIDD: First black president, right?

MARTIN: Sure, or a lawyer, or a banker, whatever; even a stock-broker.

KIDD: Like father, like son, right?

MARTIN: Like whatever you want to be. See, success isn't black or white, it's just good.

KIDD: Guess you're right about that.

MARTIN: You work hard, and the world gets better, little by little.

KIDD: Guess so.

MARTIN: We all got a reason to hate, but the strong man forgets about it, moves on.

KIDD: Guess that's true.

MARTIN: Make it true, Robert. Come with us tonight.

KIDD: To that society shindig?

MARTIN: I know you'd rather be with your friends, but it might be fun. The caterer is outstanding, and I'm sure you could have a glass of wine or two.

KIDD: Cabernet.

MARTIN: And it might be a good way to start making connections. Never too early, you know?

KIDD: Make my presence known, so to speak?

MARTIN: Exactly. Show the world what a fine upstanding young man you've become.

KIDD: Guess I'll need a costume then.

MARTIN: I think I've got a few extras in my closet, grab whatever fits.

KIDD: All right, I'll go.

MARTIN: Great! Wait'll Jane hears this. She thinks the world of you, you know. And she was right, you're turning into a fine young man.

KIDD: Turning into something.

MARTIN: Be glad of it, Robert. You'll lead a longer, happier life. All right, here we are, let's get dressed.

SCENE 11

In the Dane's living room. JANE *puts the finishing touches on her Guinevere costume.*

JANE: Did you hear the Franklins are going as Jesus and Mary Magdalene?

MARTIN: *(Offstage)* Very appropriate.

JANE: For her, anyway. And Scott Crandell's going as the Wolfman.

MARTIN: *(Offstage)* Won't need much makeup for that.

JANE: Neither will Jimmy as the Tinman.

MARTIN: *(Offstage)* Be nice.

JANE: Why am I going as this stupid Guinevere?

MARTIN: *(Offstage)* It was your idea.

JANE: It's your job to stop those ideas.

MARTIN: *(Offstage)* We can see how well that's worked.

JANE: You shouldn't say that, it's a big step for him to come tonight.

MARTIN: *(Offstage)* One giant leap for gangsta-kind.

JANE: I'm not dreading it so much now. If Kidd's there at least it won't be boring. I might even laugh once or twice.

(MARTIN enters as King Arthur.)

MARTIN: My Queen.

JANE: Wow.

MARTIN: Wow to you.

JANE: I look old.

MARTIN: You look beautiful.

JANE: Keep thinking that, you better keep thinking that.

MARTIN: Everyone at the party will think that.

JANE: As long as you and Kidd do, you're the only ones I care about.

MARTIN: Yeah, we should hurry him up—

KIDD: *(Offstage)* Ladies and gentlemen, bitches and hos, playas and gangstas, are you ready to see the next great American superhero?

JANE: Yeah! Woo-woo-woo!

KIDD: *(Offstage)* Faster than a speeding bullet, more powerful than taxes, able to assimilate races in a single smile, it's a dove! it's a paper airplane! it's a Kleenex! No, it's Wiggerman!

(KIDD *enters wearing* MARTIN*'s clothes, in white face.*)

By day, a mild mannered stockbroker named Martin Dane; by night, a race-erasing superhero called Wiggerman, saving countless inner city youths from the doom of themselves!

JANE: Oh, Kidd.

KIDD: His gaze turns crackrocks into stocks, basketballs into racquetballs, gats into yachts, ghettos into meadows, gangstas into banksters, and playas into assistants to the assistant of the associated vice president of happyland!

MARTIN: Get out of this house.

KIDD: But father, I'm only trying to be like you, an upstanding young citizen who stands for nothing. Bring me to the tea party, and I shall dazzle the upper crust by comparing the rhythmic innovations of Stravinsky to the fall of Communism!

MARTIN: I said, get out of this house.

KIDD: But Tokedog, isn't this just what you wanted? Both of you? Living proof you're not just rich assholes, but rich assholes with heart? Look at the good you've done, taking that poor little ghetto boy and making him shine. But I ain't going out like that.

JANE: Clean yourself off and go put on another costume.

MARTIN: I don't want him in my house a second longer.

KIDD: Oh I ain't staying, I just got a few things to say before I tell you to fuck off.

MARTIN: I don't give a goddamn what you have to say, get out of this house.

KIDD: Or else what you gonna do, crusader? You ain't got the fucking heart to bring it, fucking pussy-whipped pussy.

JANE: Let's start this all over—

(MARTIN *starts dialing the phone.*)

Martin, no.

KIDD: Yeah, that's right, call the cops, run away, just like a white-boy, can't stand up for himself.

(JANE *rips the phone away.*)

MARTIN: Jane, give me the phone.

JANE: He's just doing this cause he's scared.

KIDD: Bitch is right I'm scared, scared of who the fuck I'm becoming—

JANE: You deserve this, Kidd, you can't lie to yourself anymore—

KIDD: Lie to myself? This house is a goddamn palace of lies, lie to myself—

MARTIN: I'm going to count to ten. If you're not out by then—

(MARTIN *counts out loud to ten.*)

KIDD: Let's start with that pretty little lie about your love, yeah, you love your little project, Janey, and you love your mother-fucking trophy, your proof that you made it, that you just as good as any rich white man, and maybe you gave up your dream for that lie but if you admit that shit then you admitting you wasted twenty years of your motherfucking life, no, no, no, better finda new project, another trophy, some other poor fuck-er to fill your sad-ass silences and if I fucking lie along with you I can be your new shining white half-nigger baby—

(MARTIN *reaches ten, attacks* KIDD.)

KIDD: Yeah, that's right, that's right—

(JANE *breaks them up.*)

JANE: Stop it, stop it, just fucking stop it!

KIDD: Well glory be, I was wrong. Looks like when the shit hits the fan you a gangsta after all; I'm proud of you, Martin.

MARTIN: Excuse me, I lost my temper.

(*The following section all overlaps on a rising pitch to a near cacophony.*)

KIDD: No, no, no, don't go excusing yourself—

JANE: Let's just sit down and talk about this—

KIDD: —don't go all white on me—

JANE: —Kidd, Kidd—

KIDD: —I was just making progress with you—

JANE: —I know why you're doing this—

KIDD: —getting you back to your roots—

JANE: —but you don't have to—

KIDD: —taking that crown off your head—

JANE: —you deserve a good life—

KIDD: —teaching you what a real black man is—

MARTIN: You don't have a fucking clue what a real black man is—

JANE: Martin, no—

MARTIN: —you're a boy—

JANE: —don't let him suck you into this—

MARTIN: —and I'm tired of trying to talk sense into your thick-ass skull—

JANE: —he wants you to be angry with him—

KIDD: —oh keep talking—

JANE: Kidd!

KIDD: —you a real good talker—

MARTIN: You better stop talking—

JANE: Martin!

MARTIN: —boy, that's what I'm saying—

JANE: —this is so stupid—

MARTIN: —and you better hear it—

JANE: —that if you two don't stop and just listen to yourselves—

KIDD: Talk, talk, talk, talk—

JANE: —I'm gonna scream—

KIDD: —bitch, that's all you do—

JANE: —stop it before you hurt each other—

KIDD: —you know I bury you—

MARTIN: Let's find out—

JANE: —stop it, sit down and shut up—

KIDD: All right!

MARTIN: —boy, let's find out right now—

JANE: —god fucking damn it—

KIDD: Come on!

JANE: —would the two of you stop being such a pair of goddamn stupid fucking niggers!

(Silence.)

JANE: I'm sorry. I didn't mean it.

(KIDD exits slowly.)

Kidd, I'm sorry, I didn't mean—I was angry, I—Martin, you know that's not what, that's not how I think. Martin?

(MARTIN exits.)

(KATE enters and walks slowly to JANE.)

(JANE exits.)

ACT II

SCENE 1

(Six months later. In the kitchen of the Dane's Philadelphia home. Pictures of KATE, MARTIN and JANE hang on the walls.)

JANE: And where are you going, young lady?

KATE: Out.

JANE: I know out, where out?

KATE: Heading down Girard, Derrick's playing at the fire.

JANE: (Overlapping) Did you finish your paper?

KATE: (Overlapping) And yes, I finished my paper.

JANE: Well, good.

KATE: See ya.

JANE: When will you be back?

KATE: When all the fun is done.

JANE: You'll be safe?

KATE: Off the streets and out of the sheets.

JANE: That's my girl. Here, take some taxi money.

KATE: I might just walk, nice night.

JANE: Better take a taxi.

KATE: Yeah, yeah, yeah, see ya soon!

JANE: Pick up some toilet paper if you get the chance!

(KATE *exits. A gunshot.* KATE *enters.*)

JANE: And where are you going, young lady?

KATE: To Heaven or Hell, or nothing at all.

JANE: I know out, where out?

KATE: I'll smile at the wrong man.

JANE: *(Overlapping)* Did you finish your paper?

KATE: *(Overlapping)* Or the right man on the wrong night.

JANE: Well, good.

JANE: Well, good.

KATE: My smile will break him.

JANE: When will you be back?

KATE: He'll fire three times and hit me once.

JANE: You'll be safe?

KATE: The bullet will enter here and leave here and take me with it.

JANE: That's my girl. Here, take some taxi money.

KATE: The last thing I'll see is an empty Coke can.

JANE: Better take a taxi.

KATE: These are the last words you'll ever say to me.

JANE: Pick up some toilet paper if you get the chance!

(KATE *exits. A gunshot.* KATE *enters.*)

JANE: Kate?

KATE: Out.

JANE: Don't go out, stay in.

KATE: Heading down Girard, Derrick's playing at the Fire. And yes, I finished my paper.

JANE: Go some other night, not tonight.

KATE: See ya.

JANE: Don't go out there, please.

KATE: When all the fun is done.

JANE: I'll do anything you want, take you anywhere you want.

KATE: Off the streets and out of the sheets.

JANE: Please, Kate, please stay here.

KATE: I might just walk, nice night.

JANE: I love you, I love you, I love—

KATE: Yeah, yeah, yeah, see ya soon!

JANE: I love you!

(KATE *exits. A gunshot.* KATE *enters.*)

JANE: Leave me alone.

(*A gunshot.*)

KATE: Answer the door, Mother.

(*Gunshot and knock.*)

JANE: What?

(*Knock and gunshot.*)

KATE: Answer the door.

JANE: No.

(*Three knocks and fading gunshots.*)

KATE: The door, Mother, the door.

JANE: Kate, he's dead, leave me alone.

(*Three knocks.*)

KATE: Someone's waiting at the door.

JANE: He's fucking dead, what more do you want from me, leave me alone!

(KATE *opens her mouth and screams like a teakettle boiling over as the lights blink onto Scene 2.*)

SCENE 2

The Dane's living room on the Vineyard. JANE *jerks awake.* KATE *is gone.*

JANE: Oh god, oh god, it's okay, you're okay, ah the tea, the tea!

(JANE *takes the kettle off.*) You're okay.

(*Three loud knocks.*)

Ah!

(JANE *holds still. More knocking.*)

(*Under her breath*)

Go away go away go away just go away—

(*A key turns in the door.* KIDD *enters as* JANE *turns away.*)

KIDD: Hey. Still had my key, so . . . I knocked.

JANE: I was asleep.

KIDD: Hey, that's good, sleeping's good, right? Mind if I come in? Uh, don't do nothing if it's all right for me to come in. Thanks. You all right, Janey?

JANE: Yeah, good, great, fine.

KIDD: Then why you turned away if you good, great, fine?

JANE: Why are you here?

KIDD: I was in the hood, that's all.

JANE: Oh, you want money, do you?

KIDD: No.

JANE: I don't have much, I've been giving it away, charity, but—

KIDD: I don't want your money, I'm doing fine.

JANE: Good.

KIDD: Making some mad buck, matter of fact. Brothers buying up my tapes on the streets, I speak gold and they putting some in my pocket.

JANE: Good.

KIDD: Yeah, Boston showing me love, keeping it real.

JANE: What about Philly?

KIDD: Philly thinks I'm here, they find out I ain't, they bust my jive ass back to juvie.

JANE: I won't tell them, you can go, I won't tell.

KIDD: I didn't come here to tell you to tell them that I ain't here, that made sense . . .

JANE: Bye, Kidd, it was good to see you.

KIDD: You ain't seen me, Janey—

JANE: Goodbye.

KIDD: Bitch, I only came here to get some new raps from you.

JANE: Please, I'm not such a fool now.

KIDD: Fool? You was busting some tight ass rhymes, I laid your shit down for a couple playas, and they thought it was all right—

JANE: What do you want?

KIDD: Look at me.

JANE: No.

KIDD: What am I, too ugly for eyes or something?

JANE: Yeah, you are, I hate the way you look, the way you talk.

KIDD: That right?

JANE: Tried to fool myself, tried to be a good little white girl, but now I know who I am.

KIDD: And that's a big ol' hater?

JANE: I thought marry one, give birth to one, you'll learn to love them, to love those big-lipped black boys limping and pumping more misbegotten bastards into the wide hips of hos and tricks sucking like ticks on the money we make, you'll understand why history makes them killers, you'll love rap and hip hop and all the crap they call music, but I don't, I won't, and I'm through caring or trying to pretend.

KIDD: Shit, you got better, that shit was tight, how that go, "wide hips of hos and tricks sucking like ticks on the money we make", that good, but how about, "sucking like ticks on the tits of our cash" or—

JANE: Get out of here, please.

KIDD: Then get me out of here, you know how to do it.

JANE: I'm trying.

KIDD: Don't play a playa, Ku Klux Jane, you such a Hitler, just say the magic word.

JANE: I already did.

KIDD: Not to my eyes, you didn't. Come on, turn around, you

such a hater, this should be easy.

(JANE *turns around.*)

Now look me in the eyes.

(JANE *does.*)

Hi.

JANE: So now I say it?

KIDD: Now you say it, right to my eyes.

JANE: I will.

KIDD: I know, since you such a big racist.

JANE: I am.

KIDD: I'm waiting to hear it.

JANE: You're gonna hear it.

KIDD: And I can't wait to.

JANE: N—

KIDD: O, n—? I hope you didn't call me a n—, cause you in for some serious ass shit you call me an n—.

JANE: Kidd, leave me alone!

KIDD: I can't, I need your help, bitch—

JANE: I can't help you.

KIDD: I ain't fucking talking that way, I ain't talking your crusading fuckall, Janey, I'm talking my shit, my rhymes, I got some ideas, and I want—

JANE: I don't wanna hear them.

KIDD: Well you gonna hear them, they got history, you like history, right?

JANE: I don't want to hear them.

KIDD: Well here they go!

(KIDD *raps.*)

Let me start with the great emancipator, fucking playa-hater, that proclimater just the creator of an unequal nation of segregation—

(JANE *runs to the tape player and presses play. Beethoven's "Ninth Symphony," in the middle of the fourth movement, booms forth.*

As KIDD *continues,* JANE *continues to turns the volume higher and higher.)*

KIDD: *(Continues)* Jim crow cawed his laws and lord it got hard to be heard, took one hundred years to kill that bird, but being misrepresented resented is still the present, prevented from joy by the image of the black boy, mistaking the up-faking gang-banging slanger as real, now we deal for chains of gold—

(KIDD continues to rap as he runs after JANE, *trying to take the tape player away from her.)*

KIDD: *(Continues)* —four hundred years and we're still getting sold, but fuck that shit, we all get sold, get old, wither and die, thither go I , but for some God's grace, if he'd show his fucking face—

(KIDD rips the tape player away from JANE.*)*

JANE: *(Overlapping)* Kidd, would you leave me the fuck alone!

KIDD: *(Continues)* —God made this world, made this world—

KIDD: *(As the chorus of "Ode to Joy" begins,* KIDD *begins rapping, screaming in melody along with the music.)*

"God made the world and the world was good

Put love in every motherfucking neighborhood

But after creation he took a vacation

And gave us free will and eternity to fill

But look at this shit we've made of our free will

Free to fight and fuck and hate and rob and steal and kill

Christ we need a savior every generation

Instead all we've got is imagination

(KIDD turns down the music.)

So be your beats of the streets or your rhymes of crime

Or your song of the sweet and the brief sublime

When your dust you will last past ashes and chance

What's divine is the rhyme that makes the room dance."

(KIDD turns off the music.) Yeah. Yeah. Yeah.

JANE: No.

KIDD: What do you mean, no?

JANE: I mean, I don't know, Kidd—

KIDD: I don't know either, Janey, and that's the goddamn truth, and ain't that the goddamn thrill of it, though?

SCENE 3

On the beach.

JANE: No, no, no—

KIDD: What you mean, "no booty"? I say booty, that's what I say when I see some fine young thang, booty, booty, booty.

JANE: But you ain't gonna marry booty, right?

KIDD: I sure as Hell am.

JANE: You gonna marry some girl just cause she got much back?

KIDD: Not just cause she got much back, but she gotta have some back.

JANE: So, so this bitch ain't got no back, but a heart that fucks shit up, and you're like, naw, naw, naw?

KIDD: No back at all?

JANE: All I'm saying is Paris can't say to Helen, "nice booty."

KIDD: This is my rap, you just an advisor, don't forget.

JANE: Well, I'm advising you.

KIDD: All right, so Paris says, "Is this the ass that launched a thousand ships? For such a fine booty I'd make that trip, I'd—"

JANE: First off, no ships have been launched yet.

KIDD: It's foreshadowing, bitch.

JANE: And secondly, when you fall in love at first sight, you don't mention their ass.

KIDD: Yeah, but you think about it.

JANE: That's lust, Kidd—

KIDD: And Paris got plenty of that for Helen.

JANE: Fine, fine, if that's all this is, then booty away.

KIDD: It ain't all it is, Janey, but it's part of it.

JANE: What about the other part?

KIDD: Yeah, well, we're getting to that.

JANE: He's just fallen in love, bam, like that, whatever he says, it's got to show his world's changed, and he don't know where the fuck he is.

KIDD: So how you say that?

JANE: No, how you say that? I'm just the advisor.

KIDD: He could say, damn.

JANE: No.

KIDD: Back that thang up.

JANE: No.

KIDD: You all that, let's get it on.

JANE: Something nice.

KIDD: Wow.

JANE: Stop.

KIDD: Gosh, you look nice.

JANE: Come on.

KIDD: I ain't ever seen something like you.

JANE: Oh, she's a thing now?

KIDD: I'd say someone but you can't be real.

JANE: Better.

KIDD: You so fine, you must be divine.

JANE: Not better.

KIDD: Where am I now? Have I left earth behind? 'Cause you way past pretty, long beyond fine.

JANE: Close.

KIDD: The first time the night saw your eyes
    the streets came undone and roses rose
    and stars lost their clothes
    to dance naked in the night
    cause you eyes were tight—

JANE: You had me till the tight part.

KIDD: Your eyes sound like the sea
    and break me like waves

and some say get to Heaven if you want to be saved

and some say fuck it all

cause it ends in the grave

but if I could speak what your eyes say tonight

the world would burn into light.

JANE: Keep going.

KIDD: If I sang the song of your eyes, our souls would burst from our skin like fireworks.

JANE: Keep going.

KIDD: If I sang the song of your eyes, laughter would catch like the common cold.

JANE: Keep going.

KIDD: If I sang the song of your eyes . . . I'd be happy. Okay that last one was shit, gimme another try.

(MARTIN *enters.*)

MARTIN: You're out here.

JANE: Martin.

MARTIN: I checked for you everywhere, saw your car, so I knew you were here—

JANE: I didn't know you were coming, or—

MARTIN: How would you?

JANE: I wouldn't, I'd want you to, though, come, I mean, I'm glad you're here.

KIDD: So I guess I'll be busting out cause—

MARTIN: No, stay.

KIDD: Yeah, that's nice, Popdog, but I'm sure you and Janey got some shit to say—

MARTIN: I've got things to say to you, too.

KIDD: And I'm sure you do, but uh, first things first—

MARTIN: No, both of you, the three of us, that's how it is from now on, right Jane? The three of us?

JANE: That would be nice, I would like that.

MARTIN: You can have it. We can all have what we want. I have a very simple plan that can give us all what we want.

KIDD: I don't like this smiley, quiet Popdog.

MARTIN: Oh I think you'll like what I have to say, sit down.

KIDD: There ain't really no place to sit down, on account of this being the shore.

MARTIN: Right. Sorry, habit. When I make deals, people sit down.

JANE: Deals?

MARTIN: I want to start over.

JANE: I want that, too—

MARTIN: You're not my trophy, Jane.

JANE: Pretty crappy trophy, if that were true—

MARTIN: And I'm not your project.

JANE: No, I know, I know you're not.

MARTIN: Kidd disagrees, he doesn't think twenty years of marriage is real—

KIDD: Look, Popdog—

MARTIN: Let me finish, please. Twenty years of faking it, your words, Kidd. Our marriage, our daughter, Kate, none of it was real, if you're right.

KIDD: Yeah, well—

MARTIN: You were wrong. I love Jane.

JANE: And I love you.

MARTIN: And we got lost a little, I think after Katie—

JANE: I know, I know.

MARTIN: But it's over, it's going to be over now. Did I waste twenty years of my life faking it?

JANE: No, they were real, Martin, I—

MARTIN: And you called me a nigger, that's real, too.

JANE: And I'm sorry.

MARTIN: Shh, let's not raise our voices.

JANE: But—

MARTIN: I know you're sorry, no one is more sorry than you,

Jane. But you being sorry, does that fix it?

JANE: I know it doesn't—

MARTIN: Then what does?

JANE: I don't know, time.

MARTIN: What happens in time?

JANE: I make it up to, maybe you trust me again, maybe forgive me—

MARTIN: Really, you think so? You think that could happen?

JANE: I hope so, I mean I made a mistake—

MARTIN: Calling me a nigger—

JANE: Stop saying that—

MARTIN: —yes, that was a mistake—

JANE: Martin—

MARTIN: —but you've made other mistakes, Jane.

JANE: I am human that way.

MARTIN: Mistakes I don't think I could forgive you for.

JANE: Maybe you should leave, Kidd—

MARTIN: No, Kidd, stay.

JANE: I'm not taking orders here, Popdog—

MARTIN: Then take my request, please stay.

JANE: If we're going to talk about Kate—

MARTIN: We're not, why would we, what would that accomplish? Would I forgive you? Would you forgive yourself? But it's over, Jane, and I'm not going to throw away twenty years over one mistake, or several, whatever the count is now.

JANE: If you're talking about our decision to have that fucker—

MARTIN: No, I'm talking about my decision, and it strikes me as very clear. I can either throw my marriage, twenty years of life, the mother of my child, away; or I can stay, and hate you.

JANE: Martin—

MARTIN: Or we can just forget about it.

JANE: Forget about what?

MARTIN: Everything. Every stupid thing we've done to each

other, forget it. Fix it, forget it, start over, it's the only right way I can see, do you see that?

JANE: What do you mean forget it?

MARTIN: I mean, you called me a nigger, I can either think about that or forget it. I'm choosing the latter.

JANE: I can't forget the things I've done, Martin—

MARTIN: But that's the deal I'm offering.

JANE: I don't think this is a deal, I think this is you trying to hurt me.

MARTIN: Jane, if I stayed with you, and remembered these things, I might. But I won't. I love you. So let's forget about it.

JANE: How do I do that?

MARTIN: Like this. (MARTIN *takes* JANE's *hand.*) I love you.

JANE: I love you.

MARTIN: And I want to start over.

JANE: I do, too.

MARTIN: So let's move past this, Jane. Let's forget all this crap we got lost in, all right? Wouldn't that be a good thing, my baby Jane?

JANE: Yeah.

(MARTIN *kisses* JANE, *breaks away.*)

MARTIN: How about you, Kidd? You coming along?

KIDD: I was wrong about you, Martin. You are a real black man.

MARTIN: Thank you.

KIDD: Or a brown one, I guess.

JANE: Whatever he is, doesn't matter to me.

KIDD: Yeah, different shades of black and brown, same way shit is, since that's what you made of, Popdog, polished and spit-shined bullshit.

JANE: Kidd—

MARTIN: You don't like my plan?

KIDD: Naw, it's all right, sorta like stepping in dogshit and cutting off your nose, but—

MARTIN: I don't understand.

KIDD: I mean, bad shit happens, Popdog, but you can't fake it didn't.

MARTIN: Why not?

KIDD: 'Cause you lying.

MARTIN: Isn't that what you do?

KIDD: I ain't never lied about nothing—

MARTIN: No, you just forgot about it.

KIDD: Speak for yourself, fucking fertilizer in a suit—

MARTIN: Did she call you a nigger?

JANE: Why do we—

MARTIN: Shh, baby. Kidd? Did she call—

KIDD: Why you asking me a question you know the answer to?

MARTIN: Then why are you here?

KIDD: Cause I don't want to go to fucking juvie, Shitdog.

MARTIN: So you forgot about it?

KIDD: Forgot nothing, lesser of two evils—

MARTIN: How many fights did you pick in school, while you lived here?

KIDD: Not enough, tell you that.

MARTIN: How many when you lived in Philly?

KIDD: I don't keep fucking track—

MARTIN: How many people you rob? Mug?

JANE: Come on—

MARTIN: Huh? How many stores you break into—

KIDD: What the fuck you driving at, Popdog?

MARTIN: Have you ever once felt bad about it? Have you ever once expressed interest in apologizing to the multitude of people you beat up, stole from, fucked over?

KIDD: Why the fuck should I?

MARTIN: I don't think you should, forget them, fuck them, right? This is your plan, Kidd, Kidd, you even forgot your name, Robert, because it didn't suit you—

KIDD: That's right—

MARTIN: Well now I'm picking what suits me and you call me what, fertilizer in a suit?

KIDD: 'Cause all the people I fucked with deserved it, I ain't ashamed of it—

MARTIN: Did Jane deserve it?

JANE: Martin—

MARTIN: This woman who dedicated her life to making yours better, did she deserve the things you said?

JANE: Oh, he never said anything bad—

MARTIN: He called you a niggah-fly, I believe was the term, called Kate our—

JANE: *(Overlapping)* I said some pretty awful things, too—

MARTIN: *(Continuous)* —shining white half-nigger baby—and you were sorry, and we've forgotten them and moved on. Are you sorry Kidd? For dressing up in white face and calling me Wiggerman?

KIDD: Yeah, I am sorry. I should've dressed up in shit-face and called you shit-man, that—

MARTIN: After I bailed you out of every jail and job you lost—

KIDD: *(Overlapping)* What the fuck you want me to say?

JANE: *(Overlapping)* Martin, that was stupid Kidd stuff—

MARTIN: Yes. I want you to say yes.

KIDD: To any fucking thing in particular—

MARTIN: Yes to the plan. Yes to starting over.

KIDD: No.

MARTIN: Yes to forgetting what's past.

KIDD: No.

MARTIN: Yes to being part of this family.

KIDD: I don't want no part of this, Guy Smiley.

MARTIN: I'm sorry to hear that. Goodbye.

JANE: What?

MARTIN: He doesn't want to be part of our family.

JANE: That's not what he meant.

MARTIN: That's what he said.

JANE: But that's not—you know that's not what he meant—

MARTIN: Then what did you mean? Kidd?

KIDD: I mean, maybe I ain't perfect, maybe I done some cold shit, but that's part of who I am, and I ain't forgetting that—

MARTIN: No, you just don't mention it or do anything about it.

KIDD: But I don't forget it, I don't ever fucking forget it.

MARTIN: What's the difference, Kidd?

JANE: Martin, stop this—

MARTIN: I just want him to tell me what the difference is.

KIDD: So I'm a worthless motherfucker, Martin, is that what you want to hear?

MARTIN: No, I want to hear, yes.

KIDD: Fuck off.

MARTIN: Clean slate, Kidd. You can stay here, I pay for college, and then you want a record deal, that's in there, too. You know that's in my power.

KIDD: No.

MARTIN: I will treat you like my son.

KIDD: Fuck off.

MARTIN: Fine. Goodbye.

JANE: Goodbye, Martin.

MARTIN: Hmm?

JANE: Your deal is so good I don't think I can accept it.

MARTIN: What do you mean?

JANE: I mean, I don't deserve your deal.

MARTIN: Deal was the wrong word to use—

JANE: No, it was the right word, and it's a good deal. But I'm not, Martin, I'm not good—

MARTIN: Jane—

JANE: I'm a bad motherfucker, same as my best friend Kidd, and I can't forget that, so, so, goodbye.

MARTIN: I think you need some time to think this over—

JANE: No.

MARTIN: I think our marriage is very strong and—

JANE: It was.

MARTIN: —and shouldn't be thrown away over, over one word—

JANE: Martin—

MARTIN: I think we can move past this, I know we can—

JANE: Martin—

MARTIN: We just need to focus on the good and—

JANE: Martin.

MARTIN: I love you.

JANE: I loved you. And I won't forget—

(MARTIN *claps his hands hard together, rubs them briskly, then snaps them apart.* MARTIN *exits, and the door slamming is not a gun shot.*)

JANE: *(Continued)* That's right, my fucking spouse
Best steer clear of this house
Best run from my crib
'Cause I'm the cat and you the mouse
I'm Sylvester you Tweety
So you better get Speedy
Get Gone-zalez away from my palace—

KIDD: Jane.

JANE: What, that was pretty good freestyle.

KIDD: Uh, listen—

JANE: Pretty good for me.

KIDD: I think—

JANE: All right, pretty stupid, I know.

KIDD: I think I need to go.

(KATE *enters, begins walking toward* JANE, *who senses her but does not turn.*)

JANE: You want to go?

KIDD: I just need a—

JANE: I got a place.

KIDD: No, I mean—

JANE: No, come on, I got a place, perfect place—

KIDD: Look, Jane—

JANE: Come on, motherfucker!

(KIDD *and* JANE *exits as* KATE *screams, a high keen that turns into the cry of gulls over water.*)

SCENE 4

On the Dane's boat.

KIDD: So where we going?

JANE: See any more land?

KIDD: Uhh . . . no

JANE: Then we're here.

KIDD: There ain't no here.

JANE: And no one to hear.

KIDD: Then throw me overboard, right?

JANE: When we were married, Martin and I, uh, at the reception, well, people were people and we had to get out, so, we hopped on a boat, and we drove to where no one could hear us, and—

KIDD: I got an idea what you did, don't need to hear about it.

JANE: We hollered. We yelled. All these, stupid, crazy, angry things, because we could, who could hear?

KIDD: Martin?

JANE: Yeah, Martin. And when Kate—when my daughter—when that fucker was over, I came out here again, by myself.

KIDD: So this is a little yodel-fest? Nice thought, Janey, but I ain't really in the mood, tell truth.

JANE: You're fucking pissed off, right?

KIDD: I don't really know what I am.

JANE: And that's just the mood for it. You gotta want to yell something bad, scream something awful, trouble, something you shouldn't. Come on. Give it a try.

KIDD: All right, all right.

(KIDD *yells.*)

"Shit—motherfucker—shit—shit!"

JANE: Kidd, you say those things every other word, that's not trouble.

KIDD: Well gimme a better fucking example.

JANE: It's gotta be creative, more like, "Goat-Fucker!"

KIDD: Goat-Fucker?

JANE: Yeah, Goat-Fucker, goats are trouble, fucking them's worse.

KIDD: True . . .

JANE: So go ahead.

KIDD: Uh, all right, how about, Orphan-Sucker!

JANE: Orphan-Sucker?

KIDD: Yeah, Orphan-Sucker, shouldn't be sucking on no orphans, right?

JANE: No you shouldn't.

KIDD: There you go. Your turn.

JANE: Mold-Licker!

KIDD: Malt liquor?

JANE: No, mold licker, mold—sorry, that was bad.

KIDD: These ain't bad, these is just half-ass clever. You wanna yell something bad, you can't go half-ass on it.

JANE: Show me full ass.

KIDD: "Martin's got a dick too small for fishbait!" Yeah, now that's bad, and you're right, it feels good. You wanna try one?

JANE: I don't know if I can think of one like that.

KIDD: All right, I'm the mad-genius here, so, "Martin's got an ass like a kindergarten chalkboard," there, give that shit a try.

JANE: "Martin's got an ass like a kindergarten chalkboard!"

KIDD: Yeah, how'd that feel?

JANE: All right.

KIDD: Here's another, "Martin is fucking fertilizer in a suit!" Let's try that one again.

JANE: "Martin is fucking fertilizer in a suit."

KIDD: Now try yelling it.

JANE: "Martin . . . "

KIDD: You all right?

JANE: Maybe I don't want to say something bad.

KIDD: Your game.

JANE: Maybe I want to say something good.

KIDD: Something good, huh? All right, how about, like, "Kidd Trick raps wonder like Zeus bringing thunder!"

JANE: Yeah, like "Kidd Trick busts the tightest ass rhymes that could ever be!"

KIDD: Yeah, well, "Jane Williams-Dane busts some tight-ass shit herself!"

JANE: Kidd trick is gonna go gold, bitch!

KIDD: After Jane W.D. goes platinum!

JANE: Kidd Trick is the coolest motherfucker I know!

KIDD: Jane Dane is the craziest bitch I know!

JANE: Kidd Trick is the sweetest gangsta that could ever be!

KIDD: Jane Dane needs to calm down.

JANE: Kidd Trick is funniest playa that could ever be!

KIDD: Janey needs to take it easy.

JANE: Kidd is cool!

KIDD: Jane is—

JANE: Kidd is great!

KIDD: Jane—

JANE: Kidd is good!!

KIDD: Jane.

JANE: What? What's wrong?

KIDD: Nothing. Tired, I guess. Guess I just wanna go home.

JANE: What did I say?

KIDD: Just take me home.

SCENE 5

KIDD's *bedroom in the Dane's house.* KIDD *is packing as* JANE *enters.*

JANE: What are you doing?

KIDD: Jane.

JANE: Hi. What're you doing?

KIDD: Oh, just, getting back to Boston, wanna work some new shit out, see how it sounds on the street, you know.

JANE: Oh. Okay.

KIDD: I'll be back, just a couple of days.

JANE: So you can leave some of your stuff here.

KIDD: Maybe a week or two, don't how long it'll take, you know, couple days, couple weeks—

JANE: Want me to come with you?

KIDD: Naw, ain't no big thang, be back in a few, we get working on that record, just need to—

JANE: Why are you lying to me?

KIDD: How you think I'm lying?

JANE: 'Cause I know you.

KIDD: Is that right? You got me figured out?

JANE: I didn't say that.

KIDD: You my best friend, you better know me, right?

JANE: You're mine, but, but I don't have to be yours—

KIDD: Mind leaving me alone for a couple of minutes?

JANE: Mind telling me what the hell's going on?

KIDD: Don't worry about it, be back in a few weeks.

JANE: You're not coming back. You're not coming back, are you?

KIDD: In a few weeks.

JANE: What did I do?

KIDD: You didn't do nothing wrong, now please, leave me alone.

JANE: I'm not leaving you, I'm not letting you leave.

KIDD: I'll be back in a few weeks.

JANE: Don't lie to me, please don't you lie to me, Kidd.

KIDD: You lie to me, only fair.

JANE: No I don't.

KIDD: Kidd is good, Kidd is great, right?

JANE: That's not a lie.

KIDD: Did you hear a word that Martin said?

JANE: What do you care about him?

KIDD: I care about the truth, and he said it.

JANE: Martin doesn't know shit about you or the truth—

KIDD: And neither do you, and I wanna keep it that way.

JANE: Why can't I know, what's so bad about a couple of drug deals—

KIDD: That's all they caught me doing, that ain't all I done.

JANE: Well, if they didn't catch you, then fuck them, live!

KIDD: While some poor motherfucker rots in jail? For what I done?

JANE: Yes!

KIDD: What are you saying?

JANE: I'm saying I don't care about the poor motherfucker in jail, let him rot and you stay here!

KIDD: Hey, hey, what happened to that do-gooder shit, crusader?

JANE: I'm not good, not anymore, I never was, I suck, I fucking suck, I'm evil, I'm the devil—

KIDD: I'm going.

JANE: I called you and Martin that word, that's so evil, that's not good—

KIDD: That's a word, I done worse.

JANE: I'll say it again, I'll look you in the eyes and say it—

KIDD: Janey—

JANE: Nigger, nigger, nigger, nigger—

KIDD: Janey, your eyes are closed!

JANE: Shit!

KIDD: Now excuse me—

JANE: I done worse than that, I ruined my husband's dreams, that's bad—

KIDD: You don't know what you're saying—

JANE: I ain't heard worse out of you.

KIDD: And you don't want to.

JANE: And you don't want to hear the bad shit I've done—

KIDD: 'Cause it ain't really that bad, now—

JANE: Two people, I've killed two people.

KIDD: Oh really?

JANE: Yeah, now top that, motherfucker.

KIDD: How'd you go about killing them?

JANE: I killed them, what do you mean how did I kill them—

KIDD: You pulled the trigger?

JANE: Sort of, I mean, it was my decision, or decisions I made that killed them—

KIDD: Oh, yeah, you rubbing them out with your fucking decisions—

JANE: It was my decision and I said kill him, he had it fucking coming, and I feel great about it, but it's not good, Kidd, and the other's worse—

KIDD: I'm sure it is, you popped a decision in their ass, right—

JANE: It's a hell of a lot worse than drug dealing and a couple of fights—

KIDD: What if I told you I killed someone, not my bad decision, but me, myself, with this hand?

JANE: I wouldn't care, I'd forgive you.

KIDD: No you wouldn't.

JANE: It was self-defense—

KIDD: No it wasn't.

JANE: You were just a kid, you were angry, or scared—

KIDD: It was cold, Janey, cold blood.

JANE: So was mine, cold blood—

KIDD: Making the wrong fucking decision is not the same thing—

JANE: We'll never know since you don't have the balls to say it.

KIDD: Oh balls, balls—

JANE: That's right, you don't have them—

KIDD: You wanna hear about my balls, Janey?

JANE: Yeah, I don't think you got 'em—

KIDD: I don't think so, either.

JANE: I guess not, since you're too scared to tell me the truth.

KIDD: Oh, is that you wanna hear?

JANE: Yeah, that's what I want to hear.

KIDD: Then I guess I got to tell you.

JANE: I'm ready for it.

KIDD: Well, you're gonna hear it.

JANE: Then fucking do it.

KIDD: You're gonna hear the whole thing.

JANE: I'm waiting.

KIDD: And when you can't stand my worthless sight, just walk out, don't say nothing.

JANE: I'm standing right here.

KIDD: A year before you crusaders do-gooded me up I was running with a gang on Girard Avenue, toughest bunch of lost mother-fuckers you ever seen, and I was gonna be just like them. Did what they told me, any fucking thing, they was my brothers, looked out for me, and I did good, so, the day came to make me a man. They gave me a gun, a badass one, better than the pissy little peashooter I stole. Then it was time for the corner. Ain't no niggah could run with them gangstas till he paid a visit to that corner. There they were, fat ones, skinny ones, white and black, senoritas and courtesans, every kind a lonely boy could dream of, painted up like neon lights, smiling like spread legs.

"Choose one boy," they said, so I choose this little China doll, heard a couple boys snicker, my brothers there before me. "Good choice, niggah." They set us up in a fine hotel and soon as we get in her clothes are off and I'm staring 'cause I ain't ever seen that and she goes, "Get on with it" and it's funny cause she looks my age, but her voice, "Hurry up," and she spreads her legs and says I better not try kissing her. So I start in, rubbing away, her moaning like some half-ass actress bored with the part, makes me so sick I can't, you know, I couldn't, but I keep pumping away, and five minutes in she feels ain't nothing happening, starts laughing, and now that don't help none, 'cause now I'm soft as a motherfucking wet towel and what do you know but all my brothers is listening at the door, and they want to know what all the laughing's about, so they run in, and I turn round, and they see, and the little China bitch starts yipping, "He can't, he can't," and the whole of fucking Philadelphia starts laughing at it, laughing at the niggah whose dick don't work, and they saying, "What's wrong with you, boy, what's wrong, niggah, what's wrong," and keep laughing till they fucking gone.

So I go to this park near Girard, ain't nobody there, quiet, playing the whole thing out over again and again, till I'm ready to take my fucking pistol to their eyes, only I can't do that, 'cause then they bury me. I feel all Philly burn round me like murder, and I'm some furious heart in the center. Then dawn comes, and you know, some bird gets to singing, and the murder starts winking out of me like all them stars. Then she walks by.

Beautiful. Skipping along, floating along like the sidewalk moving for her, head held up high like it's tied by a string to heaven, and she's smiling, and she's singing like this whole goddamn world was made for her. She had a blue bracelet on, the kind little kids wear. And she looked at me and smiled. I ain't ever seen something more beautiful and right in all my life. I shot her three times and ran.

Ran all the way down to D.C., hid out with a cousin of mine. Didn't read the papers, didn't watch the news, didn't want to know. Couple months later, my cousin told me they caught some niggah they thought did it. Told me they convicted him. Told me they gave him life. They gave him life, and I didn't do a goddamn fucking thing about it, and then I met you.

I knew it. I knew you couldn't hear that shit, don't fucking blame you. Now you see why I got to go. Now you see why I got to set that brother free. I got to pay for what I done. Now you see, now— get the fuck out of here, Janey, please, I'm a killer and a coward, but I ain't no fucking crybaby, so get out here and let me go.

JANE: You don't have to go to jail.

KIDD: I got to set that brother free, I got to—

JANE: You can't, he's dead.

KIDD: No, he ain't. He got life, my cousin said.

JANE: No, he got the death penalty. He died a month before I met you.

KIDD: That ain't true, my cousin said he got life.

JANE: Your cousin lied.

KIDD: How the fuck do you know?

JANE: 'Cause I saw him die. I wanted him to die. It was my decision.

(Silence.)

KIDD: Martin said she died of cancer.

(JANE shakes her head.)

Oh God. Oh no. Oh God.

(Sudden, fierce, furious)

JANE: I forgive you.

(KIDD crumples to the floor.)

KIDD: Oh god oh god oh no oh no oh no oh god—

(JANE grabs KIDD hard.)

JANE: I forgive you.

(KIDD tries to pull away.)

KIDD: Oh God!

(JANE pulls him back.)

JANE: I forgive you, and I love you. I love you, Kidd, and I forgive you.

(KATE enters behind JANE and walks to her slowly.)

I forgive you.

(KATE touches JANE gently.)

I forgive you.

(Lights down.)

END OF PLAY

ABOUT PORTLAND STAGE COMPANY

The leading professional theater in northern New England, Portland Stage Company (PSC) entertains, educates, and engages its audiences by producing a wide range of artistic works and programs that explore basic human issues and concerns relevant to the communities served by the theater. PSC is dedicated to establishing a dialogue between artist and audience that inspires the energetic discussion of issues and experiences that are immediate and compelling.

An essential element of PSC's mission is a deep dedication to nurturing new writing for the theater. In addition to the theater's commitment to include new plays on its main stage, this commitment is actively and vividly expressed through PSC's annual Little Festival of the Unexpected. This weeklong festival connects vibrant writers and composers with performing artists and audiences to develop, explore and support the risk-taking required of artists creating new work. The Little Festival, now in its thirteenth year, is one of the few new works forums north of New York.

Portland Stage Company produces the Little Festival of the Unexpected with generous support from The Clauder Competition. Now in its sixteenth year, The Clauder Competition is New England's most prestigious playwriting contest supporting the development of new work. This volume contains the winning script from the 2000-2001 competition, Laura Harrington's *Hallowed Ground*, as well as Clauder finalists *Dog Act* by Liz Duffy Adams, *Apocalypso!* by William Donnelly, and *Kidding Jane* by August Schulenburg.

Daniel Pinkerton's script, *Do You Want to Know a Secret?*, was brought to Portland Stage through a partnership with The Playwrights' Center in Minneapolis. The Playwrights' Center fuels the theater by providing services that support playwright and playwriting. The Playwrights' Center was founded in 1971. Thirty years later, the Center has grown into a regional and national resource for script development, which currently provides a range of services for writers at all stages of their careers.

—Anita Stewart
Artistic Director, Portland Stage Company